RADICAL *Review*
HISTORY

Issue | 100

Queer Futures

Editors' Introduction

This issue of the *Radical History Review* assembles the voices of scholars and activists who engage with critiques of what Lisa Duggan has called "the new *homonormativity* . . . a politics that does not contest dominant heteronormative assumptions and institutions but upholds and sustains them."[1] In the time that has elapsed since the *Radical History Review*'s last explicit foray into queer history—the "Queer" issue, *RHR* 62 (1995)—this process has been abundantly evident in numerous cultural and political scenes over the past four decades, as this issue's contributors amply demonstrate. While we do not want to reinforce the notion that the concept of homonormativity originated with or is limited to the confines of academic work, the configuration of homonormativity in current circulation is part of a broader turn toward political economy in contemporary queer academic and activist work. It challenges the preoccupations and objectives of LGBT (lesbian, gay, bisexual, transgender)/queer culture and community as many of its members move toward what Gayle Rubin identified, in 1984, as "the charmed circle" of sex—those practices and identities that receive social sanction.[2] This issue of *RHR* asks what this mainstreaming will mean for queer futures. But first, we want to glance backward at the recent queer past.

A Day without Sunshine

No public figure is more renowned for fomenting antigay politics in the 1970s than Anita Bryant, whose image appears on the cover of this issue of *Radical History Review*. Bryant's notorious 1977 "Save Our Children" campaign, which led to the repeal of a civil rights ordinance protecting gay and lesbian employees from discrimination in Dade County, Florida, raised the ire of many lesbian and gay political activists who pilloried her wholesome image as a pitchwoman of orange juice and performer of banal pop songs in an effort to counter a rising tide of antigay organiz-

Radical History Review
Issue 100 (Winter 2008)   DOI 10.1215/01636545-2007-019
© 2008 by MARHO: The Radical Historians' Organization, Inc.

ing. Even today, thirty years later, it is difficult to extricate Bryant the pop singer from Bryant the political actor. While political leaders like San Francisco's Harvey Milk, the first openly gay elected public official in the United States, were making history, activists throughout the United States decried Bryant as a pop icon of uncompassionate conservatism and as a symbol of the violence and exclusion that lay beneath the surface of her particular brand of normative American nationalism.

This mobilization against Bryant and against the campaign she spearheaded typified a form of representational and performative protest, at once both confrontational and camp, that animated post-Stonewall activism.[3] One need only watch the footage of the gay activist Thom Higgins, inspired by Yippie strategies of protest, throwing a pie in Bryant's face at a news conference held in Des Moines, Iowa, in 1977 to see this performative spirit in action.[4] Indeed, one could locate the pieing of Bryant as part of an impressive genealogy of queer protest that relied on the performative: from gay, lesbian, and trans activists in the 1960s and 1970s, to ACT UP, Queer Nation, and Transgender Nation in the 1980s and 1990s, to groups in the early twenty-first century such as Gay Shame and FIERCE (Fabulous Independent Educated Radicals for Community Empowerment), both of which receive attention in this issue.

The brand of antigay politics perfected by Bryant and practiced by her followers in the late 1970s has proven more resilient perhaps than even Bryant herself could have imagined. Three decades later, the homophobic rhetoric that Bryant's campaign catapulted into public discourse in the United States remains immensely influential among social conservatives and their constituencies. The "Save Our Children" campaign also represented the first foray into organized politics by the recently departed evangelist Jerry Falwell, whose organization, the Moral Majority, mobilized the latent power of post-Watergate conservative Republicans and born-again Christians to build a large-scale and enormously well-funded network of antigay political activists. The success and popularity of the Moral Majority rested on its routine invocation of the "homosexual agenda," which, as Falwell and his followers argued, posed a dire threat to the reproduction of both the "traditional family" and national power.[5]

Committed to the idea that they were saving the families and children of the United States from an uncertain future, Bryant and Falwell believed that they were building a future for heterosexual Americans that would keep their families insulated from deviant sexualities. Bryant's protectionist crusade, rooted in her reading of the Bible and her self-identification as a mother, focused on the alleged threat that homosexuals — and especially the homosexual teacher — posed to children and thus to reproductive futurity: "I know that homosexuals cannot biologically reproduce children," she famously asserted, "therefore, they must recruit our children."[6] Bryant's and Falwell's campaigns in the 1970s to protect families and children from the homosexual menace remain a touchstone for social moderates and social conservatives alike, influencing everything from Bill Clinton's 1996 signing of the Defense of Marriage Act to bully-pulpit tactics of Rev. Fred Phelps and his organization Focus on the Family to the meager allocation of federal dollars and local resources for HIV/AIDS education and prevention.

But perhaps most surprisingly, the rhetoric and goals of the 1970s antigay movement have also exercised a profound influence on contemporary movements to secure gay and lesbian rights. Bryant could not have been more wrong about the ability of homosexuals to reproduce, as demonstrated not only by the current baby boom among gay men and lesbians and the proliferation of assistive technologies that make reproduction possible for same-sex parents but also by the centrality of same-sex marriage and gay parenting in contemporary mainstream gay and lesbian movements. Of course, reproduction has never been owned or mandated by heterosexuals, just as reactionary and even authoritarian political practices have never been owned or mandated by heterosexuals, as Licia Fiol-Matta's study of the queer Chilean poet and educational reformer Gabriela Mistral makes clear.[7] Yet the current focus within gay and lesbian movements and culture on the family and reproduction as vehicles for claiming citizenship and rights works to suture reproduction to a privatizing neoliberal agenda, rather than to disrupt nationalist and heteronormative ideologies.

As scholars and activists in the early twenty-first century consider the various forms that a queer future might take, it may be useful to cast our gaze to the recent past to identify certain usable elements in the antagonistic countercultural rejections of normative family values evinced by the anti-Bryant activists. For example, a similar rejection of the normative politics of reproductive nationalism found expression in the 1970s punk movement, the iconography of which provides one of the referents for our cover. In the same year that activists pied Bryant, the Sex Pistols released their single "God Save the Queen," the original title of which was, in fact, "No Future." As Tavia Nyong'o writes in his essay in this issue, one must not conflate "punk as a mode of revolt" with the revolutionary politics of the seventies or with any other organized political formation, nor should one place punk unequivocally within a narrative of sexual or political progress. Yet even with these caveats, one cannot ignore the interpretive resonances between the Sex Pistols' negative political act of defacing the image of Queen Elizabeth II, herself a potent symbol of national reproduction, and the performative act of defacing the image of Anita Bryant, who positioned herself as the protector of a normative national future via the "saving" of the idealized child from homosexuality. The image on the cover of this issue of *RHR* represents our attempt to link these ideas and histories—between punk and family values, homosexual panic and the rise of the homonormative, and between a queer future and no future.

Contemporary Realities and Queer Futures

Clearly, all queer futures are not alike, nor are they alike in whatever it is that makes them queer in the first place. But however surprised Bryant must be about the centrality of marriage and parenting in current discourse about homosexuality, more surprising still is that proponents of same-sex marriage now deploy the very same rhetoric of the endangered child that Bryant and her adherents used in the "Save Our Children" campaign three decades ago. As Patrick McCreery shows in his contribution to this issue, mainstream gay rights organizations such as the Human Rights Campaign and conservative antigay religious groups such as Focus on the Family participate in a discourse on same-sex marriage that focuses not on civil or human rights but on the benefits or hazards of the institution of marriage for the child, who is almost always imagined in abstract terms. In centering the figure of the endangered child, McCreery argues, same-sex marriage proponents reinforce and reproduce a normative vision that confers rights "to and through the family." The future imagined within this discourse can hardly be understood as queer. Rather, it works toward wholly normative and, one could argue, neoliberal ends, privileging the family unit as the premier site of consumption and social reproduction while simultaneously destabilizing the protections afforded to citizens' rights outside of the mode of the reproductive.

What should we make of the ideological and tactical confluences between the family-first strategies of gay rights' organizations and those of their opponents who have historically pathologized and criminalized homosexuals as "perverse" and "deviant" enemies of the family? What kind of historical amnesia produces and is produced by such alliances? It would appear that in the three decades since Bryant first emerged to sow the seeds of intolerance, some formerly non-normative categories of sexual identity are moving rapidly inside Rubin's "charmed circle." Many LGBT scholars and activists, including same-sex marriage proponents, have been at the forefront of a slow but steady normalizing process through which queers identify with, rather than challenge, the mainstream U.S. body politic. By positioning particular sexual identities as belonging to a timeless, universal, and even biological minority group, they have argued that certain categories of sexuality—especially those that are white, monogamous, gender-conforming, and middle-class—are more amenable than others to inclusion in Rubin's "charmed circle." Even in just the past five years, the North American cultural scene has manifested compelling evidence for the effectiveness of such normalizing strategies, given the tenor of the same-sex marriage debates, the successful promotion of queer consumer products in the pursuit of the "pink dollar," and the popularity of representations that appeal to wide audiences such as *Queer Eye for the Straight Guy*, *The L Word*, and *Brokeback Mountain*.

As prominent and mainstream lesbian and gay rights organizations strategically embrace agendas that vie for acceptance within contemporary economic and political systems, one could argue that they have abandoned many of the political commitments of their LGBT activist predecessors, especially their foci on the redistribution of economic resources and the protection of sexual freedoms. This shift has made strange bedfellows out of lesbian and gay rights organizations and social conservatives: both endorse normative and family-oriented formations associated with domestic partnership, adoption, military service, and gender-normative social roles; both work to marginalize and disempower those who challenge serial monogamy and those belonging to categories — including transgender, bisexual, pansexual, and intersex constituencies — that are seen as eccentric within a traditional binary gender or sex system. Moreover, much of contemporary mainstream lesbian and gay political and cultural activity is based in the neoliberal philosophy of consumer rights rather than that of citizen rights. This brand of lesbian and gay neoliberalism exercises an influence beyond borders of the United States and other Western countries through the global proliferation of so-called lavender tourism, gay- and lesbian-themed cultural productions, and economic and political interventions that claim to make "gay rights" (defined in Western terms but promoted as universal) a global human rights issue.

Some radical activists and scholars have challenged these moves, citing such developments as reactionary responses to the privatizing imperatives of a powerful, ascendant brand of neoliberal politics that coalesced in the 1990s. Along with Duggan, some queer and/or sex-positive radicals identify and reject neoliberal strategies, not because they undermine citizens' rights but because they threaten to erase the historic alliance between radical politics and lesbian and gay politics, at the core of which had been a struggle for sexual freedom. They argue that these neoliberal gains push existing sexual categories — including queer ones — toward the fixed and the exclusive. If gays and lesbians now fit comfortably within market niches and voting blocs, they ask, can these formerly marginalized sexualities also retain their radical potential? In short, activists and scholars criticize the new homonormativity because it privileges particular sexual minorities over others and because it fails to dismantle larger systems of power that position queers as threats to the economy, the nation-state, and the very fabric of civilized society.

History and the New Homonormativity

This issue of *RHR* contributes to a small but growing body of scholarship that critically reexamines the trajectory of LGBT politics and scholarship over the past several decades. In particular, "Queer Futures" takes up the task of tracing and examining the interconnected and sometimes contradictory historical moments that have produced the current state of sexual politics. We seek to complicate and challenge normative narratives of queer progress (for example, from marginalization to inclusion; from invisible to visible), as well as narratives that imagine the queer past as one exclusively characterized by radical political resistance. The contributions to this issue explore the histories of homonormativity within those discourses (medical, political, activist, capitalist, academic, etc.) that have shaped stable, safe, and normalized identities with political and cultural cache out of formerly deviant categories. In doing so, they offer new historical and analytical frameworks for talking about lesbian, gay, bisexual, transgender, and queer history that expand and challenge current models of identity and community formation.

The authors presented in this issue of *RHR* use the historian's tools to carve out of the recent past some of the precedents that have shaped the economic, political, and institutional sites responsible for bringing homonormativity into the world. In our "Features" section, for example, Regina Kunzel challenges an all-too-easy understanding of homonormative politics as a wholesale departure from the libratory movement of the Stonewall era. Examining what many have understood as one of the more radical components of the 1970s and 1980s movement, Kunzel argues that gay activism on behalf of imprisoned gay and lesbian "brothers" and "sisters" worked to produce new gay norms. Confused by and often critical of the more ambiguous and capacious sexual and gender categories that operated within prison walls, activists worked to transform "punks," "jockers," and butch "daddies" into proper minority subjects defined within a binary classification of sexual identity. Characterizing prison sexual culture as primitive, some went so far as to produce a pedagogy of socialization into emerging norms of gay culture in order to remake the homosexual prisoner as "a gay we can be proud of."

Similar to Kunzel, Dan Irving makes an intervention into narratives of liberation by challenging conventional accounts of trans subjectivity in North America. Irving argues that studies of transsexualism and transgenderism in medical, psychological, and popular literatures talk almost exclusively about liberation and self-actualization but are oblivious to how normative discourses of economic productivity and social assimilation have become the markers by which many trans people from the 1950s onward measure themselves in transitioning from one gender identity to another. Irving argues that under the free market mandates of neoliberalism, many contemporary trans writers and activists have absorbed these markers, thereby sustaining the implicit assumption that trans bodies are only viable if they can be brought into submission by the dictates of global capitalism.

Locating the ideological roots of homonormativity is also an essential component of Christina Hanhardt's history of so-called safe streets patrols in Greenwich Village in New York City and the Castro neighborhood in San Francisco. She offers a compelling reexamination of these neighborhoods in the mid- to late 1970s, the formative years during which these model "gay ghettoes" came into their own. Through innovative analyses of archival materials and oral histories with former street patrol members, Hanhardt shows how attempts to curtail homophobic violence in the 1970s and 1980s were shaped by "culture of poverty" discourses that pathologized poor people and people of color. Hanhardt demonstrates that safe streets patrols ultimately contributed to processes of urban gentrification as elite residents, including gay white men, transformed formerly marginal gay neighborhoods into wealthy enclaves and deployed oppressive quality-of-life policing strategies that disproportionately targeted people of color, including those who identified as queer.

Tracing a similar lineage to that of Hanhardt's genealogy of the homonormative in urban street activism, Margot D. Weiss contrasts two contemporary activist groups and finds surprisingly comparable results. She compares Gay Shame San Francisco, which seeks to disrupt lesbian and gay assimilation into the city's mainstream and challenges the very policing and gentrification practices that Hanhardt describes, with the National Coalition for Sexual Freedom, which disseminates a public image of practitioners of bondage/discipline/sadomasochism (BDSM), swingers, and polyamorous people as suburban minivan drivers who "look and dress like your neighbors." Weiss's study suggests that neoliberalism's relegation of sexuality into the realm of the private renders even kinky sexual practices like BDSM as normative, especially when practitioners actively work to detach potentially disruptive and deviant sexual practices from any form of radical or progressive politics.

Finally, Anna M. Agathangelou, Daniel Bassichis, and Tamara L. Spira return to themes explored by Kunzel in an essay that asserts that since September 11, 2001, imprisonment for the many and freedom for the few have come to characterize and classify the experiences of queer citizens in the era of global lockdown. Ranging from an examination of the landmark Supreme Court ruling in *Lawrence and Garner v. State of Texas* (2003) to an exegesis of a post-9/11 advertisement by the Human Rights Campaign, Agathangelou, Bassichis, and Spira trace the contours of our contemporary historical moment, one in which the liberation and protection of certain queer bodies and identities under neoliberalism coexists with the prosecution and incarceration of racialized queer bodies and identities deemed incompatible with the goals of the state.

In our "Interventions" section, Susan Stryker challenges queer studies to acknowledge the central roles that transgender communities have played in countering heteronormativity and those sexualities—including nonheterosexual ones—that it allows to access its power. Stryker turns to the history of the term *homonormativity* and its roots in transgender activism to intervene against contemporary critics that perpetuate the prioritizing of gay and lesbian subjectivities in their critiques of the homonormative. She also takes us back to the historic 1966 riot in San Francisco's Tenderloin District, in which drag queens and gay hustlers banded together at Gene Compton's Cafeteria "to fight back against police harassment and social oppression" to locate transgender action (and coalitions with other marginalized sexualities) at the very heart of LGBT history in the United States.

Sustaining Stryker's critique of institutionalized homonormativity in the space of the university, Roderick A. Ferguson provides a genealogy of the administrative embrace of difference in the post–civil rights university to show how the university aligns the homonormative with liberal discourses of diversity. Ferguson argues that such contemporary phenomena as domestic partner benefits, touted by LGBT activists as proof of social progress within mainstream academia, is a strategy to absorb gender and sexual difference by producing certain kinds of normative academic employees. Complicity with administrative recognition by LGBT people is but one example of a larger project that Ferguson identifies as the "will to institutionality."

The absorption of difference characterized by Ferguson is also readily apparent in the work of Maxime Cervulle, who examines the history of gay and lesbian political activism in France in the early 1970s. Cervulle traces how, even after the radical political upheavals of May 1968, many gay activists upheld familiar racialized tropes of the colonial French imagination and promoted the dual fetishization and subordination of men of Arab descent. Cervulle concludes his historical analysis with an assessment of the controversial Centre d'Archives et de Documentation Homosexuelles de Paris, a community history project that, as Cervulle argues, sustains many of the racist and colonial legacies of early gay activism by focusing on the contributions of white gay men.

Aaron Belkin, the director of a research institute at the University of California at Santa Barbara that studies the status of sexual minorities in the U.S. military, discusses the failure of activists who seek to repeal the military's "don't ask, don't tell" policy—both within and outside of the military—to reckon with the high incidence of male-male rape in the U.S. armed forces. Belkin argues that this glaring omission among mainstream LGBT organizations calls into question the motives behind the repeal, which seems not to stem from direct challenges to discrimination and harassment but, instead, from a reactionary position that regards the military as a normative institution upholding patriotic values.

If controlling public relations spin remains an excessive but necessary component of the military's profile, it is equally weighty for those in the gay media industries who exert a powerful and normalizing influence in a competitive marketplace of gay representations and advertising revenues. Vincent Doyle's essay explores how the organizational amnesia—the willful forgetting of its activist roots—endemic to the Gay and Lesbian Alliance against Defamation (GLAAD) has impacted its intimate relations with the very media outlets that it purports to patrol. Using extensive ethnographic research with lesbian and gay media watchdogs, Doyle looks at GLAAD's response to the Showtime series *Queer as Folk*, which was initially critical of the show's content but eventually capitulated to Showtime's demands, and argues that many queer media advocates have lost their critical potential by being themselves so deeply immersed in media industries.

In a final essay that takes the idea of gay and lesbian niche markets to its logical conclusion, Nan Alamilla Boyd shows that the U.S.-based same-sex marriage movement has become a significant factor in the global gay travel market as cities seek to commodify marriage as part of a multibillion-dollar global tourism industry. Boyd argues that this process, which insists on both intelligible modern sexual categories and reinforces a neoliberal rhetoric of privatization, "produces a new kind of queer citizen, one that participates in civic life via the social rituals of marriage and the commercial rituals of conspicuous consumption."

Last but not least, in our "Interviews" section, Jason Ruiz speaks with Mattilda aka Matt Bernstein Sycamore to discuss her history of activism and her ideas for how to build a more queer future. One of the "instigators" behind Gay Shame San Francisco and a prolific writer and editor, Mattilda has long advocated an anti-assimilationist queer politics that builds alliances across the lines of race, class, ability, gender, and sexuality. Like Stryker, she demonstrates that a critique of what we are calling the homonormative in this issue is neither new nor limited to the gilded cage of queer theory. Rather, such a critique has long been the mission of intellectuals and activists bent on disrupting the normalization of queers within oppressive economic and political systems.

This issue of *RHR* has taken the better part of eighteen months to come to fruition and throughout the process has truly been a queer labor of love. The editors would like to thank the numerous external reviewers and members of the *RHR* editorial collective who gave our contributors and us such tremendously useful feedback. In particular, we would like to thank Duane Corpis, Ezra Davidson, Lisa Duggan, Van Gosse, Tom Harbison, Molly McGarry, Conor McGrady, and Richard Morrison, who gave their time and expertise so generously to this issue. They are vivid reminders that without the collaborative efforts of many, queer futures — or futures of any kind, for that matter — remain unimaginable.

—Kevin P. Murphy, Jason Ruiz, and David Serlin

Notes

1. Lisa Duggan, *The Twilight of Equality? Neoliberalism, Cultural Politics, and the Attack on Democracy* (Boston: Beacon, 2003), 50.
2. Gayle Rubin, "Thinking Sex: Notes for a Radical Theory of the Politics of Sexuality," in *Pleasure and Danger: Exploring Female Sexuality*, ed. Carol S. Vance (New York: Routledge, 1984), 283.
3. See, for example, Tina Fetner, "Working Anita Bryant: The Impact of Christian Anti-gay Activism on Lesbian and Gay Movement Claims," *Social Problems* 48 (2001): 411–28; Molly McGarry and Fred Wasserman, *Becoming Visible: An Illustrated History of Gay Life in Twentieth-Century America* (New York: New York Public Library, 1998), 209–11; and Barry D. Adam, *The Rise of a Gay and Lesbian Movement* (Boston: Twayne, 1987), 102–5.
4. Film clip of Bryant being "pied," 1977, director unknown, viewable at PlanetOut PopcornQ Movies, www.planetout.com/popcornq/db/getfilm.html?104 (accessed May 29, 2007). On Thom Higgins, see Dylan Hicks, "Pride: An Anecdotal History," *City Pages* (Minneapolis/St. Paul), June 23, 2004, citypages.com/databank/25/1229/article12233.asp (accessed July 30, 2007).
5. See, for example, Kenneth J. Heineman, *God Is a Conservative: Religion, Politics, and Morality in Contemporary America* (New York: New York University Press, 2005).
6. Anita Bryant, quoted in "Anita Bryant's Crusade," *Newsweek* June 6, 1977, 22; see also Anita Bryant, *The Anita Bryant Story: The Survival of Our Nation's Families and the Threat of Militant Homosexuality* (Old Tappan, NJ: Fleming H. Revell, 1977), 62.
7. Licia Fiol-Matta, *A Queer Mother for the Nation: Gabriela Mistral and the State* (Minneapolis: University of Minnesota Press, 2002).

Gay college students teach Atascadero prisoners to dance and cruise in a therapeutic role-play scenario. From Rob Cole, "Behind Bars, Lessons on Being Gay," *Advocate*, June 20, 1973, 5

Lessons in Being Gay:
Queer Encounters in Gay and
Lesbian Prison Activism

Regina Kunzel

On June 28, 1970, the first gay march in New York City commemorating the Stonewall rebellion of the preceding year passed the Women's House of Detention. The march's route was not an accident. The jail was symbolically important, having held many renowned activists. Catholic radical Dorothy Day, labor organizer Elizabeth Gurley Flynn, and accused communist spy Ethel Rosenberg all had been incarcerated there in earlier decades. Radical feminist Valerie Solanas was held at the Women's House of Detention after shooting Andy Warhol in 1968, as were Angela Davis and Weather Underground member Jane Alpert in that same year. At the time of the 1970 march, two members of the Panther 21 group arrested on bomb conspiracy charges in a COINTELPRO (Counter Intelligence Program) frame-up—Joan Bird and Afeni Shakur—were inside the jail.[1]

The location of the Women's House of Detention would also have been meaningful to gay and lesbian marchers. Situated on a triangular block at the busy intersection of Sixth Avenue, Eighth Street, and Christopher Street near Sheridan Square, the jail lay in the heart of Greenwich Village and its flamboyant and newly politicized queer scene.[2] Sheridan Square was a popular gay cruising spot and home to several gay bars, including the Stonewall Inn. The jail's downtown location had long invited a boisterous exchange between women behind bars and their friends

Radical History Review
Issue 100 (Winter 2008)   DOI 10.1215/01636545-2007-020
© 2008 by MARHO: The Radical Historians' Organization, Inc.

11

and relations on the street. Joan Nestle remembered the "House of D" as "a shrine for separated lovers" where lesbians would call up to their incarcerated girlfriends late at night after the bars closed.[3]

The permeability between street and urban jail that gave rise to that social and sexualized scene facilitated political connections as well, connections in evidence at that first march in June 1970. As the demonstrators passed the jail, Gay Liberation Front members chanted, "Free our Sisters! Free ourselves!"[4] Expressions of solidarity among gay activists and prisoners became bolder and more reciprocal later that summer. On August 29, a march protesting police harassment began on Forty-second Street and proceeded downtown, concluding with a battle cry in front of the women's jail. Protestors on the street called up, "'Power to the sisters!'" and prisoners yelled back to the crowd, "'Power to the gay people!'"[5] When demonstrators happened on a police raid taking place under the guise of a fire inspection at the Haven, a popular neighborhood gay club, they responded with rage, hurling bottles at police, overturning cars, looting stores, and setting fires. The riot spread upward to the Women's House of Detention, where prisoners threw burning paper through their barred windows to the cheering crowd below.[6]

The Women's House of Detention was shut down the following year and demolished soon after. But political connections between lesbian and gay activists and prison inmates persisted as an important and underrecognized feature of the gay liberation movement of the 1970s. Many marches and demonstrations of the movement's early years chose jails and prisons as rallying sites.[7] And beginning in the early 1970s, gay activists initiated a wide range of projects on behalf of prisoners they called "brothers" and "sisters," publishing newsletters, investigating and publicizing prison conditions, offering legal counseling, organizing prison ministries, sponsoring pen-pal and outreach projects, and assisting parolees. At the same time, prisoners, some of whom identified as gay, began organizing on their own behalf against discrimination, harassment, and violence.

The unity evoked in the chants of solidarity exchanged between prisoners and activists in the summer of 1970 masked much more complicated and at times fraught connections between newly politicized gay men and lesbians and prisoners who inhabited a sexual world permeable to but different in marked ways from the one taking shape outside. This article explores the understandings, misunderstandings, and often uneasy alliances forged between queer prison insiders and outsiders. Detectable in queer encounters wrought from the most radical impulses of gay liberation were the roots of politics that were normative in their assumptions and normalizing in their aims.

"What's Outside Is Inside Too"

Gay liberationists joined others on the radical left in allying with prisoners and in theorizing connections between the worlds behind and beyond bars.[8] Indeed, leftist

Gay liberationists proclaimed unity with "brothers" and "sisters" behind bars. Collage by "Read." *We Are All Fugitives* appeared on the cover of *Gay Sunshine*, no. 14 (1972). Published with permission of the publisher, Winston Leyland

credibility in this period seemed to depend on radical prison activism. As African American, Chicano/Chicana, and Puerto Rican militants embraced prisoners as a revolutionary vanguard in the early 1970s, participants in the gay liberation movement, too, came to see gay prisoners as "victims of a vicious system." "Whether the charge emerges from their homosexuality (sodomy, solicitation, 'lewd conduct'), or indirectly (burglary, prostitution, shoplifting)," gay liberationist Allen Young insisted, "all gay prisoners are political prisoners."[9]

Advocacy on behalf of incarcerated gay people preceded the liberationist efforts of the 1970s. Soon after its founding in the early 1950s and into the 1960s, the Mattachine Society, the first organization to argue on behalf of "homophile" rights in the United States, recognized that heightened police surveillance of gay cruising spots, routine raids on gay bars, and the felonious status of same-sex sex made it likely that gay men would at some point run afoul of the law. Mattachine mobilized to protest the then-common use of entrapment against gay men and printed wallet cards with practical instructions for gay men titled "What to Do in Case of Arrest."[10] Gay men's criminalized status and vulnerability to arrest continued to inspire gay prison activism into the 1970s. The editors of *RFD*, a quarterly newsletter that announced itself as "A Country Journal — For Gay Men Everywhere," justified devoting a section called "Brothers behind Bars" to prison issues in 1976 by reminding readers of their own vulnerability to arrest. "One of the few ways rural gay men have to meet each other is at the tea rooms in parks and along highways," the editors noted, where they risked entrapment and arrest.[11] Since "anti-gay laws are most often enforced in small towns and rural areas, away from the group power of organized gayness," the *RFD* editors argued, gay men in those areas were "likely to be scapegoated for a crime." The publication envisioned "Brothers behind Bars" as a way to bring "victims of this injustice" and "potential victims" together in a common cause.[12]

The politics of gay liberation and the larger context of radical ferment in the early 1970s produced analyses that envisioned connections between gay activists and gay prisoners in newly intense, if often more analogized, terms. Mike Riegle, the founder of *Gay Community News*'s Prisoner Project in 1975, declared that "what's outside is inside too,"[13] and he proposed that the multiple oppressions faced by gay prisoners were simply exaggerated versions of those experienced by all gay men and lesbians. Riegle extended the comparison by inverting it, asserting that "what's going on inside is only an exaggeration and a distortion of what's happening right out here, in what some of my prisoner friends call 'minimum custody.'"[14] Insisting on the connections between a "politics of 'crime'" and "the general politics of social control, control of bodies, and even control of desires," Riegle asked by way of instructive provocation, "Kissed your lover in public lately?"[15]

Prison activism was "not just about giving prisoners a 'hand out,'" a group of Illinois gay activists insisted; "it's about building a new kind of community."[16] From these powerfully imagined connections emerged a rhetoric and politics of unity based on an assumed kinship between gay prisoners and gay activists. The language of brotherhood and sisterhood infused the rhetoric and ideology of gay prison advocacy and inspired strong commitments to a range of activist efforts on behalf of prisoners.

Challenging Discrimination behind Bars

Gay and lesbian activists did not have to look hard to find evidence of an array of discriminatory practices and oppressive conditions suffered by gay and lesbian prisoners. The blatant discrimination involved in segregating homosexual prisoners was one key focus of gay prison activism. A long-standing practice in men's prisons, segregation was justified by the claim on the part of prison administrators, articulated both vaguely and sweepingly, that homosexuals represented a threat to institutional order and security. By the 1970s the segregation of gay inmates was newly promoted as a form of "protective custody" intended to shelter them from harassment and assault. Gay men, especially effeminate ones, were often targets for humiliation, exploitation, and sexual violence in prison, but many experienced their recourse of last resort—a request for protective custody (PC)—as compounding rather than relieving the conditions of their incarceration. Protective custody stamped gay men with the stigma of cowardice; it was also associated with the cardinal prison sin of informing, and placement in PC could brand gay men with the damning label of "snitch." Protective custody also entailed a wide array of restrictions and penalties, and gay prisoners alerted activists to the lack of meaningful distinction between PC and punitive solitary detention. Prisoners incarcerated in PC were often held in the same physical quarters as those in solitary confinement, and they suffered the same lack of access to social, recreational, vocational, and rehabilitative opportunities. As a consequence, gay prisoners were often unable to accrue "good time" credit or build a favorable prison record toward early parole or gain placement in work-release programs. One prisoner described the conditions of his confinement: "I am here on what they are calling Protective Custody. It means I'm locked in a 9x4 cell 24 hours a day, 7 days a week and have no program of any kind." He added in understated conclusion, "I'm what you might call getting the shaft."[17]

Few women's prisons engaged in similar practices of segregating lesbians. But lesbian activists protested the policy of placing identifiable (typically butch) lesbians in a separate cell block termed the "Daddy Tank" at the Sybil Brand Institute, the Los Angeles county jail for women. Selection for the Daddy Tank was reportedly made on the basis of physical appearance and deportment, segregating women, in one gay reporter's account, "with short hair cuts or no make up, those wearing trousers with flys [*sic*], jockey shorts, T-shirts or turned up socks, those who spread their legs when they sit, and those who hold a cigarette between thumb and forefinger."[18] Women were held in the Daddy Tank under harsh and restrictive maximum-security conditions regardless of whether they were awaiting trial or serving time and regardless of their offense. Conditions there were reportedly " 'three or four times worse'" than in other sections of the jail.[19] Women confined in the Daddy Tank, lesbian activists charged, "have the least privileges; the filthiest jobs; get thrown in Lock Up without warning."[20]

In a demonstration held in mid-June of 1972, lesbian activists picketed the Sybil Brand Institute to protest its discriminatory and punitive segregation policy.[21] Although they refused to admit bowing to pressure, Sybil Brand officials modified the Daddy Tank into a medium-security "Daddy Dorm," in which inmates were housed in a dormitory rather than in small single cells, were permitted access to an open dayroom, and were newly eligible for occupational classes and recreational programs. But some inmates denied any meaningful improvement in the still segregated conditions. One former resident of the Daddy Tank reported, "they just pulled a few femmes out of the general population" in an effort to make the discriminatory punishment for gender nonconformity less obvious.[22]

Prisoners and their advocates also protested the discrimination against lesbian and gay inmates resulting from indeterminate sentencing laws and the routine denial and revocation of parole on the basis of homosexuality. The indeterminate sentence, a popular reform measure in the late nineteenth century that became the standard form of sentencing throughout the United States, gave courts wide discretion over sentencing lengths and allowed prison officials to hold prisoners beyond their minimum sentencing period for a variety of disciplinary reasons, homosexuality among them. Members of the San Francisco–based collective Join Hands—formed in 1972 and comprising gay men, some of them former prisoners—protested this practice in testimony before a state congressional committee hearing in 1974. "This negative discrimination is often for *no other reason* than the prisoner's sexuality," collective members stated. To support their claims, Join Hands representatives quoted from a letter written by Eddie Loftin, a California prisoner who had been denied parole along with other gay men: "There was 7 gays that went to the parole board, and out of the 7 only one made parole. . . . That is a 'Hell' of a average."[23] Loftin died of a heart attack three months later, still awaiting parole at Folsom.

The discretionary power that indeterminate sentencing granted prison administrators meant that parole could also be denied to inmates on the basis of gender nonconformity. One prisoner at the California Men's Colony complained that he was denied parole sixteen months following the termination of his sentence, "solely because I expressed my intention of having sexual reassignment surgery and hormonal treatment upon release." He was told that his parole would not be reconsidered "until I change my sexual identity."[24] Parole could also be revoked, and prisoners who had been released were consequently forced to hide their homosexuality and gender nonconformity to avoid reincarceration.

Outside and Inside: Queer Encounters

Gay activists arrived at their critique of incarceration in part through the politics of gay liberation and through radical politics more generally. They also did so, importantly, in conversation with gay and lesbian prisoners. Eager for genuine dialogue with prisoners, gay activists insisted that the direction of discussion not be simply one way. The Join Hands collective advertised its newsletter as "a vehicle for gay prisoners to communicate with each other and to educate those of us on the outside as to what's coming down so that we can most effectively direct our support and action."[25] The Seattle-based lesbian feminist collective that published the newsletter *Through the Looking Glass* on women's prison conditions in the Pacific Northwest likewise solicited the writing of women and lesbian prisoners, as did the feminist and lesbian journals *off our backs*, *Lesbian Connection*, and *Lesbian Tide*. Mike Riegle developed and edited "The Other Side of the Wall," a monthly section of *Gay Community News* (*GCN*) devoted to publishing articles and letters written "*by prisoners* about their experiences being in and up against the prison system." In these pages, Riegle wrote, "prisoners speak for themselves for a change, instead of being the subject of others' writings, or forgotten altogether."[26]

The gay, lesbian, and feminist press served as a crucial conduit of information from the outside in and from the inside out.[27] For some prisoners, especially for those who had been active in the movement before their incarceration, news of gay life and politics in the outside world could prove a lifeline. One prisoner who claimed to have been among the "group of shouters" in the Stonewall riots wrote to *Join Hands* that he was "still shouting" and "will not stop. . . . If you are out in those streets, shout a little bit louder for us in here. If you listen really hard you can hear us shouting with you."[28] Another prisoner in New Mexico thanked Riegle for sending him copies of *GCN* that enabled him to "maintain a modicum of pace with current events and grants some perspective to and mediates the negativity around me."[29] For a Wisconsin prisoner, receiving the *Advocate* "keeps me informed as to what is happening in the gay society."[30] Another expressed his appreciation to gay activists who demonstrated against the state penitentiary at Leavenworth, Kansas, to protest the prison's ban on gay publications: "GAY LIB WAS HERE!" he exclaimed. "WOW! Beautiful! Fantastic!! I wanted to hug every one of the protestors. . . . The Gay Community cared, and it felt good. Really great!" As a result, he wrote, "gays walked around here proud of the protestors and of themselves. . . . It's really hard to explain how much this means to gay inmates here."[31]

The value of gay publications to gay prisoners could be measured by tracking a single newspaper's circulation around an institution. "My own G.C.N.s make the rounds of gays on this floor, six of us," one prisoner wrote; "then it goes upstairs to two more gays, then goes to another section of this prison for other gays to read."[32] Another inmate in a Missouri prison on sodomy charges counted "about half a dozen other gay men in this housing unit who are lined up to read each issue of *GCN* as I get them, so we are passing it around to everyone! We're building quite a readership here, I think."[33]

Members of that prison readership learned of gay demonstrations and pride marches, the election of Harvey Milk to San Francisco's Board of Supervisors in

1977 and his assassination the following year, Florida's Dade County anti–gay rights initiative, the defeat of California's Briggs initiative that would have banned gays and lesbians from teaching in public schools, and other news of the successes and setbacks of a growing movement. Reading in *RFD* about "the 100,000 gay march in San Francisco" in 1976 inspired one prisoner in the Washington state penitentiary to exclaim, "YEH-HOO! It opened my eyes to a new world, to know that gay brothers and sisters are out there doing what we want to do, but can't at this time."[34]

Perhaps less self-consciously but no less important, the gay press alerted readers to new homosexual norms and values. In the process, gay newspapers and journals not only informed readers of news of the movement but also instructed them in new ways to be gay. The new movement was accompanied by a new ethos — informed by the affirmation that gay was good and a call to gay pride, an imperative to "come out," a belief in sexual reciprocity and mutuality, a refusal of gay stereotypes, and a critique of gendered roles. Those new norms often collided with a sexual culture in prison that had a much longer history. In a 1976 *Advocate* article, David Rothenberg wrote that "gay pride and gay self acceptance . . . challenge the lifestyle and social structure of the prison population."[35] The norms of prison sexual culture, by contrast — characterized in women's prisons by butch-femme partnerships and in men's prisons by the participation of heterosexually identified men whose masculine gender presentation and "active," penetrative role in sex with other men did not confer or connote a homosexual identity, and by their asymmetrical and sometimes exploitative partnerships with other men who were sometimes feminized by association — ran directly counter to the emerging norms of post-Stonewall urban gay life.

Prisons were far from impermeable to phenomena in the larger outside culture, and there is some evidence that the new norms of gay life were beginning to appear behind bars by the 1970s and 1980s. "Just as the gay scene has changed in the free world," one prisoner wrote, "so in prison one finds a more militant gay who values his masculinity and refuses to be a female surrogate."[36] The demographic profile of the San Francisco jail in San Bruno would hardly have been typical, but one gay man imprisoned there reported in 1983 that "every conceivable Gay subculture" was represented on the jail's "Gay tier": "drag queens, muscle men, preppies, post-op transsexuals, hippie queers, rednecks, leather men, clones — the gamut."[37] One Oklahoma prisoner, considerably further from the epicenter of gay culture, who identified as "not overly butch nor overly femme, I'm just me," wrote in 1976 about his defiance of prison gender norms in a relationship with another inmate: "We both agreed that neither of us was the dominant one . . . . Sometimes I would be in the passive role, sometimes Roger would." "The trouble started," he wrote, when straight prisoners started asking " 'what could two whores do for each other?' The fact that two guys were making it to the exclusion of all straights rankled their souls."[38] Another prisoner at Vacaville wrote in 1977 that after "bounc[ing] in and out (mostly in) of the California prison system for close to 20 years," he had "at long last" begun to "break out of the restrictions of the almost mandatory stereotyping of sexual roles imposed on us here in the penal society by our peers."[39] When he stopped plucking his eyebrows and wearing tight pants, his noncompliance with prison gender norms incited a "battle" in which he had to "fight to prove my sincerity in demanding to be allowed to be myself" and to "put up with frequent threats of being stabbed."[40] One Lompoc inmate noted the "new trend" of what he termed "'fag-on-fag'" sex that emerged in the early 1980s, a trend that he blamed for disrupting "the sex life of straights" in the prison, his own included. "Regular guys can't compete with homosexuals," he added, because they could not abide sexual reciprocity: "Homos on homos get into sixty-nining, rimming . . . . We can't deal with that. That's tough to compete with."[41]

Some gay male prisoners resisted the feminizing demands of prison sexual culture, but many found the pressures of prison sexual norms and expectations overwhelming. That collision provoked frustration and anger on the part of some inmates who were forced to adjust to a sexual code that differed markedly from the one taking shape outside. Those accustomed to gay life on the street "must set aside their 'old self' and make way for a new personality" on coming to prison, one inmate wrote.[42] A California prisoner explained, "you don't have gays here . . . . There are 'men' and 'women.' The 'men' are 'straight' and the 'women' are queer, punks, fags, etc. All of the labels that the gays on the outside fight against . . . . It's a real bummer of a trip . . . . These things merely serve to make things difficult for those who are gay and proud."[43] Another wrote to members of New York's Gay Activists Alliance that in prison, "there is no such animal as a 'Gay.' You must be a punk, a queer, a faggot, a dicksucker . . . , a bitch, a whore — but you *may not be Gay*, and *certainly cannot be proud*!"[44] Still another complained, "There simply is no room in the prison environment for a man who likes other men. The only relationship that can be understood and accepted is a man and his 'girl.'"[45]

Some lesbian prisoners voiced similar frustration with the dissonance of gay life behind bars and the one taking shape outside. While women prisoners had long organized their relationships along gendered lines, many lesbian feminists criticized butch-femme roles as imitative of heterosexuality and supportive of traditional and oppressive gender roles, and those criticisms found their way into prisons in the 1970s. One inmate told an interviewer in 1973, "there's a lot more role playing" at California's Terminal Island prison "than out on the street," and that she felt forced to participate because people said, "'Oh, look at the new daddy that's in.' 'I've never been a daddy in my life!'" she added, "but as long as you walk with an aggressive walk, then they tag you as a daddy and that's what you're gonna be."[46] She did note, however, that "now that Women's Liberation has come around, it's changed a little bit. Like I've noticed that more girls are accepting you being a woman instead of being a male image or a butch or a dyke."[47] Another California prisoner used the terminology of lesbian feminism in referencing "women loving women relationships," but complained that in prison, they "take on all the fucked up aspects of male female relationships—the dominant/passive, the games, the possessiveness, the jealousies, the role playing."[48]

The collision between new norms of gay liberation and lesbian feminism and those of prison sexual culture elicited a change in consciousness, or at least a new consciousness of appropriate sexual script, on the part of some prisoners. One inmate who had once adopted the gendered norms of prison sexual culture recalled self-critically in an interview with a gay activist that he had been "into a role thing, where I was a homosexual and [my partner] was a straight man." When asked, leadingly, if he had come to think differently, he replied, "Oh, yeah. My consciousness is entirely different now. I think that having to play those roles was extremely oppressive for many of us."[49] The inmate Bobbie Lee White testified to the transformative power of receiving *GCN* while in prison. In learning about the gay movement outside, White explained, he had come to understand that "being gay is something more than having sex with the same sex."[50]

Some who suffered the oppressive conditions of prison life were inspired both by the gay and the prisoners' rights movements to organize on their own behalf. Some of those efforts appeared to be spontaneous responses to discrimination. An Illinois prisoner recounted that "we used to have this thing where many of the gay people would organize, and do strikes, and sit-ins, and shit like that, refuse to do any work."[51] Other groups emphasized support and consciousness raising. La Toya Lewis, a male-to-female transsexual prisoner in the state penitentiary in Los Lunas, New Mexico, notified *GCN* of a group called Gays in Prison, which held "rap sessions to help each other with the problems of everyday prison life," especially with vulnerability to sexual violence.[52] Another prisoner, Tyrone Gadson, announced the start of "a self-help organization" at New Jersey's Rahway State Prison called the Gayworld Organization, for "gay inmates who are having adjustment problems with their gaylife in the institution."[53] Gay prisoners in the Louisiana state prison at Angola formed the Self-Help Alliance Group (or SHAG) in 1984 to "help, promote, and assist this segment of the prison society which has, for so long, been ignored, ridiculed, and belittled" and to develop the "creative talents of homosexuals."[54] The founders of SHAG proposed an orientation for gay men entering prison to "indoctrinate homosexuals to the various lifestyles and atmosphere of the various prison environments" and to teach them to "conduct themselves . . . so that they can live in peace, without harassment."[55]

One of the first organizations of gay prisoners was founded in 1977 at the Washington state penitentiary at Walla Walla. Initiated by members of the George Jackson Brigade, a revolutionary guerrilla organization active in the Pacific Northwest in the mid-1970s convicted for several small bombings and bank heists, the group worked to protect gay and other vulnerable inmates from sexual harassment and violence. Members met the "chain" (the bus on which new inmates were transferred to the prison) each week and provided orientation to new prisoners to tutor them in the complexities of prison etiquette and warn them of prison dangers. They also worked to secure "safe cells" and provided escort services for "those men most likely to be raped, sold, pimped, and preyed upon in the sexual meat market condoned by the administration."[56] Gay prisoners at Walla Walla boasted some remarkable successes. "The other day two prisoners 'sold' a gay cellmate to another prisoner," one prisoner wrote. "We moved into the situation and smashed the deal. The 'property' was moved into one of our cells and is under our escort."[57] They also worked to release gay prisoners from protective custody and helped integrate them safely into the general population.

The name that Walla Walla prisoners chose for their organization, Men against Sexism, articulated an analysis of prison sexual violence comprehensible to gay and lesbian activists and fully compatible with the ideological foundations of gay liberationist thought. In working toward an analysis of gay oppression, lesbians and gay men looked to sexism as a root cause, indicting in particular the patriarchal values, normative gender roles, and institutionalized heterosexuality nurtured and policed by the nuclear family. Gay Liberation Front activist Martha Shelley identified gay men and lesbians as "women and men who, from the time of our earliest memories, have been in revolt against the sex-role structure and nuclear family structure."[58] It was perhaps not surprising that lesbians would be drawn to radical feminism for analyses of their oppression. But gay male activists also located their oppression in the nuclear family's enforcement of normative masculinity. "Gay liberation is a struggle against sexism," Allen Young announced. "Within the context of our society, sexism is primarily manifested through male supremacy and heterosexual chauvinism."[59]

Those critiques inspired Walla Walla's Men against Sexism, whose members challenged the hypermasculinist prison ethos they viewed as contributing to sexual violence. Prisoners who called on feminist analyses of sexism in order to understand prison oppressions were readily comprehensible to gay activists outside. The language of gay oppression and pride used more generally by many other incarcerated activists resonated with and echoed the language used by activists outside. Gay activists could not help but be gratified by proclamations like that of the inmate La Toya Lewis that "it was a long fight to get where we are now, but now the Gay Men and Transsexuals (such as myself) can walk with pride that cannot be DIMINISHED!!!!!!!!"[60] A representative from the "gay collective" in the Florida prison at Raiford likewise proclaimed it time "for us gay people to realize that we are oppressed people," and appealed to others to "reach out and join hands with your oppressed brothers."[61] Indiana prisoners wrote to Black and White Men Together (BWMT), declaring their interest in starting a chapter of the organization behind bars and asking outside members to "please send the Starter's Kit."[62] The language of brotherhood and sisterhood infused gay prison activism, and in communicating their gratitude to outside allies, some prisoners echoed the language of gay kinship. One lesbian wrote that *GCN* offered her and other gay prisoners "a sense of belonging—of being part of a family. The family of gay and lesbian brothers and sisters."[63] Connections between activists and prisoners were also apparent in appreciative and comradely salutations in their correspondence. One inmate signed his letter to Riegle, "Sealed with a kiss of our gay struggle," and another concluded a missive to *GCN* with "Thanks Fellow Gays."[64]

For gay and lesbian activists working in solidarity with their "brothers" and "sisters" behind bars, the familial resemblance of some prisoners was striking. When those newly forged familial connections produced a shared language and shared assumptions, conversations between prisoners and activists were mutually comprehensible, productive, and gratifying. Finding (and in some cases, producing) likenesses among others took more effort. Gay activists forged critiques of sexism that condemned the forced gendered roles of prison sexual culture expressed most violently in sexual assault and coerced partnerships, but their ethos of sexual reciprocity and condemnation of gay stereotypes sometimes made it difficult to ally with those in men's prisons who identified as ladies, queens, and transsexuals and who often felt the brunt of prison misogyny most directly. Activists typically disavowed those attitudes, but they were sometimes perceived by prisoners and occasionally by prison officials. When Mattachine and Gay Activists Alliance members held a lecture and rap session with men training to be correction officers in New York City's penal facilities, one officer in training observed the masculine gender presentation of the activists and noted, "I think you should have had a feminine homosexual on the panel" since "that is the kind we have to deal with mainly in here."[65] Another trainee, perhaps referencing class and racial divisions between activists and prisoners, as well as gender differences, told the gay panelists: "I think you have a different frame of reference coming in from the outside like you do. I think most of you would look down on most of the homos, I mean homosexuals, we have in here."[66]

Not all gay activists, certainly, disparaged queens, in or out of prison. But the 1970s ushered in a new understanding of gay identity in which gender-transgressive queers would be increasingly marginalized. As the gay movement moved away from its earlier embrace of gender transgression, many gay men assumed a clonish masculinity, and lesbian feminists rejected butch-femme styles they cast as relics of an earlier, apolitical time for a purportedly gender-neutral androgyny.[67] Many prison queens who insisted on identifying as gay at a time when inclusion in that category was coming to privilege gender normativity felt looked down on by gay activists from the outside. One complained, "The gays outside are so wrapped up in saying that drag queens are a disgrace to macho gays, . . . that they forget . . . that we're all homosexuals and on top of that we're all oppressed." He criticized Join Hands as a group that "wish[es] to continue bickering about whether queens are acceptable to be part of the gay society and if we should be cast out even further into oppression *by our own brothers and sisters.*" In response to the *Join Hands* invitation to prisoners to help define gay political strategy, this prisoner stated: "First of all you should drop all your barriers about gays having to be macho."[68] Another who identified as "a gay prisoner from Illinois" who was transferred to a small male unit of a predominantly women's institution "because I have breasts resulting from hormone treatment" addressed "all you gay brothers and sisters out there," asking "why don't you give the queens a break? It's hard enough on us being put down by straights."[69] And still another spoke to the tensions between "queens" behind bars and "machos" outside: "Both are Gay," he wrote; "this . . . should be the Unity point." This prisoner urged gay activists to focus on "just being Gay brothers seeking to help other Gay brothers."[70] Other prisoners felt pressured to conform to the gendered expectations of gay men outside, ones shaped by the scripts of gay pornography that eroticized prisoners as roughly masculine. "Just because we are in prison," one wrote, "doesn't mean we are all supermen, macho, hung like mules, etc., etc., etc." He added that he had been "forced to live these lies" in order to "keep the letters coming" from gay pen pals on the outside.[71]

Some observers described the presence of prison queens and butches and the differences between prison sexual culture and gay culture in temporal terms, as the clash between "primitive" and more evolved forms of sexual organization, or the meeting of a stubbornly retrograde sexual culture with a modern one. Casting prison sexual culture in an overtly developmental narrative, some characterized its gendered roles as evidence of a less enlightened homosexual past. To Wayne S. Wooden and Jay Parker, the "prison sexual code, which works to feminize homosexuals," was "directly opposed to the goals of the modern gay movement." "A positive gay identity," in their estimation, "attempts to free men from the tyranny of rigid role-playing."[72] That tyranny was usually equated with gender deviance and most strongly with male effeminacy; masculinity for gay men was cast not as a "role," but rather as a reclamation of the manhood and the dignity long denied them and as a sign of gay modernity. Prison life, Wooden and Parker wrote, keeps gay men "bound to rigid stereotypic roles—the roles of the submissive, dependent, passive, and weak female—the same roles many in society have also rejected" (145). Prison gender norms, to Wooden and Parker, were signs that gay identity in prison "has remained at less advanced stages of development . . . compared to the gay subculture that is developing external to the prison environment" (219). Wooden and Parker contrasted prisoners' gendered pairings with relationships in the outside "gay community" that tend "*not* to be modeled along dichotomous male and female lines" (160) and were characterized instead by "a bond between two self-affirming and masculine-defined gay men" (161). Their definition of modern gay men—those "who assume both active and passive roles, and who display few if any effeminate mannerisms"—effectively removed prison queens from the category of "gay" (3).

The developmental explanation of prison sexual culture was deeply imbued with assumptions about the gender norms appropriate to modern gay identity. As in other iterations, this narrative of sexual primitivism and modernity was also deeply racialized.[73] Those assumptions were laid bare in an account by gay journalist Randy Shilts, who arranged to be booked on fake traffic charges to observe gay life behind bars. After spending several nights in the jails' gay tiers, he felt that he had entered "not only another world but another era." The "queens' tanks" in San Francisco county jails, in Shilts's account, gave rise to their "own social system and stylized sex roles reminiscent of the gay world of two decades ago." In highlighting racial and class differences in his representation of the gendered roles he observed in jail as an anachronistic marker of same-sex desire, Shilts made clear the racialized assumptions implicit in the developmental narrative of modern gay identity. Inmates of the San Francisco jails "brought back to me what I had read about poor gays from black and Latin cultures. Influenced by the more stringent sex roles of their own worlds, I found these prisoners adopting feminine roles rather than the newer, masculine gay-male roles of the educated white middle classes."[74]

Gender identity was sometimes a point of contention in advocacy efforts on behalf of gay prisoners, and emerging norms of gay masculinity and sexual reciprocity sometimes created tensions between gay activists outside and queens and transsexuals behind bars. Gay and lesbian activists' alliances with men incarcerated for sex with minors were also occasionally strained, as they struggled over how and whether to accommodate men who were attracted to boys into the larger movement. That ambivalence was, in some cases, mutual. In a 1980 *GCN* article, Tom Reeves, the founder of the North American Man-Boy Love Association, offered an analysis "of a serious oppression of gay men, among whose number I may some day find myself."[75] But Reeves was dismayed to find that few of the 125 Massachusetts prisoners convicted of having sex with minors affiliated with "the gay community." Some of them expressed their alienation from that community in class and gender terms. One man told Reeves that the gay life he knew about in Boston, "downtown, on Beacon Hill, faggots dressed up like women, gay bars," had little to do with working-class life in Revere where he grew up. Another told him, "'I knew nothing about gay organizations other than bars. If I had known, I would have thought I didn't fit in.'"[76] Reeves found it gratifying, though, that more and more of the men in prison for having sex with minors were "coming out": "More of them are asking for subscriptions to *GCN*, more are identifying as gay in prison, and more are seeking gay activist lawyers . . . . They are beginning to define themselves as a gay population suffering a particularly severe oppression."[77] Reeves and others like him made a case for their inclusion in the larger gay liberation movement, but gay advocacy on behalf of men incarcerated for having sex with minors was always contentious. The transformation of a movement for sexual liberation into a movement for civil rights, requiring in turn a respectable homosexual subject deserving of such rights, ultimately led to an effort to remove the pedophile from the category of homosexual.[78]

Before that point, however, in one California institution, men who had been diagnosed as "disordered sex offenders," most charged with having had sex with minors, were encouraged in a strikingly literal fashion to redefine and remake themselves as gay. They were led in that remarkable effort by psychiatrist Michael Serber. A strong proponent and practitioner of behavior modification, Serber had earlier pioneered what he called "shame aversion therapy," a technique that developed, he explained, as the incidental and fortuitous result of photographing a transvestite patient in the act of cross-dressing, which produced what Serber judged to be the usefully transformative shaming effects of social exposure.[79] The photography session was originally conceived as merely instrumental to the therapeutic plan. Serber had intended to project photographs of the patient dressed in women's lingerie while administering "painful electrical shocks to one of his extremities." But he found this later stage in the "therapy" to be unnecessary: the patient became "markedly anxious" and "unable to get sexually excited" while being photographed and reported that the experience had "completely 'turned him off'" and "changed his entire feeling about cross-dressing."[80] In Serber's later applications of the technique of shame aversion therapy, patients were ordered to cross-dress in front of therapists. Serber also reported positively on the use of aversive conditioning to alter the behavior of homosexuals, noting that "homosexual practices were virtually eliminated and homosexual interest was substantially decreased" in patients who were administered electric shocks when aroused sexually.[81]

Serber came to disavow such therapies when his consciousness, along with that of many other psychiatrists and psychologists, was raised by gay liberationists who challenged the psychiatric profession's homophobic and pathologizing assumptions and practices.[82] After experiencing a Gay Activists Alliance "zap" at a meeting of the Association for Advancement of Behavior Therapy in New York in 1972, Serber introduced a new treatment and "retraining" program for inmates he termed "inadequate homosexuals"—most of them convicted of having sex with minors—sentenced to California's maximum-security carceral hospital at Atascadero. One gay activist characterized Atascadero inmates as "closeted Gays on the street" who "have never experienced being Gay but have shared the common trauma of feeling different and unaccepted."[83] Serber explained the goals of his program as working to retrain sex offenders "in the social skills most rewarding in the gay community while at the same time minimizing their problems in getting along in a generally hostile world."[84] The reporter Rob Cole translated Serber's social scientific language for readers of the *Advocate*, writing that he aimed "to teach adult males how to make it with each other instead of with young boys, and not get arrested."[85]

Toward that end, Serber renounced aversion therapy and instead led group discussions with inmates, exploring topics including "the problems of being gay in a predominantly straight society," "social alternatives for homosexuals," and "situations to be avoided in order not to be subsequently arrested."[86] To help Atascadero inmates learn social skills appropriate to modern gay life, Serber solicited members of the newly formed Gay Student Union at the California Polytechnic University to serve as instructors and "appropriate behavioral models." Cal Poly students led Atascadero inmates through imagined scenarios at a gay bar, coaching them in "specific verbal and nonverbal components of gay social interaction which served as a 'behavioral base' upon which further social skills could be built."[87] Atascadero inmate Tom Close explained that "we were taught cruising from eye contact to wrapup, and given the opportunity to practice our dancing skills."[88] Phase 2 of Serber's program involved consciousness-raising, the first topic of which was titled "Gay is ___," calling on inmates to come to terms with homosexuality's negative associations and to arrive at more self-affirming definitions.[89] In the final phase of the program (and an important part of their treatment) inmates were encouraged to form and participate in a gay organization of their own, the Atascadero Gay Encounter, within the institution.[90] Minority identity group identification and political organization thus constituted the program's therapeutic denouement.

Serber's program replaced earlier treatment regimes at Atascadero and other prisons that were considerably more violent in their sexual pedagogy and more sexually normative in their aims. Stories had circulated for years in the gay press about the use of succinylcholine, a muscle-relaxing drug that produced a feeling of suffocation and was used along with nausea-inducing drugs in aversion therapy, as well as the use of electroconvulsive shock treatment as punishment for homosexual patients who "deviated" while in the hospital. Serber acknowledged that the history of treatment at Atascadero had "mainly centered around inadequate and sometimes cruel attempts at conversion to heterosexuality or asexuality," and he developed his treatment regime with considerably more humane and progressive aims.[91] Newly critical of the belief among psychiatrists that homosexuality was a psychopathic condition, Serber advanced "an alternative perspective of homosexuals," in line with the developing gay rights ideology, as "a minority group that should be provided meaningful social and psychological services in the criminal justice system."[92] "It is questionable that it is even possible to effect a change from complete homosexuality to complete heterosexuality," Serber wrote, "but even if it were possible to successfully effect complete change, does anyone have the right to revise a person's entire value system in an area of behavior that influences only himself and a consenting partner?"[93]

Serber's recognition that "a homosexual has the right to be a homosexual if he wants to" led the *Advocate* reporter Cole to call his program "revolutionary." And surely his "retraining" program was appreciated by prisoners as more humane than earlier treatment regimes.[94] But Serber's program had a disciplinary purpose as well, however benevolently intentioned: Atascadero inmates were tutored in the new gay norms being forged in the 1970s. Those pedagogical aims were clearly recognized by Cole, who titled his article "Lessons in Being Gay."[95]

The pedagogical impulses at work in Serber's program were evident in other aspects of gay prison activism as well. The Metropolitan Community Church (MCC), a nondenominational Christian church with largely gay congregations founded in 1968, began conducting services in some prisons in 1972 and was very active in advocating on behalf of gay prisoners. In addition to holding services for prisoners—resisted in many prisons and requiring a long legal battle for recognition as a legitimate church—the MCC developed pen-pal and visitation programs for gay inmates.[96] Some of the MCC's literature made clear that among the church's missions in prison activism was inculcation in new gay norms and values. The MCC's *Prison Ministry Handbook* stated that "[a] person who is homosexual by nature, by inclination, and by behavior can benefit immensely by understanding what it is to be gay."[97] This illuminating line made clear that to be *homosexual* and to be *gay* were emerging as two different things—the first simply descriptive of a sexual orientation and the second embodying a set of norms and values, no less powerful for being only occasionally articulated explicitly.

The MCC's "Homosexual's Prayer," distributed in prison services, perhaps went the furthest in delineating those norms and exposing the MCC's missionary zeal in promoting them. In it, the MCC urged the homosexual prisoner to "be a Gay we can be proud of."[98] That self-improvement project involved coming to understand homosexuality as being "on a level higher than 'messing around.' "[99] The "bona fide homosexual," the MCC instructed, should be encouraged to "come to an understanding of how gay can be good and clean and ennobling"; that person, in the MCC's understanding, "becomes a whole lot healthier when he or she can say 'I am gay and I am proud.' "[100] This process also involved an acceptance of the minoritizing assumptions of the gay movement—the understanding of oneself as "member of a minority," one united with "brothers and sisters in a true family; bound together in a common cause"; and willing to "thank God that I am a homosexual."[101]

While Serber's treatment program and the MCC's prison ministry suggested that there were proper ways to be gay, the MCC's reference to "bona fide homosexuals" suggested that some prisoners provoked more basic questions about who among the prison population, many of whom participated in homosexual sex, was truly "gay" to begin with (not just properly so). Gay activists were, for the most part, curiously silent about men who surely constituted the majority of participants in same-sex sex behind bars—those identified as "jockers" and "punks." A long-standing prison aphorism declared that "Queens are born. Punks are made."[102] A type recognized in prison argot since at least the early twentieth century, the punk was a presumptively heterosexual prisoner who submitted to same-sex sex as a result of sexual coercion and sometimes assault. Prisoners known as jockers or "men" had long been identified in prison life as conventionally, often aggressively masculine men who preserved (and in some accounts, enhanced) that status by assuming the active, penetrative role in sex with other men.

Gay activists, for the most part, had little to say about prisoners who had sex

with other men without adopting (or, in the case of jockers, being ascribed) a gay
identity. But in a section of the MCC's *Prison Ministry Handbook* tellingly titled
"Who Is Gay?" the MCC warned those involved in prison ministry to "take note
of special problems associated with sexuality in prisons," clarifying that "in prisons
there may be homosexual behavior on the part of men and women who will never be
'gay' and who probably never will identify themselves with the gay community."[103]
Because of circumstances the MCC described vaguely as "factors peculiar to homosexuality in prison," especially the "'old man – old lady' relationships that are common" behind bars, it recommended against performing the rite of Holy Union, practiced in MCC churches, in prison ministry work.[104] While some prisoners might,
with some effort, be brought into the gay fold, others stretched the notion of gay
kinship beyond the breaking point.

Anxiety about distinguishing "true" gays from their imposters arose most frequently around the subject of pen-pal correspondence with prisoners. Many gay newspapers and journals supported pen-pal initiatives with prisoners in the 1970s as a form
of outreach and support as part of the political project of connecting prisoners to gay
men and lesbians outside and intended to let gay prisoners know that "they really are
still part of the family." "Remember that . . . those who submit their names for correspondence have a lot in common with those on the outside," *Advocate* editors wrote
in 1973.[105] But ten years later, in 1983, following reports of prisoners scamming gay
pen pals out of money and gifts, the editor of the *Bay Area Reporter* prefaced the
paper's prison pen-pal request section with a cautionary note that "the paper in no way
endorses or can stand behind the integrity of the letter writer. We . . . don't even know
if they're Gay or not."[106] One reader warned, "beware of the phony and non-gay that
want to prey on us even from within the walls of Folsom, Pendleton, Michigan City,
Travis, Lucasville, or wherever. They use OUR publications even as they sit in their jail
cells as a means to get at the faggots."[107] One *Advocate* reader asked the editor of the
pen-pal section, "Isn't there any way you can weed out the non-gay mail order pimps
from your list of prisoners who want mail?" and wrote that "your column is too good to
be used by some tramp whose only aim is to 'use the queers.'" "Can't you screen these
gays out," he asked, "or at least make sure they're gay?"[108]

Distinguishing between "real" and "phony" gays, however, was not always
easy. A misunderstanding between the prisoner Troy Lewis and *GCN*'s Mike Riegle
illuminated some of the competing and unpredictable definitions of identity at work
in interactions between prisoners and gays outside. Lewis had sent a pen-pal request
to *GCN*, in which he identified himself as "straight." When Riegle rejected the ad,
specifying that the *GCN* pen-pal section was for gay prisoners, Lewis responded in
protest: "Well, Mike, I don't know how or what you consider the terms Gay, straight,
etc . . . to be but my interpretation of straight is a homosexual that partakes an *active*
role playing (i.e. fucker) during the course of homosexuality, in contrast to 'a gay,'"
who he defined as "a homosexual who partakes the *passive* role of homosexual-

ity." "When I use the term 'straight,'" he concluded, "it doesn't exclude me from being homosexual too."[109] The self-understanding of some prisoners — in Lewis's case utterly confounding the categories of the gay movement, as well as those of the larger culture — was difficult to assimilate into the sexual epistemology of even the most accommodating and expansive of gay activists.

Anxiety about the criminal as well as the sexual status of prisoners was implicit in the many warnings about pen-pal scams and "fake" gays. The suspicions and preju-dices of many gay men and lesbians who supported a politics of prison advocacy were sometimes ignited when they were confronted with actual convicts. "Never have I seen one where the writer reveals what he is in prison for," the editor of the *Bay Area Reporter* wrote of prison pen-pal ads in a warning to potential correspondents, "but when they come from the maximum security prisons, I have to imagine the reason is for more than jaywalking."[110] One reader wrote that "in fairness to us readers, I think they should send a copy of their rap sheet to be published along with their letter. I'm sure most of those guys didn't get where they are for helping grandmothers across the street."[111] One gay prisoner wrote to the *Advocate* to complain that his pen pal stopped writing when he told him that he was serving a sentence of ten years to life for armed robbery.[112] Another reader warned that gay men who wrote to prisoners were "ideal targets for everything from blackmail to murder."[113] One lesbian wrote to *GCN* in 1987 to "refuse to support the paper further as long as it continues the asinine policy of supporting 'gay and lesbian' prisoners," her quotation marks raising questions about the authenticity of their sexual identity. She added that she was "tired of seeing letters bitching about how terrible prison is. They should have thought of that before they committed a crime."[114] Comments like these reflected a marked shift from the solidary position that "we are all prisoners" to a feeling of distance and disidentification, especially on the part of the predominantly white, middle-class readers of gay magazines, from those behind bars.

Interest in gay advocacy on behalf of prisoners declined in the 1980s and 1990s, evidenced by the discontinuation of prison pen-pal projects, often following exposés of scams perpetrated by prisoners on gay and lesbian correspondents, and the dwindling coverage of prison issues in the gay and lesbian press. In 1987, *RFD* renounced the Left's (and implicitly its own) romanticized relationship with prison-ers, which it traced to "a certain resentment of authority which elevates the criminal to the rank of hero." "The simple truth," the *RFD* editors wrote, "is that most men in prison are there because they belong there," adding that "some are truly evil."[115] That change coincided with the transmutation of a movement for sexual liberation into a movement dedicated to pursuing equal rights and reflected a corresponding shift in the movement's commitments and priorities. The activist David Frey sug-gested as much, writing bluntly in 1980 that "the Gay Prisoner Activist is a role I see no future in." In part, Frey framed his objection to prison advocacy as a pragmatic calculation of winnable battles. "You cannot expect government institutions to allow magazines depicting illegal sex acts," Frey wrote, dismissing the long-standing fight against the prohibition of gay publications in prison. More broadly, Frey asserted, prison activism "serve[d] as a negative element in the overall debate" in the struggle for "Gay Rights." That struggle, Frey insisted, "must be a united one, with as little fragmentation as possible," and he worried that advocacy on behalf of the most stigmatized and marginalized members of the community threatened to fragment the "gay community." "Let's stay on the right path and keep Gay Rights a legislative issue," Frey urged. In his prescient conclusion that "legally sanctioned Gay marriage should be a primary concern for all of us," Frey anticipated the priorities of the gay and lesbian rights movement as they would evolve in later decades.[116]

Frey made these comments in 1980, a year before the ravages of the AIDS epidemic would begin to spur some gay men and lesbians toward more militant activism and radical social analysis. With few exceptions, however, gay and lesbian activists failed to take those forms of activism and analysis into work on behalf of prisoners.[117] In 1988, the ACLU (American Civil Liberties Union) prison advocate Judy Greenspan recalled discussing prison AIDS activism with Riegle, who "looked at me and said, 'Well, there's you and me.' . . . He was very depressed."[118] Riegle continued to work on behalf of prisoners until his own death from AIDS-related illness in 1992.[119]

Riegle called for gay men and lesbians to support prisoners as "the marginal people who get too far off the proper property/propriety line—the queer queers."[120] But prison sexual culture could be more capacious, heterogeneous, and troubling in its queerness than could be easily accommodated by an emerging gay rights politics. The community-building project of gay prison activism, radical in its vision and productive in many of its manifestations, confronted sexual codes and renegade forms of homosexuality that mixed awkwardly and sometimes not at all with new visions, norms, and understandings of gay identity. As Michel Foucault observed, even ostensibly liberatory discourses impose order through constructing norms of identity and practice. Activists struggled with the difficulty of assimilating some inmates into the gay and lesbian "family" being imagined into existence in the 1970s and 1980s; in doing so, they exposed the ironically normative and evangelizing impulses of gay liberation and of "modern" homosexuality more generally. Marked at various points by solidarity and a meaningful connection across the divide of prison walls, and at others by appropriation, pedagogy, misrecognition, and disidentification, the encounter of gay activists with prisoners illuminated the contours of new gay norms in the making.

In part, those new norms were advanced in the service of claims to respectability, as liberationist calls for sexual freedom and liberation gave way to liberal demands for gay rights and social inclusion. This shift locates and surveys the historical roots of a development that historian Lisa Duggan has identified as homonormativity: "A politics that does not contest dominant heteronormative assumptions and institutions but upholds and sustains them."[121] Anxiety about gay respectability was powerfully at work, certainly, in warnings about the criminal designs of prison pen pals, in the ambivalence toward men attracted to minors, and in efforts to distinguish a supposedly modern gay masculinity from the purportedly anachronistic stereotypes of gay male effeminacy. Questions of respectability, in prison activism as elsewhere, were bound up with questions of race. Racial difference, rarely marked or reflected on by lesbian and gay prison activists, shaped concerns about criminality in the 1970s and 1980s as the mass incarceration of the late twentieth century and its disproportionate effects on people of color was beginning to gain momentum. Race was implicated, too, in activists' well-worn narrative of the sexually primitive and modern.

But more than respectability was at stake in these convergences and collisions between gay activists and prisoners. These encounters reveal a broader effort to shore up and stabilize not only the respectable homosexual subject but also to impose a gay paradigm posited as modern on a more multiform prison sexual culture and to enforce a homo-/heterosexual binary system on the more complex set of identities and sensibilities of prisoners. As gay and lesbian activists would come to understand, prison sexual culture exposed the limits of the range of dominant notions of sexuality presumed to be firmly in place by the late twentieth century and undermined presumptions of stable homosexuality as thoroughly as it did those of heterosexuality.

Notes

I am grateful for generous feedback on an early version of this article from participants in the "Sexual Worlds, Political Cultures" conference sponsored by the Social Science Research Council in October 2003. Many thanks as well to Margot Canaday, Janice Irvine, Terence Kissack, Molly McGarry, Kevin Murphy, Joanne Meyerowitz, Siobhan Somerville, and Dara Strolovitch for their helpful comments.

1. The Counter Intelligence Program was an FBI program aimed at investigating and disrupting dissident political organizations within the United States. See David Cunningham, *There's Something Happening Here: The New Left, the Klan, and FBI Counterintelligence* (Berkeley: University of California Press, 2004); Ward Churchill and Jim Vander Wall, *The COINTELPRO Papers: Documents from the FBI's Secret War against Dissent in the U.S.*, 2nd ed. (Boston: South End, 2002).

2. Elizabeth Gurley Flynn, *The Alderson Story: My Life as a Political Prisoner* (New York: International Publishers, 1963), 15.

3. Joan Nestle, "Stone Butch, Drag Butch, Baby Butch," in *A Restricted Country* (Ithaca, NY: Firebrand, 1987), 77.

4. Donn Teal, *The Gay Militants: How Gay Liberation Began in America, 1969–1971* (New York: Stein and Day, 1971), 328. The Women's House of Detention was also a site of protest for activists in the early women's liberation movement. See Karla Jay, *Tales of the Lavender Menace: A Memoir of Liberation* (New York: Basic Books, 1999), 103–5.

5. Howard Blum, "Gays Take on the Cops: From Rage to Madness," *Village Voice*, September 3, 1970, 42, 44. For an account of this march, see Daniel Hurewitz, *Stepping Out: Nine Walks through New York City's Gay and Lesbian Past* (New York: Henry Holt, 1997), 23–24.

6. Blum, "Gays Take on the Cops," 44. See also Frank J. Prial, "Protest March by Homosexuals Sparks Disturbance in 'Village,'" *New York Times*, August 30, 1970; C. Gerald Fraser, "'Gay Ghettos' Seen as Police Targets," *New York Times*, August 31, 1970; Hurewitz, *Stepping Out*, 23–24.

7. In February of 1971, representatives from several New York gay liberation groups picketed outside the Men's House of Detention in lower Manhattan to protest allegations of the "routine brutality" faced by gay prisoners there ("Gays Protest Brutality in N.Y.C. Prisons," *Advocate*, April 14, 1971, 20). During Boston's Gay Pride Week in 1972, activists led a candlelight march to the Charles Street Jail, where they "chanted and sang to let the prisoners know they were there" (John C. Mitzel, "Boston's Week Includes March to Jail, Capital," *Advocate*, July 10, 1972, 14). And in 1973, gay activists in Chicago sponsored a demonstration in support of gay prisoners at the Cook County Jail (Deanna I. Sava to Jeannie, *Advocate*, June 6, 1973, 32).

8. On the relationship of the radical left and the prisoners' rights movement, see Eric Cummins, *The Rise and Fall of California's Radical Prison Movement* (Stanford, CA: Stanford University Press 1994); John Irwin, *Prisons in Turmoil* (Boston: Little, Brown, 1980).

9. Allen Young, "Out of the Closets, into the Streets," in *Out of the Closets: Voices of Gay Liberation*, ed. Karla Jay and Young (1972; New York: New York University Press, 1992), 16.

10. See John D'Emilio, *Sexual Politics, Sexual Communities: The Making of a Homosexual Minority in the United States, 1940–1970* (Chicago: University of Chicago Press, 1983), 70, 157; Nan Alamilla Boyd, *Wide Open Town: A History of Queer San Francisco to 1965* (Berkeley: University of California Press, 2003), 172–73; Molly McGarry and Fred Wasserman, *Becoming Visible: An Illustrated History of Lesbian and Gay Life in Twentieth-Century America* (New York: Viking, 1998).

11. "Behind Bars," *RFD*, no. 10 (1976): 26.

12. Ibid.

13. Mike Riegle, "Sexual Politics of 'Crime': Inside and Out," *GCN*, December 10, 1983, 4.

14. Ibid.

15. Mike Riegle, "A Brief History of *GCN*'s 'Prison Project,'" *GCN*, October 3, 1981, 8.

16. League for Lesbian and Gay Prisoners, pamphlet, n.d., Bromfield Street Educational Foundation Records, Northeastern University, Boston, Massachusetts (hereafter BSEF), Box 12, Fol. 37.

17. Ron Rose to Robert G. DeSantis, May 19, 1974, Robert G. DeSantis Papers, Gay, Lesbian, Bisexual, Transgender Historical Society of Northern California, San Francisco (hereafter GLBT Historical Society), Box 1, Fol. 16.

18. Don Jackson, "The Daddy Tank," *Gay Sunshine*, no. 1 (1972): 3.

19. "Women Hit Jail Treatment," *Advocate*, July 10, 1972, 14.

20. "We Mean Business," *Lesbian Tide* 1 (1972): 1.

21. Ibid.

22. Jeanne Cordova, "Prison Reform—New Freedoms for Daddy-Tanked Lesbians," *Lesbian Tide* 7 (1977): 6.

23. Join Hands Testimony at California State Senate Committee on Penal Institutions Hearings, December 5, 1974, ms., GLBT Historical Society, "Prisoners" file, 1.

24. Jack Hoffman to editor, *RFD*, no. 10 (1976): 29.

25. *Join Hands* subscription form, GLBT Historical Society, "Prisoners" file.

26. Riegle, "Brief History," 8.

27. Prison projects like the one initiated by Boston's *Gay Community News* were initiated
     to forge connections between gay prisoners with gay men and lesbians on the outside.
     The journal *RFD* included a section titled "Brothers behind Bars" devoted to letters and
     pen-pal requests from prisoners. In 1972, a group of gay men in San Francisco formed
     the Join Hands collective and published a newsletter "to bring together members of
     the 'free' community with gay prisoners through correspondence and visiting" (*Join
     Hands* subscription form, GLBT Historical Society, "Prisoners" File). The *Gaycon Press
     Newsletter*, also published in San Francisco, printed articles, short stories, poetry, and
     graphics by gay prisoners, provided information on prison life for gay men and lesbians,
     and listed gay publications available free to prisoners. The Metropolitan Community
     Church (MCC), a nondenominational Christian church with largely gay congregations
     founded in 1968, began conducting services in prisons in 1972 and published the
     Cellmate newsletter.
28. "Still More on P.C.," *Join Hands*, clipping, n.d., BSEF, Box 13, Fol. 2.
29. Alan Greene to Mike Riegle, April 16, 1984, BSEF, Box 13, Fol. 42.
30. Wilbert Leonard Thomas, letter to the editor, *Advocate*, August 18, 1972, 28.
31. Calvin L. Keach, "Gay Demo against Prison Censors," *Join Hands* 5 (1976): 2.
32. Louis to Mike Riegle, March 22, 1983, BSEF, Box 13, Fol. 42.
33. Danny Owen to Mike Riegle, January 27, 1984, BSEF, Box 13, Fol. 42.
34. Buddy L. to editor, *RFD*, no. 10 (1976): 29.
35. David Rothenberg, "Gay Prisoners: Fighting Back behind the Walls," *Advocate*, June 16,
     1976, 11.
36. Frank O'Rourke, "Prisons: The Nature of the Beast," *Honcho*, August 1983, 61.
37. Mike Hippler, "Where the Boys Are: Gay Inmates at San Bruno Jail," *Bay Area Reporter*,
     December 29, 1983.
38. Jack Childers, letter to editor, *Join Hands* 1 (1976): 2.
39. Chuck Hill to editor, *RFD*, no. 13 (1977): 38.
40. Ibid.
41. Quoted in Mark Fleisher, *Warehousing Violence* (Newbury Park, CA: Sage, 1989), 164.
42. Charles McLaughlin, "Homosexual Living behind the Walls," unpublished ms., n.d., BSEF,
     Box 13, Fol. 44.
43. Letter to editor, *Join Hands* 1 (1976): 2.
44. William Kissinger, "View from Within," in New York Gay Activists Alliance newsletter, n.d.,
     International Gay Information Center Archives, New York Public Library (hereafter IGIC),
     Ephemera, "Prison File."
45. Jon Wildes, "To Be Young, Gay, and Behind Bars," *Village Voice*, January 9, 1978, 21.
46. Jeanne Cordova, "Inside Terminal Island," *Lesbian Tide* 2 (1973): 18.
47. Ibid., 18–19.
48. "The Unpleasantries of Pleasanton," *Through the Looking Glass* 4 (1979): 13.
49. "Sissy in Prison: An Interview with Ron Vernon," in Jay and Young, *Out of the Closets*, 107.
50. Bobbie Lee White, "Learning to Understand," *GCN*, January 23, 1982, 9.
51. "Sissy in Prison," 104.
52. Billy LaToya Lewis to *GCN*, n.d., BSEF, Box 13, Fol. 44.
53. Tyrone Gadson, "New American Cult Gay World Behavior Notice," flyer, April 20, 1983,
     BSEF, Box 13, Fol. 42.
54. "Self-Help Alliance Group," n.d. [1984?], BSEF, Box 13, Fol. 42.
55. Ibid.

56. Quoted in Wayne S. Wooden and Jay Parker, *Men behind Bars: Sexual Exploitation in Prison* (New York: Plenum, 1982), 220. On Men against Sexism, see "Men against Sexism," *Through the Looking Glass* 2 (1977): 18; Daniel Burton-Rose, "The Anti-exploits of Men against Sexism, 1977–78," in *Prison Masculinities*, eds. Don Sabo, Terry A. Kupers, and Willie London (Philadelphia: Temple University Press, 2001); Rick English, "Men against Sexism," *RFD* 14 (1977): 49; John McCoy, *Concrete Mama: Prison Profiles from Walla Walla* (Columbia: University of Missouri Press, 1981), 92; 136–37; "Men against Sexism: Past, Present, and Future," *Join Hands* 13 (1978): 6.

57. Rick English, "Walla . . . Men against Sexism," *Join Hands* 12 (1977): 5.

58. Martha Shelley, "Gay Is Good," in Jay and Young, *Out of the Closets*, 32. On the importance of an analysis and critique of sexism to gay liberation ideology, see John D'Emilio, "Still Radical After All These Years: Remembering *Out of the Closets*," in *The World Turned: Essays on Gay History, Politics, and Culture* (Durham, NC: Duke University Press, 2002), 45–63; John D'Emilio, "After Stonewall," in *Making Trouble: Essays on Gay History, Politics, and the University* (New York: Routledge, 1992); Terence Kissack, "'Freaking Fag Revolutionaries': New York's Gay Liberation Front, 1969–1971," *Radical History Review*, no. 62 (1995): 104–34; Marc Stein, *City of Sisterly and Brotherly Love: Lesbian and Gay Philadelphia, 1945–1972* (Chicago: University of Chicago Press, 2000), 322–23; John Loughery, *The Other Side of Silence*: *Men's Lives and Gay Identities; A Twentieth-Century History* (New York: Henry Holt, 1998), 327.

59. Young, "Out of the Closets," 7.

60. Billy LaToya Lewis to *GCN*, n.d., BSEF, Box 13, Fol. 44.

61. Henry Lucas, "We Must Unify," BSEF, Box 12, Fol. 37.

62. Johnny Crawford to *BWMT Quarterly* 11 (1981): 34.

63. Mike Riegle and prisoner friends, "Why Does GCN Have a Prisoner Project?" BSEF, Box 12, Fol. 37.

64. Curly to Mike Riegle, January 29, 1986, BSEF, Box 13, Fol. 42; Denver V. Sassoon to *GCN*, n.d., BSEF, Box 13, Fol. 44; William D. Concannon to editor, *GCN*, July 12, 1980, 4.

65. "Jail Guard Trainees Hear from Gays," *Advocate*, November 22, 1972, 14.

66. Ibid.

67. See Aaron H. Devor and Nicholas Matte, "One Inc. and Reed Erickson: The Uneasy Collaboration of Gay and Trans Activism, 1964–2003," *GLQ* 10 (2004): 179–209; Joanne Meyerowitz, *How Sex Changed: A History of Transsexuality in the United States* (Cambridge, MA: Harvard University Press, 2002), 235, 237–38; Dallas Denny, "You're Strange and We're Wonderful: The Relationship between the Gay/Lesbian and Transgendered Communities," *TransSisters* 2 (1994): 21–23; Kissack, "Freaking Fag Revolutionaries," 123. Kissack underlines the importance of masculinist affirmations in new left politics and "the extent to which sexualized codes of masculinity were a highly charged component of sixties' discourse," in which gay liberationists partook (111–12). See also Richard Meyer, "Gay Power Circa 1970: Visual Strategies for Sexual Revolution," *GLQ* 12 (2006): 454–55.

68. Tracy, letter to editor, *Join Hands* 1 (1976): 1.

69. "Hard Times for Queens," *Join Hands* 5 (1976): 3.

70. M. Darrell Hay, letter to editor, *Join Hands* 2 (1976): 1.

71. "Mr. Cuddles Talks about Letter Writing," *Join Hands* 2 (1976): 7.

72. Wooden and Parker, *Men behind Bars*, 144.

73. Postcolonial theorists, anthropologists, and historians have exposed the ethnocentrism in the developmental narrative that positions a primitive other against a modern us. David Halperin, for instance, notes the "noxious political effects" of pronouncing some forms of sexual organization "modern" and others "primitive" or "backward" by comparison. Such a progress narrative, he writes, "not only promotes a highly invidious opposition between sexually advanced and sexually retrograde cultures but also fails to take account of the complexity of contemporary transnational formations of sexuality." David Halperin, "Introduction: In Defense of Historicism," in *How to Do the History of Homosexuality* (Chicago: University of Chicago Press, 2002), 18; 14. On anthropologists' use of temporal terms to communicate cultural difference and cultural hierarchy, see Johannes Fabian, *Time and the Other: How Anthropology Makes Its Object* (New York: Columbia University Press, 1983). For discussions of the intersection of white identity and homonormativity, see Roderick A. Ferguson, "Race-ing Homonormativity: Citizenship, Sociology, and Gay Identity," in *Black Queer Studies: A Critical Anthology*, ed. E. Patrick Johnson and Mae G. Henderson (Durham, NC: Duke University Press, 2006), 52–67; Martin F. Manalansan IV, "In the Shadows of Stonewall: Examining Gay Transnational Politics and the Diasporic Dilemma," *GLQ* 2 (1995): 425–38.

74. Randy Shilts, "Locked Up with the Jailhouse Queens," *San Francisco Chronicle*, April 7, 1978. Marlon Ross characterizes the narrative of development and underdevelopment as "intrinsic to the project of queer history and theory," in "Beyond the Closet as Raceless Paradigm," in Johnson and Henderson, *Black Queer Studies*, 163.

75. Tom Reeves, "The Hidden Oppression: Gay Men in Prison for Having Sex with Minors," *GCN*, December 13, 1980, 8.

76. Ibid., 9.

77. Ibid., 11.

78. On the transition from a gay liberation movement to gay rights, see D'Emilio, "After Stonewall."

79. Michael Serber, "Shame Aversion Therapy," *Journal of Behavior Therapy and Experimental Psychiatry* 1 (1970): 213.

80. Ibid., 213.

81. Michael Serber and Joseph Wolpe, "Behavior Therapy Techniques," in *Sexual Behavior: Social, Clinical, and Legal Aspects*, ed. H. L. P. Resnick and Marvin E. Wolfgang (Boston: Little, Brown, 1972), 247.

82. See Henry L. Minton, *Departing from Deviance: A History of Homosexual Rights and Emancipatory Science in America* (Chicago: University of Chicago Press, 2002), 256–64.

83. Don Altimus to Mike Riegle, October 7, 1982, BSEF, Box 12, Fol. 52.

84. Join Hands Testimony.

85. Rob Cole, "Behind Bars, Lessons on Being Gay," *Advocate*, June 20, 1973, 1.

86. Join Hands Testimony, 9.

87. Michael Serber and Claudia G. Keith, "The Atascadero Project: Model of a Sexual Retraining Program for Incarcerated Homosexual Pedophiles," *Journal of Homosexuality* 1 (1974): 95.

88. Tom Close, "A Patient's View: A Strange New World," *Advocate*, June 20, 1973, 2.

89. Ibid.

90. Close explained that AGE "is administratively a facet of the Sexual Reorientation Program but is open to all homosexual and bisexual patients in the hospital who are 18 or over. The club is designed for specific therapeutic purposes and is an integral part of many patients'

formal program. AGE will become the voice of the gay patient as well as his conscience. As acting president, I am striving to achieve our four purposes:
- Becoming more aware and accepting of our sexual identity.
- Informing members and others in the hospital about gay culture.
- Providing opportunities to meet other Gays in social settings.
- Providing useful information to members about where to go and whom to go to after release from the hospital" (ibid., 35).

91. Serber and Keith, "Atascadero Project," 93.
92. Ibid., 87.
93. Ibid., 90.
94. "Needless to say," Serber wrote, "the patients are more than grateful to receive a service that does not include stripping them of their homosexuality and personal dignity" (ibid., 94).
95. Cole, "Behind Bars," 1.
96. A class-action suit was brought by California inmates in 1973 to allow the MCC into prisons. In a decision handed down on May 20, 1975, in the U.S. District Court of Northern California, the court ruled that the MCC was a bona fide church and that the denial of MCC religious services to prisoners who requested them was an infringement of their constitutional rights guaranteed by the First Amendment. See "Court Allows MCC in Prisons," *GCN*, June 14, 1975, 1; "Gay Church Allowed in Prisons," *Lesbian Tide* 4 (1975): 19. On the MCC, see Kay Tobin and Randy Wicker, *The Gay Crusaders* (New York: Paperback Library, 1972), 19–22; Troy D. Perry with Charles L. Lucas, *The Lord Is My Shepherd and He Knows I'm Gay* (Los Angeles: Nash, 1972); Troy D. Perry with Thomas L. P. Swicegood, *Don't Be Afraid Anymore: The Story of Reverend Troy Perry and the Metropolitan Community Churches* (New York: St. Martin's, 1990).
97. Richard R. Mickley, *Prison Ministry Handbook*, 2nd ed. (Los Angeles: Universal Fellowship Press, 1976), 7.
98. Tom Purcell, "The Homosexual's Prayer," DeSantis Papers, Box 1, Fol. 16.
99. Mickley, *Prison Ministry Handbook*, 33.
100. Ibid., 33, 7.
101. Purcell, "Homosexual's Prayer."
102. See Gresham M. Sykes, *The Society of Captives: A Study of a Maximum Security Prison* (Princeton, NJ: Princeton University Press, 1958), 96; George Lester Kirkham, "Homosexuality in Prison," in *Studies in the Sociology of Sex*, ed. James M. Henslin (New York: Appleton Century-Crofts, 1971), 334.
103. Mickley, *Prison Ministry Handbook*, 8.
104. Ibid., 31.
105. "MCC Launching 'Prison Lifeline' Letters Program," *Advocate*, January 31, 1973, 14.
106. "Open Forum," *Bay Area Reporter*, June 30, 1983.
107. Lary Holvey, "Pen Pal Caution," *Bay Area Reporter*, August 11, 1983.
108. Teddy to Jeannie, *Advocate*, July 4, 1973, 38. Some prisoners acknowledged that some among them used pen-pal relationships to scam gay men. Exploiting the generosity of gay pen pals, one prisoner acknowledged, like that of "lonely women," was "one of the oldest games in the joint" (Jim Hogshire, *You Are Going to Prison* [Port Townsend, WA: Breakout, 1999], 90). One Michigan prisoner wrote to *GCN* offering to help gay men "sort the fakes from the real thing" (David Sidener to *GCN*, n.d., BSEF, Box 13, Fol. 42).
109. Troy Lewis to Mike Riegle, October 10, 1986, BSEF, Box 13, Fol. 42.
110. "Open Forum," *Bay Area Reporter*, June 30, 1983.

111. "Prison Pen Pals on the March," *Bay Area Reporter*, June 30, 1983.

112. M. B. to Jeannie, *Advocate*, October 10, 1974, 31.

113. Letter to editor, *GCN*, January 10–16, 1988, 4.

114. "A Concerned Lesbian Subscriber," letter to the editor, *GCN*, December 13–19, 1987, 4.

115. "Joint Venture," *RFD* 13 (1987): 65.

116. David Frey, "You Are a Criminal Too," *RFD* 27 (1980): 8.

117. The organization ACT-UP San Francisco had a small but thriving Prison Issues Group in the early 1990s that "was able to galvanize activists across the state to come together and fight for the rights of prisoners" (Rosenblatt, *Criminal Justice*, 89). See also Dawn Schmitz, "Activists Demand PWA Rights on the Inside," *GCN*, April 19–May 8, 1992, 1, 3.

118. Rebecca Lavine, "A Great Need," *GCN*, December 1–17, 1991, 7.

119. Riegle's work as the *GCN* office manager and his struggle with HIV/AIDS was memorably chronicled by his friend and *GCN* colleague Amy Hoffman in *Hospital Time* (Durham, NC: Duke University Press, 1997).

120. Riegle, "The March: A Focus on 'Justice' (as 'Political' Finally!)—and Still Gay/Lesbian Prisoners Are Invisible," *GCN*, October 11, 1987, 4.

121. Lisa Duggan, *The Twilight of Equality? Neoliberalism, Cultural Politics, and the Attack on Democracy* (Boston: Beacon, 2003), 50. See also Lisa Duggan, "The New Homonormativity: The Sexual Politics of Neoliberalism," in *Materializing Democracy*, ed. Russ Castronovo and Dana D. Nelson (Durham, NC: Duke University Press, 2002), 173–94.

Normalized Transgressions: Legitimizing the Transsexual Body as Productive

Dan Irving

Have yourself replaced as soon as possible and come back here, after which we shall think about the way to make a new place for you in society.
—Monsignor's advice to Herculine Barbin

In 1966, Gene Compton's eatery in San Francisco's Tenderloin district was the site of the first recorded incident of transgender resistance to police harassment.[1] The Compton Cafeteria riot broke out after police assaulted a drag queen inside the establishment; she responded by throwing coffee at them. This incident sparked an immediate reaction from other gender-variant, gay and lesbian people who frequented the restaurant. Rioters smashed windows, destroyed furniture, and set fire to a car.[2] This act of resistance to the state regulation of lived expressions of sex/gender identity lasted for the entire day, and picketing followed for another week. Those subjugated by norms regulating their sex, gender, sexuality, and occupation (many were sex workers) fought back against the disciplining of their lives. The well-known Stonewall Riots in New York three years later were also led by trans people, as well as by butch lesbians and drag queens, fighting diligently against the police for the right to transgress sex/gender binaries in public spaces free from discrimination and violence.

Radical History Review
Issue 100 (Winter 2008)   DOI 10.1215/01636545-2007-021

Who were these trans activists? Their collective militancy in the face of police brutality seems a distant memory when compared to much contemporary trans theorizing and politics. Why have we not inherited this legacy? What barriers to radical theorizations of gender variance and politics must be stormed to open emancipatory queer futures for trans people? How have possibilities for debate concerning these futures and strategies to shape them been foreclosed by efforts to construct *proper trans social subjects* that can integrate successfully into mainstream North American society? This essay addresses these questions by discussing the integral links between regimes of sex/gender and exploitative economic relations of production as mutually constitutive systems of domination. While various strands of feminist commentary,[3] along with scholarship from within critical sexuality studies,[4] have demonstrated the intersectional relations of power among heteronormative gender roles, sexuality, and the demands of capitalist (re)productive regimes of accumulation, these vital correlations have not been made explicit by most trans researchers and activists.[5]

Scholars within trans studies rarely contextualize trans identities, subjectivities, and activism within historical and contemporary capitalist relations. Much scholarship seeks to save trans identities from invisibility, as well as to counter the ongoing reproduction of the heteronormative binary of sex/gender through detailed analyses of the vast array of existing trans identities.[6] There is a tendency within this commentary to reify trans identities as solely matters of sex/gender and to challenge state and institutional dominance over trans people by emphasizing the necessity of self-determination of sex/gender. Such advocacy of self-determination is often coupled with arguments for human rights protections.[7] Progressive scholars must question the theoretical and political implications of putting forward individualistic strategies of sex/gender self-determination, especially within the contemporary neoliberal context, where the minimalist state and a free-market economy demand individual self-sufficiency.

While some texts address the impacts of capitalist socioeconomic relations on trans people's lives, a critical analysis of the exploitative labor relations that comprise the logic of capital remains lacking.[8] Although poverty, which often results from the marginalization of many trans people from the legal labor force, is a major theme, impoverishment is most often comprehended as a barrier to the full realization of sex/gender identities and their embodied expressions. When employment within the legal wage labor economy is addressed, the tenor of discussion is often assimilatory.[9] The necessity of integrating some trans people into the labor force, and of protecting the employment status of others, appear to foreclose critiques of capitalist productive relations and of the embeddedness of trans subjectivities within capitalist systems of power. Likewise, critical analyses of the impact of capitalist productive relations on trans subjectivities are rarely offered. Also underexamined are the ways in which hegemonic capitalism's socioeconomic and political relations are reproduced vis-à-vis the transsexual body.

This essay addresses these lacunae in trans studies literature by specifically addressing the ways in which medical experts, transsexual individuals, and contemporary trans researchers, activists, and allies seeking justice for gender variant people contribute to the construction of transsexual subjectivities in ways that reinforce dominant exploitative class relations. The mediation of transsexuality through capitalist productive relations carries implications extending beyond trans individuals ourselves. I argue that an emphasis on the transsexual as an economically productive body has important effects on the shaping of transsexual subjectivities and of political strategizing for emancipatory futures. Constructions of transsexuals as viable social subjects by medical experts, transsexual individuals, researchers, and allies were, and continue to be, shaped significantly by discourses of productivity emerging from and reinforcing regimes of capitalist accumulation. To move toward achieving social recognition, the transsexual body must constitute a productive working body, that is, it must be capable of participating in capitalist production processes. This legacy impacts the trajectories of political organizing to achieve social justice for trans communities.

To make this argument, this essay is divided into three sections. The first analyzes early medical approaches to the treatment of transsexuals including those made by influential doctors hostile to transsexuality (e.g., David O. Cauldwell), as well as by those considered compassionate (e.g., Harry Benjamin). Close attention is paid to the ways in which transsexuals are characterized in terms of their class, social status, and creative and employment potential. The second section highlights early trans theorization and activism spearheaded by trans people and their allies. I assert that these efforts were primarily directed at engaging with medical experts to depathologize transsexuality. This approach emphasized respect for transsexuals in order to enable increased access to state-based social services, human rights protections, and public spaces. An underlying goal of these initiatives to achieve sociopolitical, legal, and economic validation for transsexuals was to establish their worth as citizens. Appeals to mainstream society to accept transsexuals as legitimate subjects often emphasized their valuable contributions to society through their labor. The third section focuses on contemporary theorizations of transsexual identities and politics within a neoliberal context. I pay particular attention to subtexts emphasizing worthiness, value, and productivity in order to demonstrate the complicity of trans theorists and activists in naturalizing the exacerbated gendered labor relations characteristic of the neoliberal order that seeks to increase profits through decreasing wages.

The analysis offered in this essay is anchored in critical political economy. As defined by Gary Browning and Andrew Kilmister, this approach "rests on two main pillars; the drawing of links between the economic and other areas of social life and the recognition of the economic when these links are drawn."[10] Critical political economy centers on the productive sphere of capitalism while simultaneously working to cultivate a wider understanding of productive relations. This is achieved through analyzing the numerous components that comprise the sphere of the productive including the home, public space, and communities, as well as other vectors of power such as sex and gender. In addition, power operates discursively as meaning is created and circulated throughout society. For example, discourses of productivity naturalize the exploitative labor relations characteristic of capitalism; despite this naturalization, these discourses influence the treatment and conceptualizations of the transsexual body.

Clearly, sites of commodity production do not produce all meaning. Nor can we claim that all facets of life are determined by exploitative class relations, which maximize profit through the extraction of increasing amounts of surplus value. Social meanings are not created through direct and one-dimensional transference from the workplace to the bodies and consciousness of members of society. Embodied identities, such as transsexuality, are the result of complex amalgamating relations of domination, exploitation, and agency. Defining critical political economy as such begs the question: Why write an essay directing attention toward subtexts of value, worth, and citizenship within medical texts, transsexual narratives, and political agendas that correlate directly with participation in the legally paid labor economy? To be sure, regimes of accumulation—such as Fordism or late capitalism—do not, on their own, shape transsexual existences. That the organization of (re)production wields a significant influence on the social construction of sex and gender is a rudimentary point of feminist political economy. The construction of transsexual identities vis-à-vis capitalist productive relations serves to enrich our understanding of the ways that sex/gender are constructed as regulatory regimes.[11] In addition, considering transsexual subjectivities in light of past and contemporary regimes of accumulation opens new opportunities for theorizing trans identities and for strategizing an emancipatory politics that resists systemic oppression and enriches the lives of trans people.

Medically Constructing Transsexual Bodies That Work

Early discursive and physiological constructions of transsexual bodies by medical experts and their patients exemplify the reciprocal relationship between economic regimes of accumulation and sex/gender categories. Trans researchers, notably Sandy Stone and Jay Prosser, have established that medical professionals wielded enormous power over the range of possible ways that gender-variant individuals could express gendered identities.[12] This was particularly the case in North American locations, such as the Canadian province of Ontario, where the state funded hormone therapy and sex reassignment surgeries (SRS).[13] Gender Identity Clinics (GICs) required that gender-variant individuals seeking medical transition submit to numerous physical and psychological evaluations to qualify for state-funded SRS.[14] Thus qualification for paid SRS depended on a process that pathologized transsexual people as suffering from a set of mental maladies known first as "gender dysphoria" and later as "gender identity disorder."

Because they served as conduits between transsexuals and the physical expression of their sex/gender identities, doctors and psychological professionals exerted considerable authority over their patients. The reinforcement of heteronormative categories of sex, gender, and sexuality through these engagements has been well documented; however, the economic facets of these diagnoses and recommendations for treatment are less well analyzed.[15] By assessing their transsexual patients in terms of their aptitudes, earning potentials, education, and class backgrounds, medical professionals also strengthened hegemonic discourses of citizenship and productivity that buttressed the economy.

Four economic themes appear as subtexts in medical discourse on the treatment of transsexuality. The first concerns the class backgrounds of transsexual patients. Medical experts required detailed information from individuals or their families regarding their class as defined by occupation and social status. This information often appears in the writings of medical doctors as they grapple with the meaning of gender variance. For example, in documenting "Case 131" concerning Count Sandor, a female-bodied person living as male, Richard von Krafft-Ebing noted that Sandor hailed from an "ancient, noble and highly respected family of Hungary."[16]

The writings of the prolific American sexologist David O. Cauldwell (1897–1959) offer an additional example of the way class background factored into physicians' comprehension of transsexuality. Cauldwell characterized "psychopathic transsexuality" in terms of delayed development, sexual immaturity, and frivolity. For him, one's class location played a clear role in fostering this disorder; asserting a higher prevalence of transsexualism among "well to do families," he explained that impoverished people, consumed by the obligations of providing bare necessities for themselves and their families, did not have the means or time for such "deviant" pursuits. For Cauldwell, then, poverty served as a deterrent to transsexualism. The link between one's propensity toward expressing gender variance and class location is demonstrated further in his account of "Earl," a female-to-male (FTM) transsexual patient, whom he identified as having been born a "normal female" into a prominent and wealthy family. Noting that one of Earl's maternal relatives was a doctor whose son became a lawyer and that his paternal grandfather was involved in politics and civic affairs, Cauldwell interpreted Earl as one who squandered his life; in other words, he understood Earl's potential to cultivate his talents and contribute to society as thwarted due to his fixation on expressing his masculine identity. Indeed, Cauldwell asserted that such fixations would most likely result in Earl engaging in criminal activity.[17]

Class discipline also received emphasis within medical literature. The majority of gender-variant individuals who enlisted medical experts for substantive assistance were white, middle-class, able-bodied male-to-female trans people more likely to be able to finance medical transition. This class location emerged as a prominent component of the pathologization of transsexual identities. It is here that the productive body intersects with the creation of pathology as a disciplinary technique. Doctors who opposed any medical intervention enabling one to change sex did so in part because they believed that this transition would thwart the industrious potential of the middle-class, able-bodied (presumed) male and (re)productive potential of the (presumed) female. Because they understood the economic value created by individuals through their labor as a social concern, some medical professionals refused to support deliberate medical interventions that would compromise capable bodies.

Transsexuals were disciplined partially because their sex/gender variance violated social codes that contributed to the growth, development, and global expansion of the domestic economy. Like other citizens, doctors often internalized the social expectations of the upper and middle classes that undergirded hegemonic discourses of productivity. The Hippocratic oath extended beyond their professional obligation to heal individual patients to encompass a broader sense of civic duty. In other words, doctors understood their professional obligation to restore health to individuals as part of a broader imperative to act as moral, upstanding citizens. As physicians, their value lay in contributing to the vitality of the nation. In the case of physicians who adamantly refused to engage in medical transition processes, this contribution was realized through relegitimizing the normatively sexed and gendered body (i.e., one biologically genetically determined) as "the" productive body.

These sex/gendered dimensions of class discipline were clearly elucidated by Cauldwell, who highlighted the civic duty of doctors to ensure the wealth of the nation through the provision of healthy (re)productive bodies. For Cauldwell, this social responsibility trumped all other considerations, including the self-identity of transsexual patients whose understandings of sex/gender he interpreted as destructive to society. He positioned the transsexual individual who requested or demanded medical help as an adversary to the ethical, law-abiding citizen; writing in 1949, he asserted that "the psyche is already ill and sanity is seriously involved when an individual develops a compulsion to be rid of his natural organs and places his insane desires ahead of the rights of others."[18] Cauldwell proved so adamant in his understanding of sex reassignment surgery as mutilation that he claimed that "it would be criminal of a doctor to remove healthy organs."[19] The criminal nature of the surgical act is rooted in Cauldwell's belief that to operate on the transsexual body is to destroy its capacity for a (hetero)sexual life by thwarting the individual's reproductive potential.[20]

It is important to note that even experts who supported medical intervention as a treatment for transsexuality sounded the theme of class discipline. Unlike their peers who reinforced hegemonic sexed/gendered bodies as productive subjects through their refusal to assist in transition procedures, doctors who advocated for "sexual reassignment" through hormonal therapy and surgeries contributed to the economic vitality of the nation through the construction of a working body. Based on their understanding of the so-called dysphoric condition as largely unresponsive to psychotherapy, medical experts asserted the necessity of physiological interventions to construct a sexed body that reflected the self-image held by transsexuals. They grounded this hormonally and surgically assisted transformation in a social context framed in part by conceptualizing the national value ascribed to individuals in terms of their productive capacity.

While critiques by trans scholars of the gatekeeping function of medical professionals have offered compelling analyses of the investment of medical experts in heteronormative sex/gender categories, they have paid scant attention to the ways in which professionals understood these categories in relation to economic production. Prosser, for example, has directed attention to the construction of hegemonic sex/gender categories through diagnostic criteria and requirements of transsexual patients prior to their receiving hormone therapy and SRS.[21] He explains that "narrativization as a transsexual necessarily precedes one's diagnosis as a transsexual; autobiography is transsexuality's proffered symptom."[22] Prosser explains that medical experts have analyzed such narratives to ensure that supposedly proper gender norms of behavior were understood. Other scholars raise concerns regarding the reinforcement of heterosexuality by GICs: while transsexuals were required to divulge explicit details of their heterosexual fantasies, they were prohibited from acting on these fantasies prior to sex reassignment.[23] As Jason Cromwell explains, doctors governed the production of heterosexual subjects by refusing to approve surgery for transsexuals who were gay, bisexual, or lesbian.[24]

Yet the valorization of the maleness or femaleness of post-transition transsexuals hinged in part on understandings of their productive capacity. Value was ascribed to the actual contribution of one's labor power to the economy. The economic element of the "real-life test" illustrates this point. As an integral component of the Benjamin Standards of Care developed to anticipate the kinds of psychic and social challenges that the transsexual patient might encounter, the real-life test was administered by GICs to monitor the ability of the transsexual patient to live entirely as a demonstrable member of the opposite sex. If deemed successful in this endeavor by the team of doctors and psychologists managing the case, the individual was approved for hormone therapy and SRS. The real-life test functioned as an oppressive appraisal of endurance that disciplined transsexuals through the reiteration of their sex/gender variance as problematic and abnormal.[25] Transsexuals were forced to undergo the real-life test before hormone therapy modified their appearance and thereby made it easier to pass as a man or woman. Medical experts believed that the individual who succeeded in withstanding the daily harassment and discrimination that accompanied the real-life test demonstrated a genuine dedication to pursuing transition and therefore deserved to be diagnosed as transsexual.

It is important to understand that the real-life test had an economic component that cannot be conceptualized entirely as an exercise in sex/gender endurance; the test also monitored the future occupational capacities for the postoperative subject. The real-life test contained a facet of economic rehabilitation that required transsexual patients to obtain employment while living full time in their self-identified sex/gender.[26] Regardless of the personal intentions of medical experts, the employment requirements of the real-life test worked to legitimize sex/gender divisions of labor that buttressed the use of gender to maximize profits.

Within the context of heteronormativity during the post–World War II era, the ability of the male body to be economically industrious signified "authentic" manhood. Some clinical understandings of FTM transsexuals made increasingly apparent the connection between supposedly genuine maleness and productive capacity. The willingness of many FTM transsexuals to demonstrate their masculinity through an avid participation in the labor market trumped their nonnormative, nonreproductive embodiment of masculinity. According to the prominent sexologist John Money,

> There is a general consensus among professionals in transexualism that female-to-male transsexualism is not an exact homologue of male-to-female transexualism. *Whereas the gender coding of the male-to-female transsexual is prevalently that of the attention-attracting vamp, not the devoted Madonna, the masculine gender coding of the female-to-male transsexual is prevalently that of the reliable provider,* not the profligate playboy. Throughout Europe, America and the English speaking world, clinicians of transexualism agree that a successfully unobtrusive sex-reassigned life is more prevalent in female-to-male reassignment than male to female reassignment even though the success of the female-to-male sex-reassignment surgery leaves something to be desired, namely an erectile penis.[27]

For Money and other medical professionals, the binary system of sex/gender naturalized the devaluation of women, as well as of nonnormative masculinities (i.e., effeminate gay men or FTM transsexuals who do not pass as men). This sex/gender–based degradation, which resulted in systemic oppression, was not practiced only by governmental and institutional bureaucracies. It was also appropriated within spheres of capitalist production, and it is within sites of commodity production where we can witness the amalgamation of exploitation with relations of domination. Oppressed sex/gender and sexual minorities such as women, trans people, gays, and lesbians have always been overrepresented within low-wage, part-time, nonunionized, and precarious sectors of the labor market.[28]

The naturalization of these gender relations is reflected in the writings of doctors who discuss how they judged the "authenticity" of their patients' claims to sex/gender identities. For instance, the influential sexologist Harry Benjamin questioned whether male-to-female patients realized fully that they would likely be unable to maintain their vocation and would experience lower job status and lower wages as women.[29] The success of their sexual reassignment was measured partly through their complacency (an ideal mark of femininity) and their willingness to assimilate into these gendered and exploitative relations.

Social parasitism represents another theme in the medical literature that demonstrates the link between processes of wealth accumulation and the construction of productive bodies. This theme, too, reveals the linkages among transsexualism as pathology, discourses of citizenship, and the economic welfare of the nation. Often medical professionals identified transsexualism as a mental disability—a preoccupation with sex/gender identities and expressions that impeded the ability of transsexuals to contribute to society. As such, they configured the transsexual as threatening and dangerous. The writings of Cauldwell exemplify this pejorative conceptualization of transsexuality. He included "parasitism" as one of the characteristics of psychopathology and marked this quality as abhorrent in his discussion of "psychopathia transsexualis."[30] Cauldwell characterized transsexuals as "sex destructionists" and characterized such destruction as a social act. Those suffering from this "self-hating psychosis . . . turn destruction on themselves [and] impose on society by *becoming burdens to it*."[31] Cauldwell understood transsexuals as socially burdensome in part because he claimed that they refused to participate in the labor economy. In relation to the case of Earl discussed above, Cauldwell wrote: "By now we were beginning to learn something of the real Earl. We knew that her [*sic*] ambitions were to live parasitically. *She [sic] would not work*."[32]

Medical professionals' concern with social parasitism extended beyond employment; many believed that the propensity of gender-variant individuals toward social dependence also manifested in the leeching of public resources, especially those provided by state-funded institutions such as prisons and mental hospitals. Cauldwell advised one gender-variant individual who self-identified as a closeted homosexual and a transvestite to continue to live contrary to his identity for society's sake. Cauldwell explained that "if he continues to live his life in such a way as not to openly offend society he is a *far more valuable citizen* than hundreds (or thousands) of others who, because they are incapable of psychologically adjusting themselves, eventually land in public institutions."[33]

Doctors who reinforced the supposed knowledge that sex is immutable advocated punitive actions when transsexuals proved adamant about expressing freely their chosen sex/gender. They believed not only that disciplinary measures would promote emotional stability for gender variant individuals, but also that these measures would have a restorative effect on society. In response to a family requesting advice on dealing with a FTM transsexual relative, Cauldwell positioned gender variance as pathological with probable negative social implications. He proposed cutting this youth off from material resources as punishment.

Cauldwell argued that increasing the vulnerability of transsexuals would eventually construct a productive body:

Should the young women [*sic*] here involved be put fully on her own and refused financial assistance the results . . . although unpleasant for a number of people, might be the best in the long run for all concerned and this may be considered to include society as a whole. Just as it is said of people who are regarded as wayward, there always is a possibility that these individuals will in time settle down and become significantly well adjusted to avoid causing serious social concern.[34]

Analyzing critically the ways in which transsexualism as a category of sex/gender variance was isolated from other nonnormative gender identities such as transvestism (presently labeled "cross-dressing") reveals the concrete presence of such productive logics and the significant role they played in medical approaches to the treatment of transsexuality. For doctors like Cauldwell and Benjamin, cross-dressing was not as threatening because it was understood as an erotic fetish. Medical experts asserted that many cross-dressers were heterosexuals and professionals and often were happily married men with families and stable employment. Their desire to derive pleasure from dressing in feminine attire was interpreted as an activity that could be contained easily within private spaces (i.e., their own homes or at gatherings with other cross-dressers). Benjamin explains that "the typical or true transvestite is a completely harmless member of society. He derives his sexual pleasure and emotional satisfaction in a strictly solitary fashion."[35] For Benjamin and other sexologists, cross-dressing represented a nonnormatively gendered practice that contributed only to a facet of one's identity, rather than an all-encompassing compulsion that impinged on one's ability to perform the roles of husband, father, and/or worker.

Such was not the case with transsexuality. Doctors described transsexual individuals as consumed by the need to align their bodily sex and gender identity. Therefore, a hierarchy of gender-variant identities existed among medical experts, with transsexuals occupying the bottom echelons of this taxonomy. Regardless of their views concerning the mutability of sex and the scientific facilitation of transitioning, the majority of medical professionals classified transsexuals as the most damaged—and *damaging*—among nonnormatively gendered individuals. Frequently borrowing terminology from psychological professionals, doctors degraded transsexuals as narcissistic, destructive, and self-loathing.[36] This characterization extended beyond the frame of individual abnormality to encompass socially corrosive forms of deviance.

A reading of the medical literature reveals a dominant belief that transsexuality, framed as a mental disorder, renders the body unproductive. According to this literature, the sex/gender "preoccupations" of transsexual individuals undermined their productivity and created states of dependency. The transsexual burdened society rather than contributing to it. Thus, given their broad social commitment to healing, most doctors would not condone a decision to live as a transsexual. They maintained that if untreated, this disorder would likely have a devastating impact on the transsexual individual. Medical commentaries, including those of Cauldwell and Benjamin, interpreted problems faced by gender-variant individuals—including depression, substance abuse, and self-mutilation—not as evidence of the personal implications of unrealized desires to embody one's sex/gender identity but, rather, as evidence of the social and economic threats that such individuals posed to a broader public. Discourses of economic productivity contributed to the degradation of transsexuality and the systemic erasure of transsexual individuals. Within a heteronormative capitalist society organized around binary sex/gender and exploitative labor relations, transsexuality did not work.

Initiating Trans Resistance: Transsexuality Can Work!

The creation of transsexual subjectivities is a multidimensional process arising through an engagement with dominant societal institutions. In this way, transsexuals are not entirely victims of external authority. They internalize power and participate actively in disciplinary techniques that lend meaning to the transsexual body as productive. The efforts through which transsexual people seek validation for their sex/gender identities and embodied expressions have economic components. The emergence of transsexual voices in and beyond academe echo hegemonic socioeconomic and political discourses grounded in conceptualizations of citizenship defined through laboring bodies. In a manner that resonates with medical practitioners' concerns regarding the practical capacity of transsexual bodies that impacts their ability to exist as responsible citizens, transsexuals also articulate understandings of their sex/gender identity grounded in the logic that buttresses wealth accumulation. Regarding (trans) citizenship, the scholar Aren Aizura asserts that "citizenship here means fading into the population . . . but also the imperative to be 'proper' in the eyes of the state: to reproduce, to find proper employment; to reorient one's 'different' body into the flow of the nationalized aspiration for possessions, property, [and] wealth."[37]

Aizura's claims are demonstrated in transsexual autobiographies, for example, which reveal a tacit commitment to a gendered logic of capitalist production. These autobiographies are often written by transsexual participants in gender-identity programs to gain a "favorable" diagnosis necessary to undergo transition. The underlying logic of economic productivity presented in these autobiographies makes Gramscian "common sense" to both expert and patient. Whether transsexuals individually subscribe to this particular notion of productive citizenship is not at issue here. It was common knowledge among patients at GICs that only a particular transsexual narrative—one that subscribes to hegemonic and heteronormative categories of sex/gender—will be accepted as a reflection of genuine transsexualism.[38] Yet even if some individuals produce these rigid narratives only for functional purposes, the rearticulation and circulation of these narratives serves to embed transsexuality within a discourse of productive citizenship.

It is important to read these early autobiographies with an eye toward connections drawn between the reinforcement of supposedly proper gender roles and the structures of the wage labor economy. Such connections are frequently obscured given that transsexual clients of GICs did not address employment directly.[39] Nevertheless, the understood need to make social contributions is reflected in the tenor of transsexual autobiographers' expressions of their future aspirations. The prospects of life after medicalized transition are often expressed in assimilatory terms. These writings reinforce the understanding that genuine transsexuals are those who seek integration into mainstream society as "normal"—and productive—men or women. In his book entitled *The Transsexual Phenomenon* (1966), Harry Benjamin quotes from the autobiography of a transsexual woman who explained that "we prefer the normalcy's [*sic*] of life and want to be accepted in circles of normal society, enjoying the same pursuits and pleasures without calling attention to the fact that we are 'queers' trying to invade the world of normal people."[40]

While it could be suggested that the above quote privileges heterosexuality, other transsexual authors expose more clearly the economic elements of normality. Early transsexual biographies frequently narrated a trajectory of economic difficulty (and, in some cases, failure) prior to transition, followed by integration into society post-transition.[41] For example, Christine Jorgensen, perhaps the most well-known transsexual during the 1950s, wrote of her frustration living as a shy, underweight man "who was unable to find a place in society where he could earn a living and move up in the world."[42] On returning to the United States post-transition, Jorgensen enjoyed a successful career as a public transsexual. Her self-image was embedded in an understanding of the productive potential of her transsexuality. For example, she described her invited addresses at charity events (i.e., voluntary labor) in terms of supporting her community: "It seemed to me an opportunity to prove myself a useful member of the community . . . [to make] some sort of contribution."[43] Of an appearance at Madison Square Garden, Jorgensen remembered that "the brief speech I addressed to the audience was a simple expression of the honor accorded me . . . and the opportunity to be a useful citizen of New York City."[44] Unlike the shy underweight man who could not secure an upwardly mobile position and career, Jorgensen became a financially independent and cosmopolitan woman who worked as a nightclub entertainer.[45]

In addition to transsexual autobiography, research on transsexual lives reinforces the link between gendered dimensions of power and exploitative economic relations. When analyzed through the lens of critical political economy, efforts made by academic commentators to combat characterizations of transsexuals as deviant, abnormal, criminal, and socially destructive do not achieve significant distance from the experts who articulate these characterizations. The urgency to gain social legitimacy for transsexuality often forecloses possibilities for critically theorizing the formation of transsexual subjectivities within a socioeconomic and political context. For example, prominent trans scholars and activists who have made historical arguments advocating the tolerance and social integration of transsexual people have often embedded these arguments within a socioeconomic framework that invokes a model productive citizen. Such literature seeks to challenge efforts of medical professionals to make transsexuality disappear, but it does so through the construction of productive bodies. Likewise, this literature attempts to validate transsexuality as a legitimate sex/gender identity by demonstrating the productive capacity of this identity. In the influential book *Transgender Warriors*, for example, Leslie Feinberg yearns for a society that resembles a past when trans people were "viewed with respect as vital contributing members of our societies."[46] Scholars like Jason Cromwell invoke the historicized lives of gender-variant people to argue that if historical individuals whose embodied lives did not subscribe to binary sex/gender systems were alive today, these would most likely define themselves as transsexual.

In both of these cases, the authors focus not on the discrepancy between historical actors' sex/gender identity and their physical embodiment, but on their contributions as workers and dutiful citizens. Such historical narratives frequently speak to the convergence of gender and nation via accounts of the trans man as soldier.[47] Other archival efforts make contributionist claims by focusing on transsexuals in professional occupations. In most of these cases, authors focus on the ways in which these historical figures passed as men or women until illness or death resulted in the discovery of their bodily incongruence. The message one can derive from such accounts is that rather than seeking to make "gender trouble," these historical actors devoted their energies to their professions and families. Trans scholars also often succumb to working within dichotomous categorizations that effectively normalize heteropatriarchal and capitalist relations. When constructing transsexual subjectivities as deserving of social recognition, researchers and activists often employ hegemonic notions of "normal," "healthy," "able-bodied," and "productive." Therefore, since transsexuals are neither unhealthy nor mentally unstable, many of them heal the sick. They are not threats to the security of the country; they fight to defend their nations in war. They are not drains on the system; they are successful workers who provide for themselves and their families (in atypical cases, they are eccentric billionaires who fund the research of doctors like Benjamin, as did the FTM transsexual millionaire Reed Erickson).[48] They are not freaks in carnival shows; they are successful entertainers.[49]

This reactionary approach to achieving trans visibility, accessibility, and inclusion is problematic. To flip dichotomies so that the abnormal becomes normal, the unproductive becomes productive, and the uncreative becomes artistic is to plant some dangerous seeds that jeopardize the state of trans theory and politics. This particular understanding of trans people privileges those within transsexual communities who have the potential to become respectable social subjects. One must acknowledge transsexual individuals who are excluded as subjects and continue to exist on the margins of society, including transsexuals of color, those who do not pass as men or women, those with illnesses or disabilities, those who are impoverished, those who are unable or unwilling to be employed within the legal wage labor economy and thus work in the sex trade, as well as those incarcerated in prisons or mental institutions. Their narratives largely remain untold.

Neoliberal Accumulation Strategies; or, Transsexuality, Inc.

The new millennium has marked the concretization of trans studies wherein trans people have become the subjects of scholarly inquiry rather than its objects.[50] In many respects, trans scholars are setting the research agenda rather than responding to the commentary provided by medical professionals. Yet the need for legitimization that precipitates social recognition for trans people, particularly transsexuals who embody physically a reassigned sex, remains urgent. Transsexual people often live a marginalized existence in which they are unable to secure legal employment, housing, and meet other rudimentary needs. The urgency stemming from the dire circumstances in which many transsexual people find themselves fosters commentary that veers away from a critical analysis of the socioeconomic and political context that structures trans subjectivities and abjection. Much emphasis is placed on integrating trans people as nonnormatively sexed/gendered into heteronormative capitalist society. Such a focus reproduces problematic approaches to transsexuality, which began with medical doctors such as Cauldwell and Benjamin who pathologized transsexual individuals. Contemporary scholarship is haunted by the specter of pathologization due to the continuous reproduction of the heteronormative sex/gender binary system.

This specter emerges as especially troubling in our current neoliberal moment wherein claims to rights and equality have been easily subsumed within a discourse of economic productivity. While it is beyond the scope of this essay to provide a detailed discussion of the multiple facets of neoliberalism, two main pillars should be highlighted in relation to transsexual subjectivities. First, neoliberalism is defined according to an economic restructuring that marks the resurgence of the free-market economy.[51] To increase the accumulation of wealth, concentrated efforts have been made to push wages downward. Such efforts have contributed to the significant growth of certain sectors such as the service sector, as well as to the expansion of "home work" and contract work,[52] which are for the most part precarious, part-time, low-wage positions with few or no benefits.[53] These developments have also produced ever-expanding pools of un(der)employed workers whose vulnerability creates conditions of desperation.[54] Although capital's appropriation of other relations of power (i.e., colonization, race, sexuality, sex/gender) is not unique to neoliberalism, this current "policy project" has given new form to intersecting relations of dominance.[55] Many transsexual individuals, people of color, nonstatus immigrants, migrant workers, and gays and lesbians who do not pass as straight are overrepresented in the above-mentioned hyperexploitative sectors of the economy.

The minimalist state constitutes the second major pillar of neoliberalism. According to the logic of the free-market economy, the role of the minimal state is to provide the infrastructure and support necessary for the accumulation of capital. Within a North American context, this has meant the dismantling of the welfare state. Programs that provided citizens with social assistance, unemployment insurance, and publicly funded heath care have steadily declined, which has contributed to an environment hospitable to hyperexploitative labor relations and to an increased vulnerability of many segments of society, including many transsexual individuals. I will offer two examples most relevant to the critical political economic analysis of transsexual subjectivities. First, discourses concerning citizenship have shifted away from notions of social citizenship,[56] wherein one has clear expectations of the state to provide for one's well-being in cases of economic hardship. Neoliberal notions of citizenship do not carry these same expectations; instead, good citizens are defined as those who can contribute to their nation's advancement in the global political economy. Related closely to dominant notion of the deserving citizen, as revived under neoliberalism, is a second discourse, which espouses the necessity of an individual to cultivate an "entrepreneurial spirit." The onus has thereby shifted from the state to individual members of society who are expected to make adjustments and sacrifices to provide for their own material needs, as well as for those of their family and communities. This may include self-care (i.e., taking care of one's physical and mental well-being), education, and training to obtain employment.[57]

Discourses of the good, deserving citizen who cultivates an entrepreneurial spirit fuel a volatile context that Angela Harris refers to as the "cultural wars."[58] The anxieties of many middle- and working-class people resulting from neoliberal restructuring are alleviated through rendering the logic of capitalist accumulation strategies invisible. Instead of focusing on these strategies, media, state, and community institutions continuously construct socioeconomic and political discourses that represent segments of middle- and working-class populations as innocent victims and upstanding citizens while simultaneously (re)constructing others as enemies, threats, and drains on the system. It is through the predominance of these discourses among the majority of middle- and working-class society that transsexuality is rendered suspect. Therefore many commentators and LGBT (lesbian, gay, bisexual, and transgender) organizations deliberately emphasize the transsexual individual as a contributing member of society when appealing for recognition of trans subjects and for access to employment. The understanding of the transsexual body as productive provides the subtexts for differing representations of transsexuality.

For example, major newspapers have recently featured transsexuals who hold corporate positions. The *Toronto Star* published an article featuring Angela Wensley, a senior manager for MacMillan Bloedel Ltd., one of Canada's leading forestry companies, who transitioned on the job. Geared toward an audience comprised mainly of businesspeople, academics, and other professionals, these articles focus primarily on values of capability and achievement. Wensley vows continued success as head of the corporation's corrosion and materials engineering group in spite of being transsexual: "A lot of women in this company have told me they're counting on me because I'm one of only a few here to make it above the glass ceiling. I'm afraid my career advancement is on hold . . . but I'm going to prove to them that not only am I as good as the man I was before, I'm better as a woman."[59] This subtext of industriousness also permeates many contemporary transsexual autobiographies. Deirdre N. McCloskey's autobiography *Crossing: A Memoir* (2000), serves as but one example.[60] A professor of economics at the University of Iowa, McCloskey transitioned from male to female while maintaining her job and, by and large, the respect she had garnered as an economist. Transsexuality did not denote the end of McCloskey's professional success. (Trans)gender dynamics are at work here as readers are informed both that women, even transsexual women, are fully capable of flourishing within such a male-dominated discipline. While McCloskey expected to lose her job, she maintained her influential position within the field, was hired at the University of Illinois at Chicago, and was appointed to the editorial board of a major journal for the discipline. Her accounts of success reflect a narrative of continuous productivity as she explains, "I'm getting a new urban life style, more money, and a lot more autonomy to do my work among the disciplines. . . . I would not have got the job . . . if economists and others had somehow lost respect for me. If you want to change gender, get a job at a university, and publish a lot."[61]

Autobiographies by trans activists often follow a similar trajectory. For example, the internationally renowned activist Jamison Green's book, *Becoming a Visible Man* (2004), serves to buttress the idea that transsexual embodiment can translate easily to economic success. As the leader of Female to Male International (FTMI), an international resource and activist-based group for trans men, Green is widely recognized. What is particularly interesting vis-à-vis his autobiography, however, is the way that the authenticity regarding his (trans)sex/gender identity and the realization of this identity through medical transition leads to his ability to occupy a leadership role within FTM organizing. He links the right to sex/gender self-determination directly to the capacity of transsexuals to be effective within broader public spheres. Green discusses his gradual recognition of his male sex over many years and describes how the path to medical transition is mediated partially by economic anxieties. Green also concerns himself with the economic implications of transitioning, asserting that "most FTMs just are not prepared to become captains of industry"[62] due to discrepancies in female socialization and education levels, to the negative impact of visible gender variance on the job, to periods of un(der)employment, and to how women internalize their position within gendered sectors of the workplace. Similar to medical experts' concerns regarding the prospects of transsexuals living economically productive lives, Green is also anxious that personal security with one's male embodiment and masculine gender expression does not correlate directly with productive achievements. He explains that "employers are free to dismiss us because they feel our presence is too 'disruptive,' they apparently don't believe it is possible for us to *function efficiently*."[63]

To prove to employers just how efficiently transsexual people can function, trans activists and allies stress the capacity of transsexuals to be loyal and diligent employees. For example, the Center for Gender Sanity makes a case for the value transsexual people add to economic operations through their labor. In *Transsexual Workers: An Employer's Guide* (2003), Janis Wolworth makes the case for hiring transsexual workers, as well as for maintaining the employment status of those transitioning. It is here that (trans)sex and gender mediate economic needs to render the transsexual laboring body industrious, and in ways that are strikingly similar to how the neoliberal political economy renders all workers susceptible to decreasing wages, fewer benefits, and precarious positions (such as contract work). As Wolworth writes, "while in transition, transsexuals are strongly motivated to earn enough money to pay for the desired procedures and to maintain above-average performance in order to keep their jobs." Furthermore, corporations can influence the construction of effective transsexual bodies through investing in procedures for sexual reassignment and instituting antidiscriminatory policies that protect gender identity and expression. She states, "Once transition is completed, a transsexual employee is likely to become more productive."[64]

Transsexual individuals can be viewed as viable neoliberal subjects: they have proven to be flexible and fluid, self-sufficient, and major contributors to their families, workplaces, communities, and societies. To many, emphasizing the normative potential of transsexuality has been a successful strategy to counter the marginalizing effects of pathologization. The legitimizing of the transsexual worker, however, does not offer serious challenges to heteronormativity, nor does it illuminate the conditions of hyperexploitation that structure neoliberalism. In fact, these narratives dovetail with hegemonic discourses concerning the upstanding citizen and the necessity of entrepreneurialism.[65] The interest expressed by major corporations such as IBM demonstrates the ease with which capital continues to appropriate the oppressed minorities, such as sex/gender variants, into its accumulation strategies. As part of its "managed diversity" programs, IBM actively recruits trans people, racial minorities, Native Americans, gay men and lesbians, and women.[66]

The changing tides of neoliberal restructuring amid the continuation of the heteronormative sex/gender binary has created a receptive atmosphere for transsexual incorporation into the productive spheres of capital. Unlike medical experts such as Cauldwell who chastised nonnormative sex/gender identifications as frivolities that distracted from one's potential as a laborer, corporate executives view these tenuous identifications as advantageous to present regimes of accumulation. Difference is appropriated not only as a market niche but also as a resource for capital accumulation when transsexual bodies are valorized socially because of the value their labor contributes to the economy. As explained to members of sex/gender minorities by IBM, "When you join IBM's diverse team you are *encouraged to share your unique perspectives and capabilities*. At IBM we recognize individual differences and appreciate *how these differences provide a powerful competitive advantage* and a source of great pride and opportunity in the workplace and marketplace."[67]

Toward Radical Futures

Much like modern gay and lesbian movements that have veered away from liberationist approaches toward assimilatory goals, transsexuals have overwhelmingly responded to pathologization and erasure by cultivating social subjectivities that demonstrate their ability to contribute to economic progress. However, claims to self-sufficiency, morality, and a positive work ethic undermine the potential for a politics of resistance and create fractures within transsexual communities based on class, race, citizenship status, and ability (to name a few). Whose bodies are the most productive and most effortlessly absorbed into capitalist employment pools? Appealing to mainstream society through a rearticulation of dominant socioeconomic discourses comes at a cost to those within trans communities who cannot be easily assimilated into normative categories, such as those who do not pass as men or women or those who are physically or mentally ill or incarcerated.

A second division resulting from these assimilatory strategies extends beyond transsexual communities. This strategy within the context of neoliberalism distances transsexual people from other economic outsiders who are also configured as parasitic, abnormal, or deviant. Progressive trans scholars and activists ought to think through the complex ways that heteronormativity and capitalism impact the lives of many other individuals who are understood as improperly sexed/gendered such as single mothers, women and men of color, those on social assistance, and those engaged in sex work. Further, these efforts to normalize trans bodies as productive forego the possibility of establishing alliances with anticapitalist and antiglobalization activists who engage in queering all facets of political economy. While the urgent need for employment is deniable for many trans people, it is important to ask: Whose interests are ultimately served by the formation of dutiful, self-sufficient, hardworking transsexual subjectivities?

Certainly, the lasting legacy of the medicalization of trans people demands our continued resistance. We also need to acknowledge the ways in which neoliberal prescriptions for thought and behavior have influenced the lived experiences that contribute to trans theory and activism despite transsexuals' rich history of militant opposition to systemic power structures. The actions of the trans and gender-noncompliant Compton Cafeteria rioters and of those who fought police at Stonewall ought to occupy a more significant place in the queer collective memory. In the midst of a political climate in which we are told that "there is no alternative," their activism can still spark radical imaginations of a queer future.

Notes

I would like to express my gratitude to the helpful commentary provided by an anonymous *RHR* external reviewer. Much thanks goes to Melissa Autumn White for hours spent in conversation, as well as to her and David Serlin for editorial suggestions.

1. I use the term *transsexual*, a specific category that defines gender-variant individuals who communicated their desires to have their sex reassigned, as coined by medical experts. In other words, transsexual people did not create the term; rather, it was introduced by Magnus Hirschfeld in 1923, but did not become an official diagnostic category until 1980. I use the term *trans* to denote the current terminology used. It reflects a movement away from the transsexual/transgender divide and acknowledges diversity among gender-variant identities and expressions including genderqueers, transmen, transwomen, and so on. I also use the term *gender variant* to mark the exclusion of all trans people from the hegemonic sex/gender binary.
2. Larry Buhl, "Historic 1966 Transgender Riot Remembered," Intraa, www.intraa.org/story/comptons (accessed May 8, 2007).
3. For examples, see Rosemary Hennessy, *Materialist Feminism: A Reader in Class, Difference, and Women's Lives* (New York: Routledge, 1997); Gayle Rubin, "Thinking Sex: Notes for a Radical Theory of the Politics of Sexuality," 1984, in *Social Perspectives in Lesbian and Gay Studies: A Reader*, ed. Peter M. Nardi and Beth E. Schneider (New York: Routledge, 1998), 100–133.
4. Donald Morton, ed., *The Material Queer: A LesBiGay Cultural Studies Reader* (Boulder, CO: Westview, 1996); Amy Gluckman and Betsy Reed, *HomoEconomics: Capitalism, Community, and Lesbian and Gay Life* (New York: Routledge, 1997).
5. Leslie Feinberg and Dean Spade are notable exceptions to this scholarly act of omission.
6. For examples of the myriad of texts describing trans identities, see Ann Bolin, *In Search of Eve: Transsexual Rites of Passage* (New York: Bergin and Garvy, 1988); Holly Devor, *FTM: Female-to-Male Transsexuals in Society* (Bloomington: Indiana University Press, 1997); Kate Bornstein, *Gender Outlaws: On Men, Women, and the Rest of Us* (New York: Random House, 1995); Judith Halberstam, *Female Masculinities* (Durham, NC: Duke University Press, 1998).
7. For an example of literature concerning human rights debates, see Paisley Currah, Richard M. Juang, and Shannon Price Minter, eds., *Transgender Rights* (Minneapolis: University of Minnesota Press, 2006).
8. For texts that address trans poverty, see, for example, Dean Spade, "Compliance Is Gendered: Struggling for Gender Self-Determination in a Hostile Economy," in Currah, Juang, and Minter, *Transgender Rights*, 217–41.
9. For scholarly publications on trans employment, see Viviane Namaste, "Beyond Leisure Studies: A Labour History of Male to Female Transsexual and Transvestite Artists in Montreal, 1955–1985," *Atlantis: A Women's Studies Journal* 29 (2004): 4–11; Christine Burnham, *Gender Change: Employability Issues* (Vancouver: Perceptions, 1994). For trans

community publications, see Marty Wilder, "First Day on the Gender," *FTMI Newsletter* 51 (2002): 8–9; Janis Wolworth, *Transsexual Workers: An Employers Guide* (Los Angeles: Center for Gender Sanity, 1998).

10. Gary Browning and Andrew Kilmister, *Critical and Post-critical Political Economy* (London: Palgrave, 2006), 4.

11. Judith Butler, "Gender Regulations," in *Undoing Gender* (New York: Routledge, 2005), 41.

12. Sandy Stone, "The Empire Strikes Back: A Posttranssexual Manifesto," in *The Transgender Studies Reader*, ed. Susan Stryker and Stephen Whittle (New York: Routledge, 2006), 232; Jay Prosser, *Second Skins: The Body Narrative of Transsexuality* (New York: Columbia University Press, 1998), 101.

13. SRS was delisted from the Ontario Health Insurance Plan in 1998.

14. The John Hopkins Gender Identity Clinic in Baltimore is one of the most notable U.S. clinics, whereas the former Clarke Institute (presently the Centre for Addictions and Mental Health) in Toronto and the Gender Dysphoria program in Vancouver are Canadian examples.

15. For example, see Vernon A. Rosario, "Trans (Homo) Sexuality? Double Inversion, Psychiatric Confusion, and Hetero-hegemony," in *Queer Studies: A Lesbian, Gay, Bisexual, Transgender Anthropology*, ed. Brett Beemyn and Mickey Eliason (New York: New York University Press, 1996), 35–51.

16. Richard von Krafft-Ebing, "Selections from Psychopathia Sexualis with Special Reference to Contrary Sexual Instinct: A Medico-Legal Study," in Stryker and Whittle, *Transgender Studies Reader*, 22.

17. David O. Cauldwell, "Psychopathia Transexualis," *International Journal of Transgenderism* 5, no. 2 (2001), www.symposion.com/ijt/cauldwell/cauldwell_02.htm.

18. Ibid.

19. David O. Cauldwell, "Questions and Answers on the Sex Life and Sexual Problems of Transsexuals," *International Journal of Transgenderism* 5, no. 2 (2001), www.symposion.com/ijt/cauldwell/cauldwell_04.htm.

20. Cauldwell, "Psychopathia Transexualis."

21. For similar commentary, see Dean Spade, "Mutilating Gender," in Stryker and Whittle, *Transgender Studies Reader*, 325–29.

22. Prosser, *Second Skins*, 104.

23. Stone, "Empire Strikes Back," 228.

24. Jason Cromwell, "Queering the Binaries: Transituated Identities, Bodies, and Sexualities," in Stryker and Whittle, *Transgender Studies Reader*, 511.

25. While the real-life test is addressed using past tense to indicate a time in the history of transsexuality when GICs were prevalent, this requirement before any access to a medicalized transition still exists for many. Transsexuals located in suburban and rural locations, where trans awareness is lacking among medical professionals, continue to be referred to GICs still in operation.

26. It was John Money who referred to the employment requirement of the real-life test as economic "rehabilitation." Money, a psychologist and a sexologist, was a professor of pediatrics and psychology at John Hopkins University from 1951 until his death in 2006. He worked within the Sexual Behaviors Unit that researches SRS. See John Money, *Gay, Straight, and In-Between* (Oxford: Oxford University Press, 1989), 88.

27. Ibid., 92; emphasis mine.

28. Jo Hirschmann, "TransAction: Organizing against Capitalism and State Violence in San

Francisco," *Socialist Review* (2001): 4, www.findarticles.com/p/articles/mi_qa3952/
    is_200101/ai_n8932894.

29. Harry Benjamin, *The Transsexual Phenomenon* (Dusseldorf: Symposion, 1997),
    www.symposion.com/ijt/Benjamin/chapt_07.htm.

30. Cauldwell, "Psychopathia Transexualis."

31. David O. Cauldwell, "Sex Transmutation—Can Anyone's Sex Be Changed?" *International
    Journal of Transgenderism* 5, no. 2 (2001), www.symposion.com/ijt/cauldwell/cauldwell_05
    .htm; emphasis mine.

32. Cauldwell, "Psychopathia Transexualis"; emphasis original.

33. Cauldwell, "Questions and Answers"; emphasis mine.

34. Ibid.

35. Benjamin, *Transsexual Phenomenon*.

36. Ibid.; Cauldwell, "Psychopathia Transexualis"; David O. Cauldwell, "Desire for Surgical Sex
    Transmutation," *International Journal of Transgenderism* 5, no. 2(2001), www.symposion
    .com/ijt/cauldwell/cauldwell_03.htm.

37. Aren Z. Aizura, "Of Borders and Homes: The Imaginary Community of (Trans)sexual
    Citizenship," *Inter-Asia Cultural Studies* 7(2006): 295.

38. The two failed attempts to receive the necessary access to medicalized transition
    procedures by the renowned FTM activist Lou Sullivan—a gay man who refused to comply
    with the imperative that transsexual men must desire women—demonstrate the rigidity
    of this narrative. For a discussion of Sullivan, see Pat Califia, *Sex Changes: The Politics of
    Transgenderism* (San Francisco: Cleis, 1997), 186.

39. While direct references may have been made to employment elsewhere, they were not at all
    prominent within sexology literature.

40. Benjamin, *Transsexual Phenomenon*.

41. Bernice Hausman, "Body, Technology, and Gender in Transsexual Autobiographies," in
    Stryker and Whittle, *Transgender Studies Reader*, 350.

42. Ibid., 341.

43. Christine Jorgensen, "Christine Jorgensen: A Personal Autobiography," in *Sexual
    Metamorphosis: An Anthology of Transsexual Memoirs*, ed. Jonathan Ames (New York:
    Vintage, 2005), 72.

44. Ibid., 73.

45. Joanne Meyerowitz, *How Sex Changed: A History of Transsexuality in the United States*
    (Cambridge, MA: Harvard University Press, 2002), 79.

46. Leslie Feinberg, *Transgendered Warriors: Making History from Joan of Arc to Dennis
    Rodman* (Boston: Beacon, 1996), 88.

47. Jason Cromwell, *Transmen and FTMs: Identities, Bodies, Genders, and Sexualities*
    (Urbana: University of Illinois Press, 1999), 63–72; Nan Alamilla Boyd, "Bodies in Motion:
    Lesbian and Transsexual Histories," in Stryker and Whittle, *Transgender Studies Reader*,
    423–24.

48. Aaron Devor and Nicholas Matte, "ONE Inc. and Reed Erickson: The Uneasy Collaboration
    of Gay and Trans Activism," in Stryker and Whittle, *Transgender Studies Reader*, 387–406.

49. Namaste, "Beyond Leisure Studies," 4–11.

50. Viviane Namaste, *Invisible Lives: The Erasure of Transsexual and Transgendered People*
    (Chicago: University of Chicago Press, 2000); C. Jacob Hale, "Suggested Rules for
    Non-transsexuals Writing about Transsexuals, Transsexualism, or Trans," www.sandystone
    .com/hale.rules.html (accessed May 8, 2007).

51. Thom Workman, *Banking on Deception: The Discourse of Fiscal Crisis* (Halifax: Fernwood, 1996), 23–24.

52. Roxana Ng, "Homeworking: Dream Realized or Freedom Restrained? The Globalized Reality of Immigrant Garment Workers," *Canadian Women's Studies* 19, no. 3 (1999): 110.

53. Jamie Swift, *Wheel of Fortune: Work and Life in the Age of Falling Expectations* (Toronto: Between the Lines, 1995), 13.

54. Thom Workman, *Social Torment: Globalization in Atlantic Canada* (Halifax: Fernwood, 2003), 105.

55. Angela Harris, "From Stonewall to the Suburbs? Toward a Political Economy of Sexuality," *William and Mary Bill of Rights Journal* 14 (2006): 1541.

56. Stephen McBride and John Shields, *Dismantling a Nation: The Transition to Corporate Rule in Canada* (Halifax: Fernwood, 1997), 26.

57. For an example, see Thomas Dunk, Stephen McBride, and Randle W. Nelson, eds., *The Training Trap: Ideology, Training, and the Labour Market* (Winnipeg: Society for Socialist Studies, 1996).

58. Harris, "From Stonewall to the Suburbs," 1542.

59. Kathleen Kenna, "Engineer 'Just Knew' He Was Really Female," *Toronto Star*, August 4, 1990.

60. Deirdre N. McCloskey, *Crossing: A Memoir* (Chicago: University of Chicago Press, 2000).

61. Deirdre N. McCloskey, "Crossing Economics," *International Journal of Transgenderism* 4 (2000), www.symposion.com/ijt/gilbert/mccloskey.htm.

62. Jamison Green, *Becoming a Visible Man* (Nashville, TN: Vanderbilt University Press, 2004), 74.

63. Ibid., 181; emphasis mine.

64. Wolworth, *Transsexual Workers*, 54.

65. Within the Western patriarchal capitalist system, one can say that gender and economic activity have always combined to produce an understanding of fully realized humanity. It is not coincidental that the titles of many recent texts written by transsexual men make use of the notion of the economic man to attempt to access hegemonic masculinity. Examples include Henry Rubin, *Self-Made Men: Identity and Embodiment among Transsexual Men* (Nashville, TN: Vanderbilt University Press, 2003); and Paul Hewitt with Jane Warren, *A Self-Made Man: The Diary of a Man Born in a Woman's Body* (London: Headline, 1995).

66. For a general overview of the purpose of IBM's Executive Task Forces and a sample of the questions task forces comprised of GBLT people, Native Americans, and women were asked, please see IBM's Web site, especially Global Task Forces, www-03.ibm.com/employment/us/diverse/50/exectask.shtml (accessed May 12, 2007).

67. IBM, "Diversity at IBM," www-03.ibm.com/employment/ca/en/diversity.html; emphasis mine (accessed May 12, 2007).

CITY OF NEW YORK
COMMUNITY BOARD NO. 2, MANHATTAN
3 Washington Square Village • New York, New York 10012-1899 • (212) 979-2272 • FAX (212) 254-5102
Greenwich Village • Little Italy • SoHo • NoHo • Hudson Square

Aubrey Lees
Chair

Arthur W. Strickler
District Manager

Carol Yankay
1st Vice-Chair

Ann Arlen
2nd Vice-Chair

Jeanne Wilcke
Treasurer

Robert Rinaolo
Secretary

Martin Tessler
Assistant Secretary

NOTICE OF
PUBLIC HEARING

TAKE BACK OUR STREETS

Date: Monday, May 6, 2002
Time: 6:00 p.m.
Place: Sheridan Square Park
         7th Ave. & Christopher St.

RE: Summer's coming! Fight Back against our
     new neighbors; the Bloods and the Crips
     plus our old neighbors, the dealers, the
     hookers, the pimps, the johns, etc. etc.

     Sponsored by the Sixth Precinct
     Community Council, Chelsea, Greenwich
     Village Chamber of Commerce and
     Residence in Distress (RID).

     ALL ARE WELCOME TO ATTEND.

Please come and be heard. We need your input. If you are unable to
attend, please submit your comments in writing to the Community
Board #2, Manhattan office, 3 Washington Square Village, Suite 1A,
New York, NY 10012.

Aubrey Lees, Chair   Arthur W. Strickler
Community Board #2, Manhattan   District Manager

Blane Roberts,
Community Board Liaison
Man. Borough President's Office

"Notice of Public Hearing, City of New York," Community Board 2, Manhattan, New York

Butterflies, Whistles, and Fists:

Gay Safe Streets Patrols and

the New Gay Ghetto, 1976–1981

Christina B. Hanhardt

On May 6, 2002, members of the Christopher Street Patrol, a safe streets organization in New York City's Greenwich Village neighborhood, joined Residents in
Distress (or RID, a name inspired by a popular insecticide) and local politicians in
a rally called "Take Back Our Streets" in Christopher Park.[1] The location was strategic; not only is it a public space near the neighborhood's main commercial hub,
but it is also across the street from the historic Stonewall Inn, where, on June 28,
1969, the modern LGBT (lesbian, gay, bisexual, transgender) movement is said to
have begun.[2] The Stonewall riot, as it is known, has been repeatedly evoked in the
rise of gay liberation and civil rights movements. Yet today the memory of Stonewall as a long overdue, passionate expression of *selfhood* often omits that it was a
challenge to the police and but the latest clash in a continuing struggle. Moreover,
many members of the gay liberation organizations that arose in the aftermath of
Stonewall believed that gay safety would depend on coalitions with other liberation
movements, including Black Power, feminist consciousness-raising, and third world
decolonization.[3] This stood in contrast to the approach adopted by their predecessors, the so-called second wave of homophile activists who in the 1950s and into
the 1960s pushed for police accountability through cooperation. Consequently, the
post-Stonewall refusal to collaborate with the police not only marked a break from a
homophile ethos of cultural assimilation, but was also a rejection of the partnership

Radical History Review
Issue 100 (Winter 2008)   DOI 10.1215/01636545-2007-022
© 2008 by MARHO: The Radical Historians' Organization, Inc.

solutions to urban violence that were popular with policymakers in the 1960s such as community policing and War on Poverty development initiatives.

The recent actions of the Christopher Street Patrol offer one example of the changing strategic uses of lesbian and gay political goals in the intervening decades. The Christopher Street Patrol is run primarily by nongay people. But in its first incarnation in 1990, among its stated main purposes was the desire to protect against antigay violence, and the patrol was part of an informal national network that included the San Francisco Street Patrol, an offshoot of Queer Nation.[4] Although the Christopher Street Patrol originally intended to focus on "violent crime, including gay-bashing, and drug sales" and not the "public drinking, rowdiness and noisemaking" it associated with the neighborhood's identity, in the next decade such concerns became its central focus.[5]

In a campaign still active today, members patrol the streets and collaborate with other resident and block associations to organize rallies, speak-outs, and media blitzes, in which they assert that boisterous crowds and sex and drug trades are fomenting a threatening culture of crime and disorder in their neighborhood.[6] In Community Board hearings and other city-sponsored venues for neighborhood decision making, majority white residents argue for the "cleanup" of places where sexual minorities of color, many of whom identify as lesbian, gay, bisexual, or transgender, have long socialized.[7] Overwhelmingly, residents, gay and straight alike, demand policing and zoning changes with a focus on securing "safety," citing the quality-of-life laws that target low-level offenses (such as public drinking and loitering) first instituted by the former mayor Rudolph Giuliani.[8]

While the historical juxtaposition of radical liberation movements and rearguard actions on behalf of now exclusive neighborhoods like Greenwich Village does not tell the whole story behind the actions of organizations like the Christopher Street Patrol, it does point to a significant overlap.[9] The call for "safe streets" has been a rallying cry expressed by both social minorities and property owners in the eras of postwar urban decline and neoliberal development in the United States. Early in the twenty-first century, the pitch of this call heightened as the issue of national protection entered the center of American public debate. The increased attention paid to security has revealed the disparate understandings of threat held among those considered representative of and those marginal to the national body politic. This disjunction points to the need for deeper knowledge about violence and the quest for safety within local communities and contemporary social movements.

Whether to prevent crime or to allay local uprisings, the fight against urban violence has been waged by the state and the disenfranchised alike and has inspired much urban research since the tumults in American cities during the 1960s.[10] Nevertheless, research on sexual minorities' efforts to combat violence has been nominal. Some attention has been given to the formal LGBT antiviolence movement begun in the 1980s and its advocacy for hate crime laws. Social science research, in particular psychological studies of the motives and impact of violence, has supported efforts to expose the problem of antigay violence.[11] Yet these empirical studies are more likely to assess the effectiveness of advocacy than the ideologies of activism, and they almost never consider the context of urban politics. Queer theoretical scholarship on violence and hate has analyzed the ideological underpinnings of policy advocacy, but these studies overwhelmingly focus on the production of subjects of the law and not the actors of grassroots movements.[12] But the history of on-the-ground LGBT political organizing against violence has much to tell us about both sexual minority and urban life in the United States. Over the past forty years, the fight against violence and the ideal of "safe space" have been fundamental to emergent forms of LGBT identity, as well as to urban policy and social science research on violence, neighborhoods, and social "deviancy."

This essay focuses on the strategies of two patrols during the 1970s—the Butterfly Brigade in San Francisco's Castro District and the Society to Make America Safe for Homosexuals (SMASH) in New York's Chelsea neighborhood—in light of concomitant urban research and development. Specifically, I contend that grassroots activism lying outside the orbit usually associated with property ownership is one means by which neighborhoods have been claimed and marketed for exclusive urban constituencies.[13] In addition, I demonstrate how the public uptake of a racialized culture of poverty thesis based on ideas of wounded masculinity has shaped new activist understandings of the "homophobia" found in gentrifying central cities.

It is important to note that the benefit of gay concentration has been hailed not only by gay activists but also by city boosters. The Gay Index, developed by the demographer Gary Gates, has become a key tool of city agencies from Washington, DC, to Oakland, California, because of its highly touted claim to predict the regional success of high-tech industries. The policy consultant Richard Florida has popularized the Gay Index by contending that a concentration of gay men (and sometimes lesbians) reflects the region's social "tolerance," which he explains to be a draw factor for the creative class of workers at the center of the new economy.[14] Gay space becomes, then, an index of economic competitiveness in a global marketplace for business location.

This understanding of gay space is but one held by Gay Index proponents: another is that gay people tend to live in neighborhoods with a dilapidated housing stock and high crime rates. As Gates explains, "It could be that gay and lesbian people are less risk averse. They've already taken the risk of coming out of the closet, so it could be that they're willing to take more risk in other dimensions of their lives as well."[15] According to Gates and Florida, gay populations are the "canaries of the Creative Age" whose survival in urban regions is an indicator of the "last frontier" of social tolerance and diversity, and the hope of a successful economy.[16]

Yet people of color are conspicuously absent from Florida's conceptualization of diversity. As Florida observes when describing the Composite Diversity Index of which the Gay Index is a part (joined by the Melting Pot Index and the Bohemian Index): "The diversity picture does not include African-Americans and other nonwhites." He continues, "my statistical research identifies a troubling negative statistical correlation between concentrations of high-tech firms and the percentage of the nonwhite population."[17]

The debates in Greenwich Village show the contradictions of postwar urban politics, in which neighborhood activists cast racial, sexual, and gender identities, as well as economic diversity, as "liabilities" of a community best known for its gay populations and bohemianism.[18] Moreover, in residents', gay activists', and developers' shared investment in the assessment of *risk*, the debates show the discursive construction of antigay violence as a part of the history of real estate speculation fueling gentrification and gay enclave formation. Here violence is imagined as the risk of gay visibility—the dominant trope of mainstream LGBT politics since the 1970s. Yet in naming the solution to be the settling of gay identity in place, LGBT politics and urban developers invest in the race and class stratification of postwar urban space.

This essay argues that the connection between neighborhood transformation and antiviolence ideologies is not only conceptual but, in fact, organizational. Although lesbian and gay activists have fought state violence since at least the 1950s, it was not until the 1970s that activists began to design response strategies to violence perpetrated by people other than the police.[19] The most popular strategy was safe streets patrols,[20] and the members of the two patrols discussed in this essay provided some of the founding members and example strategies of the antiviolence movement that followed.[21] Borrowing from and paralleling the mainstream feminist antirape movement's turn to state power, these patrols took urban policies such as street cleanups and heightened policing, which a decade earlier had placed "sexual deviants" at odds with redevelopment and law and order and cast them as the very insurance of lesbian and gay visibility.[22] Gay vulnerability was, in effect, understood as the vulnerability of the crime victim.

This trajectory explains in part why so many lesbian and gay residents of Greenwich Village today tend to remain silent on the subject of the Christopher Street Patrol despite the fact that the majority of those targeted by quality-of-life policies in the area are themselves sexual minorities. In public hearings, both gay and straight residents cite the history of antigay violence—and activism against it—to bolster their fight against undesirable street life, and they advocate many of the very same strategies promoted by 1970s gay activists that later became the foundation of the LGBT antiviolence movement, from safe streets patrols to increased policing to enhanced criminal penalties.[23] The result is that the demands of elite residents of neighborhoods like Greenwich Village and those of the national LGBT antiviolence movement look strikingly alike.[24]

This is the "new homonormativity" as described by Lisa Duggan, in which the goals of lesbian and gay civil rights organizations resonate with the neoliberal values of individualism and privatization.[25] As Alexandra Chasin has demonstrated in *Selling*

Out: The Gay and Lesbian Movement Goes to Market, many lesbian and gay activist goals were transformed into consumer demands in the 1990s.[26] This process fueled the growth of gay enclaves as visible niche markets for retail commerce and realty speculation; the use of the Gay Index for regional growth is but the most recent development.[27] In fact, one of Duggan's defining examples of homonormativity is drawn from the antiviolence movement: in 2001, the National Coalition of Anti-Violence Programs protested antigay graffiti on a bomb destined for Afghanistan without noting the violence promised by the bomb itself.[28] The research that follows provides one piece of the historical context for the emergence of homonormative antiviolence politics and argues for their connection to gay enclave history. Nonetheless, as I note in my conclusion, this has not been the only possible model for activism.

BAGL, Gay Action, and the Rise of the Butterfly Brigade

One of the earliest gay safe streets patrols was the Butterfly Brigade. It was the main project of Gay Action, an offshoot of Bay Area Gay Liberation (BAGL), an organization established in San Francisco around 1975.[29] Founded by the labor organizer Howard Wallace with the participation of former New York Gay Activist Alliance (GAA) youth member Claude Wynne, BAGL was instrumental to some of the city's most successful gay political campaigns of the 1970s including the Coors Beer boycott and the defeat of the Briggs Initiative, which sought to prevent lesbian and gay men from teaching in California's public schools. Despite the fact that many scholars have described gay liberation as "over" by 1971, BAGL put forth a radical gay agenda based on a multi-issue critique of capitalism and the state, but, like many of the organizations that followed gay liberationism, this one aimed specifically at gay-oriented reforms.[30] The organization's initial position on policing reflected this "in-between" status. Members of the Gay Community Defense Committee advertised what would be the founding meeting of BAGL in conjunction with a citywide campaign for police accountability. "We understand the police all too well—BY THEIR DEEDS! From the racist Zebra dragnet to the Chinatown payoffs to the failure to investigate widespread reports of brutality against Chicanos and Latinos in the Mission to police infiltration of progressive organizations to the 'clean up' of pornography and prostitution on the Tenderloin to the crackdown on gays and shakedown of gay businesses—BEHAVIOR, NOT WORDS, TELLS THE STORY!"[31] The police problem was understood to be multifaceted and endemic yet open to reform.

In the fall of 1976, after only a year, BAGL split into two discrete organizations due to by-then familiar rifts over adopting a broad-based left agenda as opposed to a more explicitly gay-focused one.[32] The "Principles of Unity" put forth by the left-identified Progressive Caucus were adopted by the group, and they continued coalition work on issues as varied as farmworker support or solidarity with the Chilean resistance.[33] They argued vehemently that a struggle unilaterally focused on gay oppression would only assist "white middle class men" and that "gay people's problems cannot be solved by reacting to the symptoms of anti-gay prejudice, but must attack the system at the root . . . : Imperialism."[34] The other organization that emerged after the split, Gay Action, had a different aim in mind, as evinced by the second item in their statement of purpose: "We support the right of self-defense. We will resist violent attacks against individuals in our community."[35] In December 1976, Gay Action initiated what would be its biggest project: the Richard Heakin Memorial Butterfly Brigade, named after a gay man who had been murdered in Tuscon, Arizona. Outraged by the fact that Heakin's murderers received only probation, Gay Action members developed a community response by choosing the Castro as its main location.[36]

The Butterfly Brigade considered the Castro its territory, and its actions marked its borders. Every weekend, patrollers would meet at around 10:00 p.m. on the corner of Castro and Eighteenth Streets, the center of the area's commercial strip, with the control center a converted bakery delivery truck that they would park in an always available (and illegal) spot in front of a fire hydrant.[37] A driver occupied the truck, in keeping with an unspoken agreement with the police that it would be moved when requested. In two shifts, groups of activists would take up positions on designated street corners, including in a popular cruising park, a public transportation hub, and other spots considered central to gay night life. Armed with whistles, index cards, pens, and walkie-talkies, they mainly recorded the license plate numbers of cars that carried passengers shouting antigay epithets and blew whistles if threatening individuals approached. Later, they would look up plate numbers and send letters to the cars' owners. The letters carefully recorded "conduct" and included slurs spoken, aggressive gestures, and even questionable looks.[38] The index cards noted even more detail, including, on occasion, the race of attackers, in particular when they were people of color. This suggests that the patrollers presumed other potential offenders and all victims to be, by default (by being unremarked), white. The majority of the patrollers themselves were white men.[39]

The campaign continued for a year or so, and eventually it petered out, due not only to activist burnout but also because the Butterfly Brigade considered the project a success; they interpreted the infrequency of violent confrontation as evidence that potential attackers knew the Castro was not to be messed with. The whistle strategy became the enduring legacy of the patrol, borrowed from the feminist antirape movement and combined with general anticrime guidelines. One activist estimated that over thirty thousand whistles were distributed in a widespread campaign to furnish them as a welcome to new gay arrivals to San Francisco and, by doing so, to forge a symbolic marker of community.[40]

Although the Butterfly Brigade never worked directly with the police, it collaborated informally, even after the *San Francisco Examiner* published an inflammatory editorial calling the brigade a "semi-vigilante" group.[41] Yet members of the brigade considered themselves peaceful, with the goal of restraining attackers until the police—summoned by a chorus of whistles—arrived on the scene. Many gay San Franciscans responded proudly to the brigade. In *The Mayor of Castro Street*, for example, Randy Shilts declared, "The fact that a virile gay community was taking care of its own problems startled the city's establishment, which could barely deal with homosexuals of the Judy Garland vintage."[42] As the masculinism of Shilts's comments suggests, manhood and a desire for order linked, rather than separated, the brigade and the police.[43] That the Butterfly Brigade hoped to work with the police is crucial to understanding their analysis of urban violence and gay community. Members of the patrol were active in the push for a police reform campaign that would include increasing the number of lesbian and gay officers and the institutionalization of sensitivity training. This was not only to stem police violence but also to make officers aware of the at-once general and specific needs of gay victims. Indeed, these would be among the primary demands of the antiviolence organizations that followed on the heels of the Butterfly Brigade.

The argument for increased policing arose from activists' faith in a theoretically neutral third party, but it also stemmed from the popular conviction that antigay violence was produced by the very phenomenon of an open gay population. As Shilts writes, "Attacks came with the neighborhood's national prominence." Visibility, in other words, was often equated with the vague terms of coming out and its attendant risks and possibilities. Yet for the Butterfly Brigade, the popularity of a "gay look" as a form of visibility was troublesome, notwithstanding commonplace complaints about an emerging "clone culture" of athletic white men in mustaches and Levis.[44] Cultural activism undermined stereotypes, even while some activists had begun to acknowledge that gender nonconforming dress and comportment might increase one's risk of violence. In this way, visibility was most realized via representation or abstraction; visibility, quite simply, functioned as a shorthand for an increased presence in the public sphere from media coverage to electoral power to neighborhood. Neighborhoods came to be seen as an expressive demonstration of gay identity, and thus as the collective asset most in need of protection.

The assumption that increased visibility led to increased neighborhood violence worked in tandem with conflicted assumptions about the people who were the mostly likely to commit antigay violence. Members of the brigade later described perpetrators as young men in their late teens and early twenties, racially diverse, from a variety of areas outside the Castro.[45] Yet some brigade members' memories suggest that they also suspected that lower-income areas adjacent to the Castro, such as the majority Latino Mission District to the east and the predominantly African American Western Addition to the north, provided a particular threat.[46] Moreover, during these years there was a growing public concern about the link between gentrification and the rise of antigay sentiment in these neighborhoods.[47] By 1980 even *NBC Late Night* reported that the gentrification of the Western Addition and Mission had, in part, made white gays a target of street violence.[48]

The claim that signs of threat such as aggressive language and gestures led to violence and that increased visibility increased violence were invoked as common knowledge. Yet these correlations, like assumptions about who tended to be most violent, reflect various strains of social science scholarship from the 1960s through the 1970s that were being taken up in public policy and popular commentary. Often working toward different ends, these studies included research on the causes of disorder, violence, and hate, as well as practical blueprints for local solutions. While ostensibly independent, they overlapped in a few key understandings. One commonality found both urban violence and homophobia to be *symptoms* of other social problems. Another shared interpretation was that self-monitoring communities were best equipped to recognize threat, and that signs of threat often signaled more serious violence to come. By the end of the decade, it was the merging of these formulas that would guide the shift from grassroots patrolling to evidence gathering, as later evinced by the antiviolence movement's collection of surveys and personal testimonials.

In response to 1960s urban uprisings, policymakers and social scientists dedicated themselves to understanding the causes of urban violence and to designing appropriate remedies. In the late 1960s, Lyndon B. Johnson ordered a series of commissions to research violence including the National Advisory Commission on Civil Disorders (the 1968 Kerner Commission), the President's Commission on Law Enforcement and the Administration of Justice (1967), and the National Commission on the Causes and Prevention of Violence (1968–1969). In 1968, the Omnibus Crime Control and Safe Streets Act emphasized participatory solutions by identifying a community policing model, which included neighborhood involvement in community watch efforts, as a possible remedy for urban crime. Many on the left viewed such programs as viable alternatives to top-down policing strategies such as the Special Weapons and Tactical Squad (SWAT) formed in 1967 and the subsequent law-and-order ideologies of Johnson's successor Richard Nixon.

The sociologist David Garland interprets community policing programs as efforts to involve citizens in the process of policing themselves.[49] By the mid-1970s, such programs were common in middle-class neighborhoods gripped by fears of crime and committed to community identity; these programs linked the work of the police with that of residents and business owners. In later years, such alliances became foundational to a new wave of policy philosophy about crime that Garland dubs the "new criminologies of everyday life." This approach to crime advocates the involvement of civilian participation in the management of "criminogenic situations,"[50] which include factors such as victim conduct and criminal opportunity. Among the early proponents of this paradigm were James Q. Wilson and George Kelling, who in 1982 developed the infamous "broken window" theory of crime control that targets all signs of disorderly life in a neighborhood as encouragements to criminal behavior. The data-gathering activities of the Butterfly Brigade, which recorded not only actual violent crime but also *signs* that violence *might* follow, paralleled the development of Wilson and Kelling's argument.

To understand how the representation of threat became increasingly equated with the power of violence itself, it is important to acknowledge the relationship between the Butterfly Brigade and its avowed primary influence, the feminist antirape movement. During the late 1970s feminists began organizing "Take Back the Night" marches to reclaim city streets from violent attack. One of the most famous was held in 1978 when more than five thousand women, many attending a conference sponsored by Women Against Violence in Pornography and Media (WAVPM), marched through San Francisco's pornography-heavy North Beach district. Although activists cite the tactical use of whistles and street patrols as the most prominent links between early gay and feminist antiviolence movements, perhaps more important is the shared interpretation of certain acts as simultaneously directives to and realizations of violence. Pornography and antigay epithets (in the absence of many actual attacks) were treated as injuries unto themselves, the threat of victimization both promised and assumed manifest.[51]

The organizers of the 1978 San Francisco march through North Beach considered not only the threat of pornography but also the threat of the city, as did New York feminist antiporn activists who hosted tours of Times Square in the 1970s.[52] By merging the fight against pornography with that against street violence, activists invoked the city as one place in which the violent promises of pornography were fulfilled.[53] In the case of the WAVPM marches, merging the fight against pornography with that against unsafe streets cast the signs of the seedy city as sinister. As the preface to the book *Take Back the Night*, edited by WAVPM member Laura Lederer, reads: "We live in cities like the tame pheasants who are hand-raised and then turned loose for hunters to shoot, an activity called sport."[54]

Pornography and city streets are formally different, but they both attest to the tenuous power of visual iconography. At the start of the "Take Back the Night" movement, Kelling published his first essay on his fieldwork on the quality of life of neighborhoods.[55] This approach treats signs of disorder, from broken windows to loitering to strangers, as directives to commit violent crimes. In later years, when quality-of-life theory manifested in urban policy, the subjects of these visible (and audible) signs—that is, young people holding open drinks or talking loudly late at night—were considered the threats unto themselves.[56] One of the first places where Kelling's theories would be translated into policy was Greenwich Village—where quality-of-life violations were often interpreted as particularly threatening to the neighborhood's gay community. For this reason, it is important to note the significance of the Butterfly Brigade's earlier attention to the language and postures of antigay threat, including epithets and even the types of clothing styles and automobile makes of imagined perpetrators. That these signs carried not-so-subtle class and racial connotations demonstrates the ways in which visual markers of difference were not only subject to unjust regulation through policies of racial profiling, also first instituted during the 1970s, but were treated as *inherently* violent.

Given that the Butterfly Brigade's practices called for increased policing, especially in an area that bordered other neighborhoods home to large numbers of low-income people and people of color, one might understand the effects of their activism as contributing to patterns of neighborhood gentrification and segregation. By the late 1970s the Castro was becoming less economically diverse as property values rapidly escalated. Although Lesbian and Gay Action (the renamed organizational birthplace of the Butterfly Brigade) criticized this transformation of the Castro, its members did not appear to connect their policing practices to this change. In 1978, for example, Lesbian and Gay Action joined with BAGL and the Housing Rights Study Group to produce a flyer, "Speculators Get Out of Our Neighborhood!,"[57] which argued that gay people were being used by speculators to "bust" neighborhoods by moving white gays in and families of color out. Despite this intervention, Lesbian and Gay Action—or BAGL, for that matter—did not sponsor sustained efforts to counter gay people's involvement in gentrification, although the Housing Rights Study Group did continue to support a municipal anti-speculation tax and other BAGL members fought the evictions of Filipino and Chinese tenants at the International Hotel.[58] Instead, other gay organizations, such as Lesbians against Police Violence and the Gay Latino/Latina Alliance, continued work in the following years that explicitly examined the relationship between gentrification and white gay communities.[59]

From Police Action to the Leatherman Stroll: Patrolling in New York

Like San Francisco, New York City during the early to mid-1970s was caught between the fast demise of gay liberation politics and the equally mercurial rise of a gay civil rights agenda. At the start of the 1970s, the GAA dedicated most of its energy to the fight for the city's first gay civil rights bill. With the exception of a few scattered protests and rallies (including an explosive confrontation on Fire Island), militant forms of opposition to police abuse were largely abandoned.[60] Nonetheless, the GAA's gay geography was crystal clear: in 1974 the group organized a "Freedom Ride" to the Bronx, Brooklyn, and Queens in search of nongay support for the passage of the civil rights bill, despite the fact that, as George Chauncey has shown, gay and same-sex erotic communities already existed in neighborhoods across New York City.[61] However, the GAA proved unsuccessful in garnering support necessary for passing the civil rights bill (a version would eventually pass in 1986), and the group's membership had substantially dwindled by 1974.

Approximately two years later, in 1976, the same year the Butterfly Brigade was founded, a new gay safe streets patrol—the Society to Make America Safe for Homosexuals (SMASH)—was formed by new gay residents of Chelsea, a neighborhood just north of Greenwich Village. A mixed-use neighborhood linked to the city's waterfront economy, Chelsea was home to a decreasing number of the white working class alongside a population of poor and working-class Puerto Ricans and African Americans, especially in the public housing units on its west side. As was happening throughout New York, the departure and displacement of working-class communities from dilapidated housing stock was met by an influx of middle- and upper-income white residents refurbishing homes and businesses.[62] The neighborhood was also home to the majority of New York's gay leather and S-M bars as a result of the area's evacuated industrial spaces and its proximity to the popular public sex spot of the West Side piers.

According to its founders, SMASH's purpose was to stop a "spike" in antigay violence perpetrated by the neighborhood's teenaged boys.[63] New gay residents claimed that young men from the neighborhood had been targeting "macho" gay men as a way to assert their own masculinity. The society sent out decoys to prove to attackers the power of gay masculinity and, through the instigation and documentation of antigay violence, to elicit a formal response from the police. Indeed, SMASH explicitly directed its work to publicizing antigay violence; members even called it a "smoke and mirrors" operation in which the distribution of their press release ranked among most significant aspects of their actions.[64] Their ultimate goals were an increase in police presence and a neighborhood-wide recognition that violence against gay men was unacceptable.[65]

What is most compelling about SMASH was its attention to psychology; more than one member was a professional psychologist, and the group attributed antigay violence to psychological causes. For example, SMASH cofounders Larry Durham and Louis Weingarden gave a television interview in which he argued that the young men from the neighborhood sought to prove their masculinity, which Weingarden claimed had been damaged by the fact that "half of their fathers were out of work."[66] Due to the economic disinvestment in urban manufacturing and services of the 1970s, Durham asserted, youths did not have access to employment or youth services and instead they were "hanging out" all day long. According to Weingarden, antigay violence functioned as a "testing ground" for an insecure masculine identity and as a way to take out the frustrations of social inequality: hypermasculine gay leathermen served as an ideal target. Although the members of SMASH never publically addressed the racial identities of the young people involved, they sometimes used coded language to suggest that they were Puerto Rican or African American. Specifically, some members described the threat as coming from the area's public housing project, whose tenants were increasingly Puerto Rican and African American.[67]

This focus on low-income men of color was particularly curious due to the events of the summer of 1976. In June of that year, a fifteen–year-old boy from Greenwich Village stabbed to death a fellow Villager. Allegedly linked to violent gang activity, the incident received much attention since the killer was middle-class, an honor student, and, mostly likely, white.[68] Just three months later, in September, another murder took place in Washington Square Park; in this case, the victim was Puerto Rican and the attackers presumed Italian. The local newpaper *The Villager* included numerous editorials by residents who described the perpetrators as the real victims and declared that if the police would "do their job" to get "undesirables" out of "our" parks none of this would have happened.[69] These sentiments typified a highly racialized public discourse of social conflict among white working-class New Yorkers during the late 1960s and 1970s, which identified white ethnics as the victims of the larger social and economic changes constitutive of the so-called postwar urban crisis.[70]

Indeed, despite a context in which violence was most often associated with white youth in the mostly middle-class Greenwich Village, the members of SMASH continued to patrol areas home to mostly low-income people of color. They even sought a well-publicized "truce" with Greenwich Village youth as they continued to cite Chelsea as a problem.[71] The prevalence of this understanding of race, poverty, and violence is particularly interesting in light of the public discussion of this nexus popular in the 1970s. Wilson and Kelling's broken-window research built on the growing backlash to progressive social science commissioned by the Johnson administration. These studies examined the structural roots of violence and crime and focused on their social and psychological impact. In other words, this research underscored the damage to psyches brought about by social inequality and posited violence as a logical and pathological symptom. As Ellen Herman has argued, "All of the psychological experts affiliated with Kerner Commission research were steeped in the postwar literature on prejudice and personality damage, and their explorations of riot causation were marked by the characteristic themes of psychological work on race since 1945: social pathology, wounded masculinity, matriarchal families, and problematic self-esteem."[72]

For some, such as the social psychologist Kenneth Clark, cyclical violence represented a response to an American preoccupation with property damage and a related inattention to the structural causes of and potential solutions to problems produced by poverty.[73] Nonetheless, many researchers emphasized psychological causation and argued that poor black families, ravaged by social and psychological pathologies, had become moored in place, stuck in stagnating, crime-ridden neighborhoods. Although some early analyses of the "ghetto" challenged racial reductionism and posited institutional critiques, they also proposed narrowly predictive relationships between economic structure and psychosocial effect and defined low-income families as inherently inferior to idealized models of the "good community."[74]

This critique of the postwar "culture of poverty" received broad public attention with the response to publication of the Moynihan Report in 1965. Officially titled *The Negro Family: The Case for National Action*, the report offered an analysis of racialized poverty that described black families as caught up in a "tangle of pathologies." At the center of this indictment were female-headed households and the negative impact that they allegedly had on normative masculinity and self-esteem. Soon after its release, Lee Rainwater and William Yancey published a collection of challenges to the Moynihan Report that argued that low-income communities of color were far from pathological and that economic and political causes of poverty must be placed at the analytic fore.[75] Activists and scholars then and since pushed this critique even further by demonstrating how the construction of the heterosexual "normal" has long relied on ideas about racial inferiority and "backward" poverty.[76] Yet the racialized "cycle of poverty" paradigm typified by the Moynihan Report retained significant ideological currency in the postwar era.

Theories of damaged masculinity and low self-esteem were also invoked in another line of research during this period: studies on sexual nonconformity and the origins of homophobia. (As had, in turn, a public gay identity been correlated with high self-esteem.) Indeed, research on the "problem" of the black urban poor developed coterminously with new activist-inspired work, rooted in psychology, on the causes of antigay sentiment. This research gave rise to the term *homophobia*, which first appeared in Kenneth Smith's essay "Homophobia: A Tentative Personality Profile" and in George Weinberg's book *Society and the Healthy Homosexual*, both published in 1972.[77] These sources figured homophobia as a measurable set of negative attitudes rooted in a pathological fear of lesbians and gay men. Although coined in the 1970s, Daniel Wickberg shows that the term *homophobia* reflects long-standing psychological explanations for social inequality endemic to postwar liberalism.[78]

Despite not gaining popularity until the 1980s, the concept of homophobia was very familiar to gay psychologists in the 1970s. These psychologists were often also activists; as members of groups like the GAA and Mattachine Society, they had advocated the removal of homosexuality from the *Diagnostic and Statistical Manual* of mental illnesses and had forged new community-based alternative mental health services.[79] Thus, psychological explanations of urban violence and homophobia research coalesced in popular thinking about antigay violence. Weinberg's work (which circulated among activists) presented a psychodynamic analysis that understood homophobia as rooted in insecure masculinity and an unstable sense of self that could take expression in violent behavior. Thus, in the activist imagination, homophobia and a (racialized) culture of poverty were understood to share the same origins. Likewise, for many mostly white and middle-class reform activists who saw the end of urban poverty as unfeasible, this correlation translated into a growing fear of poor people and people of color. This mentality echoed that of earlier gay liberationists who called to challenge the police yet also diagnosed as "tenuous," as in Carl Wittman's "A Gay Manifesto" (1970), coalitions with black liberationists because of their "understandable" "uptightness and supermasculinity" and with Chicanos because of the "traditional pattern of Mexicans beating up queers."[80] These assumptions minimized the experiences of LGBT-identified people of color and also antigay sentiments among white people. And for women and men who engaged in same-sex relations but did not identify with the labels of "lesbian" and "gay," they, too, fell out of consideration, presumed to be suffering from an intractable but self-imposed low self-esteem.

Such ideas about the causal dynamics of identity, violence, and neighborhood would influence, over time, the ensuing path of antiviolence activism and determine how the public perceived homophobia. Although SMASH existed for only a couple of months, many of its members joined a new neighborhood organization, the Chelsea Gay Assocation (CGA). The CGA was the first ever block association organized under the banner of sexual identity, and it was from CGA that the Chelsea Anti-Crime Task Force—later the Anti-Violence Project (AVP)—emerged. In San Francisco, members of the Butterfly Brigade were among those who banded together to form Community United Against Violence (CUAV) in 1979. AVP and CUAV were the two major organizations behind the establishment of the National Gay Task Force's Violence Project in 1982.[81]

While the impetus came from on-the-ground action, the institutionalization of antiviolence politics was greatly influenced by the kinds of scholarly studies described in this essay. Surveys of violence provided the evidence for the newly consolidated lesbian and gay antiviolence movement and enabled a formal coalition with the crime victims' movement that also gained momentum in the early 1980s.[82] These developments shifted the emphasis from the protection of designated gay spaces to the qualification of threats; in this process new understandings of victims and intent became predicated on an understanding of local geography established just years before. More importantly, these patrols turned out to be but a first act, reappearing in major U.S. cities in the 1990s during the next strong wave of real-estate speculation and gentrification.

Conclusion

In the 1970s, in neighborhoods like San Francisco's Castro and New York's Chelsea, populations of gay residents grew as did the areas' identities as new gay enclaves. On the surface, the reasons for this dynamic appear self-evident. But as this essay has argued, the processes of population and identity consolidation were far more complex. Neighborhoods like New York's Harlem and Jackson Heights, Queens, and San Francisco's Tenderloin had long been home to same-sex sexuality and even gay residential concentration. Nonetheless, they did not join Greenwich Village and, later, the Castro and Chelsea as "gay havens" to be protected. This is due in large part to the extent of middle-class reinvestment in central cities and the concomitant growth of professionals in the urban service sector, both phenomena that included gay men.

Street patrols offer one example of how publicity about violence became a means by which geographic spaces were claimed as gay territories. As the historian Martin Meeker explains, the growth of San Francisco as a gay region is not simply a function of economic and social changes that brought single men and women together. Meeker makes a convincing argument for the role of cultural communication; namely, the publicity efforts of small lesbian and gay publications and organizations.[83] Similarly, the work of grassroots organizing can imprint ideas of urban neighborhoods in a broader gay imagination in conjunction with shifts in the urban land market. Thus in the 1970s, political interests held by mostly white middle-class gay men establishing residential concentrations in inner-city areas fit into the larger flows of urban restructuring, but they were understood locally to express new social and political demands. This is not to say that the two are the same, nor that they are responsible for one another. Rather, certain issues, such as violence, served well to connect (and even make indistinguishable) claims for property and claims for rights, through, for example, a call for policing. This process was also enabled by the circulation of public knowledge about the seemingly incontrovertible link between urban poverty and urban violence.

Far from representing a cynical reading of lesbian and gay activism, this understanding shows the cultural tugs of economic restructuring that produce the conditions for profit in the name of community.[84] In the context of antigay violence, neighborhood concentration was assumed to both protect gay communities and to highlight them as a target. What was to be guarded was, by extension, a specific *kind* of gay identity that reflected the race and class stratification of the city itself. Hence, in much the same way that people of color are excluded from the economic benefits afforded by Richard Florida's vision of "diversity," sexual minorities who do not live in Greenwich Village nor match its race, class, or gender demographics are excluded from the protections of gay "safe space."

Yet it is important to remember that there are places of nonheteronormative sexualities across the city. This essay hopes to challenge homonormative definitions of gay space so as to expand rather than barricade queer safety.[85] Indeed, this essay joins critiques that are already in circulation among organizations on the front lines of social justice, just as there were thirty years ago.[86] The New York–based FIERCE! (Fabulous Independent Educated Radicals for Community Empowerment), for example, offers compelling political challenges to the exclusionary tendencies of Greenwich Village residents. In addition to demanding participation in local decision making and calling for the scaling back of policing, FIERCE! imagines alternative queer futures outside of homonormative visions. In 2003, the Education for Liberation Project of FIERCE! created a map of what they identified as their "Dream City, " an urban planning model in which the after-hours club is connected to the post office, the theater district adjoins welfare and Section 8 offices, the airport is next to the bathhouse, and the ninety-nine–cent store is out in front of the LGBTST center. This dream city is not founded on a model of territory, even as it respects claims to place. In doing so, it makes distinctive gay spaces more inclusive and, in fact, imagines spaces *everywhere* as potentially queer, both by loosening the status of gayness as a unique — and exclusive — commodity (as Gay Index proponents would have it) and by making numerous peoples and places marginalized by heteronormativity central to broad queer political imaginations.

Education for Liberation Project of FIERCE! (Fabulous Independent Educated Radicals for Community Empowerment). Reprinted with permission

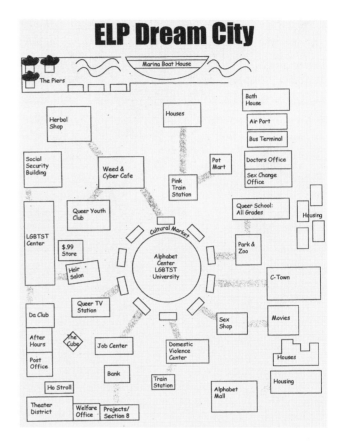

Notes

This essay would not have been possible without the mentorship of Lisa Duggan. It has also greatly benefited from the feedback of Andrew Ross and from comments by Kevin Murphy, Jason Ruiz, and David Serlin, as well as by two anonymous reviewers. Susan Stryker generously directed me to many of my sources. Kat Lewis provided key research assistance. Thanks also to Dayo Folayan Gore, Janice Irvine, and, especially, Eva Hageman. My research was assisted by a fellowship from the Sexuality Research Fellowship Program of the Social Science Research Council with funds provided by the Ford Foundation and by a Phil Zwickler Memorial Research Grant, which supported by research at the Human Sexuality Collection of Cornell University's Carl A. Kroch Library.

1.   "Notice of Public Hearing, City of New York," Community Board 2, Manhattan, New York. Author field notes, May 6, 2002.

2.   The Stonewall Inn was a popular gay bar in Greenwich Village. On June 28, 1969, patrons challenged a police raid, then a routine feature of gay bar life. The riot continued for three days and included innumerable arrests. It is also credited for inspiring the gay liberation movement. Scholars and activists tend to agree that those arrested at Stonewall were a mix of transsexual women, gay men, street kids, and lesbians. There is less of a consensus about how many were people of color and about the significance of a butch lesbian who resisted arrest and inspired the militancy of others. The elision of people of color, women, and the gender nonnormative from the story of Stonewall is often cited to support arguments that those at the center of the now mythical riot have been left out of the consolidation of a

mainstream movement. For different versions of the Stonewall riots, see Donn Teal, *The Gay Militants: How Gay Liberation Began in America, 1969–1971* (1971; New York: St. Martin's, 1995); Toby Marotta, *The Politics of Homosexuality* (Boston: Houghton Mifflin, 1981); Martin Duberman, *Stonewall* (New York: Plume, 1993); David Carter, *Stonewall: The Riots That Sparked the Gay Revolution* (New York: St. Martin's, 2004); and John D'Emilio, *Sexual Politics, Sexual Communities: The Making of a Homosexual Minority in the University States, 1940–1970* (Chicago: University of Chicago Press, 1983). For discussions of the treatment of Stonewall as myth, see Scott Bravmann, *Queer Fictions of the Past: History, Culture, and Difference* (Cambridge: Cambridge University Press, 1997); Elizabeth A. Armstrong and Susanna M. Crage, "Meaning and Memory: The Making of the Stonewall Myth," *American Sociological Review* 71 (2006): 724–51; and John D'Emilio, "Stonewall: Myth and Meaning," in *The World Turned: Essays on Gay History, Politics, and Culture* (Durham, NC: Duke University Press, 2002), 146–53.

3. Terence Kissack, "Freaking Fag Revolutionaries: New York's Gay Liberation Front, 1969–1971," *Radical History Review* 62 (1995): 104–34.

4. "A Report To Our Neighbors," flyer, National Gay and Lesbian Task Force Records, 1970–2000, Collection 7301, Box 48, Folder 4, Human Sexuality Collection, Kroch Library, Cornell University; "Police Pay Respect to Angels," *The Villager*, March 2–8, 2005. The San Francisco Street Patrol was a project of the Queer Nation focus group DORIS SQUASH (Defend Our Rights in the Streets / Super Queers United against Heterosexism). In their newsletter they listed New York street patrols with which they were associated, including the Christopher Street Patrol and OutWatch (paper insert, San Francisco Street Patrol Newszine, July/August 1993, and paper insert, San Francisco Street Patrol Newszine, September 9993 [*sic*], Box 1, Folder 1, San Francisco Street Patrol Records, 98-17, 1991–1993, Gay, Lesbian, Bisexual, Transgender Historical Society [GLBTHS]). For further discussions of the approaches taken by the San Francisco Street Patrol, the Christopher Street Patrol, and the Pink Panthers (an offshoot of New York's Queer Nation), see Edward Elhauge, "San Francisco's Queer Street Patrol," *Ideas & Action*, no. 16 (Fall 1991): 24 (included in Box 1, Folder 10, San Francisco Street Patrol Records, GLBTHS), and Sara Miles, "The Fabulous Fight Back," *Out/Look* 17 (Summer 1992): 54–59.

5. John Voelcker, Nina Reyes, and Andrew Miller, "Panthers and Angels Arrive on Christopher Street," *Outweek* 60 (1990): 18.

6. Residents claimed that the neighborhood had been taken over by "the Bloods and the Crips" and "the dealers, the hookers, the pimps, the johns" ("Notice of Public Hearing, City of New York," Community Board 2 [CB2], undated document faxed from CB2 office on April 24, 2002); "vicious drug dealers and hostile transgender prostitutes" and "rowdies" (Wendy Dixon, "Alice Certainly Doesn't Live Here," Greenwhich [*sic*] Village Block Association News, flyer, CB2); and "an army of occupation" (Albert Amateau, "Queer Youth and Residents Still at Odds on Park Use," *The Villager*, December 14–20, 2005).

7. For a discussion of the racial and sexual politics of the neighborhood, see Martin F. Manalansan IV, "Race, Violence, and Neoliberal Spatial Politics in the Global City," *Social Text* 23, no. 3 (2005): 141–55; *Fenced Out!* (video), dir. Paper Tiger Television with the Neutral Zone and FIERCE! (New York: FIERCE, the New Neutral Zone, and Paper Tiger Television, 2001). That their targets are people of color is not only coded by geography; in 2006 a neighborhood resolution explicitly named the "problems" as LGBT African American and Latino youth. It read: "Whereas problems have arisen involving noise and also involving some rowdyism resulting from large crowds of young people, mostly lesbian, gay, bisexual, and transgender youth of African-American and Hispanic origin leaving Pier 45 at 1:00am on Friday and Saturday nights." Quoted in Duncan Osborne, "Piers Fears Go

Racial: With No Christopher Street Solution, Community Board Faults LGBT Youth of Color," *Gay City News*, March 9–15, 2006.

8.   For background on quality-of-life policies in New York City, see Tanya Erzen, "Turnstile Jumpers and Broken Windows: Policing Disorder in New York City," in *Zero Tolerance: Quality of Life and the New Police Brutality in New York City*, ed. Andrea McArdle and Erzen (New York: New York University Press, 2001), 19–49. Counteractivists, primarily representing nonresident LGBT youth of color, also attend these meetings, demanding that they, too, should be eligible to give input, insisting that their safety is also at stake, and defining the area's violence in terms of police brutality, race- and gender-profiling, inflated property values, and resident vigilantism. The primary activists are members of FIERCE! (Fabulous Independent Educated Radicals for Community Empowerment), representing transgender, lesbian, gay, bisexual, two-spirit, queer, and questioning youth of color in New York City. See www.fiercenyc.org (accessed May 18, 2007).

9.   It is useful to note that Greenwich Village, like much of New York City, is primarily a renter economy. Participants at community meetings include a mix of renters and home owners, yet they all unite behind property value. But not all of them stand to gain from a rising tax base and an inflated rental market; for them, property may be something other than their home. As of 2000, the residents of Community Board 2 were 74.8 percent white; in addition, the two census tracks along the waterfront boast median incomes of $125,295 and $72,418 versus the two relevant areas of the neighborhood core at $58,202 and $57,567. Thus whiteness may be a value added to real estate, but it may also be, following Cheryl Harris's argument, a kind of property unto itself. See Cheryl L. Harris, "Whiteness as Property," in *Critical Race Theory: The Key Writings That Formed the Movement*, ed. Kimberlé Crenshaw et al. (New York: New Press, 1995), 276–91.

10.   A few examples of the immense literature on post-1960s urban politics include David Boesel and Peter H. Rossi, eds., *Cities under Siege: An Anatomy of the Ghetto Riots, 1964–1968* (New York: Basic Books, 1971); John Mollenkopf, *The Contested City* (Princeton, NJ: Princeton University Press, 1983); Roger Friedland, *Power and Crisis in the City* (London: Schocken, 1983); Thomas Sugrue, *The Origins of the Urban Crisis: Race and Inequality in Postwar Detroit* (Princeton, NJ: Princeton University Press, 1996); Rhonda Williams, *The Politics of Public Housing: Black Women's Struggles against Urban Inequality* (Oxford: Oxford University Press, 2004).

11.   Valerie Jenness and Kendal Broad, *Hate Crimes: New Social Movements and the Politics of Violence* (New York: Aldine de Gruyter, 1997); Valerie Jenness and Ryken Grattet, *Making Hate a Crime: From Social Movement to Law Enforcement* (New York: Russell Sage Foundation, 2001); Gregory M. Herek and Kevin T. Berrill, eds., *Hate Crimes: Confronting Violence against Lesbians and Gay Men* (Newbury Park, CA: Sage, 1992); David M. Wertheimer, "The Emergence of a Gay and Lesbian Antiviolence Movement," in *Creating Change: Sexuality, Public Policy, and Civil Rights*, ed. John D'Emilio, William B. Turner, and Urvashi Vaid (New York: St. Martin's, 2000), 261–78.

12.   Many of these sources also theorize the relationship between sexuality and race in the law and thus are particularly relevant to my analysis. See Judith Butler, "Burning Acts, Injurious Speech," in *Excitable Speech: A Politics of the Performative* (New York: Routledge, 1997), 43–69; Kendall Thomas, "*Corpus Juris (Hetero) Sexualis*: Doctrine, Discourse, and Desire in *Bowers v. Hardwick*," in *A Queer World: The Center for Lesbian and Gay Studies Reader*, ed. Martin Duberman (New York: New York University Press, 1997), 438–51; Siobhan Somerville, "Queer *Loving*," *GLQ: A Journal of Lesbian and Gay Studies* 11 (2005): 335–70.

13. The dominant literature on gay gentrification has focused on how the professional structure, economic activity, and electoral politics of white, upper-income gay men have transformed local neighborhood markets. See Manuel Castells, "Cultural Identity, Sexual Liberation, and Urban Structure: The Gay Community in San Francisco," in *The City and the Grassroots: A Cross-Cultural Theory of Urban Social Movements* (Berkeley: University of California Press, 1983), 138–70; Damaris Rose, "Rethinking Gentrification: Beyond the Uneven Development of Marxist Urban Theory," *Environment and Planning D: Society and Space* 2 (1984): 47–74; Lawrence Knopp, "Some Theoretical Implications of Gay Involvement in an Urban Land Market," *Political Geography Quarterly* 9 (1990): 337–52; Lawrence Knopp, "Sexuality and Urban Space: A Framework for Analysis," in *Mapping Desire: Geographies of Sexualities*, ed. David Bell and Gill Valentine (London: Routledge, 1995), 149–61; Stephen Quilley, "Constructing Manchester's 'New Urban Village': Gay Space in the Entrepreneurial City," in *Queers in Space: Communities/Public Places/Sites of Resistance*, ed. G. Brent Ingram, Anne Marie Bouthillette, and Yvette Retter (Seattle: Bay, 1997), 275–92.

14. Richard Florida, *The Rise of the Creative Class, and How It's Transforming Work, Leisure, Community, and Everyday Life* (New York: Basic Books, 2002).

15. Christopher Swope, "Chasing the Rainbow: Is a Gay Population an Engine of Urban Revival? Cities Are Beginning to Think So," *Governing*, August 2003, www.governing.com/textbook/gays.htm (accessed August 1, 2007).

16. Florida, *Rise of the Creative Class*, 256. "Canaries of the creative age" is Gates's term, and the "last frontier" is Florida's. In his follow-up to *Rise of the Creative Class*, Florida cites Lower Manhattan as a prime area for development using his theory of creativity. See Richard Florida, *Cities and the Creative Class* (New York: Routledge, 2005), 155–70.

17. In *Rise of the Creative Class*, Florida concludes, "It appears that the Creative Economy does little to ameliorate the traditional divide between the white and nonwhite segments of the population. It may even make it worse" (262–63).

18. In an article penned by Christopher Street Patrol members in 2005, they described a series of criminal acts from the area and concluded: "What have been the Village's greatest assets—its acceptance and diversity—have become its greatest liabilities." Dave Poster and Elaine Goldman, "Gay Youth Gone Wild: Something Has Got to Change," *The Villager*, September 21–27, 2005. For a history of bohemianism in Greenwich Village, see Maurice Stein, *The Eclipse of Community: An Interpretation of American Studies* (Princeton, NJ: Princeton University Press, 1960); and Sally Banes, *Greenwich Village 1963: Avant-Garde Performance and the Effervescent Body* (Durham, NC: Duke University Press, 1993). For a discussion of bohemianism and urban renewal, see Richard Lloyd, *Neobohemia: Art and Commerce in the Postindustrial City* (New York: Routledge, 2006).

19. See D'Emilio, *Sexual Politics, Sexual Communities*; and Nan Alamilla Boyd, *Wide Open Town: A History of Queer San Francisco to 1965* (Berkeley: University of California Press, 2003). For discussions of informal resistance to state violence, see Elizabeth Lapovsky Kennedy and Madeline Davis, *Boots of Leather, Slippers of Gold: The History of a Lesbian Community* (New York: Routledge, 1993); George Chauncey, *Gay New York: Gender, Urban Culture, and the Making of the Gay Male World, 1890–1940* (New York: Basic Books, 1994); John Howard, *Men Like That: A Queer Southern History* (Chicago: University of Chicago Press, 1999).

20. Safe streets patrols popped up and almost as quickly disappeared across San Francisco and New York during the 1970s. All were short-lived, and many were more stunts than sustained vigilance. The two discussed in this essay featured members and strategies that became central to the antiviolence movement that followed.

21.   The focus on New York and San Francisco is not incidental. These cities were home to the two antiviolence projects that became the anchors for the national antiviolence movement, Community United against Violence in San Francisco and the New York Anti-violence Project.

22.   Both the feminist antirape movement and the LGBT antiviolence movement grappled with debates about the role of the state in combating violence. Both were majority white movements that were slow, and often resistant, to including people of color. Both tried to balance social service provision with grassroots activism, and to better understand their relationship to crime victims in general. Both movements also experienced tension between the ethos of local organizing and the visions of national movement building, the legacies of post-1960s radicalism and the pressures of immediate reforms. See Nancy A. Matthews, *Confronting Rape: The Feminist Anti-rape Movement and the State* (New York: Routledge, 1994); Maria Bevacqua, *Rape on the Public Agenda: Feminism and the Politics of Sexual Assault* (Boston: Northeastern University Press, 2000). These commonalities existed despite that fact that many lesbian and women of color activists were taking a different approach to violence during these years, often refusing police collaboration. Lesbians against Police Violence in San Francisco and the Combahee River Collective in Boston are but two examples.

23.   Penalty enhancement is a key goal of much hate-crime legislation, which itself has been a top priority of the national antiviolence movement. For a critique, see the American Friends Service Committee (AFSC), "In a Time of Broken Bones: A Call to Dialogue on Hate Violence and the Limitations of Hate Crime Legislation," and "AFSC's Position on the Local Law Enforcement Enhancement Act (LLEEA)," www.afsc.org/lgbt/fighting-violence.htm (accessed May 15, 2007).

24.   This conflict is not restricted to New York. A similar debate erupted over the placement of housing for homeless queer youth in San Francisco's Castro in the early 2000s. See Jennifer Reck, "Be Queer . . . But Not Here! Queer and Transgender Youth, the Castro 'Mecca,' and Spatial Gay Politics" (PhD diss., University of California at Santa Cruz, 2005); Amy Donovan, "Telling Me Different: An Ethnography of Homeless Youth in San Francisco" (PhD diss., New School University, 2002).

25.   Lisa Duggan, *The Twilight of Equality? Neoliberalism, Cultural Politics, and the Attack on Democracy* (Boston: Beacon, 2003), 50–51.

26.   Alexandra Chasin, *Selling Out: The Gay and Lesbian Movement Goes to Market* (New York: St. Martin's, 2000).

27.   For an analysis of the function of retail commerce in gay enclave history, see Michael Warner, "Zone of Privacy," in *What's Left of Theory? New Work on the Politics of Literary Theory*, ed. Judith Butler, John Guillory, and Kendall Thomas (New York: Routledge, 2000), 75–113.

28.   Duggan, *Twilight of Equality*, 46–47.

29.   See "On the Frontlines with Howard Wallace," Political Affairs.Net: Marxist Thought Online, April 2004, www.politicalaffairs.net/article/articleview/113/1/29.

30.   For a discussion of the differences between the gay liberationism as represented by the Gay Liberation Front (GLF) and break-off organizations like the GAA, see Kissack, "Freaking Fag Revolutionaries." On BAGL, Arra Miller, "BAGL," *Gay Sunshine: A Journal of Gay Liberation* 24 (1975): n.p. (Xeroxed copy in Gay Sunshine, Ephemera Collection, GLBTHS); Hal Offen, "Gay Liberation Growing with BAGL," *Voice of the Gay Students Coalition*, April 18, 1975 (Bay Area Gay Liberation, Ephemera Collection, GLBTHS). Elizabeth Armstrong is among those who names gay liberation to be "over" by 1971. Elizabeth A.

Armstrong, *Forging Gay Identities: Organizing Sexuality in San Francisco, 1950–1994* (Chicago: University of Chicago Press, 2002), 81.

31. "Can Gay People Get It Together in San Francisco?" Bay Area Gay Liberation, Ephemera Collection, GLBTHS. Also see Hal Offen, "Gay liberation Growing with BAGL."

32. Randy Alfred, interview by the author, San Francisco, August 11, 2004.

33. "Second BAGL Birthday Party," flyer, n.d., Bay Area Gay Liberation, Ephemera Collection, GLBTHS.

34. "Progressive Gay Caucus—Principles of Unity," Bay Area Gay Liberation, Ephemera Collection, GLBTHS.

35. "Gay Action Statement of Purpose," Bay Area Gay Liberation, Ephemera Collection, GLBTHS; Hal Offen, "From the Left," *San Francisco Sentinel*, November 18, 1976. A year following, in August 1977, the Richard Heakin Memorial Butterfly Brigade broke off from Gay Action into an autonomous organization (letter, August 31, 1977, Butterfly Brigade subject files, Folder 1, Randy Alfred subject files and sound recordings, 1992-24, GLBTHS). Gay Action was later renamed Lesbian and Gay Action (Lesbian and Gay Action, flyer, n.d., Bay Area Gay Liberation, Ephemera Collection, GLBTHS).

36. Ron Lanza, "Butterfly Brigade: Love and Rage," *San Francisco Sentinel*, June 30, 1977. Randy Alfred, "From the Left [column]," *San Francisco Sentinel*, December 16, 1976.

37. My description of the Butterfly Brigade is culled from interviews I conducted with three former members during the summer of 2004 in San Francisco: Randy Alfred (August 11, 2004), Hank Wilson (August 9, 2004), and Ben Gardiner (August 16, 2004). Alfred's papers are held by the GLBTHS. He also helped organize a panel about the Butterfly Brigade in June 2002 at the San Francisco Public Library, which is on a video held by GLBTHS. Alfred continued his journalism and support of local gay activism. Hank Wilson did health and housing advocacy and was an original member of CUAV in the 1980s. He was also a cofounder of CUAV in the 1980s. Ben Gardiner became a vocal and contentious activist in response to AIDS. Although my analysis of the implications of the Butterfly Brigade may differ from theirs, I admire the passion and longevity of their commitments. They were also very generous in their time with me. Also see Hank Wilson and Harley Kohler, "Butterfly Brigade: Not About to Disband," *San Francisco Sentinel*, July 14, 1977; Randy Alfred, "Patrolling the Streets," *San Francisco Sentinel*, December 16, 1976; Steven Rubinstein, "CB Patrols Protects S.F. Gays," *San Francisco Examiner*, January 24, 1977; "San Francisco Police Approve Butterfly Brigade," *California View*, August 10 – September 1, 1977.

38. "Gay Action: Notice of Anti-gay Conduct," Butterfly Brigade subject files, Folder 1, Randy Alfred subject files and sound recordings, 1991-24, Box 1, GLBTHS.

39. This may also suggest that members of the brigade considered race irrelevant. Yet, as I discuss later, the Butterfly Brigade emerged around the same years that the gentrification of the Western Addition began. This was joined by a public and activist discourse that cast gays as white and local black residents as homophobic. Because the group failed to note the racial identities of those attacked, violence against gay people of color was either subsumed under the single category of antigay or risked nonrecognition. The cards and letters are filed in Butterfly Brigade subject files, Folder 1, Randy Alfred subject files and sound recordings, 1991-24, Box 1, GLBTHS.

40. Wilson, interview.

41. "Opinion: Self-Discipline in Gay Community," Editorial, *San Francisco Examiner*, June 27, 1977.

42. Randy Shilts, *The Mayor of Castro Street: The Life and Times of Harvey Milk* (New York: St. Martin's, 1982), 175.

43. Despite Shilts's own investment in the patrol's masculinity, its members often disavowed it. See Ron Lanza, "Butterfly Brigade: Love and Rage," *San Francisco Sentinel*, June 30, 1977.

44. This association was less troubling to Manuel Castells, who wrote in a footnote: "A typical gay around the Castro may be characterized as having short hair and a moustache, and dressing in a t-shirt, jeans, and leather jacket. This 'code' serves to increase visibility and communication amongst gays as well as helping to identify intruders and potential attackers." "Cultural Identity, Sexual Liberation and Urban Structure," 410.

45. Alfred, interview.

46. Gardiner, interview. Gardiner described the perpetrators as largely from the suburbs, but he also highlighted a separate problem of economic violence committed by African American men from the Western Addition. Alfred described threats as coming from a racially diverse group of young men, primarily between the ages of nineteen and twenty-three. He noted Dolores Park (a divider between the two areas) to have been a historically dangerous area and added that lesbians, rather than gay men, encountered verbal harassment in the Mission. This was in opposition to Randy Alfred's descriptions that he published in the *San Francisco Sentinel* that more systematically noted white assailants. See Randy Alfred, "Antigay Violence: Any Time, Any Place," *San Francisco Sentinel*, June 30, 1977.

47. Emphasizing that developers were the main motor of a real estate industry that excluded, among others, low-income gays, Gayle Rubin wrote that "in San Francisco, competition for low-cost housing has exacerbated both racism and homophobia and is one source of the epidemic of street violence against homosexuals." Rubin, "Thinking Sex," in *The Lesbian and Gay Studies Reader*, ed. Henry Abelove et al. (New York: Routledge, 1993). In an article discussing the range of positions gay activists were taking in response to the problem of violence (from a call for increased policing to decriminalization to police diversification), Alfred also responded to the media coverage about the "gay invasion" of San Francisco, writing that "throughout April and May, anti-gay hostility rankled in some black neighborhoods as a portion of that community's leadership openly expressed their homophobia at a series of meetings dealing with the city's housing crunch." Randy Alfred, "Why the Lid Blew Off," *Berkeley Barb*, May 24–June 6, 1979.

48. "I Left My Home in San Francisco," Tony Van Witsen, producer, *NBC Late Night*, May 17, 1980, GLBTHS.

49. David Garland, *The Culture of Control: Crime and Social Order in Contemporary Society* (Chicago: University of Chicago Press, 2001), 7.

50. Ibid., 129.

51. Judith Butler discusses how pornography and antigay language have been asserted as hate speech, speech acts that both lead to an effect and are the effect in itself. Butler explores the rhetorical and political limits of advocating for the legal regulation of speech as violence. Here I am most interested in Butler's brief analysis of how Catherine MacKinnon, in arguing for the regulation of pornography, constitutes the visual field of pornography as an injurious speech act that promises and realizes the threat it carries. This provides a link between safe streets patrols' response to the antigay threat and new anticrime theories. See Butler, *Excitable Speech*, 4, 47–52, 68.

52. See Susan Brownmiller, *In Our Time: Memoir of a Revolution* (New York: Dial, 1999).

53. Butler also discusses how lawmakers have treated rap music as an imperative to urban violence. See Butler, *Excitable Speech*, 22.

54. Marge Piercy, preface to *Take Back the Night: Women on Pornography*, ed. Laura Lederer (New York: Morrow, 1980), 7.

55. George Kelling, "Police Field Services and Crime: The Presumed Effects of a Capacity," *Crime and Delinquency—Hackensack, NJ* 24 (1978): 173–84. This article is cited by Kelling in his essay "'Broken Windows' and the Culture War: A Response to Selected Critiques," in *Crime, Disorder, and Community Safety*, ed. Roger Matthews and John Pitts (London: Routledge, 2001).

56. Activists followed MacKinnon's primary understanding of pornography as conduct that orders those addressed to do as it shows. Butler critiques this for misunderstanding the work of "visual depiction" and attaching to it the power of a verbal imperative: "Do this." As Butler explains, rather than a willful act that then constitutes women's subordination, pornography might be considered an "allegory" that "repeatedly and anxiously rehearses its own unrealizability." In the case of quality-of-life laws, the open drink is like the broken window, which due to their appearance command crime. Here the drinker is substituted for the drink, and the allegoric conduct of the drink is literalized in the person drinking. Deviant city street culture might be best described as "periperformative," Eve Sedgwick's term to describe that *nearby* the explicit speech act. She uses this concept as a way to "spatialize" the performative; it captures the everyday and signals that which acts out of place. See Eve Kosofsky Sedgwick, *Touching Feeling: Affect, Pedagogy, Performativity* (Durham, NC: Duke University Press, 2003).

57. "Speculators Get Out of Our Neighborhood!" Bay Area Gay Liberation, Ephemera Collection, GLBTHS.

58. "What Hotel Fight Means to Gays," *San Francisco Sentinel*, February 24, 1977. See also James Sobredo, "From Manila Bay to Daly City: Filipinos in San Francisco," in *Reclaiming San Francisco: History, Politics, Culture*, ed. James Brook, Chris Carlsson, and Nancy J. Peters (San Francisco: City Lights Books, 1998), 273–86.

59. See Meg Barnett Papers [Lesbians against Police Violence], 89-5, GLBTHS, and Horacio N. Roque Ramírez, "'That's My Place!' Negotiating Racial, Sexual, and Gender Politics in San Francisco's Gay Latino Alliance, 1975–1983," *Journal of the History of Sexuality* 12 (2003): 224–58. This was also the case in New York, and during the 1980s organizations like Dykes against Racism Everywhere (DARE) responded to what was increasingly perceived to be a set script. Although many of these activists flipped what had become a popular story about the violence of gentrification in which gay communities were involved, they often failed to elaborate the clearly racist overtures of such pronouncements. More to the point, they repeated the assumption that gays were white and people of color straight. Glaringly absent from both activist and mainstream accounts were the gay-identified (and nongay same-sex–oriented) experiences of people of color. This dynamic was made most manifest in discussions of San Francisco's Western Addition, in which white gay activists read critiques of gentrification as antigay invective.

60. "Brutality—Suffolk Style," *Gay Activist* 1 (1971): 1, 8–9, 13.

61. Chauncey, *Gay New York*.

62. Manhattan Community Board 4 and the City Planning Commission Documents, www.manhattancb4.org/Planning_Items/1969_Plan.html (accessed May 15, 2007).

63. The description of SMASH is based on several sources: an article by Michael Shernoff, "Early Gay Activism in Chelsea: Building a Queer Neighborhood," *LGNY* 57 (1997); Michael Shernoff, interview by the author, New York, September 13, 2004; a video in which the founders of SMASH, Louis Weingarden and Larry Durham, were interviewed by Myron Berger (a journalist for *The Villager*) on the short-lived gay public access television program *Emerald City* (Tape 1 76/00/00, Summer Final Pilot "A" 59:04, *Emerald City*

Tapes [Television program] 1976 to 1979, National Archive of Lesbian, Gay, Bisexual, and Transgender History, Lesbian, Gay, Bisexual and Transgender Community Center, New York); and a series of articles including Myron Berger, "Gays Organize Vigilante Action," *The Villager*, August 12, 1976; Myron Berger, "SMASH and Kids at Summit," *The Villager*, August 19, 1976; Myron Berger, "Friendly Persuasion Works," *The Villager*, August 26, 1976. Shernoff's article from 1997 and the interview in 2004 place SMASH in the summer of 1978; all other sources suggest it was active in the summer of 1976. As with the members of the Butterfly Brigade, Michael Shernoff was generous with his time and encouragement. My interpretation of SMASH does not detract from my admiration for the longevity and depth of his commitment to gay politics. A psychotherapist with a practice in Chelsea, Shernoff is also the author and editor of many books addressing gay men's health issues.

64. *Emerald City,* tape 1 76/00/00; Shernoff, "Early Gay Activism in Chelsea."

65. Another patrol of leathermen called the Surveillance Squad existed in the industrial South of Market District of San Francisco in 1978 soon after the end of the Butterfly Brigade. They were identified more as an anticrime than a gay safe streets patrol. Although they expressed concern about antigay violence, they were vehement that they were there to protect the gay and straight and were not identified in conjunction with any local gay organizations. See Birney Jarvis, "Volunteer Squads: The Gay Crime Fighters," *San Francisco Chronicle*, June 5, 1978; "Citizen Squad Patrols Folsom," *Bay Area Reporter*, June 11, 1978.

66. *Emerald City,* tape 1 76/00/00.

67. Berger, "Gays Organize Vigilante Action"; Shernoff, "Early Gay Activism in Chelsea." Shernoff, interview.

68. A teacher was quoted as saying that the boy's crowd had "'a thing' against blacks and Puerto Ricans." Quoted in Dan Oppenheimer, "Aftermath of a Tragedy," *The Villager*, June 24, 1976. The article also described the other members of the gang and band to which he belonged as white. Additionally, I am assuming that the youth was white due to the complete lack of reference to race in every article covering this event. This is most certainly not the case in media representations of violence purportedly done by people of color. See also Dan Oppenheimer, "Youth Confesses to Fatal Stabbing," *The Villager*, June 17, 1976.

69. Earl Jay Perel, "Police Manipulations," *The Villager*, September 16, 1976. Steve Simon, "Washington Square Tragedy," *The Villager*, September 16, 1976. Also see the response to the perpetrators' conviction: Adam Blumenthal, "Angry Rally Follows Riot Convictions," *The Villager*, March 23, 1978. Their comments about the "disorder" wrought by visitors to Washington Square Park almost exactly match those of present-day residents discussing the West Side piers. And it was during the 1980s that the ball scene moved from Washington Square Park to the piers because of police pressure.

70. See Jerald Podair, *The Strike That Changed New York: Blacks, Whites, and the Ocean Hill–Brownsville Crisis* (New Haven, CT: Yale University Press, 2002); Joshua B. Freeman, *Working-Class New York: Life and Labor since World War II* (New York: New Press, 2000).

71. Berger, "Friendly Persuasion Works," 4. Shernoff, interview.

72. Ellen Herman, *The Romance of American Psychology: Political Culture in the Age of Experts* (Berkeley: University of California Press, 1995), 219–20.

73. See Kenneth B. Clark, *Dark Ghetto: Dilemmas of Social Power* (New York: Harper, 1965).

74. See E. Franklin Frazier, *The Negro Family in the United States* (Chicago: University of Chicago Press, 1939), 39–124.

75. Lee Rainwater and William L. Yancey, *The Moynihan Report and the Politics of Controversy* (Cambridge, MA: MIT Press, 1967).

76. See Cathy Cohen, "Punks, Bulldaggers, and Welfare Queens: The Radical Potential of Queer Politics?" *GLQ* 3 (1997): 437–65; Robin D. G. Kelley, *Yo' Mama's Disfunktional! Fighting the Culture Wars in Urban America* (Boston: Beacon, 1997); and Roderick A. Ferguson, *Aberrations in Black: Toward a Queer of Color Critique* (Minneapolis: University of Minnesota Press, 2004).

77. K. T. Smith, "Homophobia: A Tentative Personality Profile," *Psychological Reports* 29 (1972): 1091–94; George Weinberg, *Society and the Healthy Homosexual* (New York: St. Martin's, 1972). There is some debate as to who coined the term, since both claim to have first started using it in the late 1960s.

78. Daniel Wickberg, "Homophobia: On the Cultural History of an Idea," *Critical Inquiry* 27 (2000): 42–57.

79. For example, the Mattachine Society organized an event with Weinberg in the early 1970s, and an affiliate of the Chelsea Gay Association (which shared members with SMASH) was a founder of the gay psychology association Identity House. Weinberg's book was reviewed by Charles Choset, *Gay Activist* 1 (1972): 19. On April 18, 1972, the Mattachine Society held a public forum with Weinberg called "Society and the Healthy Homosexual," which was reported in the May/June 1972 issue of *New York Mattachine*. "Report on Our Mettings [*sic*]," *New York Mattachine*, May/June 1972, p. 15.

80. Carl Wittman, "A Gay Manifesto," 1970, in *Out of the Closets: Voices of Gay Liberation*, ed. Karla Jay and Allen Young (1972; New York: New York University Press, 1992). Originally titled "Refugees from Amerika: A Gay Manifesto," Wittman's essay was published in leftist papers across the country in the early 1970s.

81. The National Gay Task Force later became the National Gay and Lesbian Task Force and the Violence Project later became the Anti-violence Project. See John D'Emilio, "Organizational Tales: Interpreting the NGLTF Story," in D'Emilio, Turner, and Vaid, *Creating Change*, 469–86; "The NGTF Violence Project," booklet, n.d., Papers of Larry Bush (Collection 7316), Box 5, Folder 14, Human Sexuality Collection, Kroch Library, Cornell University.

82. See Markus Dirk Dubber, *Victims in the War on Crime: The Use and Abuse of Victims' Rights* (New York: New York University Press, 2002).

83. Martin D. Meeker, *Contacts Desired: Gay and Lesbian Communication and Community, 1940s–1970s* (Chicago: University of Chicago Press, 2006).

84. See Miranda Joseph, *Against the Romance of Community* (Minneapolis: University of Minnesota Press, 2002).

85. For an analysis of when homonormativity meets metronormativity, see Judith Halberstam, *In a Queer Time and Place: Transgender Bodies, Subcultural Lives* (New York: New York University Press, 2005).

86. In addition to some of the antigentrification organizations named earlier in this essay, one might also look at the Combahee River Collective's work to end violence against women of color in the 1970s (see Kimberly Springer, *Living for the Revolution: Black Feminist Organizations, 1968–1980* [Durham, NC: Duke University Press, 2005]) or the present-day activism of INCITE: Women of Color against Violence, www.incite-national.org (accessed May 15, 2007). Some local antiviolence projects pursue alternatives to policing programs, especially the San Francisco–based Community United Against Violence.

Gay Shame's antimarriage stencil, 2004 (www.gayshamesf.org/images_endmarriage.html)

Gay Shame and BDSM Pride:

Neoliberalism, Privacy, and Sexual Politics

Margot D. Weiss

I was riding the bus over the Castro Hill during the summer of 2004, in the midst of my ethnographic fieldwork with bondage/dominance/sadomasochism (BDSM) practitioners in the San Francisco Bay Area.[1] Two men boarded at the corner of Market and 18th Streets and sat down near me. "Disgusting," one said to the other, shaking his head. He was responding to a slogan stenciled on the sidewalk by the bus stop: "End Marriage [heart] Gay Shame." In February of that year, San Francisco mayor Gavin Newsom had begun issuing marriage licenses to gay and lesbian couples. Gay Shame, a radical queer activist organization, responded by stenciling sidewalks in several San Francisco neighborhoods with antimarriage slogans. In a city with a large, well-organized gay constituency, Newsom's move — only twelve days into his mayoral reign — was widely understood as a stand for gay and lesbian equality or civil rights and a rallying point in the national same-sex marriage debate.[2] In March, however, the California Supreme Court halted the marriages, and by August of that year, it nullified all 3,955 marriages. As images of rain-soaked, gleeful couples on the steps of City Hall faded into nostalgia, Gay Shame's public critique of marriage struck many as perverse.

Gay Shame is one of several new radical queer organizations formed in the late 1990s. Resurrecting the direct action not widely used since ACT-UP, these groups use humor, satire, and camp to stage street protests, blending theatrical style with a radical political message. Gay Shame's critique of marriage weds queer and

Radical History Review

Issue 100 (Winter 2008)   DOI 10.1215/01636545-2007-023

© 2008 by MARHO: The Radical Historians' Organization, Inc.

Marxist-feminist arguments: "Marriage is the central institution of that misogynist, racist system of domination and oppression known as heterosexuality. Don't get us wrong—we support everyone's right to fuck whomever they want—we're just not in favor of supporting the imperialist, bloodthirsty status quo."[3] Accusing Newsom of "pandering to the privileged gay vote," Gay Shame's radical opposition to homo-normative gay and lesbian rights activism refuses to accept "gay marriage as the penultimate achievement on the road to 'equality' or 'rights.'"[4]

A year before, in October 2003, "concerned citizens" and religious leaders in Ocean City, Maryland, organized a protest campaign against "Free to Be Bound," Black Rose's annual BDSM conference. Black Rose (a Washington, DC–based BDSM organization) had planned to hold its seventh annual conference in Ocean City and had booked the Princess Royale hotel in preparation. When residents learned that "upwards of 2,000 kinky people" would be descending on their town, some staged a protest campaign, prompting the county's Alcohol Beverage License Board to remind the host hotel's manager that the law prohibits public nudity, flag-ellation, and sex—simulated or otherwise—in places where alcohol is sold. As the crisis developed, Jon Tremellen, the manager of the hotel, regretfully canceled his contract with Black Rose. He explained to the press that the conference would have been a "tremendous boost to the local economy" and that "they have a right to be here. Most of what they do involves married couples just trying to spice up their relationships."[5]

Tremellen's defense here dovetails the approach taken by the National Coali-tion for Sexual Freedom (NCSF). An advocacy and lobby group that represents the BDSM, swing, and polyamorous communities, the NCSF provides legal and media assistance to local BDSM organizations embroiled in public controversy. In this case, the NCSF coordinated media efforts for Black Rose, urging BDSM activists and practitioners within the greater DC area to send letters to the editors in defense of the conference and its attendees. As explained on its Web page, the NCSF's goal is to create "a political, legal, and social environment in the United States that advances equal rights of consenting adults who practice forms of alternative sexual expression," a goal they pursue through mainstream media, lobbying, legal case-work, and policy advising.[6] Thus, in the Black Rose case, they explained to the local media that the conference was "going to be a lot of sitting in chairs and . . . lecturing on how to better your relationship," and "more than 75% of the people are couples, most of them married."[7]

Marriage figures in both of these conflicts as a key site of contemporary sexual activism. Gay Shame's critique in the face of citywide support for marriage equality and the NCSF's deployment of married, heterosexual normalcy to defend a kink conference represent differing strategies available to activists in the neoliberal United States today. Both groups utilize a flexible network model of activism, rely-ing on Internet technologies and collective articulation.[8] Yet their goals, methods, and orientations are markedly different. Gay Shame, on the one hand, emphasizes a more radical approach, stages more visible public performances (e.g., street-level protests), and attempts to make connections across marginalized groups working toward collective action. The NCSF, on the other hand, embraces a more assimilationist style, enacts less visible, behind-the-scenes forms of activism (e.g., political lobbying), and represents a more narrow niche identity.

In this essay, I emphasize these distinctions to consider how these groups articulate sexual rights in the context of U.S. neoliberalism. Taking up these two iterations of rights and equality, I argue that the contrast between these organizations highlights the tension between equality as sameness with normativity (hetero- or homo-) and equality as freedom for difference from the norm. These tensions point to new relationships between equality and rights, between individual and collective action, and between privatization and public claims, relationships that have been transformed by a broader culture of neoliberalism. As Lisa Duggan has noted, "Neoliberalism in fact *has* a sexual politics."[9] Neoliberalism is typically understood as a global economic doctrine, developed and implemented in the United States (and elsewhere) in the late 1970s and early 1980s. David Harvey (among others) observes that neoliberalism "proposes that human well-being can best be advanced by liberating individual entrepreneurial freedoms and skills within an institutional framework characterized by strong private property rights, free markets, and free trade."[10]

There are cultural components to this ostensibly economic framework, of course, components that in the United States map onto social configurations of global capital, as well as onto particularly American cultural values: privatization, personal responsibility, agentic individualism, autonomy, and personal freedom. As an ideology, the supposedly free, unfettered market is understood as *the* resolution to social problems, and individual freedom becomes market choice.[11] What Duggan terms the "culture of neoliberalism" has transformed citizenship into consumption, rights, and family values.[12] Politics has retreated from the public sphere into the domestic, the intimate. In this newly privatized setting, it is the relationship within families, structured through consumption, rather than a civic relationship between individuals and the state, that serves as the locus for engagement: consumer citizenship.[13] In this context, sexuality emerges as a highly contested and conflicted zone. As the public sphere itself is increasingly accessed, debated, and imagined in private, personal, intimate terms, sexuality grafts the cultural to the economic. Neoliberalism's privatization and personal privacy dismantle a social imaginary of collective redress, public good, or what Michael Hardt and Antonio Negri term "the common."[14] In its place, the private—figured with much if not total overlap as the personal or the domestic—is newly invigorated as the site for action or belonging. These complex relationships between the economic and the sexual, the body and the social body, and individual private life and the collective management of resources are the frameworks within which sexual politics under U.S. neoliberalism must operate.

I focus here on a comparison between Gay Shame's and the NCSF's vision of sexual freedom based on particular conceptions of privacy, equality, and activism. As Duggan argues in her discussion of the Independent Gay Forum (IGF), new "homonormative" gay politics define equality as "access to the institutions of domestic privacy, the 'free' market, and patriotism."[15] In her example, the IGF and other mainstream gay and lesbian rights organizations are both responsive to and driven by neoliberal governmentality. In this short piece, I extend this concern to the NCSF, a mostly heterosexual, professional BDSM lobby organization, and Gay Shame, a radical, queer street-protest group. There are other organizations—gay and lesbian, queer, and kinky—that produce less strikingly oppositional activist languages, and my discussion of the NCSF and Gay Shame is intended neither to collapse the state of queer activism into these two examples nor to claim that either fully represents the sexual practices, experiences, or desires of their myriad constituents.[16] However, the juxtaposition of the politics of these two groups does draw our attention to the ways in which homonormativity is a politics not confined to LGBT (lesbian, gay, bisexual, transgender) activism, but rather one deeply informed by neoliberalism in a variety of guises.

Gay Shame: Performing Difference in Public

Gay Shame emerged in New York in 1998. Conceived to protest the corporate sponsorship and commercialization of Gay Pride parades, the group's local versions organized counter-Pride celebrations in New York, San Francisco, Barcelona, Seattle, London, and Stockholm, chanting "it's a movement, not a market."[17] With this anti-consumer beginning, Gay Shame has moved toward a broader social justice agenda. In New York, for example, the group's protests linked Mayor Rudolph Giuliani's so-called quality-of-life campaign, the closure of public sex spaces, and the harassment of homeless people, sex workers, and youth of color. In San Francisco, the first Gay Shame event featured speeches critiquing gentrification and the U.S. colonization of Vieques, Puerto Rico, and tried to bridge antiprison, youth, and trans activism. The San Francisco group's statement of purpose reads:

GAY SHAME is a Virus in the System. We are committed to a queer extravaganza that brings direct action to astounding levels of theatricality. We will not be satisfied with a commercialized gay identity that denies the intrinsic links between queer struggle and challenging power. We seek nothing less than a new queer activism that foregrounds race, class, gender, and sexuality, to counter the self-serving "values" of gay consumerism and the increasingly hypocritical left. We are dedicated to fighting the rabid assimilationist monster with a devastating mobilization of queer brilliance. GAY SHAME is a celebration of resistance: all are welcome.[18]

Every Saturday evening at 5:30 p.m., Gay Shame San Francisco gathers in the back room of the Modern Times bookstore to plan events and discuss strategy. Some of their recent actions include (1) spray-painting sidewalks with antimarriage and antigentrification messages; (2) organizing a protest to the "Cutest of the Castro" beauty pageant; (3) participating in the city's large Iraq war protests; and (4) holding two award ceremonies, targeting "institutions and individuals who should be ashamed of their disservice to the queer community, progressive politics, and social justice."[19] In 2002, for example, Mary Cheney (Dick's daughter) won the "Helping Right-Wingers Cope" award for acting as a liaison between the gay and lesbian community and Coors Brewery. The same year, the Pottery Barn at the intersection of Market and Castro Streets won the "Making More Queers Homeless" award for contributing to population displacement in the ongoing gentrification of the queer neighborhood.

Gay Shame reserves special ire for San Francisco's Mayor Newsom. During his 2002 mayoral campaign (while Newsom was serving as a city supervisor), Newsom proposed a ballot measure called "Care Not Cash," or Proposition N. Proposition N would have reduced the city's welfare payments to homeless residents from $395 to $59 a month, with the promise to replace this loss with (nonexistent or overburdened) social services.[20] Gay Shame marched on Newsom's campaign headquarters in the wealthy Marina neighborhood, holding a street rally. This action marked the first time the group had explicitly rallied around the privatization of social services for the city's poor. As Mattilda, a key Gay Shame "instigator," notes, these campaigns illustrate the group's shifting focus from Gay Pride, assimilation, and consumerism to broader class and race concerns.[21]

The event that has garnered the most attention for the group, however, was Gay Shame's 2003 protest of Newsom's fund-raiser at the LGBT Center in San Francisco. Members of Gay Shame stood on the sidewalk outside the center handing out anti-Newsom flyers that attempted to, as they put it, "call attention to his racist and classist policies, and to ask the Center why they would accept this influence from someone who is obviously merely trying to exploit the powerful gay vote."[22] According to *San Francisco Independent Media*, the action turned ugly when protestors tried to follow Newsom into the center. The police, who had been guarding the door, charged the activists, pushing several members of Gay Shame into the street and hitting others with nightsticks.[23] "Gays bashed at Gay Center," the group's press release stated.

This action epitomizes Gay Shame's constellation of issues. In the group's view, the fund-raiser—a $125-a-plate affair—simultaneously pandered to the gay vote and defined the gay community as those privileged enough to afford this sort of political contribution. As Gay Shame points out in its press release, the tickets "cost more than twice the monthly income of San Francisco's neediest under Newsom's new 'Care Not Cash' plan." By targeting the LGBT Community Center, Gay Shame protested the construction of the LGBT community as these particularly privileged gays, defined in opposition to the excluded poor, homeless, trans, or queer constituencies left out of mainstream, homonormative gay and (to a lesser extent) lesbian activism.

Gay Shame's actions rely on public spectacle and strategies of humiliation: performative activism through street action, drag and costuming, or public stenciling. Like the Radical Cheerleaders, Billionaires for Bush, or the Church of Stop Shopping, Gay Shame emphasizes "confrontational, fun, and participatory" actions that draw attention and create spectacle. This spectacular visibility is intended to offer a "critique of the dominant culture," as well as of the racism, classism, sexism, and transphobia inherent in those systems. For example, in 2005, when the San Francisco Department of Public Health papered the Castro neighborhood with posters featuring a shirtless, muscular black man with the caption "Don't be a bitch — Use a condom," Gay Shame produced a counterposter, retorting, "Be a bitch." The poster read, in part: "By reasserting stereotypical notions equating femininity with passivity, the Department of Public Health is rolling back decades of bitches fiercely confronting male power . . . this ad campaign makes effeminate, queer black men, gender non-conformists, and trannies invisible or powerless. . . . masculinity doesn't protect anyone from HIV. What we need is a sexual culture that encourages respect, open communication, flamboyance, gender transgression, creativity, collective pleasure, celebration, experimentation, and transformation. Turn it out, honey. BE A BITCH."[24] Gay Shame's performative campaign draws attention to the coconstruction of sexual citizenship with racialized, gendered, and classed positionality. The celebration of effeminate flamboyance — femininity in the face of "male power" — is precisely what is excluded from homonormative gay activisms. By spectacularizing the intersections of gender, race, class, and sexuality, this campaign showcases Gay Shame's strategy of "turning it out": building a loud sexual culture that is inclusive of and responsive to these vectors of difference. This open, accessible culture does not rely on a stable constituency or the privileging of sexuality as an axis of identity. Rather, in direct opposition to more mainstream gay activism (advocating the accrual of rights to a white, male, masculine, privileged subject), Gay Shame holds out the promise of a new public with the central purpose of fighting capitalism and its attendant inequalities of race, sex, gender, sexuality, and body.[25]

Stressing the interlinkage of the economy and culture, Gay Shame's actions attempt to make visible precisely the relations obscured by neoliberal ideology, including the role of class privilege in constructing multiple kinds of social marginality. Deemphasizing individuality (e.g., all members of Gay Shame are publicly identified as "Mary") and instead making public claims for the social good, Gay Shame focuses on the neoliberal collapse of public sexual culture, the privatization of care, and the (hetero- and homo-) normalization of privileged relationships between citizens and the state (like marriage and docile consumerism). As Mattilda explained in an interview with the *San Francisco Chronicle,*

I moved here [to San Francisco] in 1992 and was absolutely terrified . . . just
a few years ago, when activists first tried to set up a shelter for queer homeless
youth in the Castro, residents argued it would bring down property values! Talk
about values. . . . People need to step back and challenge . . . everything that
is normal. That's the gift that queers have. But all that's being thrown away,
discarded, just for a taste of straight privilege.[26]

In short, Gay Shame combats assimilation and an increasingly homonormative
gay mainstream by performing disidentifications with, and critiques of, privilege in
public.

BDSM Pride: Professionalization, Privacy, and Sameness

If *heteronormativity* describes the normalization of institutional relations between
particular practices, citizens, and the state,[27] and not heterosexuality as practiced by
individuals, then *homonormativity* must also describe an array of privileged relationships, not particular homosexualities. Yet normativity is not always organized
around homo- or hetero- identities.

The National Coalition for Sexual Freedom, founded in 1997 to "fight for
sexual freedom and privacy rights for all adults who engage in safe, sane, and consensual behavior," is an advocacy and PR group representing BDSM practitioners,
swingers, and polyamorous people. As the group explains on its Web page, the
NCSF is:

- A nationwide advocacy coalition

- A member of the National Policy Roundtable

- A national outreach organization, educating law enforcement, health care, and
  psychiatric professionals

- A media advocacy and training organization working to change negative portrayals of normal, alternative sexual practices among consenting adults

- A resource you can contact when discrimination or persecution related to sexual
  practices among consenting adults threatens you or your community[28]

Like Gay Shame, the NCSF relies on new forms of networked coalitional activism
such as using the Internet as a medium of communication. Unlike Gay Shame, however, the NCSF uses the mainstream media, lobbying, legal casework, and policy
advising to advance its goals. For example, the coalition issues a "media watch," a
weekly e-mail that lists news coverage of these alternative sexualities along with the
contact information of the editor so that individuals can voice their support of or,
more often, opposition to these representations. They also provide legal assistance to
individuals in custody, divorce, and job discrimination cases where BDSM practices

or polyamory factors as an issue. The NCSF responds to zoning regulations especially relevant to swingers' parties, BDSM conferences, and clubs; they have also been involved in national lawsuits. For example, in 2001, the NCSF filed a lawsuit against the United States of America, challenging the constitutionality of the Federal Communications Decency Act's obscenity statutes on free speech grounds. The case drew to a close in March 2006 when the Supreme Court refused to hear their appeal of a lower court's dismissal.[29] Neoliberal-libertarian in outlook, the NCSF is most concerned with protecting individual freedom and privacy from the interference of the state.

Providing legal and media assistance to local BDSM organizations like Black Rose makes for a large part of the NCSF's work. The conference "Free to Be Bound" was the first BDSM conference cancelled due to protest, although in 2002 and 2003 at least eight conferences throughout the Midwest were similarly targeted.[30] This selective enforcement of local zoning, liquor, and decency regulations is one facet of the discrimination directed toward BDSM practitioners, who also face widespread public condemnation, phobia, and legal risks such as job and custody loss.[31]

In the aftermath of the Black Rose cancellation, I received over two hundred e-mails from BDSM-related e-mail lists to which I subscribed. One of the first was from the NCSF, acting as Black Rose's media representative. The message urged activists and practitioners within the greater DC area to send a letter to the editor using the following as a guide:

Dear Editor,

In regards to your recent article on the BR conference, this is a private event for adults only. The attendees are just like you— they are parents, friends, coworkers, and married couples. The attendees are participating in this educational conference to get safer sex information, and to learn more about themselves and their relationships. They are responsible, law-abiding citizens who have the right to privacy.

Sincerely,
Your Name
Your City or State
Your Phone Number (for verification purposes only)

This e-mail models the rhetorical strategies of neoliberal address. Directed to the "normal" subject, it claims that BDSM practitioners are "just like you": "Responsible, law-abiding," married adult "citizens who have the right to privacy." The NCSF's public relations discourse pursues BDSM rights by attempting to shift the public's counteridentification against practitioners (described, in attacks, as trash, deviants, and perverts who practice sexual torture) to an identification with parents, friends, coworkers, and married couples. This is an argument on behalf of private individuals (not groups) who should have access to normal/good citizenship on the basis of their similarity to the norm. Attempting to position BDSM practitioners within dominant constructions of responsible citizens, the NCSF's strategy grounds sexual rights and equality in sameness. As good citizens, according to this neoliberal strategy, practitioners should be free to engage in private sexual expressions and remain free from state interference as they pursue their educational opportunities and better themselves and their relationships. The e-mail—and the NCSF in general—understands privacy as that which shields both personal, intimate sexual relations and the activities taking place on nonpublic property.[32]

Stressing sameness, individual rights, and autonomy, the NCSF attempts, in the wake of the June 2003 decision in *Lawrence and Garner v. State of Texas* (establishing that consensual sex in private is protected under due process),[33] to claim a right to sexual privacy historically denied to sexual minorities and practitioners of nonprocreative sex. At the same time, this case takes place in the context of a neoliberal privatization of politics and sociality. And so, just as homonormative gay and lesbian rights pursue the privatization of social care through same-sex marriage campaigns, the kink-normativity at work in the NCSF's rhetoric positions rights and equality as a form of sexual citizenship organized around a particularly classed, privatized consumer-citizen.

As Daniel Bell and Jon Binnie argue, when sexual dissidents make use of rights-based political strategies to demand citizenship, they must conform to a prevailing model of acceptability that they describe as "privatized, de-radicalized, de-eroticized, and confined."[34] The NCSF's sample letter argues that the attendees are "just like you"—regular, normal citizens. In an effort to correct the public's negative perception of BDSM, the NCSF is advancing a new public face: white, professional, married, heterosexual, and middle-class. As a letter to the editor of a local paper, prompted by this campaign, argues, Ocean City should expect "sober, clean and polite" middle-aged people, "many driving mini-vans" who "look and dress like your neighbors."[35]

In a media tip sheet available on its Web page, the NCSF gives advice on how to talk to the press about SM, fetish, or polyamorous lifestyles. Among the tips are

Universalize the questions.
If the reporter says something like, "you people who beat each other up . . ." or "You people who have sex with other people . . ." then respond with, "We, like you and everyone else in America, believe we have First Amendment rights to express our sexuality in any way that is safe and consensual."

Don't do anything sexual on camera.
. . . Don't let reporters take pictures of your polyamory family sitting on the bed. Don't do an SM scene in front of a camera. We need activists who will speak up for the SM-Leather-Fetish communities and explain the serious issues such as discrimination and violence against our people.

Wear appropriate attire.

This means business or casual wear, such as an activist t-shirt. Don't wear revealing fetish wear or lingerie . . . if our communities want to be taken seriously, we must present an image that the average person can relate to.[36]

Stressing sameness with the norm, professionalization, and middle-class status and bearing, the NCSF rhetorically reproduces a neoliberal relationship between individual class privilege and freedom. In this reckoning, equality is sameness, rights are rights to privacy, and sexual freedom is an individual's right to be free from state interference *in exchange for* and *as long as* that individual occupies a certain relationship to privilege.

There are many points of contrast between the NCSF and Gay Shame: business suits versus costumes, cooperation versus confrontation, and professionals versus provocateurs. Gay Shame is amateurish; its members stress difference (raced, classed, gendered, that of sexual practices) from norm and are "in your face," relying on spectacle, visibility, and performance. The NCSF is professional; it stresses sameness (raced, classed, gendered, that of sexual "lifestyle") to norm and is retracted, assimilated, and accommodationist. Unlike Gay Shame, which protests neoliberalism by attempting to create an inclusive, public, collective sexual culture and contesting the privatization and commodification of citizenship, the NCSF relies on iterations of citizenship derived from the social politics of neoliberal governance, what Lauren Berlant and Michael Warner describe as privatized citizenship.[37] As Berlant and Warner argue, these cultural forms organize citizenship around a "zone of heterosexual privacy" that serves to protect and privilege the family form by separating it from, and demonizing, queer sex/culture that is supposedly promiscuously public.[38] Privacy, here, guarantees rights and freedom, while removing public sexual culture from the activist agenda.

In Conclusion: Sexual Rights

For members of Gay Shame, sexual rights are the freedom to create collective, public spaces of transgression, pleasure, and experimentation. They seek what Duggan calls "privacy-in-public."[39] According to the NCSF, sexual rights are the ability to be free from state interference in the bedroom and to have personal privacy in a domestic, personal space understood as outside the collective public or the political commons. This is why the NCSF distances itself from the public antics of groups like Gay Shame and from representations of sexual difference and desire that are less easily recuperated into the norm. What bears recalling here is that these visions are of *rights* not of *sex*; they are representations of sexual citizenship.

Thus while many, even most, who attend the pansexual Black Rose conference are indeed middle-aged, heterosexually married, and suburban, the production of this image perpetuates and reinforces the same discursive oppositions (good, heterosexual family versus bad, kinky SM) that are mobilized in the political Right's hysterical descriptions of wild perverts.[40] When the NCSF neuters BDSM play and straightens up diverse practitioners, it reproduces the view that flogging, bondage, and play piercing are shameful and that sissy maids, pushy bottoms, and dyke daddies should keep their erotic lives out of view. The rights claimed by the NCSF are based on a new, more vigorously guarded private populated by good, neoliberal sexual subjects. On the other hand, by spectacularizing sexual difference—played out in terms of class, race, gender, and body—Gay Shame attempts to publicly "create a home for the culturally homeless," a space in which radical queers contest not only sexual marginalization but also the very hierarchies that produce these subjects.[41] This space is metaphoric but also literal: it is, for example, the Tenderloin neighborhood's "femmes, drug dealers, runaways, freaks, welfare cheats, hustlers, and homeless people" evacuated—erased—from the landscape by conference organizers promoting San Francisco's hotels.[42] For Gay Shame, rights are "strategies for survival and celebration" produced in dialogue and grounded in an open, shared public populated by defiant queer subjects.

Yet tactically, the visions of sexual citizenship produced by both these activist organizations offer possibilities as well as pitfalls. The professionalism and pragmatism of the NCSF's approach *does* breed a certain success. In the Black Rose controversy, for example, after three weeks of debate, the board decided to move the conference back into the DC metropolitan area, where it proceeded as planned. On the other hand, many people, like the men on my bus, see the street activism of Gay Shame as unfocused, annoying, and unorganized: "Just kids cutting up in the streets."[43] Perhaps the normalized sexual citizen, just as much as the more romantic rowdy queer, is a necessary "stumbling-block" in our ongoing political struggles.[44] Given these limitations, I am left wondering what strategies redress, or make the best use of, an increasingly pervasive neoliberalism.

For better or worse, sexual rights in the United States are about more than gay and lesbian equality: they are about the culture and economics of neoliberalism. For this reason, rather than parse the divergence between heteronormativity, homonormativity, and what could be characterized as kink-normativity, scholarly work on sexual activism must take up neoliberalism's particular forms of normalization outside, or in addition to, homo- and hetero-identity frames. *Homonormativity* as a key term asks us to think through the ways that sexuality structures relationships among individuals, groups, and the state. Tropes such as exclusion, erasure, pathology, recognition, or visibility point to shifting understandings of equality, freedom, and difference, and these refigured landscapes must be addressed in our activism and our scholarship. What kinds of sexual rights should we be fighting for? Is the goal a more inclusive private life or a public sexual culture that might be shared by all? If we contest the privatization at the heart of American neoliberalism, the ways in which the public is increasingly policed and controlled by corporations, we must also recognize that our claims to citizenship are grounded in this shrinking private sphere. At the same time, the obfuscation of some differences (e.g., class privilege) and the hypervisibility of others (e.g., perverts); the constriction of a defensible sexuality combined with the rapid expansion of media-saturated, marketable identities and practices; and the possibilities of new forms of alliance and social networking that carry with them many of the (same old) problems of access and privilege all create new potentials and possibilities. In this context, because sexuality is a crucial point of mediation between the intimate and the social, the private and the public, and bodies and body politics, these new forms of queer activism might point a path out of the social imaginary of U.S. neoliberalism itself.

Notes

Portions of this essay were presented at the American Anthropological Association, the Society for the Anthropology of North America, and the National Women's Studies Association meetings. I am grateful for the feedback I received from conference attendees and panel participants. I would also like to thank Mattilda, of Gay Shame San Francisco, as well as Naomi Greyser, whose support, generous assistance, and critical interlocution have been crucial to this project.

1. I use the acronym BDSM (bondage and discipline, domination/submission, and sadomasochism) to connote a diverse community that includes consensual bondage, power exchange, pain/sensation play, leathersex, role-playing, and fetish.

2. That same year, for example, same-sex marriages were authorized in Massachusetts, but eleven states banned same-sex marriage in constitutional amendments.

3. Gay Shame, "Gay Shame Opposes Marriage in Any Form," www.gayshamesf.org/endmarriage.html (accessed May 12, 2007).

4. Ibid. Lisa Duggan understands "the new homonormativity" as "a politics that does not contest dominant heteronormative assumptions and institutions but upholds and sustains them while promising the possibility of a demobilized gay constituency and a privatized, depoliticized gay culture anchored in domesticity and consumption." Lisa Duggan, "The New Homonormativity: The Sexual Politics of Neoliberalism," in *Materializing Democracy: Toward a Revitalized Cultural Politics*, ed. Russ Castronovo and Dana D. Nelson (Durham, NC: Duke University Press, 2002), 179.

5. Joe E. Carmean, "Black Rose Cancelled," *Daily Times* (Salisbury, MD), October 7, 2003.

6. National Coalition for Sexual Freedom, "Why Should You Care?" www.ncsfreedom.org/whycare.htm (accessed May 12, 2007).

7. Joe E. Carmean, "Black Rose Protest," *Daily Times* (Salisbury, MD), September 26, 2003.

8. Many theorists of contemporary activism argue that the 1999 World Trade Organization (WTO) protests in Seattle marked a new kind of activism. As Michael Hart and Antonio Negri put it, "the magic of Seattle was to show that these many grievances [agribusiness, prisons, African debt, IMF, war] were not just a random, haphazard collection, a cacophony of different voices, but a chorus that spoke in common" against global capital (Michael Hardt and Antonio Negri, *Multitude: War and Democracy in the Age of Empire* [New York: Penguin, 2004], 288). These new antiwar, anti-IMF/WTO, and anticonsumerism activisms are coalitional, networked, a "movement of movements" (Hardt and Negri, *Multitude*, 86). See also Benjamin Shepard and Ronald Hayduk, eds., *From ACT-UP to the WTO: Urban Protest and Community Building in the Era of Globalization* (London: Verso, 2002); and *Bad Subjects*'s special issue (no. 65, January 2004) on "Protest Cultures," eds. Cynthia

Hoffman, Joe Lockard, J. C. Meyers, and Scott Schafer. As many have noted, the chorus in Seattle did not include many voices of sexual activists, who tend to be analyzed in terms of gay/lesbian versus queer political strategies. This essay attempts a different reading of sexual activism in an age of neoliberalism.

9. Duggan, "New Homonormativity," 177.

10. David Harvey, *A Brief History of Neoliberalism* (Oxford: Oxford University Press, 2005), 2.

11. Neoliberalism is contradictory: it simultaneously separates the economic realm from the political, cultural, or social realm; obscures critical connections between these realms; and "organizes material and political life in terms of" these relationships (Lisa Duggan, *The Twilight of Equality? Neoliberalism, Cultural Politics, and the Attack on Democracy* [Boston: Beacon, 2003], 3). This is, in part, what accounts for the rise of neoliberalism as commonsense, so that other ways of understanding or ordering the world are seen as impractical, even silly.

12. Ibid., 12.

13. See Lauren Berlant, *The Queen of America Goes to Washington City: Essays on Sex and Citizenship* (Durham, NC: Duke University Press, 1997); Lauren Berlant and Michael Warner, "Sex in Public," in *Intimacy*, ed. Berlant (Chicago: University of Chicago Press, 2000); and Jean Comaroff and John L. Comaroff, *Millennial Capitalism and the Culture of Neoliberalism* (Durham, NC: Duke University Press, 2001).

14. In Hardt and Negri's work on the multitude and the common, they ask us to imagine "a conception of privacy that expresses the singularity of social subjectivities (not private property) and a conception of the public based on the common (not state control)" (Hardt and Negri, *Multitude*, 203–4). Whether these conceptions work as praxis is precisely the question of this essay.

15. Duggan, "New Homonormativity," 179.

16. My thanks to the anonymous reviewer who pointed out that although the National Coalition for Sexual Freedom is, perhaps, sexually conservative, BDSM practices are anything but. Unpacking the links between representation (activist discourses) and practice (what this reviewer termed the "steamy sexual jungle" of eros) is beyond the scope of this essay. However, I do address some of the tensions between a narrow definition of sexual normalcy and a broader range of what might be called queer practices briefly below and, at length, elsewhere (Margot Weiss, "Techniques of Pleasure, Scenes of Play: SM in the San Francisco Bay Area" [PhD diss., Duke University, 2005]).

17. See George Sanchez, "A Question of Pride," *Mother Jones*, June 28, 2002, www.motherjones.com/news/feature/2002/06/gay_shame.html; and Rusty Dornin and the Associated Press, "Gay Pride Parade Attracts Gay Protesters," CNN.com, June 29, 1998, www.cnn.com/US/9806/29/gay.parade.

18. Gay Shame, "About," www.gayshamesf.org/about.html (accessed May 12, 2007).

19. Gay Shame, "2003 Awards," www.gayshamesf.org/awards2003.html (accessed May 12, 2007). All subsequent references to the awards were taken from this Web page.

20. See Ilene Lelchuk, "'Care Not Cash' Thrown Out," *San Francisco Chronicle*, May 9, 2003.

21. Mattilda, aka Matt Bernstein Sycamore, "Gay Shame: From Queer Autonomous Space to Direct Action Extravaganza," in *That's Revolting! Queer Strategies for Resisting Assimilation* (Brooklyn, NY: Soft Skull, 2004), 237–62.

22. Gay Shame, "Hot Pink Protest," www.gayshamesf.org/hotpink.html (accessed May 12, 2007). All subsequent references to the protest and attendant press releases were taken from this Web page.

23. See "Queer Anti-capitalist Protestors Attacked by SFPD," *San Francisco Independent Media* (online media collective), February 8, 2003, www.publish.indymedia.org/en/2003/02/107227.html; and David Moisl, "Shame on the SFPD," *San Francisco Bay Guardian*, February 12, 2003, www.sfbg.com/37/20/news_shame.html.

24. Gay Shame, "Be a Bitch," www.gayshamesf.org/beabitch.html (accessed January 15, 2007). The ways Gay Shame uses creative reappropriation as a strategy to reveal how sexuality, race, class, and gender are not just interlinked in the production of subjects but can also be strategically expropriated by these same subjects is beyond the scope of this essay. The "Don't Be a Bitch" campaign can be viewed at www.homoboy.org/crunk.html (accessed July 13, 2007).

25. Gay Shame, "Points of Unity," www.gayshamesf.org/about.html#unity (accessed May 12, 2007).

26. Annie Nakao, "Rejecting 'Normal' in Favor of a Distinct Gay Identity," *San Francisco Chronicle*, September 19, 2004.

27. Lauren Berlant and Michael Warner offer a clear definition of heteronormativity as "the institutions, structures of understanding, and practical orientations that make heterosexuality seem not only coherent—that is, organized as a sexuality—but also privileged" in their "Sex in Public," 312.

28. National Coalition for Sexual Freedom, "Why Should You Care?"

29. The National Coalition for Sexual Freedom worked with Barbara Nitke, a BDSM photographer, and argued that the Communications Decency Act would "violate the free speech of Internet content providers and inhibit the discussion of sexual issues on the Internet among consenting adults." A New York court had dismissed the case in 2005. See National Coalition for Sexual Freedom, "Communications Decency Act," www.ncsfreedom.org/CDA/index.htm (accessed May 12, 2007).

30. The right-wing organizations AFA (American Family Association) and CWA (Concerned Women of America) have campaigned against BDSM conferences in Chicago; Southfield, Michigan; Oklahoma City, Okalahoma; and St. Louis. The St. Louis event ("Beat Me in St. Louis") also generated legislative action; the Missouri Republican state senator John Loudon introduced a resolution calling for an ongoing investigation of the legality of such events in April 2002. Two weeks after the Black Rose cancellation, perhaps building on the success of the Ocean City protests, organizers canceled a New Orleans–based BDSM conference ("Fetish in the Fall") after the police chief urged local hotels to refuse to host the event.

31. The NCSF reported that in 2001, it responded to 461 complaints regarding child custody or divorce proceedings and 392 cases of job discrimination. A survey the NCSF conducted in 1998 and 1999 indicated that among the 1,017 respondents, 36 percent had experienced violence or harassment and 30 percent had experienced discrimination because of BDSM practices (National Coalition for Sexual Freedom, "Violence and Discrimination Survey," www.ncsfreedom.org/library/viodiscrimsurvey.htm [accessed May 12, 2007]).

32. This is a reminder of the dense historical relationship between privacy and private property.

33. In *Bowers v. Hardwick* (1986), the court decided that sodomy (an act) was not protected because homosexuals (an identity) did not deserve the right to privacy, thus erroneously equating sodomy (historically, nonprocreative sexuality) with homosexuality. For more on the legal history of sodomy and *Bowers v. Hardwick*, see Nan Hunter, "Life after *Hardwick*," in *Sex Wars*, ed. Lisa Duggan and Hunter (New York: Routledge, 1995), 85–100; and Janet Halley, "Reasoning about Sodomy: Act and Identity in and after *Bowers v. Hardwick*," *Virginia Law Review* 79 (1993): 1721–1780. *Lawrence* reversed *Bowers*,

arguing that consenting adults have the right to sexual privacy in their homes. See Bernard E. Harcourt, "'You Are Entering a Gay and Lesbian Free Zone': On the Radical Dissents of Justice Scalia and Other [Post-]Queers," *Journal of Criminal Law and Criminology* 94 (2003): 503–49, for an analysis of the *Lawrence* decision in the context of queer critique. Also see Richard Green, "(Serious) Sadomasochism: A Protected Right of Privacy?" *Archives of Sexual Behavior* 30 (2001):543–550, for a discussion of the 1987 UK play party arrest case ("Spanner") in terms of UK law on privacy, consensuality, and sex acts.

34. David Bell and Jon Binnie, *The Sexual Citizen: Queer Politics and Beyond* (Cambridge: Polity, 2000), 3.

35. Nick Economidis, "Black Rose Not a Big Deal," *Maryland Coast Dispatch*, October 2003.

36. NCSF, "Media Tips," www.ncsfreedom.org/library/mediatips.htm (accessed January 15, 2007).

37. Berlant and Warner, "Sex in Public." See also Berlant, *Queen of America*.

38. Berlant and Warner, "Sex in Public," 313–14.

39. Duggan, "New Homonormativity," 181. Work on the restriction of sexuality in the public sphere includes Patrick Califia, "Public Sex," in his *Public Sex* (Pittsburgh, PA: Cleis, 1994); Samuel Delany, *Times Square Red, Times Square Blue* (New York: New York University Press, 1999); and Dangerous Bedfellows, eds., *Policing Public Sex* (Boston: South End, 1996).

40. This normalizing mode of SM politics is not, of course, the only discourse produced. Indeed, on the mailing list SM-ACT, some people expressed dismay at the denial of sexuality that forms the basis of the NCSF's defense. They pointed out that conferences were times to play, to revel in SM sexuality with other practitioners, and to celebrate SM sex, not only to sit around in rooms listening to panel presentations. As Susan Wright asks, "Why can't I wear my collar in public? Why do I have to be ashamed of my affectionate embraces or the clothes I wear? Because it makes you uneasy?" (Susan Wright, "The Joy of S/M," *Lesbian and Gay New York*, September 10, 1999). At the same time, some on the list suggested that the way to counter the public's hostility was by stamping bills with "BR" to show how much money the conference was bringing to the local economy. A more defiantly neoliberal strategy is hard to fathom.

41. Gay Shame, "Points of Unity."

42. Gay Shame, "Where Is This the Tenderloin," www.gayshamesf.org/index2.php (accessed May 8, 2007).

43. Andrew Boyd ("Phil T. Rich" of Billionaires for Bush [or Gore]), describing the Seattle protests, notes that "to some it's just kids cutting up in the streets. To others this brand of Do-It-Yourself (DIY) street politics represents a new kind of anti-corporate movement distinguished by creativity, self-organization, coalition building, and the will to take on global capitalism." (Andrew Boyd, "Irony, Meme Warfare, and the Extreme Costume Ball," in Shepard and Hayduk, *From ACT-UP to the WTO*, 245).

44. For Michel Foucault, "discourse can be both an instrument and an effect of power, but also a hindrance, a stumbling-block, a point of resistance and a starting point for an opposing strategy" (Michel Foucault, *History of Sexuality*, vol. 1, trans. Robert Hurley [New York: Vintage, 1990], 101). See also Judith Butler, "Imitation and Gender Insubordination," in *Inside/Out*, ed. Diana Fuss (New York: Routledge, 1991), 13–31.

Jordan (Pamela Rooke) outside the SEX shop owned by Vivienne Westwood and Malcolm McLaren. Courtesy Wikimedia Commons

Do You Want Queer Theory (or Do You Want the Truth)? Intersections of Punk and Queer in the 1970s

Tavia Nyong'o

In a May 11, 1978, interview on NBC television's late-night talk show *Tomorrow*, the punk poet Patti Smith assured her interviewer, Tom Snyder, that the kids were alright. Smith—whose first single, "Hey Joe/Piss Factory," had been financed by her friend and former lover, Robert Mapplethorpe—told Snyder:

I want the future to be like, I mean, I just want it to be like an open space for children. I mean, for me the future is children, and I feel like, you know, when I was younger first I wanted to be a missionary, then I wanted to be a schoolteacher, it's like, you know, I couldn't, I couldn't, uh, get through all the dogma, and I couldn't really integrate all of the rules and regulations of those professions into like my lifestyle and into the, into the generation that I was part of. And the really great thing about, umm, doing the work that I'm doing now, I have like all the ideals that I ever had to like communicate, you know, to, to, to children, or to people in general, to everybody, and to communicate with my creator, I, I can do everything all the perverse ends of it, and also, you know, all the innocence. It's all inherent in the form that I'm doing.[1]

In 1978, Snyder was one of the few cultural arbiters offering a platform to the insolent and snotty punk rockers who had sprung themselves on a surprised public in the

Radical History Review
Issue 100 (Winter 2008) DOI 10.1215/01636545-2007-024
© 2008 by MARHO: The Radical Historians' Organization, Inc.

preceding years. One invited punk set fire to a car live in Snyder's studio, but that stunt was hardly as jolting as Smith's unexpected paean to family values. The punk diva's statement seems to confirm the ideological hold of what the queer theorist Lee Edelman calls "reproductive futurity" even among radical misfits and rebels.[2] Scholars such as Edelman and Lauren Berlant have called attention to the role that reproductive futurity plays in the infantilization of politics, turning citizenship, as Berlant puts it, into something "made of and for children."[3] Because both the nation and its future belong to the child, who is never grown, we are led to believe that we must sacrifice our adult needs and desires on the altar of perpetual infancy. Edelman, in his widely discussed book *No Future: Queer Theory and the Death Drive*, identified this ideology of reproductive futurity as specifically antiqueer and called on queers to "accede" to our status as a flagrant threat to the future as "an open space for children," a future that excludes those who are deliberately nonreproductive. Identifying the "homosexual" with the "death drive"—that is, with the principle that is antagonistic to the very idea of society, politics, or the future—Edelman's book serves ultimately as a polemic against increasingly popular forms of lesbian and gay normativity such as marriage, parenting, and military service.

Edelman's polemic extends and expands on an older strand of gay male critique that is sometimes referred to as "antisocial" or "antirelational," a project with roots in the gay liberationist writings of Guy Hocquenghem in the 1970s.[4] The antirelational thesis locates the power of sexuality in its negativity rather than in any alternative community it may give rise to. As Hocquenghem argued in *Homosexual Desire*, which was first published in France in 1972, "the gay movement is thus not seeking recognition as a new political power on par with others; its own existence contradicts the system of political thought, because it relates to a different problematic."[5] In a similar vein, Leo Bersani noted in 1987 that "to want sex with another man is not exactly a credential for political radicalism," and instead valorized homosexuality as an example of "the inestimable value of sex as—at least in certain of its ineradicable aspects—anticommunal, antiegalitarian, antinurturing, antiloving."[6] Tactically embracing the seemingly homophobic charge that "homosexual desire" subverts the reproduction of the social order, Hocquenghem and Bersani propose what one of Edelman's critics has labeled a "queer post-politics."[7] Rejecting proposals to articulate alternative models of queer sociality, community, and utopia, these theorists of antirelationality aim to liberate queers from the normalizing effects of all such progressive and inclusionary ambitions and to instead proclaim a queer radicalism located outside politics as conventionally conceived, perhaps even outside of politics. As Edelman has put it: "Not that we are, or ever could be, outside the Symbolic ourselves but we can, nonetheless, make the choice to accede to our cultural production as figures—*within* the dominant logic of narrative, *within* Symbolic reality—for the dismantling of such a logic and thus for the death drive it harbors within."[8]

In the light of this approach, Patti Smith's comment to Snyder may seem so conventional as to preclude or, at the very least, warn against any retrospective affiliation between punk and queer feelings. Such a precluded affiliation would have less to do with obvious differences in gender, sexual orientation, or parental status than with Smith's choice to figure her rebellion into the dominant logic of symbolic reality. Despite her professed inability to fit into "the dogma" and "the rules" of society, Smith represents her outsiderness as even more faithful to the fantasy of reproductive futurity than a conventional career, such as that of a missionary or schoolteacher, would have been. Retaining "all the ideals that I ever had," Smith finds in punk rock and countercultural poetry precisely the connection that permits her to speak *to*—and perhaps even *through* and *for*—children.

Although Smith's utopian views on reproductive futurity are hardly unusual in themselves, they are startling coming from her. Like Mapplethorpe, Smith was a gifted *provocateuse* and malcontent whose lyrics and stage presence rejected both mainstream and countercultural stereotypes of femininity. On her single "Hey Joe" (1974), Smith fantasized about "Patty Hearst . . . standing there in front of the Symbionese Liberation Army flag with your legs spread . . . wondering will you get it every night from a black revolutionary man and his women." On the single's flip side, "Piss Factory," she sang about wiling away the time on a factory line and thinking that she "would rather smell the way boys smell . . . that odor rising roses and ammonia, and way their dicks droop like lilacs. . . . But no I got, I got pink clammy lady in my nostril." Such deviant and aggressive thoughts did not add up, in Smith's own view, to a thoroughgoing antisocial negativity. On Snyder's couch, Smith's rage, perversion and wild-child persona would paradoxically form the most pure and innocent grounds for preserving the future as "an open space for children." Rather than challenge reproductive futurity, then, punk rebellion could seem to confirm and sustain it.

Smith is an appropriate figure with which to open an exploration of the affinities and discontinuities between punk and queer feelings. I argue that Smith produces both punk and queer affect *through* her perverse narration of reproductive futurity, not despite it. Indeed, the spirit Smith embodies is ultimately one that is inhospitable to the heteronormativity queer theorists censure. In embracing naive futurity, Smith remakes the subject position of "antisocial rebel" and its associated death drive; and, rather than accept the guilt with which the pervert and the rebel are saddled by the social order, she asserts her radical innocence. The innocence Smith extols cannot be fully subsumed into the reproductive futurity that Edelman and others lament, for what is most remarkable about Smith's comment is her suggestion that childlike innocence can be "inherent in the form" of adult perversity. She suggests that, once one abandons the hope of following all the rules and regulations of straight society, the future becomes an open *space* rather than the disciplinary, delayed *temporality* of generational, Oedipal succession. In this heterotopic space of punk feelings, child and adult, pervert and innocent encounter and communicate back and forth continuously. The future is not a disciplinary ideal for Smith so much as it is that most queer of spatial tropes, an ambience.

Studies of queer temporality have reached a new threshold with recent books and essays by Edelman, Judith Halberstam, and Elizabeth Freeman, among others, as well as the appearance of special issues on the topic in journals such as *GLQ* and the present issue of *Radical History Review*.[9] In this essay, I seek to contribute to this conversation through a discussion of one historical intersection or switch point between queer and other subjects: the punk moment of the mid- to late 1970s. At stake in such a crossing of the subject of queer studies is a form of political work that I will associate, following Edelman, with the Lacanian trope of the *sinthome*.[10] Looking back to the cultural politics of the 1970s from which both antirelational theory and punk rock originate, I employ a reading of punk to qualify some of the claims made on exclusive behalf of queer antirelationality. I argue that the figure through which the dismantling of the social is narrated—in a word, the *sinthome*—is more historically multiform and thus both more dangerous and more useful than Edelman's limning of "sinthomosexuality" might suggest.

The critique of reproductive futurity connects compulsory heterosexuality and parenthood with a future-oriented, progressive politics. If one rejects the former, antirelational theory suggests, one must reject the other. This argument has raised a host of objections from within queer studies. Does politics as such require a utopian future orientation that is necessarily disciplined by the tyrannical obligation to reproduce the social? Halberstam, in one published forum on the question, has complained that antirelational theorists "cast material political concerns as crude and pedestrian," leaving little room, in their rush to critique dominant modes of conceptualizing politics, for subaltern and resistant modes of political engagement. She calls for a more expansive archive that includes a robust range of punk, feminist, antiracist, and postcolonial negativities that also subvert the fantasy of reproductive futurity and its sanctified innocent child.[11] Giving up on the future, politics, or both, critics argue, might actually serve a symbolic order if it subsumes the subject that much more securely in the social totality.

This debate about the prospects of a political negativity have gravitated toward a discussion by Edelman, Halberstam, and José Esteban Muñoz, among others, over a series of felt echoes between queer theory and punk rock. But what does punk have to do with either the future or with politics? To answer this question, I want to pursue Halberstram's suggestion that the antirelational call to "accede to our cultural production as figures . . . for the death drive" borrows significant aspects of its affective appeal from punk subcultural formations. On the surface, this suggestion might appear implausible. In one presentation of this essay, a respondent politely inquired into my pursuit of "archival specters" such as the Smith interview, asking whether or not there was a risk of both anachronism and a loss of focus in the pursuit of such an eclectic history of the present. I hope to answer such doubts by hewing to a fairly specific switch point between punk and queer: the queer content of the punk moment of the mid- to late 1970s and its postpunk aftermath. My principle contention, following Halberstam's lead, will be that the antisociality of punk subculture, while not identical to the antisociality of deviant sexuality, nonetheless emerged within a context in which queer and punk affect were continuously and productively confused and conflated by both outsiders and participants. It is the fundamental and productive misprision between punk and queer, even their potential chiasmus, that constitutes grounds for moving queer politics beyond the "binary stalemate" of having to choose between resisting the hegemonic fantasy of the homosexual or acceding to it.[12]

No Future . . . for You!

A plausible starting point for exploring the relationship between punk and queer is the shared vocabulary of "rough trade," the phrase denoting the easily recognized casual and sometimes commoditized sexual exchanges found in both subcultures. In Rob Young's excellent new history of the germinal punk music store and record label Rough Trade, he reprints a cartoon that economically summarizes that relation. In it, a cherubic, London-born Geoff Travis hitching through North America pauses to think: "Toronto was pretty cool . . . that band 'Rough Trade' must know the phrase means gay hustlers. That's even trashier than 'Velvet Underground.'"[13] This particular origin story for the label and store's name begs the question: does its founder Travis know that the same etymology of the phrase *rough trade* is also true of the word *punk*? As James Chance bluntly informs viewers of Don Letts's recent documentary *Punk: Attitude* (2003), "originally punk meant, you know, a guy in prison who got fucked up the ass. And that's still what it means to people in prison."[14] At one level, then, queer is to punk as john is to hustler, with both words referencing an established if underground economy of sexual favors and exchanges between men. That Chance could announce his definition as a ribald revelation suggests, however, that the subterranean linkages between punk and queer are as frequently disavowed as they are recognized. This suggests that alongside the "frozen dialectic" between black and white culture that Dick Hebdige famously noticed in British punk, there is also a less frequently noticed but equally furtive set of transactions between queer and punk that is hidden, like Poe's purloined letter, in plain sight.[15]

Punk may be literally impossible to imagine without gender and sexual dissidence. But the secret history, as Chance's comment suggests, also records a history of antagonisms between punk attitude and a male homosexual desire variously cast as predatory and pitiable. In a recent interview, for example, the journalist and author Jon Savage responded to the query about whether or not punk was "a sexy time" by arguing, "No. I thought punk was quite puritan, really. I didn't have a very good time during punk. I spent a lot of time feeling I was worthless . . . it still wasn't great to be gay in the late Seventies."[16] The phrasing of the question, and the whiff of pathos in Savage's response, suggests both a queer eagerness to identify with punk, as well as the hostility with which this desire was frequently met. We might consider as another example of this "53rd and 3rd" (1976) by the New York punk rockers the Ramones, in which Dee Dee Ramone recounts his hustling days at that notorious intersection on the east side of Manhattan and asks his audience, "Don't it make you feel sick?"[17] That line, ironically, is rhymed with "You're the one they never pick," suggesting Ramone's doubled abjection of failing even at being rough trade. But by contrast, Cynthia Fuchs, Mary Kearney, and Halberstam have argued that the affinities between lesbian, feminist, trans, and gay people and the punk subculture was immediate, definitive, and far more enduring.[18]

In a 2006 exchange with Edelman, Halberstam observed that his provocative title, *No Future*, was also the original title for the 1977 Sex Pistols' single, the one known more commonly today as "God Save the Queen." In the chorus to that song, the band front man, Johnny Rotten, snarled that there was "no future in England's dreaming," a line from which Savage drew the title for his celebrated history of British punk.[19] In Halberstam's opinion, Edelman's queer polemic does not stand up well in light of its unacknowledged punk predecessor. "While the Sex Pistols used the refrain 'no future' to reject a formulaic union of nation, monarchy, and fantasy," she argues, "Edelman tends to cast material political concerns as crude and pedestrian, as already a part of the conjuring of futurity that his project must foreclose."[20] Edelman, like Oscar Wilde with his rent boys, stands accused of using punks and then snubbing them as "crude and pedestrian," like the waiter whom Wilde famously, at his trial, denied kissing, dismissing him as "peculiarly plain" and "unfortunately, extremely ugly."[21]

Halberstam's comparison between the political stakes of "No Future" 1977 versus *No Future* 2004 bears some discussion. While rock stars may seem unlikely objects on which to pin our hopes for the expression of material political concerns, historians like Savage and Greil Marcus have situated "God Save the Queen" in a context of political, economic, and cultural crisis, one in which both conventional politics and the countercultural ethos of the sixties appeared exhausted and a time during which the anarchic antipolitics of punk therefore signaled something new.[22] Marcus in particular persuasively susses out the resonances, real and feigned, between anarchism proper and the anarchist poses and iconography of punk shock tactics. The offensive gestures of bands such as the Sex Pistols, the Clash, and Siouxsie and the Banshees, documented in films like Don Letts's *The Punk Rock Movie* (1978) and Julien Temple's *The Filth and the Fury* (2000), sometimes communicated a rejection of political action as traditionally conceived on the Left. But their very popularity inspired attempts, by both the Right and the Left, to appropriate punk attitude for political purposes. Paul Gilroy has given perhaps the definitive account of the contradictions involved in such attempts to incorporate punk, reggae, dance-hall, dub, and other genres associated with alterity into a new cultural front in the late 1970s.[23] The absence of formal political incorporation, Gilroy notes, does not immediately negate the possibility of a political reception or deployment.

Furthermore, cultural critiques of the political meanings ascribed to punk often elide the class context of British punk, a component of the subculture that is often missed in the United States where the *sub* in *subculture* seems to stand more often for "suburban" than "subaltern" and where punk is typically read as a mode of middle-class youth alienation. The submerged context of class struggle for British punk, however, comes to the fore in *The Filth and the Fury*'s astonishing footage of Rotten, Sid Vicious, and their bandmates smiling and serving cake to the children of striking firemen in Huddersfield, England, in 1977. Amid the moral panic, physical assaults, and public bans that had followed their incendiary early performances and record releases, the Sex Pistols played a Christmas benefit for the strikers and families. In the film, the Pistols are seen smearing themselves and the children with cake, and then performing, almost unbelievably, "Bodies" — an intensely graphic song about an illegal abortion — as the children and their parents bop around deliriously. Such a truly shocking conflation of the sentimental and the obscene, the perverse and the innocent, produced a moment of saturnalia that served as an outright rejection of the manufactured consensual fantasy of the queen's jubilee year. That moment was political in spite of, or even because of, the absence of a formalized politics among the callow, gangly lads that the pop Svengali Malcolm McLaren had cannily spun into cultural terrorists. Like Patti Smith, the Pistols in Huddersfield did not outright reject the mainstream scenarios of family, child rearing, and working-class politics. Rather, they insinuated themselves into the very space that their rebellious stance ostensibly foreclosed to them. In both cases, Smith's and that of the Pistols, there is a countersymbolic charge to such a performative enactment that cannot simply be subsumed as antisocial behavior.

For Edelman, however, such a countersymbolic charge goes mostly unappreciated. Edelman has objected that the Pistols' "God Save the Queen" "does not really dissent from reproductive futurism," and he has argued that punk rebellion is merely caught up in the Oedipal dynamic of the young claiming the future from their corrupt and complicit elders: "No future . . . for you!" Instead of with the *sinthome*, Edelman associates punk anarchy with the derisive category of kitsch, ever the mandarins' term for that which the masses take seriously but which they consider intellectually or politically puerile. "Taken as political statement," Edelman argues, "God Save the Queen" is "little more than Oedipal kitsch. For violence, shock, assassination, and rage aren't negative or radical in themselves." While Edelman concedes that "punk negativity" may succeed "on the level of style," he takes such success to reinforce rather than undermine his position on the grounds that stylistic revolt is best achieved through the "chiasmic inversions" of his erudite polemic. Edelman warrants that the punks — and Halberstam in her critique — have confused "the abiding negativity that accounts for political negativism with the simpler act of negating particular political positions." We cannot preserve its negativity by making "the swing of the hammer an end in itself," as Edelman puts it, but only if we "face up to political antagonism with the negativity of critical thought."[24] Johnny Rotten, meet Theodor Adorno.

Punk as a mode of revolt indeed begins in fairly blunt affects such as stroppiness and rage. But to reduce its message to the negation of particular political positions (such as repudiating the queen's jubilee) means that Edelman accounts for the Pistols' song only at the level of the lyrics and neglects a consideration of punk in the context of performance. This is a shame, as punk performers are highly cognizant of precisely the challenge of abiding negativism that Edelman raises. In the case of the Pistols, this challenge emerges at least in part from the original negation of musical skill and technical virtuosity that had occasioned punk's three-chord breakthroughs in the mid-1970s. Letts's documentary *Punk: Attitude* reflects retrospectively on the problematic prospect of a virtuoso punk rebellion. If punk rock dissented in part by rejecting musical virtuosity for pure attitude and ecstatic amateurism, how precisely could it sustain that stance? The more committed to punk one was, the quicker one acquired precisely the expressive fluency the genre ostensibly disdains. Either that, or one transforms into a cynical parody of adolescent fumbling such as that exhibited by former Bromley Contingent member Billy Idol, the bottle blond who transformed Vicious's wild snarl into the knowing smirk of eighties megastardom. Punk, like adolescence, quickly becomes its own archival specter, and for many purists, the moment was over almost as soon as the first punk singles were released. Simon Reynolds explores the extremely fruitful terrain of "postpunk" music (some of which preceded punk proper, or developed adjacent to it) that rose to prominence almost as soon as the style of punk had congealed into a recognizable, repeatable form.[25] The challenge of an abiding negativism, whether or not one agrees with the various solutions proposed, is a core feature of punk performance. Punk and postpunk styles are anything but the static, generational revolt caricatured by Edelman's analysis. The punk spirit cannot be decoded from a single lyric, song, or band, no matter how iconic the text or performer seems to be.

Part of this spirit, of course, is the traceable charge of erotic frisson detectable in much of the seemingly hostile overlap between punks and queers, which are often mirrored in the social and economic dynamics that crystallize the relationship between john and hustler. Those dynamics derive from a history of attitudes toward male homosexuality; but it strikes me that 1970s punk represents the moment at which those specifically male homosexual associations lose their exclusivity and punk becomes a role and an affect accessible to people within a range of gendered embodiments who deploy punk for a variety of erotic, aesthetic, and political purposes. The asymmetric, hostile, and desirous relations preserved in punk from the dynamics of rough trade do not always produce an open, inclusive punk community. But the forms of exclusivity punk has historically produced tend to fail abjectly at the reproduction of hegemonic and identitarian logics, even when they seek to engage in it.

For this reason it may prove useful to acknowledge and meditate further on the historical switch points between punk and queer. Let me offer two that would bear a more extensive analysis than I have space for here: a 1975 photo session of the Sex Pistols done by Peter Christopherson, a member of the legendary performance art and music group Throbbing Gristle, and Derek Jarman's 1977 film *Jubilee*. Christopherson, whose early work, by his own description, was "of white trash kids, a bit like Larry Clark's work," was contracted in the summer of 1975 by McLaren to photograph the Sex Pistols. This was at a time when McLaren and his partner, Vivienne Westwood, ran a shop called SEX on Kings Road in London that featured men's and women's street fashions inspired by S-M, gay porn, and various fetishes, like bondage trousers, that were both intentionally shocking and knowingly Warholian. But wearing the iconography or style of the homosexual—such as the gay cowboy T-shirts the Pistols would sometimes sport in concert—was apparently not the same thing as subjecting oneself to the stigma of being perceived as homosexual, or being willingly identified as "gay for pay." When Christopherson posed the Pistols to resemble rent boys in a YMCA toilet, McLaren was apparently shocked and threatened by the explicitly homoerotic images, and he turned down the pictures.[26] The photos nevertheless reside as one archival switch point between the queer and punk seventies.

Similarly, Jarman's *Jubilee* is considered by some the first punk movie, and to make it he recruited a number of nonprofessional actors from the punk scene, including Jordan (Pamela Rooke), Adam Ant, and (in a cameo) Siouxsie Sioux. According to Chuck Warner, the punk Steve Treatment guided Jarman through the punk scene, vouching for the gay outsider when necessary.[27] The film, originally intended as an impressionistic documentary of punk London, evolved into a powerful depiction of urban dystopia as seen from the fantastic vantage point of a time-traveling Queen Elizabeth I. A historically and theatrically erudite iteration of the Pistols' "God Save the Queen," *Jubilee* literalized the disjunction between present-day reality and an anachronistic monarchy by juxtaposing Elizabeth with the anarchic punks. The film proved prophetic in a number of ways, but it was not universally well received at first, with Westwood delivering her review on (where else?) a T-shirt: "The most boring and therefore disgusting film . . . a gay boy jerk off through the titillation of his masochistic tremblings. You pointed your nose in the right direction then you wanked."[28] Westwood's rhetorical condensation of Jarman's camera—first onto his nose, then onto his penis—made particularly explicit the structures of cruising and slumming that made the production of the film possible. And yet to freeze the queen/queer at the other end of a voyeuristic lens would prematurely foreclose the transmissions of desire and affect that were clearly at play in both directions, and to which *Jubilee* stands as an important testament. As Peter Hitchcock notes, while "slumming is an ideologeme of class discourse . . . the slummer also fantasizes what the culture must otherwise hide, the ways in which the porous conditions of class augur the concrete possibilities of change."[29] Rough no doubt, but trade no less.

The Three-Chord *Sinthome*

Chiasmus is a good term with which to capture the relationship between antirelational theory and punk. As a rhetorical figure, chiasmus highlights our entrapment within language, from which neither the future nor the past affords any exit. It is this entrapment within language that belligerent punks want to bust out of. Chiasmus is also the rhetorical instantiation of "sexual inversion," perverting the end of linguistic meaning in the same manner as homosexuality perverts the end of sexuality. The inverted elements of chiasmus are apparent in such formulations as Edelman's Wildean description of homosexuality as that which "leads to no good and has no other end than an end to the good as such." Edelman names the socially and sexually inverted subject of queer theory the "sinthomosexual." This word is a condensation of the word *sinthome*, an archaic way of writing the word *symptom* that Lacan began to use in the course of a seminar on James Joyce (primarily because it seems to offer so many opportunities to make his beloved puns), and the word *homosexual*. Edelman's call for us to "accede" to or "embrace" our social role as "sinthomosexuals" contains more than echo, I would warrant, of Wilde's famous comment, as recorded by Neil Bartlett, about how delicious the accusations made against him at trial would be if he himself were the one who was making them.[30] In other words, in making sense of affinities and disjunctions between the punk and the queer, it may be useful to unlock this condensation of the *sinthome* and the homosexual and, in so doing, restore greater historical specificity and political pertinence to the discourse of political negativity they both augur.

Without seeking to recuperate the death drive for some dialectically positive and progressive project, I take issue with Edelman's conflation of the homosexual with the *sinthome*, that is, with antisocial, countersymbolic *jouissance* as such. As has repeatedly been suggested, the "queer" in queer theory is most supple when it does not take as its sole referent the homosexual desire of classical psychoanalysis. "Queer" bears at least the potential to name a series of historical intersections at which the body and its potential deviations from the social have been assimilated to the figure of the *sinthome*, and several of those intersections seem to connect with the social imaginary of mid- and late 1970s punk, as we have already seen. But if this is the case, then antirelationality is in part a new articulation of deviancy theory and bears an unspoken debt to the literature emerging from radical sociology and cultural studies. This observation is not in itself a criticism, but it does suggest an expanded purview and deeper historical genealogy than that provided by the presentist and ultimately identitarian basis on which Edelman erects sinthomosexuality.

Antirelational theorists argue that the pursuit of *jouissance* is a quest for self-shattering, not for ego stabilization, and that all attempts to domesticate homosexual desire, rendering it socially productive, are therefore quixotic. Calling this approach to homosexual desire "antirelational" is somewhat misleading, insofar as it is in fact a theory of relationality, albeit not the preferred fantasy of social relations most of us possess. It depends rather on the Lacanian assertion that "there's no such thing as a sexual relationship," by which is meant that we do not relate to each other, but to a third term—the other—and to the other's desire.[31] There is, in other words, a relationship, but just not the one we believe there to be. I make this point to clarify that the virtues and faults of antirelationality lie in nothing so simple as the metaphysical question of whether society, the future, or relationality "exists" but, rather, in what the theory enables us to grasp of a reality that can never truly be grasped. In Lacan's presentation, symptom (*sinthome*) and symbol interlock with each other and provide the joint tether between the real and the imaginary. Not dialectical opposites, they are instead two loops in a complex topology of the psyche and the social. Strictly speaking, the *sinthome* is neither within nor without the symbolic order, neither negating nor sustaining it. If we associate the symbolic with closure and ideology, it might be helpful to associate the *sinthome* with flows of affect such as those Edelman identifies with an embrace of the death drive, and which I wish to extend to certain forms of punk performativity.

Edelman's condensation of *sinthome* and homosexuality, I should note, departs from conventional interpretations of Lacan, who did not originally deploy the term to explain homosexual desire. Rather, as Christine Wertheim writes in an economical summary:

In Lacan's original knotty model, the psyche is (re)presented as a space
bounded by the three interlocked rings of the Real, Symbolic, and Imaginary.
However . . . Lacan felt compelled to add a fourth ring to the configuration,
turning it from a link into a lock. Called the *sinthome* . . . this fourth
element—the symptom—is what keeps a psyche locked up. From this
perspective, the aim of Lacanian analysis is to unlock the link by breaking the
sinthome's hold. . . . Analysis then, as a practice, rather than a theory, is for
Lacan simply the operation of this unlocking—the separation of the *sinthome*
from the body of the psychic link.[32]

The *sinthome*, however, holds chiasmic properties that are elided by this therapeutic reading insofar as the separation of the *sinthome* from the psyche can also be thought of as the production of the *sinthome* by the psyche. Unlocking can be a matter not merely of "getting rid" of the *sinthome* but, more ambiguously, of "making" the *sinthome*, as is evident in Lacan's observation that *Ulysses* was Joyce's *sinthome*. Insofar as Lacan and Edelman alike associate the *sinthome* with writing, it is subject to the indefinite deferral of meaning to which deconstruction calls our attention. But if the *sinthome* can include countersymbolic writing or inscription such as that ostensibly represented by Joyce's prose, it is also worth asking whether it can be thought of in relation to expressive forms of creativity, such as music and performance, that are not primarily linguistic in structure. And furthermore, if the *sinthome* is a problem, it may also be, perversely, a solution. Hence Edelman's ambiguous instructions to "accede" and "embrace," which sound like a kind of resignation, of letting homophobia have its way, but which alternately can be figured as instructions for queer world making. Edelman's term *reproductive futurity* is helpful to the degree that it highlights a central grievance of the homophobic imaginary: that it is society that is obliged to undergo the labor of reproducing itself so that the homosexual may emerge from within it, while the homosexual is a freeloader under no obligation to reproduce society in turn. Edelman's call for queers to accede to this position is persuasive insofar as it girds us to resist the double blackmail of gay marriage and parenting as homonormative sacrifices to the altar of family values. Only by embracing the antagonism we create by our presence can we bring into view the actual labor of queerness in the processes of world making. Queerness is our *Ulysses*, our *sinthome*.

But queerness was also punk's *sinthome* insofar as punk's most powerful affects were employed in unknotting the body from its psychic link to the social. Here Lacan is especially helpful in moving our analysis beyond semiotic readings of punk subcultures by scholars like Hebdige. The emphasis on reading the symbols of punk, we can now see, elides the complex relationship between symbol and symptom. Here I evoke and diverge from the Chicago School sociologist Ned Polsky's admonition that "the researcher should forget about imputing beliefs, feelings, or motives (conscious or otherwise) to deviants on the basis of the origins of words in their argot."[33] From Polsky's perspective, Chance's connecting of the word *punk* with situational homosexuality would be as illegitimate as reading a junkie's slang for heroin ("shit" and "garbage") as signaling unconscious guilt or internalized inferiority. Even Geoff Travis's conscious borrowing of a phrase like *rough trade* for his record label cannot be read, in such a paradigm, as linking punk and queer, because his motivation was primarily to find a name even trashier than the Velvet Underground. But just because the word does not function symbolically does not prevent it from serving as a *sinthome*, and thinking of queer as punk's *sinthome* gets us further down the road of understanding the frozen dialectic between them.

In conducting my research for this project, I have had to explain repeatedly that I am not seeking to prove or disprove that 1970s punk was gay. Although such information would indeed delight me, my principal interest has been in the transmission of affect, specifically a bad or rebellious attitude, through the paraphernalia and symbols of various queer subcultures. Approaching the circulation of homosexuality or queerness as a symptom of culture has proved enormously helpful for making sense of a late 1970s group like the Homosexuals, who were mostly taking the piss out of the predictability of punk, already visible by 1978. In taking punk's flirtation with overt gay symbols to a switch point with the symptom within punk itself, they ended up serving "as figures—within [punk] for the dismantling of [punk] and thus for the death drive it harbors within."[34]

While my reading so far has accepted much of Edelman's argument, I part ways at his ahistorical presentation of the sinthomosexual. There is a fair amount of nostalgia in Edelman's chiasmic description of homosexuality as that which "leads to no good and has no other end than an end to the good as such." In the era of popular and openly gay musical acts like the Scissors Sisters, television programs like *Queer Eye for the Straight Guy*, and even networks like Logo TV, it stretches credulity to maintain that "the homosexual" as a figure always stands in the cultural imagination for pure and uncompromising complicity with the death drive. To the contrary, it seems that Halberstam is persuasive in arguing that queer theory's bad attitude is a secret sharer of the immature, kitschy, and revolting behavior of punks and other uppity antisocial types.

Historicism gets a bad rap, especially from psychoanalytic and deconstructionist critics. Some of this rap is deserved, and it may even be, as with Edelman, necessary to critique the fiction of a "motionless 'movement' of historical procession obedient to origins, intentions, and ends whose authority rules over all."[35] The *sinthome* may indeed obey the logic of repetition (the death drive) that undoes such a fantasy of progressive, developmental time, as Edelman argues; but that atemporal kernel of *jouissance* does not obviate historical time as such. Without historical perspective, we are insufficiently defended from the nostalgic impulse to exaggerate the radical negativity of a given symbol such as queer or homosexual desire. The problem of enduring political negativity is only whisked away by an overreliance on a by now hypostatized moment in queer theory.

A more productive response can be found in a recent album by the Soft Pink Truth, the name of which I have paraphrased for the title of this essay. This self-described "comparative analysis of ideological positions in English punk rock and American hardcore songwriting" provided the sonic ambience that enabled me to complete this essay. The title pays homage to a track from the Minutemen's opus, *Double Nickels on the Dime* (1984), a declaration of hard-core purism that serves as an ironic counterpoint to the Soft Pink Truth's musical hybridizations, which consist of ten cover versions produced out of what is described, in the CD cover art, as a "circular rationale vortex": "Reversing time . . . stopping time . . . street credibility . . . distraction from political misery . . . escapist nostalgia . . . dissertation avoidance . . . suspended dialectics . . . regressive fantasy . . . sweating to the oldies."[36] Such self-parody and free association is suggestive rather than definitive in making a connection between historicist and rhetorical approaches. The Soft Pink Truth's cover versions canvas the range of sometimes ugly feelings that survive in the punk archive, from Nervous Gender's jittery "sex worker rant" ("Confession") to the Angry Samoans' "quasi-parodic hate speech" ("Homo-Sexual"). Like Patti Smith, the Soft Pink Truth performs not so much an ideology as an ambience, one in which the question of political negativity is raised but never definitively answered. The album instead constructs what Josh Kun has called an "audiotopia," a space within sound that both mirrors and negates the world that produced it.[37]

I persist in locating such efforts to produce a usable past between punk and queer, both as a political negativity and an emotive, affective unity. In this, it seems, the songs are more faithful to Hocquenghem's Freudo-Marxian synthesis of the early 1970s than are the antirelational theorists. In chapter 6 of *Homosexual Desire*, "The Homosexual Struggle," Hocquenghem leaves open the space for the delinking of the homosexual and the *sinthome* in a revolutionary praxis founded on a transgressive "subject group," a term he adopts in contrast to the ordinary condition of being a "subjected group": "In the subject group, the opposition between the collective and the individual is transcended; the subject group is stronger than death because the institutions appear to it to be mortal. The homosexual subject group—circular and horizontal, annular and with no signifier—knows that civilization alone is mortal."[38]

"Homosexual desire," he adds in what amounts to a preemptive riposte to Edelman's identification of queer theory with the death drive some three decades later, "is neither on the side of death nor on the side of life; it is the killer of civilized egos."[39] Rather than opposing politics, relationality, and the future in toto, Hocquenghem merely rejected their expression prior to revolutionary transformation.

It is important to remember the original historical context of Hocquenghem's homosexual antirelationality because when it is invoked—especially in the early twenty-first century when the possibility of socialist revolution appears to be off the table, to put it mildly—it gives queer theory's rejection of reformist and utopian politics an entirely different meaning. We seem to succumb very easily to a disorienting left melancholy that attempts to substitute a radical critical negativity for the absence of a robust radical politics. In saying this I am not advocating Hocquenghem's particular vision of emancipation. But we may well begin to think about the relations between punk and queer outside of Hocquenghem's own limited horizons of the gay Western male. Chiasmus does such important work in both the Sex Pistols' and Edelman's iterations of "no future" because it apparently stabilizes the infinite play of inversions into a neat paradox to which, as Edelman repeatedly argues, we might ultimately accede. The verbs *accede* and *embrace* constitute critical pivots in Edelman's polemic insofar as they appear to ground his radicalism in something we can do while ensuring that this thing we can do retains its grammatical radicalism only *within* chiasmus. *Accession* and *embrace* serve as potentially positive terms for Edelman only as long as they remain fully reversible. But accession is itself a chiasmic inversion insofar as it can lead *either* to participation in the fantasy of reproductive futurity or the embrace of its stigmatized core of negativity, variously labeled the *sinthome*, the death drive, *jouissance*, and homosexuality itself. By rethinking the grouping or networking expressed across the social figurations of punk and queer in a nonidentitarian way, we may be able to uncouple the *sinthome*-homosexual metonymy, which compels us to see social negativity in an unnecessarily limited frame. Expanding the networks and linkages that produce collective subjects in the present is neither a return to a 1970s-style revolution à la Patty Hearst nor a dewy-eyed faith in perpetual progress. It is a politics of a quite different sort than that which Edelman both rightly disparages and wrongly associates with politics as such.

Notes

The author would like to thank Henry Abelove, Heather Lukes, David Watson, Sheila Ghose, Kevin Murphy, and two anonymous reviewers for comments that strengthened this essay.

1. *The Tomorrow Show with Tom Snyder: Punk and New Wave* (Shout! Factory, 2006), DVD.
2. Lee Edelman, *No Future: Queer Theory and the Death Drive* (Durham, NC: Duke University Press, 2004).
3. Lauren Berlant, *The Queen of America Goes to Washington City: Essays on Sex and Citizenship* (Durham, NC: Duke University Press, 1997), 262.
4. Guy Hocquenghem, *Homosexual Desire* (Durham, NC: Duke University Press, 1993); Leo Bersani, *Homos* (Cambridge, MA: Harvard University Press, 1995).
5. Hocquenghem, *Homosexual Desire*, 137. The English translation of this work contains a useful preface by Jeffrey Weeks that places Hocquenghem within the political and cultural context of his day. For more of an assessment of his relation to queer theory, see the introduction to Tim Dean and Christopher Lane, eds., *Homosexuality and Psychoanalysis* (Chicago: University of Chicago Press, 2001), 3–42.
6. Leo Bersani, "Is the Rectum a Grave?" *October* 43 (1987): 205–15.
7. John Brenkman, "Queer Post-politics," *Narrative* 10 (2002): 174–80.
8. Edelman, *No Future*, 22; emphasis original.
9. Elizabeth Freeman, ed., "Queer Temporalities," special issue, *GLQ* 12 (2007).
10. The *sinthome* was the topic of Lacan's Seminar 23, given in 1975–76. Jacques Lacan, *Livre XXIII: Le sinthome; 1975–1976*, ed. Jacques-Alain Miller, Le Séminaire de Jacques Lacan (Paris: Seuil, 2005). In deference to readers unfamiliar with psychoanalysis, I present the concept here with the aid of (undoubtedly simplified) English-language exegesis.
11. Robert Caserio et al., "Forum: Conference Debates; The Antisocial Thesis in Queer Theory," *Proceedings of the Modern Language Studies Association* 121 (2006): 824. In a comparable vein, in the *GLQ* forum on queer temporality, Annamarie Jagose recommends that we "acknowledge the intellectual traditions in which time has also been influentially thought and experienced as cyclical, interrupted, multilayered, reversible, stalled—and not always in contexts easily recuperated as queer." Carolyn Dinshaw et al., "Theorizing Queer Temporalities: A Roundtable Discussion," *GLQ* 13 (2007): 186–87.
12. José Estaban Muñoz has written about the intersections between punk and queer subcultural spaces in the photographs of Kevin McCarty. See José Esteban Muñoz, "Impossible Spaces: Kevin Mccarty's *The Chameleon Club*," *GLQ* 11 (2005): 427–36.

13. Rob Young, *Rough Trade: Labels Unlimited* (London: Black Dog, 2006), 11.

14. For more on *punk* as a keyword, see Tavia Nyong'o, "Punk'd Theory," *Social Text* 23 (2005): 19–34.

15. "For, at the heart of the punk subculture, forever arrested, lies this frozen dialectic between black and white cultures—a dialectic which beyond a certain point (i.e. ethnicity) is incapable of renewal, trapped, as it is, within its own history, imprisoned within its own irreducible antimonies." Dick Hebdige, *Subculture: The Meaning of Style* (London: Routledge, 1979), 70.

16. Alex Needham, "Jon Savage," *Butt*, Winter 2006, 62.

17. The Ramones, "53rd and 3rd," on *The Ramones* (1976), Audio CD, Sire.

18. Judith Halberstam, *In a Queer Time and Place: Transgender Bodies, Subcultural Lives* (New York: New York University Press, 2005); Mary Celeste Kearney, "The Missing Links: Riot Grrrl—Feminism—Lesbian Culture," in *Sexing the Groove: Popular Music and Gender*, ed. Sheila Whiteley (New York: Routledge, 1997) 207–29; Cynthia Fuchs, "If I Had a Dick: Queers, Punks, and Alternative Acts," in *Mapping the Beat: Popular Music and Contemporary Theory*, ed. Thomas Swiss, John Sloop, and Andrew Herman (Malden, MA: Blackwell, 1998) 101–18.

19. Jon Savage, *England's Dreaming: Anarchy, Sex Pistols, Punk Rock, and Beyond* (New York: St. Martin's, 2002).

20. Caserio et al., "Forum," 824.

21. Michael S. Foldy, *The Trials of Oscar Wilde: Deviance, Morality, and Late-Victorian Society* (New Haven, CT: Yale University Press, 1997), 17.

22. Greil Marcus, *Lipstick Traces: A Secret History of the Twentieth Century* (Cambridge, MA: Harvard University Press, 1989).

23. Paul Gilroy, *"There Ain't No Black in the Union Jack": The Cultural Politics of Race and Nation* (London: Hutchinson, 1987).

24. Caserio et al., "Forum," 822.

25. Simon Reynolds, *Rip It Up and Start Again: Postpunk, 1978–1984* (New York: Penguin, 2006).

26. Simon Ford, *Wreckers of Civilisation: The Story of Coum Transmissions and Throbbing Gristle* (London: Black Dog, 2000), 4–10, 5–13. Some of the photos are reproduced in Savage, *England's Dreaming*.

27. Chuck Warner, personal conversation with author, August 13, 2005.

28. Quoted by Tony Peake in "Derek Jarman's *Jubilee* (1977)," an essay accompanying the Criterion Collection release of *Jubilee*, www.criterion.com (accessed May 10, 2007).

29. Peter Hitchcock, "Slumming," in *Passing: Identity and Interpretation in Sexuality, Race, and Religion*, ed. María C. Sánchez and Linda Schlossberg (New York: New York University Press, 2001), 184–85.

30. Neil Bartlett, *Who Was That Man? A Present for Mr. Oscar Wilde* (London: Serpent's Tail, 1988).

31. Bruce Fink, *The Lacanian Subject: Between Language and Jouissance* (Princeton, NJ: Princeton University Press, 1995), 104–25.

32. Christine Wertheim, "To Be or a Knot to Be," *Cabinet* 22 (2006): 35.

33. Ned Polsky, "Research Method, Morality, and Criminology," 1967, in *The Subcultures Reader*, ed. Ken Gelder (New York: Routledge, 2005), 64.

34. The Homosexuals, *Astral Glamour* (Messthetics, 2004), audio CD.

35. Dinshaw et al., "Theorizing Queer Temporalities," 180.

36. The Soft Pink Truth, *Do You Want New Wave or Do You Want the Soft Pink Truth?* (Tigerbeat6, 2004), audio CD.

37. Josh Kun, *Audiotopia: Music, Race, and America* (Berkeley: University of California Press, 2005).

38. Hocquenghem, *Homosexual Desire*, 147.

39. Ibid., 15.

Intimate Investments:

Homonormativity, Global Lockdown,

and the Seductions of Empire

Anna M. Agathangelou, M. Daniel Bassichis, and Tamara L. Spira

What forms of intimacies do we need to develop to truly realize social transformation?
—M. Jacqui Alexander, Pedagogies of Crossing

Imperial Project(s) of Promise and Nonpromise

As the killing of those at the margins of liberal and neoliberal sovereignty continues to be glamorized and fetishized in the name of 'democracy,' we are confronted with urgent questions about the ways in which life, death, and desire are being (re)constituted in the current political moment. The intensification of carnage wrought by empire has brought with it a renewed thrust to draw in precisely those who are the most killable into performing the work of murder. As we are seduced into empire's fold by participating, often with glee and pleasure, in the deaths of those in our own communities as well as those banished to the 'outsides' of citizenship and subjectivity, we must ask: How are these seductions produced and naturalized?[1] What forms of (non)spectacular violence must be authorized to heed the promises being offered by empire? These are the central problematics this paper engages.[2]

Radical History Review
Issue 100 (Winter 2008) DOI 10.1215/01636545-2007-025
© 2008 by MARHO: The Radical Historians' Organization, Inc.

In 2003, a host of U.S. LGBT (lesbian, gay, bisexual, transgender) organizations lauded the Supreme Court's six to three majority in *Lawrence and Garner v. State of Texas*, a ruling that rendered sodomy laws unconstitutional, calling it "a legal victory so decisive that it would change the entire landscape for the LGBT community."[3] One major LGBT legal advocacy organization stated, "the good feeling we get from watching *Will & Grace* has been transformed into social legitimacy and legal protection that LGBT people can take to the bank."[4] Anthony M. Kennedy, writing for the court majority, expressed the unconstitutionality of the 1986 *Bowers v. Hardwick* case by stating, "When homosexual conduct is made criminal by the law of the state, that declaration in and of itself is an invitation to subject homosexual persons to discrimination both in the public and in the private spheres."[5] Pregnant with the promise of democratic freedoms and futures severed from histories of colonization and other forms of violence and degradation, much of the mainstream LGBT movement rejoiced at the "decriminalization of gay sexuality" with no mention of the continued forms of conduct that are made criminal, and thus remain subject to state-sponsored and state-sanctioned violence in both the public and private spheres.

The expansive effort to repeal sodomy laws coincided with, and was bolstered by, a national push on the part of a variety of LGBT organizations to legalize same-sex marriage. Both campaigns were launched under the banner of privacy rights—the National Gay and Lesbian Task Force's (NGLTF) campaign to repeal sodomy laws was aptly dubbed the Privacy Project. Not coincidentally, such efforts were spearheaded by a class of queer subjects in the leading strata of the neoliberal world order, those who "benefited" most from the increasing dominance of free market capitalism, structural adjustment policies, and the privatization of public space and welfare apparatuses.[6] Both campaigns, fought in the name of equality, proved instrumental in consolidating precisely the political and material conditions they purportedly sought to contest. In the case of sodomy laws, mainstream LGBT organizations consisting largely of media strategists, lobbyists, and attorneys—a far cry from earlier incarnations of queer social movements—heralded the "decriminalization of gay sexuality," all the while leaving unnoted and undisturbed the ongoing criminalization and pathologization of "other sexualities." Meanwhile, such desires continued to be rendered deviant by the U.S. state. We see this contradiction embodied in a statement from the executive director of NGLTF following the *Lawrence* decision: "In 2003, it's appalling that states would still argue that there's nothing wrong with the police kicking down the bedroom doors of a gay or lesbian couple and arresting them for having intimate relations with the person they love."[7] The statement makes clear which doors will and should continue to be kicked down, and which forms of intimate relations remain outside the bounds of state-sanctioned love. This newly accorded privacy (part and parcel of constituting neoliberal "individual liberty") annexes state repression to a perverse past by embracing a more tolerant future. In the case of gay marriage, the push for state-sanctioned kinship reconsolidates the exclusionary practices of the institution of marriage. This move recodes "good" forms of national kinship (monogamous, consumptive, privatized) while punishing those that fall outside of them, particularly those forms of racialized and classed kinship that continue to be the target of state violence and pathology. Thus both campaigns actively court a limited and precarious equality in exchange for leaving the foundational antagonisms of capitalist liberal democracy unscathed.[8]

If it is no longer the bedroom of a "gay and lesbian couple" arrested for having "intimate relations with the person they love," whose doors, then, will continue to get kicked down? And, precisely, which "gay and lesbian couple" is even conceivable in this statement? Eluding the grasp of the looming prison–police apparatus, the newly christened "love" of this imagined "gay and lesbian couple" can only come into relief in contradistinction to those forms of desire and intimacy whose deviance renders them commonsensical property of the state. It is no coincidence, then, that the police are being called up to legislate good and bad love during this political moment. To be sure, the ruling coincides with two decades of the rapid proliferation of an increasingly privatized and corporatized prison apparatus, police state, and militarized regime of repression. During the past three decades of neoliberal (re) consolidation, the number of mostly brown, black, and poor people locked away in the U.S. system alone has increased nearly three hundred–fold.[9] As we will argue, it is against this backdrop of, borrowing the phrase from Julia Sudbury, "global lockdown" that the "love" mentioned above becomes imaginable and attainable.[10]

In this essay, we wish to follow Sudbury in expanding analyses of "global lockdown" to "other spaces of confinement" to account for the affective economies of the diffuse networks of punishment, mass warehousing, and criminalization that come to constitute overlapping carceral landscapes.[11] By "affective economies," we refer to the circulation and mobilization of feelings of desire, pleasure, fear, and repulsion utilized to seduce all of us into the fold of the state—the various ways in which we become invested emotionally, libidinally, and erotically in global capitalism's mirages of safety and inclusion. We refer to this as a process of seduction to violence that proceeds through false promises of an end to oppression and pain. It is precisely these affective economies that are playing out as gay and lesbian leaders celebrate their own newfound equality only through the naturalization of those who truly belong in the grasp of state captivity, those whose civic redemption from the category of the sodomite or the criminal has not been promised/offered (which one, it might not matter . . .) by the Supreme Court. It is precisely the aforementioned "good feeling" strategically deployed through homonormativization—mobilizations that barely mask the bloody, violent consequences of neoliberal privatization, the mass warehousing and liquidation of mostly brown and black bodies, and of imperial(ist) war—that we wish to locate alongside the pleasure and glee that we were all compelled to perform in the wake of Saddam Hussein's execution. It is this circulation of desire and relief continually shored up in support of the relentless lockdown and torture of prisoners in both declared and nondeclared sites of global war.

To (re)consolidate itself, empire requires and solicits the production of certain ways of being, desiring, and knowing (while destroying others) that are appropriately malleable for what comes to be constituted as the so-called new world order.[12] Just as the strategies of execution and criminalization are crucial to the practices of global war, including prisons, this strategy of creating and liquidating enemies is offered, quite importantly in the wake of trauma, as a solution for fear and insecurity. In other words, as the imperial hold grows all the more tenuous, more and more violence is required to maintain its virulent mirage.[13] To deal with pain, fear, and insecurity, this logic tells us, the demonization and demolition of the racially and sexually aberrant other must be performed again and again.[14] Moreover, within this imperial fantasy, this production, consumption, and murder of the other is to be performed with gusto and state-sanctioned pleasure, as a desire for witnessing executions becomes a performance of state loyalty.[15] Likewise, in the case of prisons, it is the continual and powerful mobilization of discourses of "protection," "safety," and "victim's rights" that elicit support for what seems to be limitless prison expansion.[16] Lastly, it is our argument that this promise project is always reliant on a series of (non)promises to those on whom the entire production is staged. Offering certain classes of subjects a tenuous invitation into the folds of empire, there are always the bodies of (non)subjects that serve as the raw material for this process, those whose quotidian deaths become the grounding on which spectacularized murder becomes possible. Thus, while it is central to our thesis that the sexualized production of the racialized other holds together these ostensibly different moments, this is a variegated and heterogeneous process that simultaneously creates others as monolithic and draws up and exacerbates internal divisions within different communities. There are, thus, the "enemy Others" and the "other Others" whose life and death do not even merit mention or attention.[17]

Importantly, as we shall argue, we must locate what many have called "the homonormative turn" within this broader (heterogeneous) imperial logic: following the traumas of state-sanctioned repression of queer communities, the creation and obliteration of new outsides become the answer for ongoing pain and devastation. As exemplified in the U.S. state-supported HIV/AIDS pandemic — and the broader war on the poor, people of color, and dissidents launched in the wake of the radical social movements of the 1960s and 1970s — we are told that only an insatiable appetite for annihilation could soothe the pains of our pasts. We would thus locate the mobilization of highly individualized narratives of bourgeois belonging and ascension within a larger promise project that offers to some the tenuous promise of mobility, freedom, and equality.[18] This strategy is picked up in a privatized, corporatized, and sanitized "gay agenda" that places, for example, gay marriage and penalty-enhancing hate crimes laws at the top of its priorities. This also helps us to understand the ways in which revolutionary and redistributive yearnings that would challenge the foundations of the U.S. state, capital, and racial relations have been systematically replaced with strategies for individualized incorporation into the U.S. moral and politico-economic order. It is this promise project that has been crucial in rerouting so much of queer politics and longing from "Stonewall to the suburbs."[19]

Resituating the Homonormative Turn

What bodies, desires, and longings must be criminalized and annihilated to produce the good queer subjects, politics, and desires that are being solidified with the emergence of homonormativity? As we have already suggested, it is a highly privatized, monogamous, and white(ned) docile subjectivity that has been decriminalized and ostensibly invited into the doors of U.S. national belonging through recent shifts in the gendered and sexual order. As we have also suggested, it is not only sexual and gendered arrangements that have been rendered flexible in the wake of neoliberalization but an entire retooling of the possibilities for life that is attempted through a neoliberal narrative of private rights, peace, and security. This move works hand in hand with a deeply racist and imperialist symbolic, affective, and material order that increasingly requires the soldiering, gatekeeping, and prison-guard labor of so-called formerly and currently marginalized subjects to this order.

One site where we might begin to explore how this process operates is a recent advertisement from the Human Rights Campaign's (HRC) "Million for Marriage" campaign. The ad, partially reproduced on the next page, tells the story of Keith Bradkowski, a middle-aged white businessman, and his quest for state recognition of his relationship with his late partner, a flight attendant on the first plane that struck the World Trade Center on September 11, 2001 (see fig. 1).[20] In stark black and white, the ad exudes a grave authority: a blurry American flag waves behind Bradkowski's sharply framed head, his photograph flanked by a quotation from his testimony before the U.S. Senate. The quotation reads: "Terrorists killed people not because they were gay or straight—but because they were Americans." The ad produces the prototypical good queer citizen: white, upwardly mobile, and willing to die in the battlefields to protect the security of the homeland, both within and outside of its borders. To proclaim that the terrorist attack was launched against a nation regardless of its citizens' sexualities is to unite an imagined community of Americans in their common victimhood at the hands of foreign others. Through this move, the good queer citizen gains entrance into the nation through the displacement and explicit effacement of racial, sexual, and class antagonisms and inequities.

Theories of homonormativization, in part, offer us some insight into the moves performed in this advertisement, highlighting the turn embodied in the image of a white gay male–turned–imperial gatekeeper in the competition for (apparently limited) marriage rights. As defined by Lisa Duggan, "homonormativity" refers to "a politics that does not contest dominant heteronormative assump-

"The terrorists killed people not because they were gay or straight –

but because they were Americans."

—Keith Bradkowski, Sept. 4, 2003, testifying before the U.S. Senate

Like many Americans, my life was shattered on September 11, 2001. Jeff Collman, my devoted partner of 11 years, was an American Airlines flight attendant on Flight 11, the first plane to hit the World Trade Center. The last time I spoke with Jeff, he called to say, "I love you and I can't wait to get home."

Losing him was the hardest thing I have ever experienced. But because gay and lesbian couples in long-term, committed relationships do not have the same rights and protections under the law, Jeff's death was only the beginning of my nightmare. For two years, I suffered through an expensive and stressful legal battle just to hold onto the life we built together.

Although we both always paid Social Security and other taxes, I wasn't eligible for the death benefits offered to spouses. Even obtaining his death certificate was a monumental task.

Why talk about this now? Because extreme political organizations like Focus on the Family and the Family Research Council are playing politics with the lives of people like me and Jeff. These so-called "pro-family" groups claim that providing basic protections to devoted gay couples would bring about "the end of society as we know it."[1] They even want to amend the U.S. Constitution to deny any legal protections for gay partners and our families.

Meanwhile, gay and lesbian couples in long-term, committed relationships aren't eligible for government-issued civil marriage licenses and the legal protections they provide. Although no government should ever tell religious institutions who they can marry, the government should not discriminate in providing civil marriage licenses to any devoted couple.

America has problems – an uncertain economy, the loss of millions of jobs, and threats to our national security – but loving couples like us are not one of them. Like every other couple in America, gay and lesbian couples in long-term, committed relationships deserve the same benefits and protections under the law.

HUMAN RIGHTS CAMPAIGN FOUNDATION

[1] Sandy Rios, President of Concerned Women for America, October 2, 2003, National Press Club

Love and Commitment Deserve Protection.

To learn more please visit us at www.hrc.org

HRC commends the excellent representation provided to Keith by Lambda Legal, www.lambdalegal.org.

Figure 1. The Human Rights Campaign "Million for Marriage" advertisement featuring Keith Bradkowski, whose partner, Jeff Collman, a flight attendant, died on September 11, 2001. Photograph taken by Judy G. Rolfe. Image © 2003 The Human Rights Campaign

tions and institutions, but upholds and sustains them, while promising the possibility of a demobilized gay constituency, and a gay culture anchored in domesticity and consumption."[21] Through the stress on monogamy, devotion, and a relationship constrained within the bonds of privacy and propriety, the ad participates in the demonization of all other forms of sexual expression, practices, and relations — as per Duggan's argument, heteronormative logics are refueled in the production of the good gay subject. His taxes paid and his tie tightened, Bradkowski is called up to declare his allegiance to the U.S. nation-state through a moral economy of value in which (normative) queerness might be offered incorporation into the parameters of citizenship in exchange for violence. It is crucial to note that this is a bargain brokered in exchange for closing his eyes to other kinds of violence committed daily on bodies of other queers, indigenous, black, and other people of color, the terrorists, and members of the working class. Moreover, the ad reveals the interpenetration of the state's war-making agenda, the mandates of capitalist interests, and the officially declared gay and lesbian agenda. This convergence of agendas can only occur within an assumed economy of scarcity in which the white gay male competes with the imagined terrorist and with job-stealing immigrants for limited recognition. Also implicit within this ad is the veiling of legacies and ongoing processes of slavery, colonialism, and imperial plunder that have enabled capital accumulation. "Although we both always paid Social Security and other taxes," Bradkowski laments, "I wasn't eligible for the benefits offered to other spouses." Recapitulating a narrative of the deserving versus the undeserving (non)citizen, Bradkowski places himself in the category of the rightfully entitled and legal citizen who deserves rights, resources, and recognition not because he is alive but because he pays his taxes.

Many scholars who have taken up the homonormative to address the specifically racialized dimensions of neoliberal (re)structuring. Martin Manalansan, for example, has argued that a consolidating racist order is encoded within narratives of gay assimilationism and ascendancy in gentrifying neighborhoods in New York. Examining the gentrification that increasingly displaces queers of color through the criminalization of racially pathologized spaces, Manalansan shows how (certain) spaces of public queer sex and practice have become sites for the rounding up of immigrants and people of color in the ongoing war on terror. Juxtaposing this increased criminalization of queers and broader communities of color in the face of new elite gay spaces in gentrified neighborhoods, Manalansan productively traces the collaboration of neoliberal urban restructuring and the politics of homonormativity.[22]

Manalansan's analysis of the production of people of color as terrorists and criminals is helpful in unraveling the process of enemy production performed in the advertisement. In exchange for begging for state rights and recognition, Bradkowski participates in the process of creating new outsiders and outsides, those whose racial, sexual, and economic aberrance bear the mark of counter-national, as decidedly un-

American difference. The advertisement, then, operates as a homonormative revision of the "heteronormative patriotism" that Jasbir Puar and Amit Rai articulate in their essay, "Monster, Terrorist, Fag." For Puar and Rai, the collaboration between heteronormativity and patriotism allows for certain forms of queerness (or sexual "deviance") to be incorporated into the project of national reproduction while others are rendered continually abject, unworthy or unable to be assimilated into either hetero– or homonormative citizenship. They call this a "dual process of incorporation and quarantining," whereby those sexualities and embodiments that fall outside of white heteronormativity must be contained and banished for the sake of national sexualities, even queer ones. The HRC ad dramatizes this dual process by allowing white, middle-class lesbian, and gay sexualities to enter citizenship while simultaneously participating in the policing and criminalizing of racially pathologized sexualities seen as threatening to the nation: the terrorist, the inmate, the "welfare queen," the illegal alien. Importantly, as this process of creating spectacularized or exceptional enemies unfolds, there is always a simultaneous production of nonspectacular others, those whose lives and deaths do not even register within this moral economy. These are the forms of predatory and pathological sexualization that must be marked and liquidated for good (queer) citizens to stage their entrance into the body politic.

M. Jacqui Alexander has helped to articulate the ways in which this process of "incorporation and quarantining" is part of larger processes of "enemy production," which are foundational to projects of nation- and empire-building. For Alexander, enemy production elicits the labor of gatekeepers in exchange for seductive promises of membership into the (so-called) new world order. Turning to the 2001 and 2002 forms of the U.S. PATRIOT Act, as well as to the National Security Act of 2004, Alexander traces how such acts exemplify the logics of empire that rouse desire to "explicitly and simultaneously link the imperial project to militarization and nation building." In this production, a certain mooring of desire and the production and mobilization of pleasure is summoned up in the affective calling toward "enemy production." This process, she argues, is crucial in the ongoing solidification of the prison industrial complex as a (re)colonizing gesture. As she writes:

> Nation building can be . . . accurately understood as a form of hypernationalism with constituent parts: the manufacture of an outside enemy to rationalize military intervention, and secure the annexation of lands; the production of an internal enemy to rationalize criminalization and incarceration; the internal production of a new citizen patriot; the creation and maintenance of a permanent war economy, whose internal elements devolve on the militarization of the police and the resultant criminalization of immigrants, people of color, working class communities through the massive expansion of a punishment economy whose center is the prison industrial complex.[23]

A populace increasingly willing to engage in this process must also participate in the production of an external enemy in the form of the "terrorist," as well as the formation of an internal enemy in the form of the "criminal." Such simultaneous formations anchor a desire for safety and security to the violent work of colluding with the state and the market in producing enemies, in turn justifying nothing less than murder. Stated otherwise, once such enemies and criminals are produced, their degradation and murder is ostensibly justified. Furthermore, these formations depend on the mobilization of racialized psychic and libidinal economies: "It is [a] dark inside threat that must be cordoned off, imprisoned, expulsed and matched simultaneously with the extinction of the dark, external threat, in order that the borders of the fictive, originary nation be secured."[24]

With this in mind, we might return to the HRC advertisement to consider the process of nation- and empire-building operating through the practice of enemy production and the mobilization of desire. Looking more closely at the visual economies on which the advertisement draws, it is clear that the image of a white gay man holding a picture of his dead lover harkens back to other moments of mourning and loss within collective queer memory, especially those of the HIV/AIDS epidemic.[25] The photograph invokes an earlier moment of mass death (which, evidently, has shifted its target since the rise of the epidemic in predominately white gay communities in the late 1980s). The reader, constructed as queer or queer friendly, is meant to breathe a sigh of relief: this is not a death caused by egregious neglect and disavowal on the part of the state, the medical establishment, or our own families. Nor shall this particular death be blamed on poverty, discrimination, or the lack of any substantial welfare state or safety net to care for the working poor. Rather, in a swift and powerful reversal, the enemy is no longer the establishment but rather the "terrorist." Killed or left to die not because he is queer but because he is American, Bradkowski's lover's death constitutes a neoliberal replay of queer mourning that solicits racist, xenophobic protection as the only way to redress the pain, insecurity, and even homo- and queerphobia that is left intact throughout this process.

Consigned now to the "past" is the ever-ravaging pandemic that continues to steal the lives of millions of poor and working-class people and people of color worldwide. Thinly covered over as well is the threat of death, the ongoing pain, despair, and grief that Bradkowski and his generation, race, and class of queers faced two decades ago. As we discuss, these forceful forgettings and re-memberings of life lost and discarded are vital strategies for the consolidation of the new world order.

Technologies of Empire: Sodomizations, Lockdowns, and Other Punishments to Come

With this analysis in mind, we argue that the homonormative turn must be located within a larger imperial project of promises and nonpromises that, while contingent on incitements to fantasy and the mobilization of desire, cannot be confined to questions of "queer politics" as such. It is thus critical to connect various forms of homonormativization that fall outside of what is commonly identified as "the homonormative"—or even "the sexual"—to expose how this strategy of seduction as an affective calling is issued in varied and contradictory sites. For instance, as critical postcolonial and women of color feminists have pointed out, many social movements in the process of acquiring funds have "NGOinized" themselves, albeit contradictorily, as a "non-profit-industrial-complex" has been built up. In exchange for funding, this critique argues, NGOization has served to reroute radical political goals to desires for legitimacy, professionalization, and (relative) power.[26] Thus it is not only queers in the first world context whose intimate desires, feelings, needs, and hopes are sites of value for empire and neoliberal capitalism to draw into their fold, but all of us.[27] In these instances, seduction toward something better promises subjects an end to pain, marginalization, and violence in exchange for being recognized as legitimate subjects who can potentially participate in global capitalist relations and its futures—collusion becomes the cost of belonging. Lest we slip (back) into the realm of the hated, the despised, the killable, and the disposable (that is, if we ever had a chance to leave), we must actively support and often embody the threat of force that lies on the other side of this tenuous promise, or so the logic goes.

Stressing this politico-economic context, it becomes possible to read many of the contradictions of the homonormative moment *alongside* and *within* the recent intensification of the war on terror and of global lockdown. One could argue that it is not a coincidence that the Supreme Court reversed its decision on sodomy during the period in which the United States penetrated Afghanistan and Iraq. One may wonder what is at stake in these simultaneous modes of power relations: war and death, on the one hand, and the reinsertion of the constitutional rights of "sodomites," on the other. If, for a second, we read the granting of constitutional rights to queer subjects as the moment at which a war becomes deployed on the bodies of Afghanis and Iraqis, then we may wonder what is at stake with regard to the imperial order and its necessary subjects. Are the imperial order and its necessary subjects in crisis? Do these become strategies of reinserting a particular order and granting legitimacy to specific subjects, or do these become strategies of discipline and control within defined borders while anarchy and death are unleashed on others?[28]

First, we must contextualize the *Lawrence and Garner v. State of Texas* decision. It is important to note that while Chief Justice John Roberts called for the support of the U.S. queers rights, he simultaneously called for the Guantánamo Bay detainees' loss of rights in the United States Court of Appeals, for the District of Columbia Circuit, on July 15, 2005. What, then, does it mean to endorse queer rights within the borders of the United States while simultaneously justifying the nonspectacular "(non)scenes" of torture on other others?[29] We argue that these are not incidental or nonconnected moves, but form part of a continuous episteme: the privatization of the freedom of the queer subject enshrines a culture of loss of rights for non-U.S. citizens while naturalizing the backdrop of (specifically black) (non) subjects within the United States whose civically dead or dying status has rarely been assigned rights to lose. The violence and torture of the detainee comprises the raw material on which the privatized, territorially contained (and also national) freedom of the U.S. queer is articulated. Here we see how the support of queer rights in *Lawrence and Garner v. State of Texas* becomes a stage for both the playing out as well as the masking of racial, class, and national contestations.[30]

In taking a close look at the *Salim Ahmed Hamdan, Appellee v. Donald H. Rumsfeld, United States Secretary of Defense, et al.* case that Chief Justice Roberts supported twice in his appellate courts, we read:

> Afghani militia forces captured Salim Ahmed Hamdan in Afghanistan in late November 2001. Hamdan's captors turned him over to the American military, which transported him to the Guantanamo Bay Naval Base in Cuba. The military initially kept him in the general detention facility, known as Camp Delta. On July 3, 2003, the President determined "that there is reason to believe that [Hamdan] was a member of al Qaeda or was otherwise involved in terrorism directed against the United States." This finding brought Hamdan within the compass of the President's November 13, 2001, Order concerning the Detention, Treatment, and Trial of Certain Non-Citizens in the War Against Terrorism, 66 Fed. Reg. 57,833. Accordingly, Hamdan was designated for trial before a military commission.[31]

This case essentially grants to the president all power to make decisions regarding the future of those deemed terrorists. In this case, Hamdan, considered a member of al-Qaeda, had no rights to make any claims in U.S. or international courts, but rather had to be tried before military commissions. While his appellate court was considering this case, Roberts met with officials in the White House and was interviewed by George W. Bush to become the next judge on the Supreme Court. He ended up supporting twice the Bush administration's desire to legally acquire the presidential power to "try battlefield captives and foreign terror suspects before military commissions."[32] As Bob Egelko writes, "In the 3–0 decision, written by another judge and joined by Roberts, the court allowed Hamdan's military trial to proceed and said that the U.S. courts cannot enforce the Geneva Conventions on behalf of individual detainees. On another issue, the court ruled 2–1 —with Roberts in the majority—that the Geneva Conventions apply only to nations and not to alleged combatants for terrorist groups." Of course, we may argue, along with many legal scholars, that he "was not required to remove himself from all government cases, but this was no ordinary case—Bush himself was a defendant, and the issues were crucial to his claims of presidential power."[33] Roberts's support of Bush's presidential power here ends up assuming and hierarchizing the episteme that claims and assumes the power of the legal sovereignty of states in world politics thereby voiding individuals of any legal claims especially through the Geneva Conventions.

A reading territorialized and constrained to the United States might suggest that Roberts's position indicates a "liberal" or pro-queer stance. Moving away from such U.S.-centric readings, however, much more is revealed. In juxtaposing these two decisions, we come to recognize some of the tensions that emerge in the consolidation of the "new world order." Roberts's position in the sodomy case is informed by liberal principles of power and social relations if the focus is only inside the United States. With Justice Antonin Scalia's articulation of his position in the sodomy case we observe a shift from Roberts's dichotomization of the world (a strategy nevertheless of power) into sovereign nation-states, internally ordered and organized and with anarchy outside them. Scalia's position is based on moral grounds and seems to be informed by a neoconservative moment upholding as its basic normative subject a heteronormative one. In sum, both strategies enable the "re-privatization" of sexuality whether in the name of hetero- or homonormativity.

It is important to turn to Scalia's narrative to understand the nuances of this homo-/heteronormative (re)production of imperial bodies as raw material in the making. Scalia dissented, labeling the decision "a massive disruption of the current social order." It is crucial to highlight that Scalia's decision, while ostensibly on the other side of the fence, is also made possible through a set of similar epistemic assumptions of privatization and the production of a privatized subject. This (re)privatization of sexuality, that is, the constriction of sexual and affective ties through individual citizens, is given greater latitude within the democratic liberal context. Take, for example, the first part of Scalia's statement: "I have nothing against homosexuals or any other group, promoting their agenda through *normal democratic means.*"[34] This articulation is informed by the assumption that the liberal (capitalist, of course) democracy is the most productive site of regulating and mediating social relations. This (liberal capitalist) democracy comprises citizens that operate within very narrow confines of behavior and subjectivity. The borders of these permissible modalities of existence and interaction are signaled by Scalia's definition of "normal democratic means." Indeed this "normalcy" becomes the sole space in which this new decriminalized (homo)sexuality can operate. Clear, then, is the tension between this unmarked liminal boundary that demarcates even this newly found (neo)liberal promise of freedom and the fantastical national manly subject of empire. The outside is always marked by the tension between the national (i.e., always bound to the territoriality of the state) and the transnational (i.e., flexible subjectivity not bound by anything).[35] To (re)invoke earlier terms, freedom depends on the (re)founding of unfreedoms.

Scalia continues: "Social perceptions of sexual and other morality change over time, and every group has the right to persuade its fellow citizens that its view of such matters is the best. . . . But persuading one's fellow citizens is one thing,

and imposing one's views in absence of democratic majority will is something else."
Here we see the delimiting of legitimate forms of protest that once again reinscribe
boundaries of the normal. As with, for example, critiques of NGOization and the
so-called non-profit-industrial-complex, we see how certain forms of liberal protest
are enabled precisely through the disenabling of others. For Scalia, imposing one's
views (i.e., protest, revolution, movement building, to name but three examples) is
tantamount to criminal activity. What, one may wonder, constitutes such democratic
citizens, and for what project?

First, what we see through the decision is that granting rights to the sodomy
subject becomes crucial toward the constitution of the heteronormative/imperial
fantasy subject. Scalia's position on this decision gestures to the tensions that exist
among negotiable interests (what we term here neoconservative and neoliberal).
Along this liberal mode of deliberation, we see another strand of interest—that of
the neoconservative position expressed by Clarence Thomas, who states, "Punishing
someone for expressing his sexual preference through noncommercial consensual
conduct with another adult does not appear to be a worthy way to expend valuable
law enforcement resources. Notwithstanding this, I recognize that as a member of
this court I am not empowered to help petitioners and others similarly situated."[36]

What, exactly, is "noncommercial consensual conduct"? Embedded within
this phrase is a market (and indeed, the interests of its agents must be protected)
in which the democracy and the social order on which Scalia commented can only
be envisioned. This noncommercial consensual conduct remaps the subject/being
within a consent-force binary that cordons social protest, and alternative racial,
sexual, class, and colonized positioning, to the terrain of the chaotic, unlawful, and
hence killable zone. Such a construction of "noncommercial sex" effectively dichoto-
mizes sex and the market, and, effectively, capitalist relations. However, as women
of color, Marxist, socialist, and materialist feminists have argued for nearly three
decades, sexual and economic relations are always already inscribed within one
another. Forging such dichotomies between sex and the market hence silences the
myriad interconnections aptly detailed by such thinkers regarding the imbrication
of sexuality, the market, colonial, racial, and class relations.[37] In addition to eclipsing
these connections, the marking of sex as outside of capitalism masks precisely how
this homonormativization serves the interests of capital. Moreover, by silencing the
sexualized dimension of the market, thwarted and covered over are multiple histories of struggle, such as feminist and anticolonial struggles that have long acknowledged how imperial and slave relations are gendered, sexualized, and racialized
within the context of a capitalist patriarchy.[38]

More specifically, the move to privatize and contain intimacies and sexuality
within the realm of the private is at the same time another facet of a neoliberal strategy that absolves collective accountability and public intervention. Indeed, the state,

as the defender of the primacy of the ontology of profits and resources needed to enable such accumulations and productions,[39] refuses to perform particular services necessary for the reproduction of neoliberal capitalist relations. Thus, the disciplinary nature of this ruling, which effectively guarantees unfreedom to less flexible and upwardly mobile subjects, obfuscates power relations of violence and death. Despite the reference to a noncommercial-conduct sodomite sex that is morally unacceptable, the true force of the market emerges in the next sentence. Stripping away the affective, erotic, and dangerous dimensions of sex, and particularly of queer or deviant sex, it is reduced to "conduct." What demarcates the boundaries of this acceptable sex/relationality/being, of course, are the confines of profitability, expendability, and the "retention of law enforcement resources."

Thomas's claim that if he were a member of the Texas legislature he would vote for the ruling also points to some disjunctures. He suggests that at the state level, he would relegate the decision-making capacity and power to the state because ultimately a state decision would benefit the individual (i.e., a more libertarian position here). What guarantees profitability of a different kind other than the flexible and the flexibility accorded to sex and intimacy by the U.S. Supreme Court—a Texan lifestyle choice? This profitability is guaranteed by drawing on global lockdown to ensure and embody social relations of violence, exploitation, (non)safety, and/or (non)freedoms.

Global Lockdown and the Ends of Pain

We now turn to the threats of pure force and discipline that go hand in hand with the newfound freedoms of empire's (non)promise projects. In her introduction to the anthology *Global Lockdown*, Sudbury offers an understanding of lockdown to connect diffuse and varied networks of captivity, punishment, and mass liquidation with transnational practices of empire-building and neoliberal globalization: "'Lockdown' is a term commonly used by prison movement activists to refer to the repressive confinement of human beings as punishment for deviating from normative behaviors. Although prisons and jails are the most visible locations for lockdown, the term encourages us to think about connections with other spaces of confinement such as immigrant detention centers, psychiatric hospitals, juvenile halls, refugee camps, or Indian boarding schools."[40] In this foregrounding passage, Sudbury seeks to create analytical and political possibilities for bringing together various spaces and technologies of confinement that discipline nationally, racially, psychically, and culturally "aberrant" subjects, or those, as she will later theorize, who are "surplus or resistant to the new world order."[41]

Sudbury further elaborates on theorizations of the slavery-prison continuum, which have been compellingly argued by W. E. B. Du Bois, Angela Davis, and Joan Dayan. These scholars and activists, among others, have posited that in the wake of the failed project of Emancipation, a vast network of cultural, legal, and politico-economic apparatuses were inaugurated to (re)criminalize blackness and ensnare black subjects within intensified forms of punishment, confinement, and expropriation. These included the Thirteenth Amendment's recodification of slavery in the prison, convict lease systems, black codes, paramilitary terror, and increasingly complex systems of captivity and servitude to extract profit from locked-up black and brown bodies. As the legal scholar Guyora Binder has argued, if we expand our definition of slavery beyond a specific iteration of forced labor and instead look to the culture, custom, and institutions of race themselves, it becomes more difficult to assert that the project of Emancipation has ever been completed.[42] Additionally, as Linda Evans, Eve Goldberg, Christian Parenti, and Ruth Wilson Gilmore have argued in their respective works, in the era of globalization, the U.S. government's successive wars on drugs, poverty, crime, and terror have consolidated a prison industrial complex in which transnational corporations run globalized for-profit prisons, manufacture federal and local military- and law-enforcement technologies, expropriate prison labor, and bid for multibillion-dollar contracts for prison construction.[43] These analyses foreground the multiple, overlapping private, public, national, and international investments in the mass lockdown of poor people and people of color transnationally, and the naturalized and strengthened long-term lockdown of black people within U.S. borders. Many of these theorizations of the slavery-prison continuum and of the expansion of the prison industrial complex help us articulate how global lockdown not only naturalizes but also *produces* capitalist racial, gender, national, and sexual social formations. In this way, global lockdown and its technologies function as central sites for ontological production, for *making* subjects on all sides of prison walls: those who can and must be killed, warehoused, and watched, and those whose civic duty requires their complicity in the killing.

The prison, thus, cannot be understood as outside of social production, but rather as foundational to it. In *Are Prisons Obsolete?* Angela Davis shows how the prison functions as a mode of social production through her analysis of the "human surplus" produced at the confluence of an intensified capitalist economy and the mobilization of white supremacist imaginaries:

In the context of an economy that was driven by an unprecedented pursuit of profit, no matter what the human cost, and the concomitant dismantling of the welfare state, poor people's abilities to survive became increasingly constrained by the looming presence of the prison. The massive prison-building project that began in the 1980s created the means of concentrating and managing what the capitalist system had implicitly declared to be a human surplus. In the meantime, elected officials and the dominant media justified the new draconian sentencing practices, sending more and more people to prison in the frenzied drive to build more and more prisons by arguing that it was the only way to make our communities safe from murderers, rapists, and robbers.[44]

In the wake of the neoliberal gutting of an already precarious and punitive welfare state, the prison stepped in to produce, mark, and manage human surplus. It is through the mobilization of racist sexualized fears of "murderers, rapists, and robbers" and through misguided yearnings for safety that the prison binge of the 1980s and its progeny *(re)produce* subjects who must be locked down, as well as those who must do the locking. These same economies of panic and security legitimize the systematic dismantling of revolutionary social movements that oppose state repression through the mounting use of torture, imprisonment, disappearance, and massacre,[45] both within and outside of the United States, and a litany of technologies of anti-black, anti-immigrant, and anti-poor terror narrating the history of racial state formation including lynching, execution, and rape.

Continuing her line of thought, Davis argues that the prison operates to naturalize and intensify the generalized violence deployed by the state and its citizens against communities marked as criminal, specifically black, Latino, Native, and poor communities, as well as poor and racially pathologized communities in the global South. In particular, she writes, "prison is a space in which the threat of sexualized violence that looms in the larger society is effectively sanctioned as a routine aspect of the landscape of punishment behind prison walls."[46] In this way, the widespread sexual abuse of people in prison, and particularly women, queer people, and transgender people of color, emerges not as exceptional, but rather as indicative and productive of a larger regime of gratuitous force that marks bodies as surplus *through* the use of violence and imprisonment. Sexualized violence against those in lockdown should thus not be understood as "cruel and unusual" spectacles aberrant to the political order, but rather as *foundational to it*, and as central to the production of civil society as well as its outsides.[47] This is a move difficult to understand if we do not pay attention to how feelings are mobilized to garner legitimacy for the prison project. The construction of those in lockdown as "murderers, rapists, and robbers" and the pervasiveness of sexual violence in prisons thus should not be seen as coincidental, but rather as indicative of the powerful imbrications of desire, fear, and safety in the production and disposal of those who are "resistant or surplus to the new world order." Just as we have argued that promises of belonging, value, recognition, and worth are issued to certain marginalized subjects, it is always on the ground of other (non)subjects. Heeding the same logics of expendability, once again a promise for safety and happiness can only be issued as a simultaneous call for murder and human demolition. This is but one of the central affective economies that produces the prison industrial complex as a seductive facet of our collective common sense.

Through the mystifying narratives of "'crime and punishment'" and "'law and order,'" the prison is offered as an end to pain and as a catch-all solution to violence of all kinds. The prison promises citizens and subjects a future filled with freedom, security, and safety. Individualizing pain and harm such that they might be reduced to "crime" and "perpetrators," the prison promises safety, order, and redress severed from the persistence of structural murder and the exploitation fundamental to the capitalist democracy itself. Importantly, the futures that global lockdown promises its docile disciples can only be imagined through the unending creation and preservation of outsiders, nonsubjects, nonfutures, and nonhumans. In effect, the citizen-subject cannot be free or perhaps even alive without the captivity and (social, corporeal, and civic) death of the noncitizen, nonsubject, and those cordoned off to the realm of human surplus or, as Davis calls it, "detritus."[48]

We understand the promise project playing out through global lockdown in a variety of ways, from ongoing prison expansion efforts to soothe the crisis of prison overcrowding and fatal prison conditions, to the proliferation of citizen-led reformist measures in the name of rehabilitation and redemption, to our daily reliance on police as the primary way we might feel safe. To return to the site of (recognizable) queer politics, penalty-enhancing hate crimes legislation is proposed and supported as a solution to systemic transphobic and homophobic violence. In these campaigns, the prison offers the seductive promise of security if we might authorize and support the ongoing roundup and lockdown of subjects marked as threatening. As the HRC advertisement demonstrated, safety can only be called into being through a hypernationalism that requires the cordoning off and disposal of those deemed criminal, enemy, and surplus. It is specifically through the sexualized violence inherent in being "brought to justice" that enables the end of pain offered by global lockdown. Very clearly, then, the neoliberal empire has quite effectively commandeered our affective yearnings for safety, security, redress, and peace and collapsed them with carnage, punishment, and confinement such that they might appear synonymous. It should come as no surprise, then, that so many of the gains made by formerly marginal subjects over the past many decades have been simultaneous with intensified forms of violence and abjection against surplus populations. It is precisely *through* these forms of aggression that those gains have been made possible.[49]

Global lockdown thus functions as one of the looming underbellies and conditions of possibility of the (un)freedoms and (non)futures being promised by neoliberal empire. Consigning the collective traumas of slavery and colonization to a remote and irrelevant past while drawing on their logics to instantiate its rule, global lockdown shows itself to be neither cruel and unusual nor exceptional, but rather as foundational. Importantly, these (un)freedoms and (non)futures carry very different promises and pleasures depending on our relationship to the human surplus motoring the global political economy. Global lockdown, then, is not simply the newest outside, but quite literally the material redefining off what life can even mean in the wake of so much "necessary" death.

Toward an Intimate Politics of Decolonizing Abolitionism

We have thus far argued that across diffuse spaces and moments—the homonormative turn, the neoliberalization of the economy, the war on terror, and global lockdown—we see different dimensions of a promise project, which is also a project forever seeking to (re)consolidate empire. On the one hand, there are those for whom subjectivity, capital, and satiating pleasures and rights are being forever promised. This occurs, we argue, at the expense of compliance with, or perhaps distraction from, the larger structural underpinnings of social relations and processes. On the other hand, there are the (non)subjects for whom the same promise has not been issued, the abject(s) whose lives and deaths are completely nonspectacular within the dominant imaginations. Adding to this contradiction is the dimension that even the promises themselves are tenuous: indeed, as elite queers privilege homonormativity over more radical political and economic praxes, neoconservative forces continue to criminalize queerness. While first and foremost queers outside this elite or national racial strata are produced as exterminable sodomites, the category of the abject and killable always threatens even elite queers in first world spaces. This is part of the politico-economic and affective logics that have fueled a frenzied search for an end to pain: continue imperial soldiering in exchange for a mirage of security, or spend your energies fighting other queers for a prized space as most radical. With such a paucity of choices, our energies are directed away from building solidarities and exhausted by fixing on individualized solutions and fueling the (re)production of neoliberal, neoconservative, homonormative, and ultimately heteronormative worlds.

If the neoliberal turn has been part of a larger strategy of counterinsurgency mobilized in the wake of revolutionary decolonization movements threatening capitalism, (hetero)sexism, and white supremacy, it is important to pause on some of the impacts of that (counter)mobilization. In this paper we have worked to foreground the affective logics that function on the level of feeling and desire in the service of a neoliberal project of a world remade. To begin to articulate the ways in which our most 'intimate' sensibilities—our fears, desires, mourning, and yearning—are being mobilized by a regime of global lockdown is to make urgent the production of solidarities not premised upon exploitation, profit, or death. For those engaged in movements dismantling the prison industrial complex and any form of imperial violence, it is precisely these affective economies to which we must be attentive. If we do not work to articulate the ways in which we become libidinally and erotically invested in the status quo of mass lockdown—in effect, the various promises that the prison issues—we run the risk of reproducing the racialized and sexualized economies of benevolence and exploitation that fortify so much of conservative, liberal, and even radical praxis. However, as we have sought to argue, the price of such dismissals is nothing less than participation in imperial violence that, ultimately, impacts us all. Amidst the many affective callings and seductive offerings we are issued, we must continue the work of imagining alternative ways to feel, be, and love in this moment of intensified empire-building. To become completely drawn into challenging homonormativization without attention to the larger structural underpinnings of social relations and processes may ultimately prove unproductive as it misses the larger imperial logics that may be embodied differentially in other sites. Moreover, it becomes impossible to discern the relationship between our own struggles and the set of promises and nonpromises offered to other others. Foreclosing potential and increasingly crucial solidarities, we are drawn into our own corners and ultimately diverted from the possibilities of massive, cross-bordered mobilizations, movements and revolutionary projects.

In the place of this vision, we offer first and foremost a disruption of complicity, a refusal of empire's promise project. The series of wars in which empire asks us to participate are utterly genocidal, rather than constituting processes that enable our security and healing. As members of different and overlapping communities and struggles, the authors have each grappled personally with this process. As activists and intellectuals who are engaged in struggles around war, migration and trafficking, labor and homelessness, mass imprisonment, and state violence against queer and transgender communities, we are confronted with the seductive — yet ultimately murderous — promises that are described in this essay. Moreover, as members of the academy at different levels (undergraduate student, graduate student, and faculty member), we have witnessed how the strategies of promise and nonpromise projects have worked to fragment, divide, and conquer people of color, working-class people, queers, transgender people, postcolonial subjects, and others within powerful academic zones of knowledge production. Recognizing that we can never be outside empire's seductive offerings, we engage these questions out of rage, hope, and the desire to form life-sustaining solidarities and intimacies. We strive with others toward a politics that enables intimacies as both means and ends, as a strategy of movement-building in which relationships are formed not to instantiate empire's incessant production of internal and external enemies, but to disrupt it. This is a politics that would challenge histories that dichotomize and fragment our worlds, and instead offer praxes of erotic resistance in which we might be able to glimpse a breathing space for reconstituting connections and relations based in collectivity and healing.

With this analysis in mind, all attempts to separate and make discrete struggles for social justice and transformation — those working for prison abolition, sexual and gender freedom, decolonization, and the end to war, for example — prove unsuccessful. They are always already imbricated in one another. When one struggles to resist coercive sexual or gender regimes — heternormativization as well as homonormativization — one is already engaging in a politics deeply implicated in the wars on terror, poverty, and drugs, and in the (neo)slaveries of the prison industrial complex.

This is true not only because of the devastating impacts these wars have had on queer communities and sexually aberrant (non)subjects locked away, and because of the ways in which a racializing "sodomotification" is drawn on to produce the criminal and the terrorist. Indeed, the violence and death that we authorize and face operate through and within our libidinal, erotic, and affective investments, investments that we must engage directly and rigorously if we are to disrupt the seductive workings of power in their most intimate dimensions.

If, then, all queer politics are already organizing around and implicated in the buildup of global lockdown and imperialist war, the question is not *if* a praxis of decolonization and abolitionism is pertinent to queer struggles, but *how* and *why* it is. If it is true that our deepest desires, feelings, and arousals are tapped into for imperial production, it also becomes crucial to ask how we might organize, mobilize, and form alternative intimacies and desires. These alternatives, which continue to be nurtured in radical and revolutionary movements and collectivities, are forged as a disruption to individualized, consumptive, and privatized erotics in the name of broader collective projects of freedom and transformation that cultivate the pleasures of substantial connection and the production of more egalitarian relations. These are the intimacies that form the core of decolonizing imaginaries, those that understand sexual freedom only through collective self-determination. It is only when we engage the traumas *as well as* the yearnings of our pasts and our futures that we might be able to seize the possibilities increasingly foreclosed by empire's seductive promises.

Notes

We wish to thank the many people whose support and struggles offer us glimpses into the solidarities and intimacies that inspired this paper. Particularly, we would like to mention Cindy Bello, Kyle D. Killian, Thomas J. Lax, Alexander Lee, Diane Machado, Alison Merz, Dean Spade, and Heather Turcotte.

1. The idea of seductions of empire comes from a larger project that Agathangelou is co-authoring with L. H. M. Ling and is (forthcoming) *Empire and Insecurity in World Politics: Seductions of Neoliberalism* (Routledge). For a definition of seductions see more specifically Anna M. Agathangelou and Kyle D. Killian "Electronic Attachments: Desire, the Other, and the Internet Marital Trade in the Twenty-First Century," in *Cross-Cultural Couples: Transbordered Relationships in the Twenty-First Century*, ed. Terri Karris and Kyle D. Killian (Binghampton, NY: Haworth, forthcoming).

2. The idea of promises and non-promises comes from a larger book project that Agathangelou is working on. It is more specifically on the terror-necrotic practices of "empire" and the "rewards" promised to participate in the formation and reconsolidation of such projects. Please see Anna M. Agathangelou, "Ontologies of Desire, Empire, and Capital: Recolonizations, "Security" and the 'Near East.'" Invited by the Institute of Political Science, National Sun Yat-sen University, Taiwan. Presented at the International Academic Conference, "Asian Security Facing Hegemony: Nationalism, Immigration and Humanity," June 2, 2006.

3. Lambda Legal, "Seismic Shift," www.lambdalegal.org/our-work/publications/impact/2003/fall/page.jsp?itemID=31989920 (accessed May 9, 2007).

4. Ibid.

5. Sodomy Laws, "*Lawrence and Garner v. State of Texas*," www.sodomylaws.org/lawrence/lawrence.htm (accessed May 9, 2007).

6. We place "benefit" in quotes not to underscore the contradictory material acquisition and privilege gained by this (whitened) class of queers or to understate the violence performed, but to suggest that this so-called membership in the new world order is indeed precarious. In this neoliberal content of instrumentality and competitive advantage, anyone can be used as a friend or an enemy, as friends and allies of yesterday become the enemy to be hunted and killed today. One need only look at the history of U.S.-backed regimes and the state-sponsored coups in Argentina, Chile, and Central America of the 1980s and 1990s. Saddam Hussein and the Taliban are good contemporary examples of friends turned enemies of the U.S. state. On the other side of this, for example, is the ongoing persecution of Assata Shakur, who currently has a 1 million dollar price on her head, and the recently rearrested so-called San Francisco 8. These are figures who are persistently produced as enemies of the state and as threats to public safety. See Committee for the Defense of Human Rights, "FBI Hunting the Dead: Can John Bowman Ever Rest in Peace?" www.cdhrsupport.org/what_to_do.html (accessed May 9, 2007); and New Jersey State Police, "New Jersey's 12 Most Wanted," www.state.nj.us/njsp/want/chesimard.html (accessed May 16, 2007).

7. Matt Foreman, "National Gay and Lesbian Task Force Welcomes Supreme Court Sodomy Decision—Calls Opinion Major Advance for Individual Liberty," National Gay and Lesbian Task Force, www.thetaskforce.org/press/releases/pr551_062603 (accessed May 9, 2007).

8. For a more in-depth discussion of these contradictions, see Dean Spade and Craig Willse, "Freedom in a Regulatory State? Lawrence, Marriage, and Biopolitics," *Widener Law Review* 11 (2005): 309.

9. Sentencing Project, "Facts about Prisons and Prisoners," www.sentencingproject.org/Admin/Documents/publications/inc_factsaboutprison.pdf (accessed May 16, 2007).

10. Julia Sudbury, "Introduction: Feminist Critiques, Transnational Landscapes, Abolitionist Visions," in *Global Lockdown: Race, Gender, and the Prison-Industrial Complex*, ed. Sudbury (New York: Routledge, 2005), xxii.

11. Ibid.

12. By referring to "empire" we in no way see this as a complete project, but one whose heterogeneous consolidation is both continually in the (un)making. See also Neferti X. M. Tadiar, "Cultures of Empire" (keynote address presented at the "Convening US Empire Conference," University of Michigan, Ann Arbor, January 8–10, 2004), cffsc.focusnow.org/NT-cultures.html.

13. Highlighting the symbolic work that 9/11 does in the imperial imagination does not mean to trace it as the source of instability and conflict in the Middle East, as most U.S. narratives would report. For instance, Anna M. Agathangelou argues that 9/11 becomes a "fetish object" within discussions of democracy and that the war on terror forecloses the possibility of asking other questions that (1) locate historically the attacks on the World Trade Center towers; and (2) engage with conflicts and tensions globally, including with what come to be constituted as civilizational clashes. See Anna M. Agathangelou, "A Transborder Feminist Critique of the Epistemologies of Militarized Neoliberalism: Solidarities and Practices of Substantive Democracy" (paper presented at the International Studies Association, Chicago, February 28, 2007; conference was held from February 28 to March 3, 2007).

14. For important analyses of the conflations between the racially and sexually aberrant within the post–9/11 landscape, see Jasbir K. Puar and Amit S. Rai, "Monster, Terrorist, Fag: The War on Terrorism and the Production of Docile Patriots," *Social Text* 20:3 (2002): 117–48.

15. For a more detailed analysis of desire and the production of the other in the war on terror, please see Anna M. Agathangelou and L. H. M. Ling, "Power, Borders, Security, Wealth: Lessons of Violence and Desire from September 11," *International Studies Quarterly* 48 (2004): 517–38.

16. It is precisely the mobilization of victim's rights and rehabilitation that California legislators recently used to justify the most recent of the state's ongoing prison expansion efforts—the biggest in the history of the world—agreeing to spend over $7.3 billion to build nearly fifty-three thousand more prison beds to address the state-proctored crisis of prison overcrowding and the lack of rehabilitative programs. To look at the history of prisons in the United States is to see this logic of the "bigger, friendlier" prison behind almost every prison-building project. As a state with one of the highest imprisonment rates annually in the country, California is a testament to the seductive slippage between supposed safety and carnage.

17. See Anna M. Agathangelou and Kyle D. Killian, "Epistemologies of Peace: Poetics, Globalization, and the Social Justice Movement," *Globalizations* 34 (2006): 453–83; and Achille Mbembe, "Necropolitics," *Public Culture* 15 (2006): 11–40.

18. Anna M. Agathangelou, *The Global Political Economy of Sex: Desire, Violence, and Insecurity in Mediterranean Nation States* (New York: Palgrave Macmillan, 2004).

19. Angela P. Harris, "From Stonewall to the Suburbs? Toward a Political Economy of Sexuality," *William and Mary Bill of Rights Journal* 14 (2006): 1539–82.

20. The full advertisement is available online at www.hrc.org/millionformarriage/hrc_adcenter/keith.pdf (accessed May 9, 2007).

21. Lisa Duggan, *The Twilight of Equality? Neoliberalism, Cultural Politics, and the Attack on Democracy* (Boston: Beacon 2004), 50.

22. Martin F. Manalansan IV, "Race, Violence, and Neoliberal Spatial Politics in the Global City," *Social Text* 23:3–4 (2005): 141–55.

23. M. Jacqui Alexander, *Pedagogies of Crossing: Meditations on Feminism, Sexual Politics, Memory, and the Sacred* (Durham, NC: Duke University Press, 2005), 234.

24. Ibid.

25. The emergence of the HRC follows much of the logic we trace. Founded in the 1980s as an advocacy organization primarily around issues of decriminalizing homosexuality and HIV/AIDS, the HRC was instrumental in such struggles as barring insurance firms from denying coverage to those testing HIV positive. Now the largest and most well-funded LGBT advocacy organization in the United States, the HRC has shifted its agenda since the early 1990s to focus almost solely on measures that bolster neoliberal privatization and militarization: military entrance, hate crimes legislation, same-sex marriage rights, and adoption. As many activists and theorists have articulated, this professionalizing and neoliberalizing impulse has gained increased fervor and support in queer politics over the past two decades.

26. Sonia E. Alvarez, "Latin American Feminisms 'Go Global': Trends of the 1990s and Challenges for the New Millennium," in *Cultures of Politics/Politics of Cultures: Revisioning Latin American Social Movements*, ed. Sonia E. Alvarez, Evelina Dagnino, and Arturo Escobar (Boulder, CO: Westview, 1997), 293–324. INCITE! Women of Color against Violence, *The Revolution Will Not Be Funded beyond the Non-Profit Industrial Complex* (Boston: South End, 2007).

27. See Agathangelou, *Global Political Economy of Sex.*

28. Anna M. Agathangelou, "Militarizations and Neoliberalism(s): Empire, Terror-Necrocies, and Death," forthcoming.

29. Our analysis of the often contradictory and antagonistic histories of torture(s) both within and outside of the U.S. borders draws from Dylan Rodriguez, "(Non)Scenes of Captivity: The Common Sense of Punishment and Death," *Radical History Review*, no. 96 (2006): 9–32.

30. For more on this, see Anjali Arondekar, "Border/Line Sex: Queer Postcolonialities or How Race Matters outside the U.S.," *Interventions: International Journal of Postcolonial Studies* 7 (2005): 235–49.

31. United States Court of Appeals, *Salim Ahmed Hamdan, Appellee v. Donald H. Rumsfeld, United States Secretary of Defense, et al., Appellants*, www.asil.org/pdfs/Hamdanv .Rumsfeld.pdf (accessed May 9, 2007).

32. See Bob Egelko, "Roberts' Ruling in Bush's Favor Debated: Terrorism Case Came as White House Was Interviewing Him," *San Francisco Chronicle*, September 22, 2005.

33. Ibid.

34. *Lawrence V. Texas*, www.law.cornell.edu/supct/html/02–102.ZD.html

35. See Agathangelou, "Militarizations and Neoliberalism(s)."

36. In Thomas's dissenting opinion, he wrote that were he a member of the Texas legislature, he would vote to repeal the antisodomy law.

37. See Maria Mies, *Patriarchy and Accumulation on a World Scale* (London: Zed, 1998).

38. See Angela Davis, *Women, Race, and Class* (New York: Vintage Books, 1983); Angela Davis, *Are Prisons Obsolete?* (New York: Seven Stories Press, 2003); Anne McClintock, *Imperial Leather: Race, Gender, and Sexuality in the Colonial Contest* (New York: Routledge, 1995); A. M. Agathangelou, "Colonising Desires: Bodies for Sale, Exploitation and (In)Security in Desire Industries," in *Cyprus Review* 18, no. 2 (2004): 37–73; and A. M. Agathangelou, "Gender, Race, Militarization, and Economic Restructuring in Former Yugoslavia and the US–Mexico Border," in *Women and Globalization*, ed. Delia D. Aguilar and Anne E. Lascamana (New York: Humanity Press, 2004), 347–86.

39. See Anna M. Agathangelou and Kyle D. Killian, "Electronic Attachments: Desire, the Other, and the Internet Marital Trade in the Twenty-First Century," in *Cross-Cultural Couples: Transbordered Relationships in the Twenty-First Century*, ed. Terri Karris and Killian (Binghamton, NY: Haworth, forthcoming).

40. Sudbury, *Global Lockdown*, xxii.

41. Ibid.

42. Guyora Binder, "The Slavery of Emancipation," *Cardozo Law Review* 17 (1996): 2063–102.

43. Please see Linda Evans and Evan Goldberg, *The Prison Industrial Complex and the Global Economy* (San Francisco, CA: AK Press Distribution, 1998); Ruth Wilson Gilmore, *Golden Gulag: Prisons, Surplus, Crisis, and Opposition in Globalizing California* (Berkeley: University of California Press, 2007); and Christian Palenti, *Lockdown America: Police and Prisons in the Age of Crisis* (New York: Verso, 1999).

44. Davis, *Are Prisons Obsolete?* 191.

45. Ruth Wilson Gilmore, "Globalization and U.S. Prison Growth," *Race and Class* 40 (1998): 171–88.

46. Davis, *Are Prisons Obsolete?* 191.

47. This discussion of gratuitous (sexualized) violence as paradigmatic of antiblack racism and the production of civil society's prison regimes is hugely informed by Jared Sexton, "Racial

Profiling and the Societies of Control," in *Warfare in the American Homeland: Prisons and Policing in a Penal Democracy*, ed. Joy James (Durham, NC: Duke University Press, 2007); Frank B. Wilderson III, "Gramsci's Black Marx: Whither the Slave in Society," *Social Identities* 9 (2003): 225–40; and Dylan Rodriguez, *Forced Passages: Imprisoned Intellectuals and the U.S. Prison Regime* (Minneapolis: University of Minnesota Press, 2006).

48. Davis, *Are Prisons Obsolete?* 16.

49. A number of radical and transformative political formations challenging the intersections of the prison industrial complex and racist heteropatriarchal capitalism have emerged in the wake of these double-edged gains made by many activists fighting for prison reform and LGBT rights, including the Audre Lorde Project, Critical Resistance, FIERCE!, Justice Now, the Sylvia Rivera Law Project, and the Transgender, Gender Variant, and Intersex Justice Project. In their struggles for collective self-determination, many of these formations explicitly work to develop and nourish alternative intimacies that might counter neoliberal empire's seductive offerings of individualization, commodification, and corporatization as the only models for building social justice. This paper is deeply indebted to the political and social praxes produced through and within these formations.

Fortieth anniversary of Compton's Cafeteria riot, June 22, 2006. Photo by Philipe Lonestar.
Reprinted by permission of the photographer and the San Francisco Bay Area Independent
Media Center

Transgender History, Homonormativity, and Disciplinarity

Susan Stryker

The current attention to homonormativity has tended to focus on gay and lesbian social, political, and cultural formations and their relationship to a neoliberal politics of multicultural diversity that meshes with the assimilative strategies of transnational capital. Lisa Duggan's *The Twilight of Equality? Neoliberalism, Cultural Politics, and the Attack on Democracy* (2003), which describes a "new homonormativity that does not challenge heterosexist institutions and values, but rather upholds, sustains, and seeks inclusion within them," is generally acknowledged as the text through which this term has come into wider currency.[1] There is, however, an older formulation of *homonormativity* that nevertheless merits retention, one closer in meaning to the "homo-normative" social codes described in 1998 by Judith Halberstam in *Female Masculinity*, in accordance with which expressions of masculinity in women are as readily disparaged within gender-normative gay and lesbian contexts as within heteronormative ones.[2] It is this earlier sense of homonormativity that is most pertinent to the thoughts I offer here on homonormativity and transgender history, both as an object of scholarly inquiry and as a professional disciplinary practice.

Terminological History

Homonormativity, as I first heard and used the term in the early 1990s, was an attempt to articulate the double sense of marginalization and displacement experienced within transgender political and cultural activism. Like other queer militants,

Radical History Review

Issue 100 (Winter 2008)   DOI 10.1215/01636545-2007-026

© 2008 by MARHO: The Radical Historians' Organization, Inc.

transgender activists sought to make common cause with any groups—including nontransgender gays, lesbians, and bisexuals—who contested heterosexist privilege. However, we also needed to name the ways that homosexuality, as a sexual orientation category based on constructions of gender it shared with the dominant culture, sometimes had more in common with the straight world than it did with us.[3]

The grassroots conversations in which I participated in San Francisco in the first half of the 1990s used the term *homonormative* when discussing the relationship of transgender to queer, and queer to gay and lesbian. *Transgender* itself was a term then undergoing a significant shift in meaning. Robert Hill, who has been researching the history of heterosexual male cross-dressing communities, found instances in community-based publications of words like *transgenderal*, *transgenderist*, and *transgenderism* dating back to the late 1960s.[4] The logic of those terms, used to describe individuals who lived in one social gender but had a bodily sex conventionally associated with the other, aimed for a conceptual middle ground between transvestism (merely changing one's clothing) and transsexualism (changing one's sex). By the early 1990s, primarily through the influence of Leslie Feinberg's 1992 pamphlet *Transgender Liberation: A Movement Whose Time Has Come*, *transgender* was beginning to refer to something else—an imagined political alliance of all possible forms of gender antinormativity. It was in this latter sense that *transgender* became articulated with *queer*.[5]

This "new transgender" marked both a political and generational distinction between older transvestite/transsexual/drag terminologies and an emerging gender politics that was explicitly and self-consciously queer. It began for me in 1992, when the San Francisco chapter of Queer Nation distributed one of its trademark Day-Glo crack-and-peel stickers that read "Trans Power/Bi Power/Queer Nation." The transsexual activist Anne Ogborn encountered someone on the street wearing one of those stickers, but with the words "Trans Power" torn off. When Ogborn asked if there was any significance to the omission, she was told that the wearer did not consider trans people to be part of the queer movement.[6] Ogborn attended the next Queer Nation general meeting to protest transphobia within the group, whereupon she was invited, in high Queer Nation style, to organize a transgender caucus.[7] As a result, Transgender Nation, of which I was a founding member, came into being as the first explicitly queer transgender social change group in the United States. The group survived the soon-to-be-defunct Queer Nation and became, in its own brief existence from 1992 to 1994, a touchstone in the transgender inclusion debates then raging in San Francisco's emerging Lesbian, Gay, Bisexual, and Transgender (LGBT) community.

In a contradictory environment simultaneously welcoming and hostile, transgender activists staked their own claims to queer politics. We argued that sexual orientation was not the only significant way to differ from heteronormativity—that homo, hetero, and bi in fact all depended on similar understandings of "man" and "woman," which trans problematized. People with trans identities could describe themselves as men and women, too — or resist binary categorization altogether — but in doing either they queered the dominant relationship of sexed body and gendered subject. We drew a distinction between "orientation queers" and "gender queers." Tellingly, *gender queer*, necessary for naming the minoritized/marginalized position of difference within queer cultural formations more generally, has stuck around as a useful term; *orientation queer*, naming queer's unstated norm, has seemed redundant in most contexts and has not survived to the same extent.

When San Francisco gays and lesbians who were active in queer politics in the first half of the 1990s were antagonistic to transgender concerns, we accused them of being antiheteronormative in a homonormative fashion. The term was an intuitive, almost self-evident, back-formation from the ubiquitous *heteronormative*, suitable for use where homosexual community norms marginalized other kinds of sex/gender/sexuality difference. Although I do not recall specific instances where the term *homonormative* was used, or who used it, the general discussions in which the term would have been deployed were playing themselves out in any number of places in which transgender inclusion was being contested: within Queer Nation and ACT-UP and AIDS agencies; at community meetings to organize for the March on Washington in 1993 and the twenty-fifth anniversary of the Stonewall uprising in 1994; at town-hall meetings about gays in the military and domestic partnerships during the hopeful early days of the first Clinton administration; during policy discussions about including gender identity in the proposed federal Employment Non-Discrimination Act; in catfights over who could attend the Michigan Women's Music Festival; at meetings of the Harvey Milk and Alice B. Toklas Democratic Clubs; at Pride Parade meetings; at membership meetings and board meetings of practically every lesbian and gay nonprofit organization in the city; at the San Francisco Humans Rights Commission committee on lesbian and gay issues; in flame wars in the letters-to-the-editors columns of the *Bay Times* and the *BAR* (*Bay Area Reporter*); and in coffee shops, bars, dance clubs, dungeon spaces, and bedrooms throughout the city.

The homonormative accusation tended to be leveled against a handful of favorite targets: gays and lesbians who saw transgender issues as entirely distinct from their own and who resisted any sort of transgender participation in queer politics and culture; lesbians who excluded male-to-female transgender people but nervously engaged with female-to-male people, on the grounds that the former were really men and the latter were really women; and, putting a somewhat finer point on the matter, those who conceptualized "T" as an identity category analogous to "GLB" and who advocated for a GLBT community on that basis. In the first instance, homonormativity was a threat to a broadly conceived politics of alliance and affinity, regardless of identity; it aimed at securing privilege for gender-normative gays and lesbians based on adherence to dominant cultural constructions of gender, and it diminished the scope of potential resistance to oppression. In the second instance, homonormativity took the shape of lesbian subcultural norms that perversely grounded themselves in reactionary notions of biological determinism as the only legitimate basis of gender identity and paradoxically resisted feminist arguments that "woman" and "lesbian" were political rather than ontological categories. The third instance requires a more subtle and expansive explication.

In this case, homonormativity lies in misconstruing trans as either a gender or a sexual orientation. Misconstrued as a distinct gender, trans people are simply considered another kind or type of human than either men or women, which leads to such homonormative attempts at "transgender inclusion" as questionnaires and survey instruments within GLBT contexts that offer respondents opportunities for self-identification structured along the lines of

___ Man

___ Woman

___ Transgender (check one)

Misconstrued as a sexual orientation category, trans appears as a desire, akin to kink and fetish desire, for cross-dressing or (more extremely) genital modification. The "T" in this version of the LGBT community becomes a group of people who are attracted to one another on the basis of enjoying certain sexual practices—in the same way that gay men are attracted to gay men, and lesbians are attracted to lesbians, on the basis of a shared desire for particular sexual practices. "T" is thus homonormatively constructed as a properly distinct group of people with a different orientation than gays, lesbians, and bisexuals (or, for that matter, straights). In this model of GLBT intracommunity relations, each identity is happily attracted to its own kind and leaves the other groups to their own devices except in ceremonial circumstances (like pride parades and other public celebrations of diversity), or whenever political expediency calls for coalitional action of some sort.

In either homonormative deformation, "T" becomes a separate category to be appended, through a liberal politics of minority assimilation, to gay, lesbian, and bisexual community formations. Trans thus conceived of does not trouble the basis of the other categories—indeed, it becomes a containment mechanism for "gender trouble" of various sorts that works in tandem with assimilative gender-normative tendencies within the sexual identities.[8] Transgender activism and theory, on the other hand, tend to treat trans as a modality rather than a category. Trans segments the sexual orientations and gender identities in much the same manner as race and class—in other words, a transsexual woman (someone with a transsexual mode of embodiment who lives in the social category woman) can be a lesbian (someone who lives in the social category woman and is sexually oriented toward women), just as a black man could be gay, or a bisexual person could be poor. In doing so, transgender theory and activism call attention to the operations of normativity within and between gender/sexual identity categories, raise questions about the structuration of power along axes other than the homo/hetero and man/woman binaries, and identify productive points of attachment for linking sexual orientation and gender identity activism to other social justice struggles.

A decade before *homonormative* became a critically chic term elsewhere, I thus suggest, transgender praxis and critique required an articulation of the concept of homonormativity. The border wars that transgender activists fought within queer communities of the 1990s had important consequences for shaping contemporary transgender politics and theorizing, and for charting a future path toward radical activism. Transgender relations to gay and lesbian community formations necessarily became strategic — sometimes oppositional, sometimes aligned, sometimes fighting rearguard actions for inclusion, sometimes branching out in entirely different and unrelated directions. Central issues for transgender activism — such as gender-appropriate state-issued identification documents that allow trans people to work, cross borders, and access social services without exposing themselves to potential discrimination — suggest useful forms of alliance politics, in this instance with migrant workers and diasporic communities, that are not organized around sexual identity. One operation of homonormativity exposed by transgender activism is that homo is not always the most relevant norm against which trans needs to define itself.

Antihomonormative Transgender History

As important as queer identitarian disputes have been for present and future transgender politics, they have been equally important for reinterpreting the queer past. I first started researching the transgender history of San Francisco, particularly in relation to the city's gay and lesbian community, while participating in the Bay Area's broader queer culture during the early 1990s. In 1991, during my final year as a PhD student in U.S. history at the University of California at Berkeley, the same year I began transitioning from male to female, I became deeply involved with an organization then known as the Gay and Lesbian Historical Society of Northern California. That organization, now the GLBT Historical Society, houses the preeminent collection of primary source materials on San Francisco Bay Area gay, lesbian, bisexual, and transgender communities, and one of the best collections of sexuality-related materials anywhere in the world. I started there as a volunteer in the archives, joined the board of directors in 1992, and later became the first executive director of the organization, from 1999 to 2003.

Through my long and intimate association with the GLBT Historical Society, as well as through two years of postdoctoral funding from the Sexuality Research Fellowship Program of the Social Science Research Council, I had ample opportunity to exhaustively research the status of transgender issues within gay and lesbian organizations and communities in post–World War II San Francisco. I was able to scan all the periodical literature, community newspapers, collections of personal papers, organizational records, ephemera, and visual materials—tens of thousands of items—for transgender-related content. This research was motivated by several competing agendas. It was first and foremost a critically queer project, one informed by theory, guided by practice, and framed by my historical training at Berkeley in the decade between Michel Foucault's death and Judith Butler's arrival; I wanted to account for the precipitation of new categories of personal and collective identity from the matrix of possible configurations of sex, gender, identity, and desire; trace their genealogies and modes of discourse; and analyze the cultural politics of their interactions with each other and society at large. It was also a project to recover the history of transgender experience specifically, in a way that resisted essentializing transgender identities, and to make that knowledge available as content for transgender-related social justice work. Only those who are "crushed by a present concern," and who want to "throw off their burden at any cost," Friedrich Nietzsche wrote in "On the Use and Abuse of History for Life," have "a need for a critical . . . historiography."[9] And finally, I was motivated by polemical and partisan considerations; I wanted to offer an empirically grounded account of transgender history that recontextualized its relation to gay and lesbian normativity and countered the pathologizing, moralizing, condescending, dismissive, and generally wrongheaded treatment of transgender issues so often found in gay and lesbian discourses of that time.

Over the course of my research, gender-policing practices came into focus as an important mechanism for shaping the landscape of sexual identity community formations described in the major historiographical accounts.[10] As homosexual communities in mid-twentieth century San Francisco redefined themselves as political minorities, they distanced themselves from older notions of "inversion" that collapsed gender transposition and homosexual desire into one another; they simultaneously drew their boundaries at least partly in relation to new and rapidly evolving scientific discourses on transgender phenomena and related medico-legal techniques for changing sex. Homophile groups such as the Mattachine Society and the Daughters of Bilitis were not initially antagonistic to transgender issues; they sometimes fielded queries from people questioning their gender or seeking a community in which to express a transgender identity, but they tended to redirect such queries elsewhere.[11] Transgender issues tended to be seen within the homophile movement as parallel rather than intersecting, at least partially due to the central role that gender normativity played in the homophile movement's public politics of respectability in the 1950s and early 1960s. In lesbian contexts this took the form of class-based criticisms of butch-femme roles, while in the gay male world it expressed itself through the condemnation of the hypermasculine styles found in the leather, motorcycle, and cowboy subcultures, as well as in the femininity of "swish" styles and public female impersonation. Drag remained an important subcultural idiom, especially for gay men and working-class lesbians, but one typically confined to clubs, bars, and private parties; street drag was almost universally condemned and largely relegated to territories coextensive with prostitution, hustling, and other economically marginalized activities. Thus, from the outset of the post–World War II gay rights movement, transgender practices and identities marked communal boundaries between the normative and the transgressive.

One particular archival discovery seemed so perfectly attuned to all my research motivations, however, and so seemingly significant yet almost entirely unknown, that I initially questioned whether it could possibly be true. In the centerfold of the program for the first Gay Pride Parade in San Francisco, held in 1972, I found a description of a 1966 riot in San Francisco's Tenderloin District, in which drag queens and gay hustlers banded together at a popular late-night hangout called Gene Compton's Cafeteria to fight back against police harassment and social oppression. The key text reads as follows:

In the streets of the Tenderloin, at Turk and Taylor on a hot August night in 1966, Gays rose up angry at the constant police harassment of the drag-queens by the police. It had to be the first ever recorded violence by Gays against police anywhere. For on that evening when the SFPD paddy wagon drove up to make their "usual" sweeps of the streets, Gays this time did not go willingly. It began when the police came into a cafeteria, still located there at Turk and Taylor, Compton's, to do their usual job of hassling the drag-queens and hair-fairies and hustlers setting at the table. This was with the permission of management, of course. But when the police grabbed the arm of one of the transvestites, he threw his cup of coffee in the cop's face, and with that, cups, saucers, and trays began flying around the place, and all directed at the police. They retreated outside until reinforcements arrived, and the Compton's management ordered the place closed, and with that, the Gays began breaking out every window in the place, and as they ran outside to escape the breaking glass, the police tried to grab them and throw them into the paddy wagon, but they found this no easy task for Gays began hitting them "below the belt" and drag-queens smashing them in the face with their extremely heavy purses. A police car had every window broken, a newspaper shack outside the cafeteria was burned to the ground, and general havoc was raised that night in the Tenderloin. The next night drag-queens, hair-fairies, conservative Gays, and hustlers joined in a picket of the cafeteria, which would not allow drags back in again. It ended with the newly installed plate glass windows once more being smashed. The Police Community Relations Unit began mediating the conflict, which was never fully resolved, which ended in a group called VANGUARD being formed of the street peoples and a lesbian group of street people being formed called the STREET ORPHANS, both of which later became the old GAY LIBERATION FRONT in San Francisco, and is today called the GAY ACTIVISTS ALLIANCE.[12]

The story seemed important in several respects. First, what reportedly happened at Compton's Cafeteria bore obvious similarities to the famous Stonewall uprising in New York in 1969, where the militant phase of gay liberation is commonly supposed to have begun, but reputedly preceded it by three years. How the San Francisco gay activist community positioned the Compton's story vis-à-vis Stonewall in their first commemorative Gay Pride Parade was clearly intended as an early revisionist account of gay liberation history. Furthermore, the inciting incident of the riot was described as an act of antitransgender discrimination, rather than an act of discrimination against sexual orientation. At the time I came across this source in 1995, the role of drag queens in the Stonewall riots had become a site of conflict between transgender and normative gay/lesbian histories—transgender activists pointed to the act of mythologizing Stonewall as the "birth" of gay liberation as a homonormative co-optation of gender queer resistance, while homonormative gay and lesbian commentators tended to downplay the significance of antidrag oppression at Stonewall—and whatever I could learn about the Compton's incident would certainly inform that debate. The 1972 document also related a genealogy of gay liberation activism at odds with the normative accounts—one rooted in the socioeconomics of the multiethnic Tenderloin sex-work ghetto rather than in campus-based activism oriented toward countercultural white youth of middle-class origin. For all these reasons, the Compton's Cafeteria riot became a central focus of my research into San Francisco's transgender history and its intersectional relationship to the history of gay and lesbian communities.

Although the 1972 document proved factually inaccurate in several particulars (the picketing happened before the riot, for example), I was ultimately able to verify its basic account of the Compton's Cafeteria riot, and to situate that event in a history of transgender community formation and politicization that both complemented and contested homonormative gay and lesbian history. Most important, I was able to connect the location and timing of the riot to social, political, geographical, and historical circumstances in San Francisco in ways that the Stonewall story had never connected gay liberation discourse to similar circumstances in New York—thereby opening up new ways to think about the relationship between identity politics and broader material conditions. The 1966 riot at Compton's Cafeteria took place at the intersection of several broad social issues that continue to be of concern today, such as discriminatory policing practices in minority communities, the lack of minority access to appropriate health care, elitist urban land-use policies, the unsettling domestic consequences of foreign wars, and civil rights campaigns that aim to expand individual liberties and social tolerance on matters of sexuality and gender. A fuller treatment of this material exceeds the space limitations of this essay, but it can be found elsewhere in works cited below.

Homonormative Disciplinarity

Although the history of the Compton's Cafeteria riot provides a productive point of critique and revision for homonormative accounts of the recent history of sexual identity communities and movements, most knowledge of this event has circulated through works of public history (most notably the 2005 public television documentary *Screaming Queens: The Riot at Compton's Cafeteria*), work by nonacademic writers, and in community-based publications, rather than through professional academic channels.[13] In those few instances in which this history has been examined in peer-reviewed journals, the articles have been placed, as this one has been, in sections of the journals set aside for uses other than feature articles. In the one instance where this has not been the case, the article was written by another (nontransgendered) scholar who interviewed me and made use of primary source documents I directed her to, in order to relate the Compton's Cafeteria riot to her own research interest in the sociology of historical memory.[14] I point this out not as a complaint—it was my own decision to pursue the public history dissemination of my research findings; I actually guest-edited a journal issue that put my own research into the back matter and anonymized my authorship, and I have eagerly collaborated with other scholars who have never failed to accurately and appropriately cite the use of my research in their own projects. My aim, rather, is to call needed attention to the micropolitical practices through which the radical implications of transgender knowledges can become marginalized. Even in contexts such as this special homonormativities issue of *Radical History Review*, which explicitly called for transgender scholarship that could generate "new analytical frameworks for talking about lesbian, gay, bisexual, transgender, and queer history that expand and challenge current models of identity and community formation as well as models of political and cultural resistance," transgender knowledges are far too easily subjugated to what Michel Foucault once called "the hierarchies of erudition."[15]

In my original abstract for this issue, I proposed not only to recount the little-known history of the Compton's Cafeteria riot but also to call attention to the multiple normativizing frames of reference that kept the Compton's story "hidden in plain sight" for so long—the confluence of class, race, and gender considerations, as well as the homonormative gaze that did not construct transgender subjects, actions, embodiments, or intentions as the objects of its desire. I wanted, too, to make methodologically explicit the critical role of embodied difference in the practice of archival research. As a range of new scholarship on the recent so-called archival turn in the humanities begins to make evident, embodiment—that contingent accomplishment through which the histories of our identities become invested in our corporeal space—not only animates the research query but modulates access to the archive, in both its physical and its intellectual arrangement. Discussing how my transsexual embodiment figured into reading a gay and lesbian archive against the grain served the larger purpose of calling critical attention to homonormative constructions of knowledge embedded in the content and organization of the archive itself. My goal was to offer a radical critique not just of historiography but of the political epistemology of historical knowledge production.

Because the tone of what I proposed was deemed "personal," however, due to how I situated my own research activities as part of the narrative, and because, I suspect, I tend to work outside the academy, I was invited to contribute an essay to either the "Reflections" or "Public History" section of *Radical History Review*, rather than a feature article. I felt some reservations in doing so because my intent had been to do something else. "Reflections" are not as intellectually rigorous as the documented arguments expected in feature articles, and "Public History," as distinguished from what academic historians do, can come off as a form of popularization in which knowledge produced by specialists is transmitted to the consuming masses through less intellectually accomplished intermediaries. The journal's own division of knowledge into "less formal" and "more formal" categories, and the positioning of my work within this two-tiered economy, would replicate the very hierarchies I had set out to critique by containing what I had to say within a structurally less legitimated space.

The most basic act of normativizing disciplinarity at work here is not directly related to the increasingly comfortable fit between gender-normative homosexuality and neoliberal policy. It is rooted in a more fundamental and culturally pervasive disavowal of intrinsically diverse modes of bodily being as the lived ground of all knowing and of all knowledge production. In an epistemological regime structured by the subject-object split, the bodily situatedness of knowing becomes divorced from the status of formally legitimated objective knowledge; experiential knowledge of the material effects of one's own antinormative bodily difference on the production and reception of what one knows consequently becomes delegitimated as merely subjective. This in turn circumscribes the radical potential of that knowledge to critique other knowledge produced from other bodily locations, equally partial and contingent, which have been vested with the prerogatives of a normativity variously figured as white, masculinist, heterosexist, or Eurocentric—as feminism, communities of color, and third world voices have long maintained, and as the disabled, intersexed, and transgendered increasingly contend.

The peculiar excitement of academic humanities work at this moment in time lies, in my estimation, in the potential of interdisciplinary critical work to produce new strategies through which disruptive knowledges can dislodge the privileges of normativity. Breaking "personal voice" away from the taint of "mere" subjective reflection, and recuperating embodied knowing as a formally legitimated basis of knowledge production, is one such disruptive strategy. Deploying disciplinary distinctions that foreclose this possibility is not. But that is precisely why the opportunity provided by the editors of this volume for my words to occupy these pages under the heading of an "Intervention" was ultimately such a welcome one. In the end, it has enabled the critique I intended to offer all along, albeit not in the form or manner I initially proposed, while opening up the space to push the argument one turn further.

Homonormativity, I conclude, is more than an accommodation to neoliberalism in its macropolitical manifestations. It is also an operation at the micropolitical level, one that aligns gay interests with dominant constructions of knowledge and power that disqualify the very modes of knowing threatening to disrupt the smooth functioning of normative space and that displace modes of embodiment calling into question the basis of authority from which normative voices speak. Because transgender phenomena unsettle the categories on which the normative sexualities depend, their articulation can offer compelling opportunities for contesting the expansion of neoliberalism's purview through homonormative strategies of minority assimilation. And yet, even well-intentioned antihomonormative critical practices that take aim at neoliberalism can fall short of their goal when they fail to adequately account for the destabilizing, cross-cutting differences within sexual categories that transgender issues represent. Such critical practices can function in unintentionally homonormative ways that circumvent and circumscribe, rather than amplify, the radical potential of transgender phenomena to profoundly disturb the normative — even in so seemingly small a thing as where an article gets placed in a journal. Creating a proper space for radical transgender scholarship, in the double sense of scholarship on transgender issues and of work by transgender scholars, should be a vital part of any radically antinormative intellectual and political agenda.

Notes

1. Lisa Duggan, *The Twilight of Equality? Neoliberalism, Cultural Politics, and the Attack on Democracy* (Boston: Beacon, 2003), 50.
2. Judith Halberstam, *Female Masculinity* (Durham, NC: Duke University Press, 1998), 9.
3. I posted an earlier version of these observations on the genealogy of *homonormative* on qstudy-lL@listserv.buffalo.edu, November 7, 2006.
4. Robert Hill, personal communication, October 6, 2005; see also Robert Hill, *A Social History of Heterosexual Transvestism in Cold War America* (PhD diss., University of Michigan at Ann Arbor, 2007).
5. I have made this argument elsewhere; see Susan Stryker, "The Transgender Issue: An Introduction," *GLQ* 4 (1998): 149–53; Susan Stryker, "Transgender Studies: Queer Theory's Evil Twin," *GLQ* 10 (2004): 212–15; and Susan Stryker, "(De)Subjugated Knowledges: An Introduction to Transgender Studies," in *The Transgender Studies Reader*, ed. Susan Stryker and Stephen Whittle (New York: Routledge, 2006), 4–8. On Feinberg's use of "transgender," see Leslie Feinberg, *Transgender Liberation: A Movement Whose Time Has Come* (New York: *World View Forum*, 1992); reprinted in Stryker and Whittle, *Transgender Studies*

Reader, 205–20. On page 206, Feinberg, after listing a variety of what s/he terms "gender outlaws," that is, "transvestites, transsexuals, drag queens and drag kings, cross-dressers, bull-daggers, stone butches, androgynes, diesel dykes," notes that "we didn't choose these words" and that "they don't fit all of us." Because "it's hard to fight an oppression without a name connoting pride," s/he proposes "transgender" to name "a diverse group of people who define ourselves in many different ways." While acknowledging that this term itself may prove inadequate or short-lived, s/he intends for it to be "a tool to battle bigotry and brutality" and hopes that "it can connect us, that it can capture what is similar about the oppressions that we endure."

6.   Ann Ogborn, interview by the author, July 5, 1998, Oakland, California.

7.   Gerard Koskovich, an early member of Queer Nation–San Francisco, recalls "lively critiques regarding the group's awareness and inclusiveness regarding transgender and bisexual issues." He writes: "I recall a telling incident at one of the earliest QN meetings that I attended: A lesbian in her early 30s made comments to the general meeting to the effect that she didn't appreciate gay men wearing drag, an act that she portrayed as an expression of misogyny—in short, she offered an old-school lesbian-feminist reading. This led to a group discussion of the uses of drag as a critique of gender norms—a discussion that ultimately changed the woman's mind. That early anti-drag moment quickly gave way to Queer National celebrating personal styles that transgressed gender norms in various ways—a phenomenon that fit well with the in-your-face politics of representation that drove many QN actions." Personal communication, December 8, 2006.

8.   David Valentine, "I Went to Bed with My Own Kind Once: The Erasure of Desire in the Name of Identity," *Language and Communication* 23 (2003): 123–38; David Valentine, "The Categories Themselves," *GLQ* 10 (2003): 215–20.

9.   Friedrich Nietzsche, "On the Use and Abuse of History for Life," 1874, trans. Ian C. Johnson, www.geocities.com/thenietzschechannel/history.htm (accessed May 12, 2007).

10.   John D'Emilio, *Sexual Politics, Sexual Communities: The Making of a Homosexual Minority in the United States, 1940–1970* (Chicago: University of Chicago Press, 1983); Elizabeth Armstrong, *Forging Gay Identity: Organizing Sexuality in San Francisco, 1950–1994* (Chicago: University of Chicago Press, 2002), Nan Alamilla Boyd, *Wide Open Town: A History of Queer San Francisco to 1965* (Berkeley: University of California Press, 2003); Martin Meeker, *Contacts Desired: Gay and Lesbian Communications and Community, 1940s–1970s* (Chicago: University of Chicago Press, 2006); Marcia Gallo, *Different Daughters: A History of the Daughters of Bilitis and the Rise of the Lesbian Rights Movement* (New York: Carroll and Graf, 2006).

11.   Joanne Meyerowitz, *How Sex Changed: A History of Transsexuality in the United States* (Cambridge, MA: Harvard University Press, 2002), 176–85.

12.   Raymond Broshears, "History of Christopher Street West—SF," *Gay Pride: The Official Voice of the Christopher Street West Parade '72 Committee of San Francisco, California*, June 25, 1972, 8.

13.   *Screaming Queens: The Riot at Compton's Cafeteria*, dir. Victor Silverman and Susan Stryker (Independent Television Service/KQED-TV, 2005); Susan Stryker, "The Compton's Cafeteria Riot of 1966: The Radical Roots of the Contemporary Transgender Movement," *Critical Moment*, no. 12 (2005): 5, 19. Susan Stryker, "'The Riot at Compton's Cafeteria: Coming Soon to a Theater Near You!" *Transgender Tapestry*, no. 105 (2004): 46–47; Mack Friedman, *Strapped for Cash: A History of American Hustler Culture* (Los Angeles: Alyson, 2003) 129–33; David Carter, *Stonewall: The Riots That Sparked the Gay Revolution* (New York: St. Martin's, 2004), 109–10.

14. Members of the Gay and Lesbian Historical Society, "MTF Transgender Activism in San Francisco's Tenderloin: Commentary and Interview with Elliot Blackstone," *GLQ* 4 (1998): 349–72; Elizabeth Armstrong and Suzanna Crage, "Movements and Memory: The Making of the Stonewall Myth," *American Sociological Review* 71 (2006): 724–51; see also Meyerowitz, *How Sex Changed*, 229.

15. Michel Foucault, *Society Must Be Defended: Lectures at the College de France, 1975–1976*, trans. David Macey (New York: Picador, 2003), 7–8.

Administering Sexuality;
or, The Will to Institutionality

Roderick A. Ferguson

What changes does a mode of difference undergo in administrative contexts? What is the nature of those transformations when "the administrative" defines not only discrete institutions but an entire historical ethos? What contortions does sexuality, in particular, suffer while passing through institutional realms? These questions, for me, undergird every analysis of what we have come to name "homonormativity," an analysis whose purview presumes an unpacking of the metastases of institutional affirmation, recognition, and legibility.

We can begin to assemble such a critique by reviewing Michel Foucault's theorizations of power and sexuality, by ruminating a little on well-trodden territory. In the first volume of *The History of Sexuality*, Foucault retheorizes power as a potentially productive rather than exclusively negative force. Power is not only that which says "no." For Foucault, power is also that which says, "Yes, tell me more. Yes, say that. Say that and say much more than that." Power is that which speaks in the affirmative. Foucault elaborates on this aspect of power and its appeal to subjects in an interview entitled "Truth and Power": "If power were never anything but repressive, if it never did anything but to say no, do you really think one would be brought to obey it? What makes power hold good, what makes it accepted, is simply the fact that it doesn't only weigh on us as a force that says no, but that it traverses and produces things, it induces pleasure, forms knowledge, produces discourse."[1] By linking power and knowledge through their affirmative properties, Foucault argues that the

Radical History Review
Issue 100 (Winter 2008)   DOI 10.1215/01636545-2007-027
© 2008 by MARHO: The Radical Historians' Organization, Inc.

modern subject invites power, in part, because of power's productive qualities. In sum, the modern subject, constituted by power, speaks in the affirmative.

The History of the Sexuality was originally entitled, in the French version, *The Will to Know*. It seems to me that this distinction is significant beyond the semantic differences of what American and French publishers consider a more marketable name. The French title reminds us that, for Foucault, sexuality was not an object to analyze in and of itself but a reason to assess the productive and discursive nature of power—power realized through knowledge, as well as power realized through the *desire* for knowledge. Moreover, for Foucault, sexuality also referred to manifestations and mutations of power. It is this sense of sexuality-as-power that I want to retain in an analysis of institutionality, particularly that of the university. That is, I want to examine how sexuality as an artifact of power and knowledge serves a way of assessing the forms of power deployed by the university in the current historical moment.

The critical scholarship on the university theorizes power within the contemporary setting as emanating from and culminating in administrative arrangements. Indeed, in the humanities and particularly within cultural studies, this critique has been most famously advanced by the literary scholar and cultural theorist Bill Readings in *The University in Ruins* (1996). For Readings, the crisis of the university can be seen in the increased ascendancy of the administrator and the resulting displacement of the scholar/professor. Applying Jacques Barzun's *The American University: How It Runs, Where It Is Going* as an unfortunately prophetic text, Readings states, "The central figure of the University is no longer the professor who is both scholar and teacher but the provost to whom both these apparatchiks and the professors are unanswerable. . . . Barzun has realized what kind of liberal individual it is that must embody the new University. The administrator will have been a student and a professor in his time, of course, but the challenge of the contemporary university is a challenge addressed to him as administrator."[2] In this narrative of maturation, the student becomes a professor who evolves into the administrator and assumes stewardship of the university toward its latest historical incarnation. In possessing a greater degree of influence, force, and power than the scholar, the administrator has the kind of managerial and economic profile appropriate for the contemporary moment of globalization. Readings also addresses the rhetorical power of the category of "excellence" deployed by administrators as an institutional mode: "'Excellence' . . . functions to allow the university to understand itself solely in terms of corporate administration. . . . This primarily administrative approach is explicitly situated as a result of the University's need to 'become part of the international scene.' Globalization requires that 'greater attention is given to administration' in order to permit the integration of the market in knowledge."[3] While the American academy has always been influenced by market forces,[4] the administrative transformation of the university, and the infiltration of administrative regimes into virtually all sectors of university life — both large and small, both structural and corporeal — is propelled by unprecedented social and economic processes. As Sheila Slaughter and Larry Leslie argue in *Academic Capitalism: Politics, Policies, and the Entrepreneurial University*, "During the second half of the twentieth century, professors, like other professionals, gradually became more involved in the market. . . . In the 1980's globalization accelerated the movement of faculty and universities toward the market."[5] Multinational corporations emerged in the 1970s and 1980s at the moment that industrialized countries began to lose market share to Pacific Rim competitors (6). To compensate for such losses, such corporations made more and more claims on public monies, diverting funds away from entitlement programs, social services, and public education. In addition, multinational corporations began to "devote more resources to the enhancement and management of innovation so that corporations and the nations in which they were headquartered could compete more successfully in the world markets" (7). As Slaughter and Leslie contend, a "quiet revolution . . . has taken place. Within public research universities, fewer and fewer funds are devoted to instruction and more and more to research and other endeavors that increase institutional ability to win external funds" (12). Hence much of the research on the entrepreneurial transformation of the Western university corroborates Reading's analysis of the spread of an administrative ethos that nurtures market tendencies within the university.

But there is a troubling aspect to Readings's critique, particularly for those of us interested in race, gender, and sexuality as social processes constituting the contemporary university. For instance, Readings makes the following claim about the roles of culture and difference in the administrative university: "[Since] the nation-state is no longer the primary instance of the reproduction of global capitals, 'culture' — as the symbolic and political counterpart to the project of integration pursued by the nation-state — has lost its purchase. The nation-state and the modern notion of culture arose together, and they are . . . ceasing to be essential to an increasingly transnational global economy."[6] Readings assumes here that culture belongs to the national and thus emanates from the global imperial formations in which nations determine cultural institutions, identities, and markets. Thus as contemporary globalization declares its identity through economic processes that weaken and dilute national authority, those same forces — for Readings — dilute and weaken the significance of culture. In terms of the university, Readings argues that

the University no longer has to safeguard and propagate national culture, because the nation-state is no longer the major site at which capital reproduces itself. Hence, the idea of national culture no longer functions as an external referent toward which all of the efforts of research and teaching are directed. The idea of national culture no longer provides an overarching ideological meaning for what goes on in the University, and as a result, what exactly gets taught or produced as knowledge matters less and less.[7]

Readings argues that as contemporary globalization—signified through the birth of multinational corporations and global markets—undermines nationalism, culture no longer has any ground to stand on and must consign itself to insignificance within the university. Culture, in this formulation, is not hegemonic in any way, and is useless as a mode of ideological struggle precisely because its nationalist foundation is no longer operational.

     We might contrast Readings's uses of globalization and culture with that of Stuart Hall. In his essay "The Local and the Global," Hall writes,

> I simply do not believe in the notion of globalization as a noncontradictory, uncontested space in which everything is fully within the keeping of institutions that know where globalization is going. I think the story points to something else: that in order to maintain its global position, capital has had to negotiate, has had to incorporate and partly reflect the differences it was trying to overcome. It has had to try to get hold of, and neutralize, to some degree, the differences. It is trying to constitute a world in which things are different. Some seem to take pleasure in that, but, for capital, in the end, the differences do not matter.[8]

Unlike Readings, Hall presumes that culture and difference are not simply exhausted by institutions under globalization. Instead, Hall argues that the forces of globalization are in constant negotiations with difference in an attempt to ingest it. While culture for Readings signifies that which globalization nullifies to such an extent that it provides no possibility for critical ruptures, for Hall culture and difference are pursued by global systems of commodification precisely because they have the capacity for rupture. Within a global capitalist system, the commodification of difference produces new forms of critique and agency, or, as he says, "new subjects, new genders, new ethnicities, new regions, and new communities."[9]

     In what ways has the modern university, as the sometimes sycophant of contemporary globalization, attempted to negotiate, incorporate, and reflect the differences that it was trying to overcome? Put another way, how does global capital's commodification of difference intersect with the commodification of difference in the contemporary university? Might the university intersect with corporate capital not only through self-congratulatory categories such as "excellence" but also through the attempt to incorporate and thereby neutralize difference? After Hall, we might ask ourselves: To what trials do the university and administrative power subject forms of difference? And how might we provide a chronicle of those trials?

     Determining the relationship of sexuality to administrative power means that we must first attempt to trace a genealogy of the incorporation of institutionally anterior forms of difference. As Chandra Mohanty argues,

The origins of black, ethnic, and women's studies programs, unlike those of
most academic disciplines can be traced to oppositional social movements. . . .
Between 1966 and 1970 most American colleges and universities added courses
on Afro-American experience and history to their curricula. This was the direct
outcome of a number of sociohistorical factors, not the least of which was an
increase in black student enrollment in higher education and a broad-based call
for a transformation of a racist, Eurocentric curriculum.[10]

Mohanty goes on to argue that the university responded to those social movements
by increasing black student enrollment and calling for curricular transformations
that rendered race and gender as individualized matters rather than as structural or
institutional ones. She writes:

Any inroads made by such programs and departments in the seventies are
being slowly undermined in the eighties and the nineties by the management
of race through attitudinal and behavioral strategies, with their logical
dependence on individuals seen as appropriate representatives of their race or
some other equivalent political constituency. Race and gender are reformulated
as individual characteristics and attitudes, and thus an individualized,
ostensibly unmarked discourse of difference is being put into place. This shift
in the academic discourse on gender and race actually rolls back any progress
that has been made in carving out institutional spaces for women's and black
studies programs and departments.[11]

If contemporary globalization, as Hall argues, incorporates differences as a way to
neutralize any ruptural possibilities, we might say that the administrative university
unmarks and reabsorbs difference, one of the familiar imprints of globalization. We
can think of this moment as unleashing a new mode of power, one characterized
generally by the commodification of difference as part of an emergent global capital,
and specifically as part of the university's own efforts to incorporate and commodify
differences of race and gender. We might even think of the historical formations
that Mohanty discusses as part of the moment in which — to use Hall's words — contemporary capital tries to "get hold of and neutralize difference." If neoliberalism,
as Lisa Duggan defines it, represents the forcible curtailment of liberal, left-liberal,
and leftist social movements of the 1960s and 1970s, then neoliberalism can be
understood as a component of those historic processes that attempt to "get hold of
and neutralize difference."[12] Indeed, we might think of neoliberalism as the latest
expression of contemporary globalization's effort to cannibalize difference and its
potential for rupture. In such a context and with regard to the academy, differences
that were often articulated as critiques of the presumed benevolence of political and
economic institutions become absorbed within an administrative ethos that recast

those differences as testaments to the progress of the university and the resuscitation of a common national culture.

The historic arc that begins in the late 1960s signifies a profound change within modern institutions in the West. Administrative power had to restrict the collective, oppositional, and redistributive aims of difference at the same time that administrative power had to affirm difference to demonstrate institutional protocols and progress. We must read this affirmation as not simply a moment of encouragement but as a moment of subjugation. As the university affirms forms of difference, what histories and critical capacities will it attempt to conceal or try to overcome? As power has negotiated and incorporated differences, it has also developed and deployed a calculus by which to determine the specific critical and ruptural capacities of those forms of difference. We may call this incorporation of modes of difference and the calculus that seeks to determine the properties and functions of those modes *as a will to institutionality.* The will to institutionality not only absorbs institutions and modern subjects; it is itself a mode of subjection as well. We might consider this rumination on administrative power in relation to Judith Butler's observation in *The Psychic Life of Power* that " 'subjection' signifies the process of becoming subordinated by power as well as the process of becoming a subject."[13]

Discussing sexuality as a complex apparatus of truth-seeking and truth-producing practices, Foucault writes, "[Nearly] one hundred and fifty years have gone into the making of a complex machinery for producing true discourses of sex: a deployment that spans a wide segment of history in that it connects the ancient injunction of confession to clinical listening methods. It is this deployment that enables something called sexuality to embody the truth of sex and its pleasures."[14] As part of that "complex machinery for producing true discourses of sex," sexuality is thus a discursive effect. As the linchpin between "ancient injunctions of confession" and "clinical listening methods," sexuality accounts for the discursive outlines of practices geared toward extracting the truth of sex and gauging the pleasures presumably embodied in it.[15] In other words, Foucault's revision of power exposes its affirmative rather than repressive itineraries. Similarly, we might argue that sexuality is part of administrative power's affirmative posture as well. What particular calculus has power applied to sexuality to discern and neutralize its ruptural possibilities? As Foucault notes, sexuality has been as easily located in the religious arena of the church as it has been in the secular arena of modern epistemes. Now we are in a moment in which sexuality finds itself within the realm of administration.

To illustrate this point, we might examine the text of a memo written in 1997 by Richard Atkinson, then the president of the University of California (UC) system, to the UC's board of regents on the topic of "limited domestic partner benefits." The memo begins by stating that

The first prerequisite would be to meet the University's definition of domestic partner—an unmarried partner of the same sex as the University employee who is eligible for benefits. In addition, both partners must be at least 18 years of age; unmarried to any other person and uncommitted to any other domestic partner; not related by blood to a degree of closeness that would prohibit legal marriage in California; living together in a long-term relationship of indefinite duration with an exclusive mutual commitment similar to that of a marriage; and financially responsible for each other's well-being and for each other's debts to third parties.[16]

We can think of this section of the memo as emblematic of the ways in which sexuality is incorporated into the structural logic of the university. In the language of Gayle Rubin's essay "Thinking Sex: Notes for a Radical Theory of the Politics of Sexuality" (1984), those queers who can conform to the requirements of the memo "are rewarded with certified mental health, respectability, legality, social and physical mobility, institutional support, and material benefits."[17] That incorporation, that recognition, indexes the subjugation of a whole diversity of sexual practices and subjectivities—transsexuality, nonmonogamy, cross-generational intimacies, endogamous and nondomiciled relationships, to name but a few—to the privileges of normative and socially sanctioned domestic practices. In doing so, the memo works to marginalize the very queer subcultures that worked to alienate gender and sexual normativity.

The administrative memo also becomes a site for the emergence and recognition of homosexuality. Indeed, the second prerequisite requires would-be domestic partners to "sign and file with the University an affidavit declaring that the abovementioned conditions have been met and that the partners have shared a common residence for at least twelve consecutive months. The third prerequisite would be to supply documentary proof of mutual financial support." With this documentary proof of mutual financial support, the legitimacy of domestic partnerships is determined according to their participation in market processes. The domestic partnership memo thus becomes a crucial element within the entrepreneurial and administrative ethos that characterizes contemporary Western universities.

As an appeal for recognition and legitimacy, we might also situate the memo within what Martin Manalansan refers to as "gay and lesbian transnational politics."[18] In his article "In the Shadows of Stonewall: Examining Gay Transnational Politics and the Gay Diasporic Dilemma" (1997), Manalansan discusses the ways in which international gay and lesbian social movements make appeals for recognition through constructions of gay and lesbian identity as "'out,' 'politicized,' [and] 'modern . . . ,'"[19] a construction that racializes non-Western and subaltern queer practices and identities as premodern and backward. As "In the Shadows of Stonewall" suggests, queer appeals for recognition and legitimacy in the contemporary moment are always articulated globally as well as nationally. Thus we might understand the memo not simply as a local and national declaration of same-sex recognition but as part of a global constellation in which queerness seeks to attain status as a modern and normative mode of difference. And in doing so, queerness becomes the engine for a series of exclusions and alienations, particularly around class, gender, and race.

In its performative stipulations, the memo resembles not so much the genre of the confession but the terms of the psychoanalytic encounter between the analyst and the analysand. Like these two encounters theorized in the first volume of *The History of Sexuality*, the Atkinson memo is a procedure for telling the "truth" of sexuality. But unlike the confession and the psychoanalytic encounter, this decla-ration is not necessarily for the production of a *scientia sexualis* to "constitute the 'political economy' of a will to knowledge" but for an *administrative sexualis* geared to a form of institutionality/power. [20] The will to institutionality names the processes by which sexuality becomes claimed by administrative realms and protocols.

Such a claim is just one instantiation of contemporary globalization's inges-tion of forms of difference. Again, as Hall argues, contemporary globalization can-not simply be grasped as a purely economic phenomenon but indeed as one that attempts to rule through culture and difference. As Hall and Mohanty suggest, we can also think of the historical moment in which difference became a commodity of capital and of the corporate university as the moment in which a new type of aca-demic subject came into being, one that spoke in terms of the institutionalization of difference. The reasons for that institutionalization varied, but most often it hinged on the promise of permanence. Modes of inquiry and histories of difference that were once threatened with extinction, existing only as ephemera, would now enjoy the consistency and reliability that the institutional form could presumably offer. The demand for the institutionalization of difference requires subjects that treat the administration as a matter of the libido. As Foucault wrote, paraphrasing Friedrich Nietzsche, "the desire for [institutionality] has been transformed among us into a passion which fears no sacrifice, which fears nothing but its own extinction."[21] This subject's agency depends on the very administrative forms of power that manage and commodify forms of difference.

This is the historical, political, and ideological context in which queerness enters the landscape of modern academic institutions. The administrative univer-sity adapts to modes of difference by attempting to normalize them. Inasmuch as the grammar for queerness's incorporation into the administrative university is derived from the university's incorporation of race and gender, understanding the procedures by which queerness is brought into the administrative ethos means that we have to comprehend both the administrative management of race and gen-der and theorize and the relation of those forms of difference to queerness as an administrative object. This is the political economy that queerness — as a mode of embodiment and as a mode of critique — must negotiate. We are now in a moment in which we must analyze sexuality and other modes of difference as effects of a will to institutionality.

We might in fact read Foucault's early theorizations about discourses as theorizations about institutions and their exploitation of discourses. For instance, in "The Discourse on Language," a lecture that he gave at the College de France on December 2, 1970, Foucault begins by addressing the relationship between knowledge and institutions:

Inclination speaks out: "I don't want to have to enter this risky world of discourse; I want nothing to do with it insofar as it is decisive and final; I would like to feel it all around me, calm and transparent, profound, infinitely open, with others responding to my expectations, and truth emerging, one by one. All I want is to allow myself to be borne along, within it, and by it, a happy wreck." Institutions reply: "But you have nothing to fear from launching out; we're here to show you discourse is within the established order of things, that we've waited a long time for its arrival, that a place has been set aside for it — a place which both honors and disarms it; and if it should happen to have a certain power, then it is we, and we alone, who give it that power."[22]

Foucault begins with the subject that is anxious about the unruly and disobedient nature of discourse, its penchant to steal away from human intentions. The subject desperately wishes for the innocence of discourse and for the promise of truth. The voice of comfort comes from the institution, telling the subject that discourse will bend to human agency and institutional protocols. Under the will to knowledge, the institution arises as that which will help the subject produce and tame discourse. And so we have the narrative of the rational and authoritative subject and of the artifact known as truth — the dramatis personae and the central props that comprise the will to knowledge. As Foucault states, "this will to truth . . . relies on institutional support: it is both reinforced and accompanied by whole strata of practices such as pedagogy — naturally — the book system, publishing, libraries, such as the learned societies in the past, and laboratories today" (219).

Foucault argues that the will to truth and the will to knowledge depend on a distinction between reason and folly or evidence and falsehood. This distinction has several functions. First, it becomes the organizing principle of discourse — think here of the argument that sexuality constitutes the "ultimate" truth of the individual. The distinction also operates as a system of exclusion, admitting only those forms of knowledge that operate under a will to truth and excluding those subject and social formations marked as irrational. In addition, the division between truth and untruth works to conceal the very thing that it constitutes. As Foucault states, "The will to truth, having imposed itself upon us for so long, is such that the truth it seeks to reveal cannot fail to mask it . . . thus only one truth appears before our eyes; wealth, fertility, and sweet strength in all its insidious universality. In contrast we are unaware of the prodigious machinery of the will to truth, with its vocation of exclusion" (220).

The will to truth was constituted in the eighteenth century, a historical moment organized around the discourses of universal humanism, homogeneity, and canonicity. But what world, exactly, has come into being in the poststructuralist era of feminist theory, ethnic studies, postcolonial studies, queer theory, and other forms of identity politics–engaged scholarship and activism? One could argue that the will to institutionality among groups and communities associated with difference emerged precisely after the critical upheavals of race, gender, and sexuality of the post–civil rights era. But what is the machinery of this will to institutionality? We might say that the will to institutionality is founded on divisions between legitimacy and illegitimacy. For example, capital and the academy have to work through and with difference in the global moment if they can claim any integrity at all. The will to institutionality also seems to presume another distinction — that between the promise of formality and the presumed ephemeral nature of informality. Formalizing certain forms of difference gives those forms permanence and institutional protection, and will lift difference from the netherworld of marginalization and informal curiosity. The will to knowledge, according to Foucault, obliges discourse to truth. That obligation represents an engagement with institutionality as well. In "The Discourse on Language," Foucault states, "education may be, as of right, the instrument whereby every individual, in a society like our own, can gain access to any kind of discourse. But we well know that in its distribution, in what it permits and in what it prevents, it follows the well-trodden battle-lines of social conflict. Every educational system is a political means of maintaining or of modifying the appropriation of a discourse, with the knowledge and the powers it carries with it" (227).

What positions, functions, and viewpoints does the will to institutionality impose on modern subjects? And how does the genealogy of institutional incorporation become the horizon for determining the useful and the effective? Put simply, how is it that we understand agency in terms of our ability to formalize knowledge and thus incorporate it into academic institutions? How did the desire for institutionalization become the common denominator for subjects differentiated in terms of gender, race, sexuality, and ideology? As knowledge is obliged to institutionalization under the will to institutionality, by what routes does the subject of knowledge become the subject of administration? By what genealogy can we understand institutionalization as the affirmation of difference and thus analyze the will to institutionality as power's most recent enactment?

We must pause and interrogate the subtle and silent transformations that the tasks of knowledge and we — the subjects of knowledge — have undergone. We must also scrutinize this will to institutionality if we are to create alternative forms of agency and subjectivity not beholden to bureaucratization. We are now in a moment in which institutionalization is the standard of the evolved and developed critical subject. What would it mean to maneuver and retheorize genealogy to make sense of the subject who understands its progress through institutionalization? If genealogy is a form of history that can account for the constitution of knowledges, discourses, and domains of objects, how can we make genealogy into a form of history that can account for the institutionalization of knowledge, modes of difference, and critical agency? Put simply, by what countercalculus can we maneuver difference for the purposes of rupture?

Notes

1. Michel Foucault, *Power/Knowledge: Selected Interviews and Writings, 1972–1977* (New York: Pantheon, 1980), 119.
2. Bill Readings, *The University in Ruins* (Cambridge, MA: Harvard University Press, 1996), 8.
3. Ibid., 29.
4. See, for instance, Christopher Newfield's deeply insightful book *Ivy and Industry: Business and the Making of the American University, 1880–1980* (Durham, NC: Duke University Press, 2003).
5. Sheila Slaughter and Larry Leslie, *Academic Capitalism: Politics, Policies, and the Entrepreneurial University* (Baltimore: Johns Hopkins University Press, 1997), 5.
6. Bill Readings, *The University in Ruins* (Cambridge, MA: Harvard University Press, 1996), 13.
7. Ibid.
8. Stuart Hall, "The Local and the Global," in *Dangerous Liaisons: Gender, Nation, and Postcolonial Perspectives*, ed. Anne McClintock, Aamir Mufti, and Ella Shohat (Minneapolis: University of Minnesota Press, 1997), 182.
9. Ibid., 183.
10. Chandra Talpade Mohanty, "On Race and Voice: Challenges for Liberal Education in the 1990s," in *Beyond a Dream Deferred: Multicultural Education and the Politics of Excellence*, ed. Becky Thompson and Sangeeta Tyagi (Minneapolis: University of Minnesota Press, 1993), 46.
11. Ibid., 58.
12. See Lisa Duggan, *The Twilight of Equality? Neoliberalism, Cultural Politics, and the Attack on Democracy* (Boston: Beacon, 2003).
13. Judith Butler, *The Psychic Life of Power: Theories in Subjection* (Stanford, CA: Stanford University Press, 1997), 2.
14. Michel Foucault, *The History of Sexuality: An Introduction*, vol. 1, trans. Robert Hurley (New York: Random House, 1978), 68.
15. Ibid.
16. For a complete text of the memo, see psychology.ucdavis.edu/rainbow/html/dp-atkinson.html (accessed May 16, 2007).
17. Gayle S. Rubin, "Thinking Sex: Notes for a Radical Theory of the Politics of Sexuality," 1984, in *The Lesbian and Gay Studies Reader*, ed. Henry Abelove, Michèle Aina Barale, and David M. Halperin (New York: Routledge, 1993), 12.

18. Martin F. Manalansan, "In the Shadows of Stonewall: Examining Gay Transnational Politics and the Gay Diasporic Dilemma," in *The Politics of Culture in the Shadow of Capital*, ed. Lisa Lowe and David Lloyd (Durham, NC: Duke University Press, 1997), 486.

19. Ibid., 487.

20. Foucault, *History of Sexuality*, 73.

21. Michel Foucault, "Nietzsche, Genealogy, History," in *Language, Counter-Memory, Practice: Selected Essays and Interviews*, ed. Donald Bouchard (Ithaca: Cornell University Press, 1977), 163.

22. Michel Foucault, *The Archaeology of Knowledge and the Discourse on Language*, trans. A. M. Sheridan Smith (New York: Pantheon, 1972), 215–16.

"Arab or leftist?" "Faggot." Cartoon taken from Front Homosexuel d'Action Révolutionnaire, *Rapport contre la normalité* (Paris: Champ Libre, 1971)

French Homonormativity and
the Commodification of the Arab Body

Maxime Cervulle

Not one of our words, not one of our gestures, not one of our attitudes, escapes
the rule that positions the individual as imprisoned by a (social or sexual) role,
possessed by what he thinks he owns, fascinated by the "object" of his desire in
the same way that we are all fascinated by *commodities*.
—Front Homosexuel d'Action Révolutionnaire (Homosexual Front for
Revolutionary Action), 1971

Many historians date the birth of the lesbian and gay movement in France to the
day in March 1971 when a group of activists in Paris disrupted the public recording
of Ménie Grégoire's radio program, the title of which was "The Painful Problem
of Homosexuality" ("L'homosexualité, ce douloureux problème"), screaming "Down
with the hetero-cops!"[1] This protest marked the moment when a still loosely formed
community of activists discovered its identity in action and, soon afterward, became
known as the FHAR, the Front Homosexuel d'Action Révolutionnaire (Homosexual
Front for Revolutionary Action). The formation of the group, which had originated as
the Pederastic Committee for Revolutionary Action (Comité d'Action Pédérastique
Révolutionnaire) during the Paris student riots of May 1968, signaled an unprecedented turning point in French sexual politics and has exerted enormous influence
on the subsequent development of lesbian and gay identity politics in France.

Yet despite its radical origins, the public voice of the FHAR has often been

Radical History Review
Issue 100 (Winter 2008)   DOI 10.1215/01636545-2007-028
© 2008 by MARHO: The Radical Historians' Organization, Inc.

a paradoxical one. At times inclusive, at times exclusive, it constitutes a primary historical base for contemporary French homonormativity since, like other French institutions, it is premised on the rhetoric of equality and also bound up in oppressive vectors of race, gender, and class. Indeed, one could argue that the FHAR paved the way as much for the assimilationist lesbian and gay movement as for the various queer anarchist and anticapitalist movements with which it is usually associated. Through a rereading of the main texts published by the FHAR, this essay's goal is to unsettle the subject that lay at the heart of the group's political action, the subject on which it based its radical demands. Tracing the roots of the homonormative already lurking within the FHAR's original texts enables us to examine its continuing influence within LGBTQ (lesbian, gay, bisexual, transgender, queer) politics in France today, and to destabilize the very subject position through which radical groups often make political demands (the deployment of the speaking position of "I" and "we") while simultaneously stifling other voices.

"We'll All Be Normal When You're All Homosexual!"

In the famous manifesto *Report against Normality* (*Rapport contre la normalité*), published in 1971, the FHAR positioned itself as a far-left revolutionary group fighting against the various regimes of the normal that oppress lesbians and gay men.[2] The group's analysis of the multiple vectors of surveillance, discipline, and repression (mainly contained in the figures of the hetero-cop and the homo-cop) described how capitalism, state regulation, and patriarchy were bound together in French political culture. The three elements, argued the FHAR, combined to constitute "normality," whereby homosexuals were forced either to conform (i.e., to identify publicly as heterosexual, hide their homosexuality, not identify as gay, not engage in same-sex relations, etc.) or else suffer confinement at the bottom of the social heap: "Along with women we are the moral doormat on which you wipe your conscience" (9).

For the FHAR, however, this pending process of normalization did not only constitute an external threat; the group's writings were also intended to bring to light the threat of normalization from within. Despite the explicit wish to organize the manifesto according to the group's various dissonant, multiple, and uncoordinated voices, a central thread appears to run through the text.[3] While the FHAR activists did strategize to combat the oppressions of women, workers, and people of color, the FHAR's main political catalyst was sexual oppression, which its members termed "fascist sexual normalcy" (11). The attention the FHAR paid to the sexual component of normalcy pushed to the margins other intersecting dynamics such as feminism, anticapitalism, and antiracism, thus excluding from its discursive frame subjects and groups whose political interests were not exclusively and primarily rooted in antihomophobic activism. Moreover, lesbian voices were relegated to a special chapter (entitled "Lesbians," 79–96) in which they were seemingly given no choice but to challenge the male-centered analysis, rhetoric, and political strategies deployed elsewhere in the book by the group's "fags." Even though FHAR had emerged out of a meeting of members of the MLF (the French Women's Liberation Movement, Mouvement de Libération des Femmes) and of the Pederastic Commit-tee of Revolutionary Action in May 1968—and, as the activist Anne-Marie Fauret argued in 1971, although the FHAR's commitment was established at the "intersec-tion of the women's and the gay liberation movements"—the political divergence between the lesbians and gay men led to a split in the movement.[4] Criticizing the theoretical abstraction of their "homosexual brothers" who only addressed other men (straight or gay), the FHAR's lesbians viewed patriarchy and "phallocentrism" as the main vectors of oppression, thus extending the scope of their combat beyond antihomophobia to all "women folk" (*le peuple des femmes*; 81). The lesbians left in April 1971 to form a separatist group called the Red Dykes (Les Gouines Rouges), whose members included, among others, Christine Delphy and Monique Wittig.

Likewise, despite the importance of the Marxist rhetoric to radical move-ments in France during the late 1960s and early 1970s, there is an apparent absence of lower-class voices in the FHAR's writings, a fact that is all the more striking considering that the FHAR constantly invoked the male proletariat to support its various arguments. These proletarian invocations can probably be understood not so much as a kind of "normalization" strategy for gays who wanted to be aligned with a certain kind of working-class masculinity, but rather as a discursive strategy to make the FHAR's claims more intelligible in a French political sphere mostly defined by the vocabulary of the revolutionary left. The *Rapport* asks, for example, "Do you have any idea of the difficulties of being in the closet for a young working-class gay man? You, who believe in the virtues of factory training, do you know what it's like to be treated as a faggot by your coworkers? We *do* know what it's like *because we know about it from one another*" (8–9; emphasis mine). Instead of putting forward a notion of experience in its conception of the modalities of oppression, the FHAR's gay male contingency instead privileged the idea of a homosexual people united in its condition. According to this logic, gay workers would not speak out in the name of their personal experiences but, instead, speak from the supposedly universal homosexual condition that united all gay men against all forms of sexual oppression. Broadly speaking, this was the message of the FHAR's article "Pour une concep-tion homosexuelle du monde" ("For a Homosexual Conception of the World,") in which it was apparent that far from working through multiple sites of oppression, or through the connections that cemented the relationship between capitalism and heterosexuality, the FHAR tended to prioritize sexuality above all else, therefore inadvertently maintaining privileged positions of class, gender, and race through the figure of the universal homosexual: "I think that a gay man is able to view the whole world, including the political world, in which he finds himself. It's precisely because he lives in acceptance of his own *singular* situation that he believes it to be universal; this is why we don't need revolutionary *generalities* or clichéd abstrac-

NOUS SOMMES PLUS DE 343 SALOPES

Nous nous sommes faits enculer par des arabes

NOUS EN SOMMES FIERS ET NOUS RECOMMENCERONS.
SIGNEZ ET FAITES *signer* AUTOUR DE VOUS

"We are more than 343 sluts. We've been fucked by Arabs. We're proud of it and we'll do it again. Sign and circulate this petition." Parody of the famous 1971 "Manifesto of the 343" circulated by French feminists who advocated legalizing abortion in France. Taken from Front Homosexuel d'Action Révolutionnaire, *Rapport contre la normalité* (Paris: Champ Libre, 1971)

tions" (73). This universal homosexuality rests obviously on Enlightenment rhetoric, a kind of normalization project in and of itself inasmuch as it erases the differences among homosexuals, therefore assuming all homosexuals to be equal in conditions, oppressions, and struggle. This minority version of the abstract French universal Republican model tends, as it still so relentlessly does, to wipe out race, class, and gender power differentials to the advantage of a normalized white male middle-class model of homosexuality.

Erotic Revolutions?

Even more surprising was the controversy over a fictional text contained in the *Rapport* and entitled "15 berges" ("Fifteen Years Old"), written by an underage boy who recounts picking up an Arab man on the banks of the Seine. The text blithely invokes stereotypes of Arab masculinity in a postcolonial France that still assumed its "immigrant workers" would one day be sent "home."[5] At the time, most immigrant workers were from North Africa, and particularly Algeria, a former French overseas colony.[6] Hypersexual, violent, rank, and threatening, the Arab man described here seems to embody every racist stereotype of Arabs circulating in the French cultural imagination of the period:

The guy I'm talking about had an ugly Arab mug, and let's put it this way, he didn't exactly smell of roses . . . , he tried coming on to the kid in the toilet. But it stank in there. . . . Smiling nastily, he stroked his dick. Love between men, what a load of shit. But the Arab bloke didn't give up—he tried to get the boy on his front, then spurted his oily come all over him, before turning nasty all of a sudden. He found the boy too obstinate. A good punch in the face and the fun was over like a shot. (102–3)

As this text was perceived as "racist by some nongay comrades" (104), it was followed by a brief response by members of the FHAR documenting their position on racism and their sexual relations with Arab men in particular. Apart from recognizing that French gay men are "*in one respect* racist" (104; emphasis mine) due to the surrounding climate of racism, the FHAR members claimed to feel a certain "solidarity as oppressed people with Arabs" (104). Even though the cliché of the "old European queer who picks up Arabs" is brushed aside on the pretext that "in France it is our Arab friends who fuck us and *never* the other way around" (104; emphasis mine), the possibility of a man of Arab descent identifying publicly as gay, or even joining the FHAR, is never considered. Likewise, since it seems inconceivable to the FHAR members that an Arab man might enjoy the sexually passive position, both homosexuality and sexual passivity become implicitly linked to whiteness, thereby conflating the sexually active position taken by Arab men with the privileges of heterosexuality and the other regimes of the normal imagined by the activists.

Curiously, even though one of the two collective manifesto statements that introduce the *Rapport* are addressed "to people like us" and call for the abolition of "active/passive role playing" (11), these same roles appear to structure the racial division of same-sex relations. If we take the FHAR's imagined gay subject as white and unable to imagine nonwhite homosexuality, then this attack on sexual roles would seem not to concern Arab men at all, but would serve instead to support the FHAR's belief that being fucked by Arab men might represent "our consensual revenge on Western colonization" (104), the ultimate gay challenge to the legacies of racism and imperialism. Clearly, it is important to read the obligatory division of sexual roles (in which the French partner is passive and the Arab partner active) alongside the so-called porno-trope of the nonwhite hypersexual stud embedded within French colonial (and postcolonial) culture.[7] This same porno-trope is reproduced in the famous FHAR petition that parodied the famous French feminist "Manifeste des 343 salopes" ("Manifesto of the 343 Sluts") in favor of abortion: "We are more than 343 sluts. We've been fucked by Arabs. We're proud of it, and we'll do it again. Sign and circulate this petition" (104).

The centrality of the white subject position and the erotic politics of the Arab body in French gay culture prefigure a form of commercial racism produced some years later that has since become central to French mainstream gay culture. In Jean-Daniel Cadinot's pornographic film *Harem* (1984), a cornerstone of gay male erotic production in France that led the way for a whole subgenre of "ethnic porn," a young white Frenchman traveling across Morocco is initiated into same-sex activity by the locals.[8] The sexual relations between white and Arab men seem to fit the model mapped out by the FHAR—the Arab men are systematically active, preferably aggressive, and decidedly well hung. *Harem* perfectly captures what Anne McClintock has judiciously termed "commodity racism," a spectacle in which race is commodified as an object of fascination.[9] But this surprising convergence of the FHAR's revolutionary political subject and Cadinot's sexual tourist also points to how the French gay subject has been historically inscribed within the capitalist flows of geographical, cultural, and erotic mobility by virtue of his positioning as "universal." The proximity between Cadinot and the 1970s revolutionary fags is such that, as Christian Fournier remarks, "*Harem* . . . seems to illustrate the famous FHAR manifesto claiming 'the right and the desire of French fags to go off and get laid in Morocco.'"[10]

    Harem promotes the concept of a political solidarity formed by dissident desire and activated by sexual relations in a manner not unlike that of Jean Genet, who self-consciously recognized the erotic significance of his political commitment to the Black Panthers in the 1960s. But while this model of sexual/political solidarity could potentially lead to an awareness of race, class, and gender as multiple sites of oppression, it does not allow for an *intersectional* account of such politics.[11] Caught between the politics of porn and the erotic charge of politics, the nonwhite subject is reduced to a body to be exploited by white pornographers and revolutionaries alike as both a sign and a mode of exchange, as both a battlefield and a playground. This reduction retrospectively reframes the FHAR's own "Manifesto of 343 Sluts": the Arab body is of exchange value between those white subjects who speak out and to whom the text is addressed, since the perceived political value of their action lies precisely in the act of sleeping with Arab men. Thus "gay pride" for these FHAR members meant a false transgression of white middle-class norms that, rather than questioning the commodification of Arab bodies, transforms it into a "necessary" sign of value for so-called revolutionary politics.

French Homonormativity: Back to the Future?

The FHAR's normative gay subject, co-opted a decade and a half later by ethnic porn's commercial production of a desire for difference, continues to lurk in the shadows of contemporary gay politics. One recent local instance that positions gay identity as white and middle-class has been the gay archive project in Paris—the Centre d'Archives et de Documentation Homosexuelles de Paris (CADHP, the Paris Center for Homosexual Archives and Documentation)—the development of which after six years of negotiations now seems to be at a dead end despite having been one of the electoral promises made by Betrand Delanoë, the openly gay socialist mayor of Paris. Initially, the CADHP overlooked the histories and lives of lesbians, trans people, sex workers, HIV-positive people, nonnationals living in France, and all nonwhite people. Social exclusions based on race, class, gender, and sero-status aimed to bolster the hegemonic reputation of the "gay ghetto" model of homosexual identity as typified locally by the denizens of Paris's Marais district. From 2002 onward, several activist groups and associations including ArchiQ, ArchiLesb, Vigitrans, LopattaQ, GayKitschCamp, and the Académie Gay et Lesbienne, denounced the homonormative politics of the AP-CADHP (Association de Préfiguration du Centre d'Archives et de Documentation Homosexuelles de Paris [Prefiguration Association for the Paris Center for Homosexual Archives and Documentation]), the group responsible for the implementation of the CADHP. The AP-CADHP claimed to take on board the activists' demands for a more inclusive project, but it simultaneously blocked any power-sharing initiative by denying them access to the scientific board that coordinated the Homo Archives. The activists argued for a collegial board of representatives to avoid the predictable stewardship by a white gay socialist, thus potentially allowing for the presence of other minorities — that is, transgender and intersexed people, and/or people of color — at the head of the board. While the AP-CADHP committee accepted and voted through this proposal, it subsequently chose to exclude the activists from all further meetings. While this almost exclusive focus on the lives of white middle-class gay men harks back to the position of the FHAR, there has been at least one significant change in the time between. The Arab body has quite simply disappeared from the political framework of gay assimilationist politics, appearing only as a domestic commodity that has been banished from the public sphere. There is no room for queers of color as speaking subjects; rather, they appear as erotic bodies in ethnic porn, in productions by the Dargos, Replay, and Jean-Noël René Clair studios, or else as suffering bodies called on to confess all on the set of the gay channel Pink TV.

It is vital that we resist the gravitational pull of the homonormative in community-based projects — even in commercial projects, like Pink TV, or in public projects, like the archives, that are ostensibly made "by us and for us." In contrast to the normative conception of the archive upheld by the CADHP's administrators — not

Cover image of *Harem* (dir. Jean-Daniel Cadinot, 1984), which arguably led the way for the subgenre of ethnic porn in France (French Art and Videovision)

to mention the CADHP's fixed, teleological, and naturalizing version of history — the group ArchiQ put forward (and continues to defend) a performative notion of the archive that, in the view of Marie-Hélène Bourcier, "understands the archive as not solely lodged in the past, or in the present — in 'immediate history,' but rather as belonging to the future. . . . This notion of performativity points to the operations the archive endures in order to exist and to the operations that map out its future, even if such operations are smartly disguised by the appointed experts."[12] How might we formulate a critical queer history that acknowledges its in-built Eurocentrism and whiteness and its biases of class and gender? How might we produce an archive of the archive, one that underlines certain tendencies toward invisibility and appropriation, such as the silencing of workers or Arabs in the FHAR's critical writings, which we might consider as an "auto-archive"? How might we produce an archive of the archivists? And ultimately, how might we produce, to borrow Bourcier's productive term, a "living archive," the autoreflexive and performative nature of which would allow us, as Michel Foucault suggested long ago, to archive the silences, the gaps, and the absences to resist the hegemonic regime of the current gay culture that seeks to normalize the history of sexual minorities and, in so doing, produces a white past and a white future?[13]

Notes

This article has been translated from the French by Nick Rees-Roberts. Thanks to David Serlin for his valuable comments on earlier versions of this essay, which is dedicated to Marco.

1. *Hetero-cop (hétéro-flic)* and *homo-cop (homo-flic)* were terms used by the FHAR to designate those, whether hetero or homo, who sought to regulate and police the field of sexuality and desire.

2. The title for this subsection of the essay is one of the FHAR's slogans, reproduced in FHAR, *Rapport contre la normalité: Le Front Homosexuel d'Action Révolutionnaire rassemble les pièces de son dossier d'accusation; Simple révolte ou début d'une révolution?* (Paris: Champ Libre, 1971), 4. Further citations from this book will be given parenthetically in the text.

3. "Some of these texts are theoretical or general; others are simply testimonies, none of which represents the FHAR as a whole, and some of which may be contradictory—they serve merely to represent our movement in its present state" (7).

4. Anne-Marie Fauret, "Homosexuels—elles, arrêtons de raser les murs : Lesbiennes et homosexuels . . . nous prenons la parole," *Tout ! Journal du groupe "Vive la Révolution,"* no. 12 (1971): 6.

5. As Thomas Deltombe and Mathieu Rigouste put it: "The reformulation of the split between a threatened [white French] identity and a threatening [Arab] otherness occurred when it became clear that the 'immigrants' who first appeared in the media in the 1970's, were destined to stay in France and that they were or inevitably would become 'French,' and therefore legally inseparable." In the 1970s, after the polemics surrounding the immigrant slums around Paris and the visibility of immigrant workers through the May 1968 strikes, the Arab became the French "enemy from within," soon to be invariably framed by the media as threatening to a "true French identity" unless fully "integrated," that is, divested of difference. Thomas Deltombe and Mathieu Rigouste, "L'ennemi intérieur: La construction médiatique de la figure de 'l'Arabe,'" in *La fracture coloniale: La société française au prisme de l'héritage colonial*, ed. Pascal Blanchard, Nicolas Bancel, and Sandrine Lemaire (Paris: La Découverte, 2005), 192.

6. As Michelle Zancarini-Fournel points out, in 1972 Algerians were the most numerous foreigners on French soil, with more than 720,000 people. Michelle Zancarini-Fournel,

"La question immigrée après 68," *Plein Droit*, no. 53–54 (2002), www.gisti.org/doc/plein-droit/53–54/question.html.

7. On the influence of this trope on contemporary French gay pornography, see Maxime Cervulle, "De l'articulation entre classe, race, genre et sexualité dans la pornographie 'ethnique,'" in *Études Culturelles et Cultural Studies*, ed. Bernard Darras (Paris: L'Harmattan, 2007), 221–28; and Maxime Cervulle, "Die Kings des Geschlechts und der Vorstadt: Frankoarabische Männlichkeitsperformanzen in Frankreich," in *Unbeschreiblich Männlich: Heteronormativitätskritische Perspektiven*, ed. Robin Bauer, Josch Hoenes, and Volker Wolsterdorff, trans. Volker Wolsterdorff (Hamburg: Männerschwarm Verlag, 2007), 230–44.

8. The expression *ethnic porn* is clearly problematic, defining as it does those films in which the bodies of Arabs, blacks, and ethnic others are eroticized while white bodies (including those of the assumed spectator) are implicitly nonethnic.

9. Anne McClintock, *Imperial Leather: Race, Gender, and Sexuality in the Colonial Context* (New York: Routledge, 1995), 16–17.

10. Christian Fournier, "Cadinot, Jean-Daniel," in *Dictionnaire de la pornographie*, ed. Phillipe Di Folco (Paris: Presses Universitaires de France, 2005), 71.

11. On intersectionality as a mode of theorizing a radical politics of social change, see Cathy J. Cohen, "Punks, Bulldaggers, and Welfare Queens: The Radical Potential of Queer Politics?" in *Sexual Identities, Queer Politics*, ed. Mark Blasius (Princeton, NJ: Princeton University Press, 2001), 200–28.

12. Marie-Hélène Bourcier, *Sexpolitiques : Queer Zones 2* (Paris: La Fabrique, 2005), 108–9.

13. See the proposals for an archive of sexual minorities written by Bourcier for the group ArchiQ: Marie-Hélène Bourcier, "La fièvre des archives: Pistes de réflexion et d'animation proposées par ArchiQ pour le projet de Centre d'Archives 'Homosexuelles' de la Ville de Paris" (unpublished manuscript, 2003).

Spam Filter: Gay Rights and the Normalization of Male-Male Rape in the U.S. Military

Aaron Belkin

At a recent conference on the "don't ask, don't tell" policy (hereafter DADT) held at the University of Hawai'i Law School, I was stunned to find that half the speakers spent their time at the podium taking potshots at the U.S. military. I have participated in many conferences on the gay ban, and such a critique of the military is atypical. At most events, it is assumed that the military is a noble institution whose readiness must be preserved at all costs. Because the integration of openly gay and lesbian service members would enhance the military's ability to fulfill its mission, the argument usually goes, the ban should be repealed. At the Hawai'i conference, by contrast, critiques of the armed forces were so vehement that, during one question-and-answer session, an audience member asked the leader of a mainland organization dedicated to DADT's repeal whether he suffered any internal turmoil in the course of doing his job. "No," he responded, "the military is an outstanding institution."

Perhaps it is no accident that LGBT (lesbian, gay, bisexual, transgender) advocates in Hawai'i seem more attuned to critical understandings of the armed forces than do their mainland counterparts. Several prominent scholars have argued that the U.S. military's presence in Hawai'i has been particularly heavy-handed and that its imprint can be seen on museums, highways, schools, cemeteries, parks,

Radical History Review

Issue 100 (Winter 2008)   DOI 10.1215/01636545-2007-029

© 2008 by MARHO: The Radical Historians' Organization, Inc.

houses, and other social and cultural institutions. "The military order," some have concluded, "is heavily written onto Hawai'i, marking literal and figurative spaces in manners both subtle and gross."[1] At the University of Hawai'i conference on DADT, participants expressed concern with the pervasiveness of the military's physical presence in the islands but seemed even more concerned by a related phenomenon: the militarization of civilian society.

The scope of the armed forces' physical presence in Hawai'i and elsewhere is one aspect of militarization. American forces are deployed in 766 foreign bases around the world, to say nothing of the 77 bases in American territories and the 2,888 bases in the United States.[2] But militarization is not only characterized by a physical military presence; it refers to how the broader civilian culture thinks about the use of armed force. According to Cynthia Enloe, militarization is "the step-by-step process by which a person or a thing gradually comes to depend for its well-being on militarist ideas."[3] We might see militarization, for example, when John Kerry saluted the audience at the 2004 Democratic National Convention in Boston and announced that he was "reporting for duty!" It is also apparent when the public comes to regard soldiering as the epitome of citizenship, when the military seems like the most ideal embodiment of patriotism (such as in the undifferentiated message of "Support Our Troops" offered on bumper stickers), and when promoting the military's interests is believed to enhance the overall welfare of a population. Militarization prevails when unbridled support for the military seems natural and unproblematic.

Many U.S. citizens perceive the military as a benign force in the world. But accepting the militarization of American society as an unremarkable phenomenon can be problematic, in part because of the central place of violence in military culture. Consider, for example, male-male rape. Based on a series of interviews with victims and mental health providers who counsel service members, I have come to understand how something as violent as male-male rape can actually shore up coercive forms of military masculinity through a range of actions, including punishment, the enforcement of the pecking order, and the expression of homophobia. A soldier at Fort Jackson in 1972, for example, reported that he "found about forty guys lined up eagerly near the latrine. The other recruits had realized there was a faggot in the barracks, and two of the bigger guys had pushed him down on his knees and held him in the shower while the entire platoon lined up for blowjobs. The next day, the soldier was gone."[4] This incident is not unique. While estimates must be interpreted with caution, available evidence suggests that each year approximately 12,500 men in the military are the victims of rape or attempted rape.[5]

Naturalizing militarization requires sanitizing this and other forms of brutality, either by hiding or reframing or, when things get badly out of control, excusing such behavior as the exception rather than the rule. Hiding such brutality is important because few Americans would want to believe that male-male rape is a central feature of military culture, and few would want to join the ranks of men who rape other men or men who cannot fend off sexual assault. This is not, of course, to imply any fault or essential weakness on the part of the victims of rape, but rather to gesture at the ways in which many recruits, in particular men, equate going through military training with becoming tough. If they realized that even military training is insufficient to prepare a man to fend off rape, they might be less inclined to enlist.

In addition to domestic implications that would follow from widespread public awareness of male-male rape in the armed forces, the international consequences could be dire. Similar to other imperial projects, the American empire requires local collaborators who govern in ways that are consistent with U.S. interests, not least of which is to downplay their countries' subordinate positions to U.S. hegemony. Given this particular historical moment in which thousands of Iraqi civilians have been killed in the ongoing war, the subjects of American imperialism do not need any outside help to think about and remember the ways in which the American military project is undermining their well-being. That said, anti-imperialists around the world can and do use information about American military brutality as political ammunition against collaborators who do the heavy lifting for American imperialism. For that reason, concealing or at least smoothing over such evidence so as not to provide additional propaganda ammunition is crucial. It may not be much of a stretch for subjects of U.S. imperialism who learn of male-male rape in the U.S. military to think about the ways in which they get screwed by the American military project.

How, then, does militarization get naturalized, given the prevalence of brutal conduct like male-male rape? Ironically, stigmatized out-groups — those condemned by the military as rapists — have played a central role in making militarization seem natural and unthreatening. Gay men, for example, have long been accused of being rapists who cannot control their desires around other troops. General Norman Schwarzkopf exemplified such an outlook while testifying before the Senate Armed Service Committee in 1993: "I am aware of instances where heterosexuals have been solicited to commit homosexual acts, and, even more traumatic emotionally, physically coerced to engage in such acts."[6] Stigmatized as sexual predators, gay men help construct and reinforce silences surrounding male-male rape by pursuing strategies that conceal militarization in plain sight.[7]

Some LGBT rights organizations tend to depict the armed forces as noble and upstanding; and they also rely on spokespersons that reflect homonormative, loyal, and harmless gendered archetypes. Despite the fact that most perpetrators of male-male sexual violence in the military are heterosexual and many victims identify as gay, most LGBT organizations rarely mention male-male rape or assault, even in the context of opposing gay abuse in the armed forces. Many who are working to repeal DADT believe that directing the public's attention to male-male sexual violence might undermine their case by connecting gay men with rape.

The choice to ignore male-male rape and to depict the armed forces as an unproblematic institution reflects movement leaders' convictions that the best strategy for convincing legislators, the military, and the public to repeal DADT is to demonstrate that gay men and lesbians are equally capable of conforming to the military's expectations of discipline, honor, and self-sacrifice. At the same time that LGBT organizations and activists have made such strategic decisions, they have had to face the perception of being antimilitarist. I have not been immune to such influences. Recently, an assistant to a U.S. congresswoman asked me to review a documentary film about a gay Christian Marine from Alabama who had come to oppose both the ban and the Iraq war. The congresswoman wanted to know if her office should circulate the film to other members of Congress to generate support for repeal. Although I found the narrative to be compelling, I told her that the Marine's story would make anti-DADT efforts seem antiwar, and antiwar efforts seem pro-gay, and I recommended that her office refrain from endorsing the film. To take another example, at the now defunct Center for the Study of Sexual Minorities in the Military at the University of California at Santa Barbara, a gay veteran removed himself from the organization's mailing list when it declined to post a banner on its Web page expressing support for U.S. troops in Iraq.[8]

Advocacy groups for LGBT people follow the same strategies used by many advocates for women and racial and ethnic minorities, who tend to depict the U.S. armed forces as a virtuous institution when calling for the right to serve in uniform on an equal basis with others. This does not mean that stigmatized outsiders respond like firefighters dousing the flames of controversy every time that the military faces a crisis in its public perception, nor does it mean that they find consensus in their relationships to militarization. Rather, decades of positive portrayals of the armed forces have created a reservoir of favorable attitudes about the military, dispersed widely throughout civil society, that can be activated to repair cracks in the military's reputation when they do appear.[9] These strategies reflect the tradition of extreme normalization within mainstream civil rights activism. These tactics are almost likely to work since it seems that the gay ban will someday be lifted. Gay men and lesbians who seek a place at the military's table surely will have their desires fulfilled.[10]

But how much do queers have to pay, ultimately, for a seat in the military mess hall? Some answers to this question emerged during a November 2006 panel at the annual meeting of the American Anthropological Association in San Jose, California, where I heard an outstanding presentation by Christopher Ames, a doctoral candidate in anthropology at the University of Michigan at Ann Arbor.[11] According to Ames, Okinawa, like Hawai'i, is home to several U.S. military bases, and Japanese and American officials have had trouble making the U.S. military presence there seem unremarkable. After three American service members raped a twelve-year-old Okinawan girl in 1995, protesters questioned not just the U.S. military's influence over the islands, but the militarized dimensions of U.S.–Japanese relations as well. Ames described a "town resort" in Okinawa known as American Village, "conceived by the local mayor as a theme park wherein 'only the good things about America' are incorporated." According to the presentation, restaurants in American Village enable visitors to ascertain what it means to live the good life in the United States by serving American food like Spam. American Village may seem innocuous, but anti-militarist activists in both Okinawa and Hawai'i understand that the processes by which militarization gets normalized can be subtle. As Enloe notes, militarization can take "humdrum forms" in addition to the explicit ones and "insinuate itself into ordinary daily routines where it is rarely heralded or even deemed noteworthy."[12] Perhaps residents of Okinawa and mainstream LGBT rights activists in the United States are implicated in the same subtle commodity chain, one that invites us to affably disavow our own complicities in militarization.

When Okinawans buy Spam, they generate profits for Hormel Foods, the company that produces and distributes it. In turn, Hormel Foods has been a pri-mary source of wealth for James C. Hormel, the former U.S. ambassador to Luxem-bourg and a generous donor to numerous LGBT rights organizations, including those that fight for the repeal of DADT. In consuming Spam, residents of Okinawa internalize what are imagined to be the good things about America, literally absorb-ing those things into their bodies while they are summoned to experience their homeland as a benign approximation of the United States itself, not a site where, as antimilitarists argue, American soldiers rape or where local priorities have taken a backseat to U.S. military interests. And at the same time, the profits generated by visitors to American Village help gay rights groups promote the message that the repeal of DADT would enhance the quality of the American armed forces. When LGBT rights advocates make this argument, they wear away at the edifice support-ing discrimination, but they also simultaneously gloss over male-male rape and the Pentagon's efforts to blame gay troops for it. When we reinforce the notion that the U.S. military is a noble institution worthy of loyalty and praise, we make the jobs of antimilitarist activists in Hawai'i, Okinawa, and everywhere more difficult. The staying power of both empire and homonormativity, it seems, turns on its capacity to induce accomplices into uttering good-natured silences that gently confirm that all is well in the U.S. military.

Notes

1. Kathy E. Ferguson and Phyllis Turnbull, *Oh Say, Can You See? The Semiotics of the Military in Hawai'i* (Minneapolis: University of Minnesota Press, 1999), xiii, xiv. At the time of writing, Ferguson was a professor of political science and women's studies, and Turnbull was an associate professor of political science, both at the University of Hawai'i.

2. *Baseline Structure Report* (Washington, DC: U.S. Department of Defense, 2006), quoted in Seungsook Moon, "Politics of Gender and Sexuality in the Global U.S. Military Empire: A Case of South Korea" (paper presented as part of the Division of World Cultural Studies 2007 Lecture Series, California State University, Dominguez Hills, April 26, 2007).

3. Cynthia Enloe, *Maneuvers: The International Politics of Militarizing Women's Lives* (Berkeley: University of California Press, 2000), 3. The argument and language in this paragraph are drawn from a proposal for a new project on the study of militarization and democracy that I coauthored.

4. Randy Shilts, *Conduct Unbecoming: Gays and Lesbians in the U.S. Military* (New York: Ballantine, 1993), 179.

5. By comparison, my lower-bound estimate is that at least 6,500 women in the military, approximately, are raped or experience attempted rape each year. My estimate hinges on the fact that many surveys of military personnel confirm that 1 percent of men and between 3 and 6 percent of women say that they experienced rape or attempted rape during the previous year. Other sources confirm that about the same number of men and women become victims of sexual violence while serving in the military. A comprehensive Veterans Administration (VA) study, for example, found that "the actual numbers of men and women who screen positive for MST [military sexual trauma] in VA are about equal." See *Military Sexual Trauma* (Washington, DC: Department of Veterans Affairs, 2004), 3.

6. Other portrayals of gay service members as rapists are discussed in Aaron Belkin, "Breaking Rank: Military Homophobia and the Production of Queer Practices and Identities," *Georgetown Journal of Gender and the Law* 3 (2001): 83–106. The Schwarzkopf quote is from "Policy Concerning Homosexuality in the Armed Forces, Hearing Held by Senate Armed Services Committee," 103rd Cong., 2nd sess. (Washington, DC: Government Printing Office, 1993), 598.

7. The argument in this section depends heavily on Enloe, *Maneuvers*, 15–23.

8. For a history of queer movement's roots in antimilitarism, see Justin David Suran, "Coming Out against the War: Antimilitarism and the Politicization of Homosexuality in the Era of Vietnam," *American Quarterly* 53 (2001): 452–88.

9. Rhonda Evans, *A History of Ethnic Minorities in the U.S. Armed Forces* (Santa Barbara: Center for the Study of Sexual Minorities in the Military, 2003).

10. Bruce Bawer, *A Place at the Table: The Gay Individual in American Society* (New York: Touchstone, 1993).

11. Christopher Ames (University of Michigan), "Okinawa's American Village; Reversing the Gaze" (paper presented at the 2006 Annual Meetings of the American Anthropological Association, San Jose California, November 16, 2006.

12. Enloe, *Maneuvers*, 3.

Save Our Children/Let Us Marry: Gay Activists Appropriate the Rhetoric of Child Protectionism

Patrick McCreery

O n September 14, 2005, Massachusetts state senators and representatives voted 157 to 39 against amending the state constitution to ban same-sex marriage. The "no" vote represented a substantial shift for many legislators; they had easily passed an identical amendment the year before. Massachusetts was, at the time of the second vote, as it remains at the time of this writing, the only state in the nation to sanction same-sex marriage. Thus the vote against the proposed amendment represented a victory for lesbian and gay civil rights. James Timilty, a Democratic state senator who supported the restrictive amendment in 2004 but voted against it in 2005, explained his change of heart this way: "When I looked in the eyes of the children living with these [same-sex] couples . . . I decided that I don't feel at this time that same-sex marriage has hurt the commonwealth in any way. In fact I would say that in my view it has had a good effect for the children in these families."[1]

No student of American politics should be surprised that a legislator like Timilty invoked children in the context of a debate over same-sex marriage—an institution in which, by definition, children are not the primary participants. For more than a century, legislators and activists of all political stripes have foisted much of the weight of political change in the United States onto the back of the figure of the endangered child. Historically, social conservatives have often deployed child-protectionist rheto-

Radical History Review
Issue 100 (Winter 2008) DOI 10.1215/01636545-2007-030

ric to argue that the public display or governmental sanction of homosexual desire endangered children's physical and moral well-being. In some instances, conservatives even claimed that gay men or lesbians, emboldened by the acquisition of civil rights, might seek to seduce or molest impressionable children. While those arguments linger, today advocates of same-sex marriage routinely argue that gay civil rights in general, and the right to marry in particular, are necessary to protect the children of same-sex couples from social prejudice and legal discrimination.

In the following essay, I argue that the political use of the endangered child by advocates of same-sex marriage represents a fundamental and wholly norma-tive shift in gay-rights rhetoric. I will leave it to others to determine whether or not same-sex marriage is itself an inherently normative structure; my goal is to argue that the particular model of same-sex marriage that many gay-rights organizations currently embrace relies on the symbolic child, rather than on the child's same-sex parents, for structure and justification. This reliance on the symbolic child fore-closes two opportunities to change the social, legal, and ethical conceptualizations of *family* in the United States. First and foremost, in deploying the rhetoric of child protectionism, advocates of same-sex marriage forfeit an opportunity to affirm the legal, emotional, and sexual bonds that can unite two adults of the same sex regard-less of their parental status. In doing so, they paradoxically imply that same-sex relationships are somehow perverse or unworthy of consideration in their own right and that the full benefits of citizenship should accrue not individually but through membership in a family. Second, by invoking the symbolic child, a malleable social construction that is at heart a mere abstraction, lesbian and gay-rights organizations miss their chance to empower actual children to speak on their own behalf, a move that has the potential to democratize the traditional family.

I realize that I am in some ways advocating competing agendas here. On the one hand, I want gay-rights organizations to pose more "adult" and fewer "child-centered" arguments for same-sex marriage; on the other hand, I want them to allow children to speak for themselves. If this sounds contradictory, it is because the contentious issue of same-sex marriage has opened a space for activists to champion a number of necessary changes to popular understandings of the family, even if some of those individual changes conflict or overlap. Alas, the normative arguments that many gay-rights organizations make in favor of same-sex marriage do nothing to transform *any* fundamental facet of family life, so a certain sense of ambivalence is inevitable.

In order to historicize and contextualize the deployment of child-protectionist rhetoric, I compare representations of the child figure in Anita Bryant's 1977 cam-paign to repeal a gay-rights measure in Dade County, Florida, with representations culled from today's debates over same-sex marriage. I believe that comparing these two moments allows us to understand three key factors that have contributed to the production of a homonormative culture of same-sex marriage supporters: the mainstream LGBT (lesbian, gay, bisexual, transgender) movement's pragmatic political shift over the past thirty years from a focus on human rights to a focus on the acquisition of material benefits; the movement's deployment of the endangered child figure as one strategy to acquire those benefits; and, perhaps most important, the indisputable centrality of the child figure to any conceptualization of normative culture.

The rhetoric of child protectionism has a long and varied history in the United States, reflecting in many ways changing conceptualizations of childhood itself. Following the influential work of Philippe Ariès in the early 1960s, most historians agree that childhood as we commonly understand it has its roots in the early modern era.[2] The emergence of mass literacy and the development of mercantile and, later, industrial capitalism profoundly affected family life, especially for those individuals who inhabited the new middle classes. Previously integrated into community life, youngsters were increasingly relegated to separate, often highly protected, spheres such as the nursery, the school, and the playground. This separatism, effected gradually over several centuries, both reflected and generated a growing understanding of children as inherently different from adults. *How* children differ is a question that has kept academics, physicians, advice columnists, and pundits employed for more than a century. In these realms of popular culture, children have been variously understood as naturally ignorant and preternaturally wise; happily asexual and sensually hedonistic; irretrievably lost and inherently redeemable.

While there is little agreement over how to understand childhood, two characteristics of the debate remain remarkably consistent. The first is that invocations of childhood typically remain untroubled by the voices of actual children. Regardless of the particular vision of childhood that adults embrace—innocence or emptiness, the child as Jean-Jacques Rousseau's noble savage or John Locke's blank slate—they tend to project their own hopes, desires, and beliefs onto the silent young people for whom they claim to speak. Second, while adults do not necessarily agree on how to understand childhood, they concur that children are routinely threatened by dangerous social forces and thus are in dire need of protection. From as far back as the early twentieth-century movements of the Progressive Era, political activists of both the right and left have routinely exploited popular concerns about endangered children. Today, whether the desire is to curb illegal immigration or increase motor vehicle safety, to ban smoking or make health care affordable, the symbolic endangered child who might benefit from political change is often highlighted while the just-as-impacted adult is all but ignored.[3] The rhetoric of child protectionism is so embedded in our culture, so naturalized, that to encourage its demise seems not only cruel but also pointless. Nonetheless, I believe the debates over same-sex marriage offer a crucial opportunity to destabilize the figure of the symbolic child and thereby begin a progressive reconceptualization of the family.

The Endangered Child: Dade County, Florida, 1977

Anita Bryant lives today in seclusion in rural Oklahoma. The former beauty queen, pop singer, orange juice promoter, and antigay activist does not grant interviews to reporters or academics, so we can only speculate about her views on same-sex marriage. Nonetheless, it is difficult to believe that she can miss the irony of much of the current child-centered rhetoric in support of same-sex marriage. In 1977, she made child protectionism the center of her successful, six-month-long, nationally publicized campaign to repeal a gay-rights measure in Dade County. Bryant, a fundamentalist Southern Baptist who then lived in the Dade County community of Miami Beach, argued that the conferral of civil rights on homosexuals would endanger children by giving gay people — and especially gay teachers — access to children's innocent bodies and impressionable minds.

The measure Bryant decried was an amendment to the Dade County Code that effectively banned discrimination against gay people in the realms of housing, employment, and public accommodation.[4] The amendment's passage by the Dade County Metro Commission in January 1977 was due to the lobbying efforts of a small group of local gay men who formed the Dade County Coalition for the Humanistic Rights of Gays in 1976. They included Jack Campbell, the owner of the national Club Baths bathhouse chain; Bob Basker, an activist who had founded the Chicago chapter of the Mattachine Society; and Bob Kunst, the codirector of a so-called human potential center where individuals could explore their sexual desires.[5]

The amendment's passage aroused heated emotions at Miami's Northwest Baptist Church, which Bryant attended with her husband, Bob Green, and their four children. Northwest Baptist's pastor, William Chapman, preached that the amendment "was designed to give special privileges to homosexuals."[6] He further warned that the change would allow homosexual teachers to work unimpeded at Northwest Christian Academy, the church-affiliated school attended by the Green children.[7] At Chapman's urging, Bryant soon formed Save Our Children from Homosexuality Inc., an organization whose mission was to force a voters' referendum on the amendment. With Bryant as its president and primary spokesperson, Save Our Children quickly collected sixty-four thousand signatures in support of a referendum. The vote took place in June 1977, and Bryant scored a clear victory: Dade residents repealed the amendment by a two-to-one margin.

Those of us too young to remember 1977 may not understand Bryant's position in mid-1970s popular culture. As a cover singer of pop tunes and religious anthems, she was never a musical superstar. However, Bryant enjoyed an increasingly lucrative career through the mid-1970s, charging up to $7,500 per show and earning more than $500,000 in 1976.[8] A substantial portion of her income came from her work as the national spokeswoman for the Florida Citrus Commission and corporations such as Coca-Cola and Singer, the sewing-machine manufacturer. As a spokeswoman for the orange growers, Bryant appeared in numerous national television and print advertisements, repeating the slogan, "A day without orange juice is like a day without sunshine." Green and the couple's four children appeared with her in many of the ads, either in a grove picking oranges or in the family's kitchen watching her prepare breakfast.

Public familiarity with Bryant and her family allowed her to play the "mommy card" like few activists before or since. Such a tactic was not a stretch for Bryant, as not only the orange juice ads but also the numerous media articles in the early to mid-1970s highlighted her experiences as a mother. During the campaign, she claimed that extending civil protections to gay men and lesbians could harm children:

> My primary concern was voiced as a mother . . . . Known homosexual
> schoolteachers and their possible role-model impact tore at my heart in a way
> I could not ignore. Two things in particular troubled me. First, public approval
> of admitted homosexual teachers could encourage more homosexuality by
> inducing pupils into looking upon it as an acceptable life-style. And second,
> a particularly deviant-minded teacher could sexually molest children. These
> were possibilities I was unwilling to risk. Added to these concerns was my
> deep-rooted biblical orientation which condemns the act of homosexuality.
> For me not to have stood up in protest would have been something my
> conscience could not tolerate. I had that right as a mother, a citizen, a voter,
> and a tax-paying resident of Dade County.[9]

As this quote suggests, Bryant's religious faith prescribed her antigay activism. Her belief system, which she articulated in numerous media interviews and in nine inspirational books published between 1970 and 1978, was complex: God designed a natural order for the universe that he required everyone to follow; in endowing people with free will, he constantly tested their allegiance to his design; people who deviated from this design were sinners who risked damnation. In short, it was the general possibility that children may be led from God's natural design, not the specifics of homosexuality itself, which most concerned Bryant. As she wrote shortly after the campaign, "It has been said that I am a one-issue person, which is not true. I hate 'sins' in the plural just as Billy Graham, Oral Roberts, and other public religious figures have expressed. I have spoken out on the issue of homosexuality because it is the one we were confronted with."[10] Bryant feared that governmental protections of homosexuals would suggest to children that they, too, could ignore God's design—could commit a sin, *any* sin—without repercussion. As she argued, "Homosexuality is a conduct, a choice, a way of life. And if you choose to have a life-style as such, then you are going to have to live with the consequences."[11]

Dade County voters who may have been put off by Bryant's moralism still had plenty of reasons to be suspicious of lesbians and, in particular, gay men. No one of voting age in the mid-1970s could have avoided the messages circulating through much of popular culture that painted homosexuals as dangerous individuals not to be trusted with children. Indeed, Florida in particular had witnessed several well-publicized antigay campaigns in the previous two decades.[12] The advent of the gay and lesbian liberation movement in the late 1960s and early 1970s ameliorated the homophobic rhetoric only slightly. In 1976, for example, a national moral panic erupted over the alleged existence (later almost entirely disproved) of a huge child pornography industry largely produced by, and catering to, gay men.[13] In May 1977, just three weeks before the vote in Miami, the *Chicago Tribune* ran a four-day series on the "kiddie porn" industry, a series that made the national wires. According to the *Tribune*:

Chicago is the headquarters of a nationwide ring trafficking in young boys—"chickens," in the argot of the streets—and placing them in various homes to serve male customers, or "chicken hawks." . . . Adult exploiters pick up the runaways at bus stations, hamburger stands, and amusement arcades, and offer them money and gifts in exchange for sexual favors. Frequently they show the children pornography to arouse them sexually, and give them drugs and alcohol to lower their inhibitions. With small children . . . dolls and candy are used.[14]

Bryant made broad use of the *Tribune* stories, repeating their assertions at news conferences and reproducing their headlines in her campaign literature. Save Our Children ran several versions of a full-page advertisement in the *Miami Herald*, southern Florida's largest newspaper, in which the slogan "THERE IS NO 'HUMAN RIGHT' TO CORRUPT OUR CHILDREN" was superimposed against a background of newspaper articles with headlines like "Boys Used in Film for National Sale," "Why a 13-Year-Old Is Selling His Body," and "Homosexuals Used Scout Troop." All three articles came from the *Tribune* series.[15] Those stories and similar ones from other publications provided Bryant with a wealth of provocative material: supposed evidence that homosexual men were not only highly sexual but predatory, especially in regard to young boys. As she famously argued, "Homosexuals cannot reproduce—so they must recruit. And to freshen their ranks, they must recruit the youth of America."[16]

Bryant's refusal to acknowledge that lesbians and gay men could and did reproduce explains why, during the campaign, she never discussed the children of homosexual parents. Indeed, the children whom her campaign rhetoric envisioned were decidedly homogeneous: all had seemingly heterosexual parents; none had the ability to resist the unwanted attentions of adults; and none experienced same-sex desires of their own.

Save Our Children's mention of a "human right" in the headline of the advertisement discussed above clearly referred to Miami's gay activists, who made the acquisition of human and civil rights the cornerstone of their campaign. Bryant's opponents considered her claims about homosexual recruitment and molestation of children to be shrill and absurd, and so they seldom sought to rebut them. Instead, they portrayed lesbians and gay men as the next logical group, after women and African Americans, on a historical continuum of marginalized populations struggling for expanded civil rights.

Miami's gay activists did not enjoy the unity of their counterparts in Save Our Children. In early 1977, Kunst abruptly left the Dade County Coalition for the Humanistic Rights of Gays, claiming it was too cautious. He quickly founded a competing organization, Miami Victory Campaign, and began issuing a series of pamphlets and press releases that not only attacked Bryant and her "vicious hate campaign" but promoted sexual exploration for everyone.[17] Distributed primarily at bathhouses, gay bars, and at his own Transperience Center, the pamphlets probably had little influence on the outcome of the repeal referendum. More important to the campaign, however, was Kunst himself, who like Bryant was an engaging but polarizing character always willing to talk to reporters. By drive and personality, he became the de facto lead spokesman for the pro-amendment side, despite the fact that his organization was chronically understaffed and underfunded.[18]

Journalists and historians sometimes portray the two competing gay-rights groups as representing generational divisions within the broader gay-rights movement.[19] In this formulation, the brash and idealistic Kunst represented the heady days of gay liberation in the early 1970s, whereas Campbell and his Dade County Coalition functionaries portended the coming dullish decades of institution building and political pragmatism, while Basker recalled the button-down homophile era of the early 1960s. Absent from such characterizations is the fact that all of Dade's gay activists generally ignored Bryant's warnings about endangered children and instead staked their claim to human rights. Kunst may have been considerably more outspoken than Basker or Campbell, but his arguments against the amendment's repeal were very similar to theirs.

With a budget of more than $200,000, the coalition was able to buy numerous full-page newspaper advertisements in the *Herald*. A typical advertisement the organization ran there featured a drawing of the Bill of Rights engraved in stone, with the headline "Don't Let Them Chip Away at the Constitution."[20] Another advertisement displayed a photograph of a voting booth with the headline "Freedom in America Begins and Ends Here" in capital letters next to it. Should any reader fail to infer the message of that image, the caption beneath the photo read in part: "We have faith that a majority of the citizens of Dade County believe in the Declaration of Independence and the Constitution of the United States. So we feel we can win the battle to save human rights in the election coming up this Tuesday."[21] Similarly, Clergy and Laity for Human Rights, an ad hoc organization of liberal clerics affiliated with the Dade County Coalition, ran a newspaper advertisement stating that the group "deplores the character of the current public debate over the Dade County Ordinance extending equal protection of the law to all persons. The issue at stake is clearly a matter of individual human rights. . . . Basic to our religious heritage is the emphatic affirmation that all persons are entitled to have their human and civil rights ensured."[22] Kunst's organization had less money to buy newspaper advertisements, but when it did, those ads also invoked rights. One claimed that Bryant was attempting to "convince Dade County to vote away human rights."[23] Another insisted that the key issue of the repeal ballot "is — HUMAN RIGHTS!"[24]

It was only toward the end of the campaign, after Bryant's arguments had taken their toll and polls showed a tightening race, that the Dade County Coalition directly addressed Bryant's molestation charges. An advertisement titled "Myths and Lies" noted that Save Our Children officials had reprinted and disseminated "unfavorable" newspaper articles about homosexual men molesting children.[25] This tactic was unfair, the ad claimed: "It would be easier to scour the nation's newspapers and pick out and reprint stories about heterosexual men raping women because statistics show that the overwhelming number of forcible sex acts are committed by heterosexual males."[26] Having made that point, the ad quickly returned to the issue of rights: "But does this mean we should take away the basic human rights of heterosexuals, like the right to work, to rent a home or to be served in a restaurant?"[27]

While Dade's two main gay-rights organizations emphasized the issue of rights above all else, they did little to explain to voters their or the legal system's understandings of the term. Indeed, pro-amendment flyers and advertisements regularly used the terms *human rights* and *civil rights* interchangeably, as if the concepts they named were identical. This vagueness confused the public: Were lesbians and gay men seeking the right to *be* homosexual, to live their lives without fear of overt social discrimination or governmental intrusion? Or were they asking for the right to *act* homosexual, to "flaunt" their sexual desires publicly, as Bryant constantly suggested?

The failure of the gay-rights organizations to explain what they meant by *rights* was echoed in their vague references to the three areas in which the ordinance provided protections from discrimination: housing, employment, and public accommodation. Whereas Bryant's literature regularly reproduced detailed media reports, however false or exaggerated, of predatory men molesting innocent boys, gay-rights activists did little to substantiate their own claims of discrimination in the realms the ordinance addressed. For example, they did not detail instances in which lesbians or gay men had lost their jobs due to their sexual orientation, or been turned down for apartments, or been denied entrance to restaurants or movie theaters. They could rightly have argued that the social climate in the mid-1970s was so repressive that it generally prevented homosexuals from publicizing their experiences of discrimination, but they did not make even this claim.

This lack of specificity raised questions about the extent to which lesbians and gay men actually experienced discrimination, thus suggesting they were, as Bryant argued, seeking "special privileges."[28] This issue clouded gay-rights activists' rhetoric from the beginning of the campaign onward. For example, at the January 1977 meeting at which Metro Commissioners passed the amendment, Kunst stated that "we already have the jobs. We're already teaching in the schools."[29] The real issue, he said, was that he and other homosexuals could not disclose their sexuality publicly without fear of retribution. Such acknowledgments, coupled with long-standing stereotypes of homosexuals as disproportionately educated and wealthy, led many to question the need to include lesbians and gay men under the county's protective ordinance. As the daily *Miami News* noted in one of several editorials it published opposing the amendment:

Homosexuals are not concentrated in low-paying jobs. They are not refused the use of public water fountains or denied access to public education. Those were the extreme conditions that prompted Congress in 1964 to extend to blacks some extraordinary protections to compensate for hundreds of years of oppression and deprivation. Gays are much better represented at the top echelons of Dade's social, economic and professional life than are blacks. There is many an expensive, exclusive club in this community that bars blacks and Jews but welcomes wealthy homosexuals.[30]

The issue of discrimination was highlighted in February 1977, when officials at Singer informed Bryant that her activism had compelled them to cancel plans for her to host a nationally televised daytime sewing program.[31] Local pundits objected to Singer's move immediately. Ralph Renick, the news director at Miami's largest television station, WTVJ, editorialized on air that Bryant was the victim of a modern-day blacklisting.[32] Similarly, John McMullan, the executive editor of the *Miami Herald*, wrote that gay activists and Singer officials were "treading callously on a fundamental right precious to all of us: the right of free speech."[33] He implied that it was Bryant, not gay activists, who could factually complain of discrimination: "None of the gays presented any evidence they were being discriminated against."[34]

Bryant, for one, indicated that she understood very well what gay activists meant by *human rights*—they meant the right to be public and forthright about their sexual desires. This for her was not only morally anathema but completely separate from the issue of discrimination. As she argued, "Homosexuals do not suffer discrimination when they keep their perversions in the privacy of their homes.

They can hold any job, transact any business, join any organization—so long as they do not flaunt their homosexuality and try to establish role models for the impressionable young people—our children."[35]

Here, as she did so often, Bryant returned to the issue she realized had the most political traction—the desire to protect children from perceived harm. In comparison, the gay rights activists who opposed her rarely discussed children, threatened or otherwise. That Basker had been married and was the father of three was briefly noted in a few media profiles, but otherwise no one discussed the issue of gay parenting. When questioned by reporters, Kunst and Campbell occasionally mentioned their own early same-sex experiences (both with youths their own age), though their comments seemed intended to show that they had not been "recruited" into homosexuality by predatory adults, not to illuminate their experiences as gay adolescents.[36]

We may speculate that Dade's gay activists did not engage Bryant's argument that children are impressionable because they believed in that instance that she was correct. Of course, contrary to Bryant's understanding of sexual orientation as a simple choice and of children as pawns who are easily seduced into homosexuality, Kunst, Campbell, and their colleagues understood childish impressionability from a different angle: having a gay teacher or other adult gay role model would not turn a straight child gay but might inspire a straight child to learn how to be tolerant of homosexuals or inspire a gay child to be comfortable with his or her sexuality. Yet ultimately these arguments were not ones the public would have accepted in 1977. What was palatable in that historical moment was the rhetoric of rights. And while lucid and compelling rights-based rhetoric can often instigate progressive change, that was not the type of rhetoric Dade's gay activists put forth.

The Endangered Child: Same-Sex Marriage Today

Whereas Dade's gay activists almost never focused on endangered children in their campaigns for gay rights, today's supporters of same-sex marriage sometimes seem to discuss little else. In researching this essay, I examined the rhetoric of six activist organizations—three socially conservative and three gay-oriented—that have been integrally involved in debates over same-sex marriage.[37] The conservative groups are American Values, Concerned Women for America, and Focus on the Family. The gay rights organizations are Lambda Legal, the Human Rights Campaign (HRC), and the National Gay and Lesbian Task Force (NGLTF).

The three conservative organizations all support some version of the proposed Marriage Protection Amendment to the U.S. Constitution, which would define marriage as a union between a man and a woman. In general, all three organizations base their opposition on three related claims, most of which rearticulate claims made in Bryant's campaign: same-sex marriage is immoral because it upends thousands of years of tradition; it privileges homosexual adults' desires for social legitimacy over children's natural need for both a mother and a father; and, last but not least, it creates definitionally dysfunctional families that in turn expose children to a plethora of physical and moral dangers.

The assertion that same-sex marriage is immoral because it is nontraditional echoes Bryant's earlier arguments about the need to respect God's natural design. Conservative activists today argue that governmental approval of same-sex marriage suggests to children that traditions can be questioned or even discarded with no harmful repercussions. A representative example of such rhetoric comes from James Dobson, the founder and president of Focus on the Family. In an article titled "Eleven Arguments against Same-Sex Marriage," Dobson's first argument states that "the legalization of homosexual marriage will quickly destroy the traditional family."[38] "When the State sanctions homosexual relationships and gives them its blessing," Dobson claims, "the younger generation becomes confused about sexual identity and quickly loses its understanding of lifelong commitments, emotional bonding, sexual purity, the role of children in a family, and from a spiritual perspective, the 'sanctity' of marriage."[39]

Dobson's bracketing of the "spiritual perspective" is one instance in which today's conservative activism around same-sex marriage differs from Bryant's rhetoric. While Protestants such as Dobson still retain disproportionate power in the hierarchies of the new right, the movement as a whole has struggled in recent years to include like-minded Roman Catholics, Jews, and even the religiously unaffiliated. Dobson's articulation therefore carefully brackets the issue of faith, with which some secular conservatives might take issue, while still evoking the value of tradition, which should not arouse any conservative's antipathy.

Furthermore, the conservative argument that same-sex marriage privileges the selfish desires of queer adults while ignoring the needs of children manages to avoid the potentially contentious issue of faith. This argument, which is pervasive in the literature of conservative organizations, has at its heart an anxiety that children should learn proper gender roles. Thus it incorporates more than just a critique of same-sex marriage—it condemns any form of gay parenting, whether the parents are male or female, single or coupled. For example, Glenn Stanton, the director of social research and cultural affairs at Focus on the Family, writes that "a wise and compassionate society always comes to the aid of children in motherless or fatherless families, but a wise and compassionate society never intentionally subjects children to such families. But every single same-sex home would do exactly that, for no other reason than that a small handful of adults desire such kinds of families."[40] A policy analyst for American Values argues more aggressively that "same-sex parents subject their children to disproportionate risks including gender confusion . . . increased . . .

promiscuity, teen pregnancy, substance abuse, school dropout, depression, suicide, and other emotional difficulties."[41]

Interestingly, it is that same desire to protect children from a chaotic culture that many lesbians and gay men cite as a key reason for why they support same-sex marriage. In advocating for same-sex marriage, Lambda Legal, the HRC, and the NGLTF consistently invoke visions of same-sex couples struggling against discriminatory government policies that endanger their—and often their children's—emotional comfort, physical welfare, and economic security. Pro–same-sex marriage organizations deploy the rhetoric of child protectionism in three ways. First, they present as fact what are actually subjective and arguably inflated estimates of the numbers of same-sex couples and their children in the United States. Second, they repeatedly enumerate the material benefits for which the children of same-sex couples are ineligible because their parents are not legally married. Third, they portray families led by same-sex couples as being remarkably similar to families led by heterosexual parents. Certainly, the first two arguments contain elements of truth: many same-sex couples do raise children, and homophobic marriage laws do negatively impact the material and emotional livelihoods of their children. However, taken together, these arguments suggest that the *typical* same-sex couple raises children and that those children, and not the partners who comprise the couple itself, are the primary victims of the nation's restrictive marriage laws. The inability of adult same-sex couples to wed is thus recast as a social problem regarding children—the children of same-sex couples who are denied necessary benefits.[42] Of course, making such a claim succeeds only when the resultant problem is politically acceptable. Children being harmed is acceptable as a problem. Adults being denied rights because of their nonnormative sexual desires is not.

All three of the gay-rights organizations I studied for this article highlight census data indicating that sizable numbers of same-sex couples are raising children in every region of the country. However, the groups have cherry-picked only the most useful statistics to include in their publications—they leave more troubling figures unmentioned. For example, the U.S. Census Bureau counted 594,000 same-sex couples living in the United States in 2000.[43] None of the three groups publicize this figure, apparently because it seems to them to be low. Indeed, staffers at the HRC, arguably the most politically conventional and unashamedly pragmatic of the three groups, estimate that 3.1 million people live together in 1.55 million same-sex relationships.[44] However, the Census Bureau's discredited count of 594,000 same-sex couples is useful for establishing a higher percentage of such couples raising children, so the HRC uses that figure to calculate that 34.3 percent of lesbian couples and 22.3 percent of gay male couples are raising children.[45] (Were the HRC to use its own 1.55 million figure, those percentages would be much lower.) Finally, the

HRC estimates that up to 9 million children in the United States are being raised by lesbian or gay male parents, a figure that should make any statistician's head spin regardless of whose figures are being used.[46]

I would argue that this fixation on empirical evidence is an indication of the normative assumptions that marriage advocacy organizations make about childhood and the family. The realpolitik of the same-sex marriage movement depends on large numbers of gay parents and their children who are adversely affected by current policy. In reality, because sexual identity is both fluid and often contested, it is impossible to estimate accurately how many lesbians and gay men live in the United States, how many are coupled, and how many raise children. We can say with some certainty that the number of same-sex couples raising children has increased substantially in recent decades as more gay men and lesbians have formally established relationships, as technological advances have made in vitro fertilization and other forms of assisted conception easier, and as some states have eased or eliminated restrictions on adoption and child custody by gay and lesbian singles and couples. But this acknowledgment is not enough—the rhetorical campaigns that these advocates for same-sex marriage are running demand concrete numbers of innocent victims, and the higher those numbers are, the better.

Inflating estimates of the numbers of same-sex couples and their children constitutes only one part of the strategy these gay-rights organizations use to make their case for same-sex marriage. Another part is the repeated enumeration of the material rights and benefits that accrue through marriage—rights and benefits that same-sex partners and, especially, their children cannot access. There is certainly a great deal of truth to the argument that marriage as an institution generally aids children materially. The Government Accountability Office (formerly the General Accounting Office) reports that the legal act of marriage conveys some 1,100 federal protections, benefits, and responsibilities to married partners and their children.[47] Such benefits include a child's access to both parents' health insurance and Social Security survivor's payments, and the couple's own ability to take advantage of federal tax credits for married people. However, in advocating for same-sex marriage, gay-rights organizations list these out-of-reach rights and benefits in extreme detail. Possibly they learned a lesson from the losing efforts of their counterparts in Dade County—gone are most lofty but vague claims to human rights; in their place are tables and charts that address everything from workers' compensation benefits to intellectual property rights.[48] Few question, however, why it is that such rights and benefits accrue through marriage and not, for example, through households or broader kinship relationships.[49] For social conservatives, such alternatives to the traditional family would be morally anathema; for the mainstream gay-rights organizations I studied, such changes might prove too radical to be politically viable. Fortunately, these gay-rights groups always have the endangered-child figure to help them make their mainstream case. For example, in a report pointedly titled "The Cost of Marriage Inequality to Children and Their Same-Sex Parents," writers for the HRC conclude that "the lack of universal access to marriage for same-sex couples in the United States . . . means that there are children in 96 percent of all counties in this nation that are deprived of the expansive range of protections available to their classmates, neighbors and other children being raised by heterosexual parents."[50]

Given the widespread social anxiety over same-sex marriage, even showing that millions of children in the United States are endangered by their parents' inabilities to wed legally may not be enough to change public opinion, however. Consequently, gay rights organizations also emphasize the supposed ordinariness of families led by same-sex couples. The HRC, in particular, makes this normative claim. For example, "The Cost of Marriage Inequality" report opens with the claim that the 2000 census shows numerous "similarities between the family lives of same-sex and heterosexual couples with children."[51] (We apparently should accept this information as being self-evidently positive, as the report's authors do not bother to explain how it is.) An early version of another HRC publication, "Answers to Questions about Marriage Equality," represents the typical family headed by same-sex parents much more personally and therefore more insidiously. It opens with a one-page introduction by Cheryl Jacques, the HRC's then president. Jacques begins by writing that "when I kiss my children good night after a long day's work, I sometimes wonder what they will learn in school about this moment in history—when Americans are wrestling, once again, with questions about who should have access to one of the most cherished, joyful freedoms in the world, the freedom to marry."[52] Throughout Jacques's short piece, she exalts a normative vision of family that Bryant herself would applaud—if only the parents were heterosexual. For example, Jacques writes that she wants to "protect" and "ensure security" for her family; she expresses "great faith" in Americans; and she is certain her sons want to "know that their moms . . . are married . . . under the law."[53]

Portraying same-sex couples as being virtually identical to their heterosexual counterparts is at best an unintended result and at worst an unspoken goal of much of the rhetoric advocating same-sex marriage. This rendering can be explicit, as in the examples above, or it can be indirect, as through the manipulation of census data. Of course, even the reliance on census figures, whatever their accuracy, to make the case for same-sex marriage is itself conceptually problematic given that the census requests information about households and so by definition imagines couples as cohabitating.[54] While literally hundreds of thousands of same-sex couples live together in the United States, many others do not. The establishment of the cohabitating same-sex couple as the norm therefore denigrates couples that may find cohabitation unnecessary, or even a hindrance, to developing respect, meaning, and integration in their relationships, or who see their relationships as containing erotic or emotional complexities that cannot be accommodated by cohabitation.

The Never-Changing Endangered Child

The fact that social conservatives who oppose same-sex marriage make largely the same arguments today as Bryant did in 1977 suggests both a rhetorical limitation and a larger ideological exhaustion. Is there nothing more they can say except that "same-sex marriage hurts children"? Of course, rhetorical limitations also apply to advocates for same-sex marriage. On many political issues, deploying the rhetoric of child protectionism can achieve remarkable short-term results, but it is a limited strategy that can have unintended consequences. I am not convinced that the gay-rights organizations I studied have considered some crucial questions: Does the deployment of the endangered-child figure represent a genuine concern for the children of same-sex couples, or is it mere strategy? If the former, why is marriage the only way to address the child's needs? If the latter, what risks does the deployment of this child-centered rhetoric pose? And, finally, what do we adults lose when we abandon the rhetoric of individual rights?

Two points emerge as especially salient when we compare Bryant's 1977 rampage against gay rights with struggles over same-sex marriage in the early twenty-first century. First, Dade's gay activists demanded expanded rights for the individual, whereas today's same-sex marriage advocates limit their goal to rights conferred to and through the family. Second, the potency of the discourse of child protectionism remains unchallenged; only its invokers have changed. Taken together, these points suggest that we have made little progress toward destabilizing normative visions of the family that for centuries have served to promote sexism, to disempower children, to repudiate individual rights, and to regulate the expression of sexual desire. While it is an overstatement to suggest that most gay-rights organizations champion these negative outcomes, it is not too far fetched to say that they clearly operate from a position of fearful pragmatism.

Today's advocates for same-sex marriage base much of their argument on a litany of material benefits that gay and lesbian would-be spouses and their children are denied. Here the rhetoric of rights, as practiced by Kunst and Campbell in Dade County during the late 1970s, has been supplanted by what often sounds like a gospel of greed. While Dade's gay activists were admittedly rhetorically clumsy, surely their expansive vision of equal citizenship was more dynamic and potentially more transformative than today's detailed accounts of lost veterans' benefits and the inability to file joint tax returns.

Some may argue that the successes of the gay-rights movement in the three decades since the Dade County campaign make broad and grand demands unnecessary, that gay men and lesbians have largely won social acceptance from the broader public and so now should devote their attention to filling in the cracks of missing material benefits.[55] I do not agree. While the movement has certainly had its successes—most notably the U.S. Supreme Court's 2003 ruling in *Lawrence and Garner v. State of Texas*, which overturned state sodomy laws—basic rights such as the ability to work, to raise children, and, yes, to marry are still often denied. Indeed, the stunning victory of *Lawrence* now seems at best something like an elaborate new gadget no one is quite sure how to operate, and at worst a moment of political opportunity that has passed. For example, in their literature, few established gay-rights organizations cite *Lawrence* as an occasion to demand expanded civil rights such as same-sex marriage, and practically none celebrate it as an affirmation of sexual diversity. Indeed, gay-rights organizations that advocate for same-sex marriage offer little in the way of lofty rhetoric or far-sighted vision. At best we have statements like the one from a Lambda Legal report titled "Decisions, Decisions: Deciding Whether to Get Married in Canada or Massachusetts," which tells the soon-to-be-wed gay adult that "your personal example of love and commitment will be an important contribution to expanding equality."[56] The suggestion, of course, is that marriage is symbolically such a powerful institution that achieving it will represent a major expansion of social and political equality. As with so much of the rhetoric supporting same-sex marriage, the message implicates children. We are asked to infer that "expanding equality" will especially benefit younger generations of queer youth—the gay kids of today who will constitute the gay brides and gay grooms of tomorrow.

That the child exists in this formulation only as an abstraction is typical of the discourse of child protectionism. To give the endangered child a name and a voice would destroy his or her supposed universality. In the debate over same-sex marriage, neither side discusses in any depth the experiences of actual children who were raised, or who are being raised, by same-sex couples. Conservatives apparently ignore such experiences because what sociological data exists—and there is not much—suggests that children raised by same-sex couples are by no means ill affected by the experience.[57] Furthermore, with organizations ranging from the American Academy of Pediatrics to the American Bar Association endorsing parenting by same-sex couples, it is difficult to make a factual—as opposed to moral or ideological—case against the practice. The silence of the gay-rights organizations on this topic only underscores their normative visions of the family. Regardless of whether or not same-sex marriage receives wider legal recognition in coming years, it seems clear that the number of children raised by lesbians and gay men, alone or coupled, will only increase. Rather than focus our attention on the abstract figure of the endangered child to make the case either for—or against—same-sex marriage, it seems to me that if we genuinely care about children's well-being we should attempt to understand how children raised by same-sex couples experience and make sense of their upbringings.

To do this effectively, we have to empower them first to speak. Fortunately, this has begun to occur, though on a very limited scale. Numerous local organizations for the children of lesbian and gay parents exist in the United States, many of them chapters or affiliates of Children of Lesbians and Gays Everywhere (COLAGE). This organization is somewhat remarkable in that it is not only one *for* the children of lesbian and gay parents but also one, to some extent, *by* them as well. For example, teenagers attend the organization's conferences, and the group's *Just for Us* newsletter routinely contains articles submitted by children as young as ten. Indeed, a 2004 newsletter that focused on same-sex marriage contains arguments and analyses that are as nuanced as those published in most adult gay-rights organizations.[58]

For same-sex marriage to have a transformative impact on society, its proponents must reject the pragmatic impulse to reify a normative vision of family. This means accepting couples who choose to remain childless; acknowledging that individuals have the right to complicated sexual histories, desires, and activities; and respecting children as autonomous individuals who must have a space to develop as intellectual, moral, and sexual people. None of this is a given, and even if it does occur, the results might not mirror anyone's vision of a progressive utopia. Nonetheless, the campaign for same-sex marriage offers a rare opportunity to reconceptualize the family. To everyone's loss, no one is seizing the opportunity.

Notes

An early and much shorter version of this article was delivered at the annual meeting of the American Studies Association in Washington, DC, in 2005. I thank the organizers of that conference for inviting me to participate. Several friends and colleagues offered insightful comments on early drafts of this article. I especially want to thank Rebecca Amato, Kitty Krupat, Michael Palm, Kimberly Phillips-Fein, and James Polchin for their time and encouragement. Finally, I would like to acknowledge here two of my favorite people, Zachary Lentz Larew and Zachary Dale McMillan. Each in his own way has challenged me to think more deeply and thoughtfully about how children raised by gay parents experience and understand their upbringings.

1. The 2005 vote was the second step in the three-step, multiyear process of amending the Massachusetts constitution. Massachusetts law requires that the combined legislature pass proposed amendments in two consecutive years; if that occurs, the measure is then sent to voters as a referendum in the third year. Quote from Pam Belluck, "Massachusetts Rejects Bill to Eliminate Gay Marriage," *New York Times*, September 15, 2005.

2. See: Philippe Ariès, *Centuries of Childhood: A Social History of Family Life*, trans. Robert Baldick (New York: Knopf, 1962).

3. For a sociological analysis of the deployment of the discourse of child endangerment, see Joel Best, *Threatened Children* (Chicago: University of Chicago Press, 1990). For

historical analyses, see Judith Sealander, *The Failed Century of the Child: Governing America's Young in the Twentieth Century* (New York: Cambridge University Press, 2003); and Philip Jenkins, *Moral Panic: Changing Concepts of the Child Molester in Modern America* (New Haven, CT: Yale University Press, 1998). For analyses of how the rhetoric of child endangerment is used to police adult sexual activity, see James R. Kincaid, *Erotic Innocence: The Culture of Child Molesting* (Durham, NC: Duke University Press, 1998); and Michael Bronski, *The Pleasure Principle: Sex, Backlash, and the Struggle for Gay Freedom* (New York: St. Martin's, 1998).

4. Specifically, the amendment added the phrase *affectional or sexual preferences* to the list of protected conditions enumerated in the code's Human Right Ordinance. Protected conditions that already existed included race, sex, and religion.

5. The commission passed the amendment unanimously in December 1976, but county law required a second vote to amend the code. The January 1977 vote took place after Bryant first spoke out against the measure; that vote was eight to three. Coincidentally, the commissioner who proposed the amendment was Ruth Shack, a Democrat from Miami Beach and the wife of Bryant's longtime agent, Dick Shack. Bryant, who had publicly endorsed Ruth Shack in her campaign, later said she was appalled at the commissioner's political views. Bryant and Dick Shack parted ways professionally in the middle of the campaign. For a background on the events leading up to the amendment's proposal and initial enactment, see Dudley Clendinen and Adam Nagourney, *Out for Good: The Struggle to Build a Gay Rights Movement in America* (New York: Simon and Schuster, 1999), 293–95; for similar characterizations, see John Loughery, *The Other Side of Silence: Men's Lives and Gay Identities: A Twentieth-Century History* (New York: Henry Holt, 1998), 372–76. Bryant herself wrote extensively about the campaign in two books. See Anita Bryant, *The Anita Bryant Story: The Survival of Our Nation's Families and the Threat of Militant Homosexuality* (Old Tappan, NJ: Fleming H. Revell, 1977); and Anita Bryant and Bob Green, *At Any Cost* (Old Tappan, NJ: Fleming H. Revell, 1978). For more on Ruth Shack's support of the amendment, see Morton Lucoff, "Homosexual Groups Urging Anti-bias Law," *Miami News*, November 16, 1976.

6. Anita Bryant, *Raising God's Children* (Old Tappan, NJ: Fleming H. Revell, 1977), 30.

7. A home-rule amendment in the Dade County Code exempted the county school board and all state and federal offices operating in the county from having to observe the county's antibias laws relating to employment. The gay rights amendment thus affected private schools, both religious and secular, but not public ones. See "How Ordinance Can Affect Gays and Everyone Else," *Miami Herald*, June 6, 1977.

8. See Alan Ebert, "Couples," *People*, January 24, 1977, 33–35.

9. Bryant, *Anita Bryant Story*, 114.

10. Bryant and Green, *At Any Cost*, 18.

11. Frank Greve and Gerald Storch, "Anita Bryant: Homosexuality Is a Sin," *Miami Herald Tropic Magazine*, May 29, 1977, 6–13.

12. Miami saw several moral panics related to homosexuals in the years prior to Bryant's campaign. One occurred in 1954 after a young girl was kidnapped, sexually abused, and murdered. See Fred Fejes, "Murder, Perversion, and Moral Panic: The 1954 Media Campaign against Miami's Homosexuals and the Discourse of Civic Betterment," *Journal of the History of Sexuality* 9 (2000): 305–47. Florida's infamous "Johns Committee," named after a state senator, waged a decade-long campaign against "subversives" in state

employment. Although it was formed to identify communist sympathizers, it ended up targeting gay men and lesbians who worked in the state university system. See James A. Schnur, "Closet Crusaders: The Johns Committee and Homophobia, 1956–1965," in *Carryin' on in the Gay and Lesbian South*, ed. John Howard (New York: New York University Press, 1997), 132–63.

13. For more on the panic, see Jenkins, *Moral Panic*, esp. chaps. 6 and 7.

14. Ray Moseley, "Child Porno: Sickness for Sale," *Chicago Tribune*, May 15, 1977.

15. The main text of Save Our Children's ad read in part: "Parents are confused and don't know the real dangers posed by many homosexuals—and perceive them all as being gentle, non-aggressive types. The other side of the homosexual coin is a hair-raising pattern of recruitment and outright seduction and molestation . . . a growing pattern that predictably will intensify if society approves laws granting legitimacy to the sexually perverted" (*Miami Herald*, June 6, 1977).

16. Bryant, *Anita Bryant Story*, 62.

17. See "Pro-Ordinance Campaign Theme: Human Rights Are Absolute," March 15, 1977, a four-page press release issued by Miami Victory Campaign, located in the uncataloged files of the Stonewall Archives, Fort Lauderdale. Kunst and Alan Rockway, Kunst's business partner and also the codirector of Miami Victory Campaign, issued numerous press releases and several pamphlets during the course of the campaign.

18. With Kunst gone and Campbell, the bathhouse king, hardly the person to counter Bryant's moralistic arguments, the coalition hired as its managers two well-known activists from opposite ends of the country, Ethan Geto from New York and Jim Foster from San Francisco. One of Geto's first moves was to drop the word *gay* from the group's title, changing it to the simpler and less divisive Dade County Coalition for Human Rights. Geto was an aide to the New York politician Robert Abrams; Foster had been the political chairman of San Francisco's Society for Individual Rights (SIR), one of the city's first gay-rights organizations.

19. See esp. Loughery, *Other Side of Silence*, 378–79.

20. Dade County Coalition for Human Rights, "Don't Let Them Chip Away at the Constitution," *Miami Herald*, June 5, 1977. The ad appeared in the *Herald* on other days as well.

21. Dade County Coalition for Human Rights, "Freedom in America Begins and Ends Here," *Miami Herald*, June 3, 1977.

22. Clergy and Laity for Human Rights and Dade County Coalition for Human Rights, "Clergy and Laity for Human Rights," *Miami Herald*, June 2, 1977.

23. Miami Victory Campaign, "The Underdog Is Your Best Friend," *Miami Herald*, May 19, 1977.

24. Miami Victory Campaign, "NO is the answer . . . the question is HUMAN RIGHTS." The ad originally appeared in the *Weekly* (Miami), May 5, 1977, 23. Kunst reprinted it in an undated pamphlet now located in the uncataloged files of the Stonewall Archives, Fort Lauderdale. Interestingly, this advertisement was one of the very few in the campaign that was produced by a gay-rights group and that also mentioned children. It asked in part: "Would you sacrifice your children to Anita Bryant? . . . Could you allow the creation of official second-class citizenship for your children and grandchildren and other American citizens?"

25. Dade County Coalition for Human Rights, "Myths and Lies," *Miami Herald*, June 6, 1977.

26. Ibid.

27. Ibid.

28. Bryant specifically invoked the phrase *special privileges* in Bryant and Green, *At Any Cost*, 131.

29. Theodore Stanger, "Dade Approves Ordinance Banning Bias against Gays," *Miami Herald*, January 19, 1977.

30. "Vote FOR Repeal of Gay Ordinance," *Miami News*, June 6, 1977. The *Miami Herald* also questioned the extent to which homosexuals faced discrimination. In an article published one week before the referendum, the newspaper reported that only three complaints of antigay discrimination had been filed in the five full months in which the ordinance had been in effect. See Theodore Stanger, "Only a Few Gays Filing Bias Complaints," *Miami Herald*, May 30, 1977.

31. Beth Dunlop, "Bryant's Fight against Gays Costs Her a Host Spot on TV," *Miami Herald*, February 25, 1977.

32. Ralph Renick, "The Blacklisting Returns," Channel 4 News, CBS-TV, WTVJ, February 24, 1977.

33. John McMullan, "Anita versus Gays: Who's Discriminated Against?" *Miami Herald*, February 27, 1977.

34. Ibid.

35. Bryant, *Anita Bryant Story*, 62.

36. For several such examples, see Carl Hiaasen, "Out of the Closet, and Then Some," *Miami Herald Tropic Magazine*, June 5, 1977, 8–14.

37. I purposely studied well-established multi-issue organizations because I believe they are more representative of their respective movements than are newer organizations that focus solely on marriage. Such single-issue organizations do exist, however, especially on the part of those advocating same-sex marriage. See, for example, the Web sites of the Freedom to Marry Collaborative, www.freedomtomarry.org (accessed May 15, 2007); and of Marriage Equality USA, www.marriageequality.org (accessed May 15, 2007). A major conservative organization that focuses on same-sex marriage is the Arlington Group, a coalition of so-called pro-family organizations (www.thearlingtongroup.org; accessed October 15, 2005).

38. James Dobson, "Eleven Arguments against Same-Sex Marriage (Part 1 of 5)," www.family.org/cforum/extras/a0032427.cfm (accessed October 15, 2005).

39. Ibid.

40. Glenn T. Stanton, "Are Same-Sex Families Good for Children? What the Social Sciences Say (and Don't Say) about Family Experimentation," Focus on the Family, Colorado Springs, 5; see www.citizenlink.org/pdfs/fosi/marriage/Citizen_Health_of_SSF.pdf (accessed May 17, 2007).

41. Daniel Allott, "Questions and Answers about Homosexual 'Marriage,'" American Values, Washington, DC, July 23, 2004, www.amvalues.org/press_releases.php.

42. For more on the construction of social problems (and a fascinating analysis of the role of the child victim in contemporary U.S. culture), see Best, *Threatened Children*.

43. All three organizations made clear that the census figures were rough estimates given that the census itself did not include questions about sexual orientation. The figure of 594,000 includes only those situations in which the person filling out the census form identified as his or her "husband/wife" or "unmarried partner" a person of the same sex. Single lesbians and gay men raising children are therefore not included in this figure. See Gary Gates, "Same-Sex Couples and the Gay, Lesbian, Bisexual Population: New Estimates from the American Community Survey," Williams Institute on Sexual Orientation Law and Public

Policy, University of California at Los Angeles School of Law, October 2006, www.law
.ucla.edu/williamsinstitute/publications/SameSexCouplesandGLBpopACS.pdf; see also
Lisa Bennett and Gary Gates, "The Cost of Marriage Inequality to Children and Their
Same-Sex Parents," Human Rights Campaign, April 13, 2004, 2-7, www.hrc.org/Content/
ContentGroups/Publications1/kids_doc_final.pdf.

44. Bennett and Gates base their theory of a census undercount of same-sex couples on the
belief that some same-sex couples would not identify themselves as such to a government
agency, while others would eschew the "husband/wife" and "unmarried partner"
terminology the Census Bureau employed. They base the figure of 3.1 million people living
together in same-sex relationships on an estimate that 5 percent of the U.S. adult population
is gay or lesbian and that 30 percent of those individuals are coupled. Both figures are
conjectural. See Bennett and Gates, "The Cost of Marriage," 5. Nonetheless, the HRC
actually uses the 3.1 million figure in its publication "Answers to Questions about Marriage
Equality." In a note, the group states that the "estimated number of people in same-sex
relationships has been adjusted by 62 percent to compensate for the widely reported
undercount in the Census." See Human Rights Campaign, "Answers to Questions about
Marriage Equality," updated 2005, www.hrc.org/Content/ContentGroups/Publications1/
marriage_brochure_2006.pdf (accessed May 17, 2007).

45. Bennett and Gates, "Cost of Marriage," 3.

46. Human Rights Campaign, "Answers to Questions about Marriage Equality" offers no basis
for this figure.

47. General Accounting Office, "Defense of Marriage Act: An Update to Prior Report,"
Washington, DC, 2004, www.gao.gov/new.items/d04353r.pdf.

48. See, for example, the National Gay and Lesbian Task Force's fact sheet titled "Why
Civil Unions Are Not Enough," www.thetaskforce.org/downloads/reports/fact_sheets/
WhyCivilUnionsAreNotEnough.pdf (accessed May 15, 2007).

49. A notable exception is a group of activists and intellectuals loosely affiliated with the
organization Queers for Economic Justice. In a 2006 position paper titled "Beyond Same-
Sex Marriage: A New Strategic Vision for All Our Families and Relationships," the group
called for "separating basic forms of legal and economic recognition from the requirement
of marital and conjugal relationship." See www.beyondmarriage.org/BeyondMarriage.pdf
(accessed May 15, 2007).

50. Bennett and Gates, "Cost of Marriage," 13.

51. Ibid., 3.

52. Cheryl Jacques, "A Message from HRC President Cheryl Jacques," in Human Rights
Campaign, "Answers to Questions about Marriage Equality." Jacques was president of the
HRC for only one year. She was ousted shortly after the 2004 elections, in which same-sex
marriage bans passed in the eleven states that had them on the ballot. In her time at the
HRC, Jacques had focused on defeating both the same-sex marriage bans and also George
W. Bush's reelection efforts.

53. Ibid.

54. In raw figures, the census data actually suggests that cohabitating same-sex couples raising
children constitute less than 0.5 percent of all households with children in the United States.
This is decidedly *not* a figure that advocates of same-sex marriage advertise. See Bennett
and Gates, "Cost of Marriage," 14–15.

55. See esp. Andrew Sullivan, *Virtually Normal: An Argument about Homosexuality* (New
York: Knopf, 1995).

56. Lambda Legal, "Decisions, Decisions: Deciding Whether to Get Married in Canada or Massachusetts," November 29, 2004, www.lambdalegal.org/our-work/publications/facts-backgrounds/page.jsp?itemID=31988461.

57. For two important studies, see Timothy Biblarz and Judith Stacey, "(How) Does the Sexual Orientation of Parents Matter?" *American Sociological Review* 66, no. 2 (2001): 159–83; and William Meezan and Jonathan Rauch, "Gay Marriage, Same-Sex Parenting, and America's Children," *Future of Children* 15 (2005): 97–115.

58. The newsletter is located at www.colage.org/programs/justforus/JFUsp04.pdf (accessed May 15, 2007). For an informal ethnography of young people involved in COLAGE, see Abigail Garner, *Families Like Mine: Children of Gay Parents Tell It Like It Is* (New York: HarperCollins, 2004).

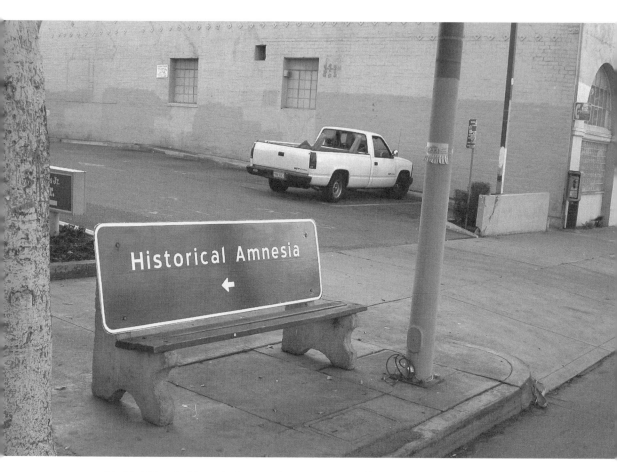

"Untitled (Historical Amnesia)," Kerry Tribe's 2002–2003 public project for Jacob Fabricius at Highland Avenue and Sunset Boulevard, Los Angeles. Courtesy of Kerry Tribe

"But Joan! You're My Daughter!"
The Gay and Lesbian Alliance against
Defamation and the Politics of Amnesia

Vincent Doyle

In October 1999, the executive director of the Gay and Lesbian Alliance against Defamation (GLAAD) gave a speech to the gay and lesbian employee group of Bell Atlantic. In this speech, Joan Garry described herself as someone from a corporate background who, until she came to GLAAD, "did not consider myself political at all." "My activism was all about my family," she said. As a partnered lesbian with kids living in the New Jersey suburbs, Garry claimed, she brought a unique ability to put herself "in the other guys' shoes." She went on to describe her sense of how GLAAD evolved: "Things have changed in fifteen years. We've made solid progress culturally. . . . And as a result of that progress, GLAAD's strategies have changed. Today I see our work is largely . . . about building relationships and much about education." In a key section of the speech, Garry invited her audience of corporate managers and executives to "revisit the images we conjure up when we consider the word 'activist.'" Activism, she said, is no longer just the "direct action methods" that "helped create a picture for America of a gay rights activist." Referring to the early years at GLAAD, she stated, "Back then, no one was paying any attention, and the only strategy that made any sense was of the 'in your face' variety," a mode of activism she compared to banging on the door. "Their job," she said, "was simply to be heard and to do what they could . . . to get that door open." The new professional

Radical History Review

Issue 100 (Winter 2008)   DOI 10.1215/01636545-2007-031

© 2008 by MARHO: The Radical Historians' Organization, Inc.

activism, by contrast, was about building relationships and educating corporate decision makers. The ground of advocacy, she implied, had shifted away from the unruliness of the street to be replaced by the efficiency of the boardroom.[1]

In recent years, much critical attention has been paid to major structural changes in the institutionalized LGBT (lesbian, gay, bisexual, transgender) movement. Lisa Duggan, for example, has argued that the large organizations of the gay and lesbian movement have abandoned progressive politics in favor of a conservative politics of visibility and equality aligned with neoliberalism.[2] Other movement critics such as Michael Warner, Alexandra Chasin, Eric Clarke, and Urvashi Vaid have claimed that movement organizations have betrayed many of the principles of gay liberation and lesbian feminism and instead have become instruments of normalization and assimilation. The mainstreaming of the movement, they charge, has produced partial and unevenly distributed accommodations that benefit only those gays and lesbians who best conform to mainstream standards of middle-class respectability.[3] Yet from an empirical perspective, comparatively little has been written about LGBT organizations themselves and the people who lead them. How does the mainstreaming of the movement manifest itself on the ground? Who are the movement's new leaders and how do they understand LGBT politics, culture, and history? What dispositions lead them to make the decisions they do? To what extent is the movement's conservative turn a result of a deliberate takeover, and to what extent is it a reflection of structural and historical factors outside the conscious purview of movement agents?

These are some of the questions I had in mind when I approached my study of cultural politics in the institutionalized LGBT movement. I hoped to understand something about how, why, and to what extent the mainstreaming of the movement has occurred and, given those realities, what avenues of residual or emergent political possibility still existed. Such an endeavor required investigating the subjectivities of movement leaders and methods that are seldom used in social science studies of movement politics. If we are to move beyond the impasses of visibility politics in the age of mainstreaming, I contend, we need living accounts of the practice of both politics and representation.

Between 2000 and 2001, I conducted an ethnographic study of the professionalization of media activism at GLAAD. As one of the consequences of this professionalization, new entrants to GLAAD had constructed and institutionalized a historical narrative that justified their newfound prominence. This narrative was characterized by a kind of structurally embedded amnesia, a strategic forgetting—though not necessarily a deliberate one—born of a felt need to graft the professionalization of media activism onto a past imagined as the early stage of a natural evolution away from the confrontation with dominant institutions toward the supposed equality that visibility politics continually promises but perpetually defers.

Narrating Movement History

Historians conventionally narrate the history of the LGBT movement in terms of the dialectical tug and pull between liberationism, which seeks the radical redefinition of gender and sexual norms and the dismantling of oppressive structures, and assimilationism, which refers to the legitimation of homosexuality within existing social norms and institutions. In 1999, however, GLAAD's board of directors devised a three-year strategic plan that constructed these tensions not as a tug-of-war but as a quasi-teleological evolution away from a confrontation with the dominant culture and toward the promised land of full integration. The alliance's strategic direction, its leaders wrote, was focused on "all that is explicit and implicit in the phrase 'we want in,'" which they borrowed from an essay by the historian John D'Emilio. In that essay, D'Emilio states explicitly that his characterization of the movement's current emphasis on mainstream integration is "meant to be descriptive rather than prescriptive."[4] Ignoring this caveat, GLAAD's strategic plan positioned D'Emilio as a sanctioning authority, someone who guaranteed that history was indeed on the organization's side as it envisioned a future predicated on "access and inclusion . . . constructive engagement and winning allies outside our own community."[5]

From its grassroots beginnings in the mid-1980s, GLAAD had, by the end of the 1990s, become a national organization led by a self-perpetuating board of directors and staffed by skilled professionals who hailed from corporate media and public relations. Before becoming GLAAD's executive director, Joan Garry had been an executive at Showtime and MTV, both part of the Viacom media empire. Steve Spurgeon, the GLAAD director of communications at the time of my fieldwork, had been a vice president at one of the top public relations firms in the United States. Scott Seomin, the GLAAD director of entertainment media, had been a producer at *Entertainment Tonight*.

At the time of her speech to the Bell Atlantic gay and lesbian employee group in 1999, Joan Garry had good reason to believe that the doors of corporate America had swung wide open. Ellen Degeneres had already been out for two years, *Will and Grace* was a big success on NBC, and corporations seemed to be tripping over themselves to land a piece of the burgeoning gay and lesbian consumer market. But Garry's speech also spoke to a lack of knowledge of movement history and a narrow conception of direct action as little more than a prelude to the more serious business of walking through the corporate door with briefcase in hand to hold polite discussions. The role of direct action in community building and identity formation had completely disappeared, as had the circumstances and motivations that first gave rise to GLAAD.

At one point in the speech, Garry went so far as to say that the "folks who founded GLAAD back in 1985 probably did not consider themselves activists either but rather just a group of writers fed up with how the *New York Post* was covering the AIDS epidemic."[6] This would no doubt have come as news to GLAAD founders Marty Robinson, Jim Owles, Vito Russo, and Arnie Kantrowitz, all of whom cut their teeth in the militant Gay Activists Alliance in the early 1970s. In an interview, Kantrowitz told me that when he introduced himself to Garry at a GLAAD function held toward the beginning of her tenure, she responded with an "uh-huh" that betrayed a complete lack of recognition. Said Kantrowitz, chuckling under his breath, "I felt very nice about that." Then, in a high campy voice, he added, "But Joan! You're my daughter!"[7]

I was struck throughout my fieldwork by how little new entrants to GLAAD knew about the history of gay and lesbian media activism or even about GLAAD's own organizational history. Another early GLAAD board member, Jewelle Gomez, told me about an otherwise pleasant encounter with a new board member who she said displayed no interest whatsoever in learning about GLAAD's early days. Seomin, the director of entertainment media, had no idea that a one-man organization called the Gay Media Task Force had performed duties virtually identical to his in the mid- to late 1970s. Addressing college students in the fall of 2000, GLAAD's director of communications, Spurgeon, stated that GLAAD had existed "ten to twelve years," as though GLAAD's 1985 founding was so far in the past that the date could only be approximated.

Although the new professional breed at GLAAD sometimes acknowledged their lack of prior involvement in the movement as a limitation, they pointed to their professional skills and connections as compensation. Spurgeon, for example, told me in an interview that the movement now requires people who have what he called a "sophisticated understanding of how the world works," which was presumably a product of extensive corporate experience like his own. When he interviewed for the post of GLAAD director of communications, he said, someone with a long history of movement activism told him that they could not picture him "chained to the fence in front of the *New York Times*." He replied, "Why would I chain myself when I can just call them up for a meeting?" Spurgeon told me that he could not have taken the GLAAD job a few years prior to his appointment because, he said, he was not ready for the movement, and the movement was not ready for him. Landing the job with GLAAD was a "fortuitous intersection of need and opportunity," he told me.[8]

Elizabeth Birch, the former director of the Human Rights Campaign (HRC), expressed a similar sentiment when she told a reporter, "in the 1990s, there had to be a meeting of minds between raw activist spirit and the communications and marketing techniques that define a new voice for gay America. . . . It came together in the person of Elizabeth Birch."[9] Birch's statement is not merely an example of "personal arrogance," as Chasin has suggested, but it is symptomatic of how profoundly the structural position of the movement shifted in the 1990s, largely as a result of the production of a gay and lesbian market.[10] It is this shift that provided the underlying conditions for people like Birch and Spurgeon to feel strongly that they were the right people to lead the movement at this historical moment. It was also this felt sense of the seemingly "miraculous adjustment"[11] between position and disposition that made it possible for Birch to add: "Imagine what you would have done if three years ago you woke up and found that someone had handed you the movement. . . . I'll bet you would have made most of the decisions I've made."[12]

Birch's comments suggest the extent to which changing structural conditions in the movement required by necessity something akin to historical amnesia. What had felt to many longtime movement activists like a hostile takeover felt to the movement's new entrants like a historically sanctioned handover. When I asked Spurgeon how he felt about being accused of partaking in a takeover, he became visibly emotional and answered that he had found the "resentment and distrust" toward him "hurtful" and could not understand, echoing the words of Rodney King, why there could not be enough room for everyone to get along. "I can contribute something," he said. "I am here to be used."[13]

Spurgeon and other new entrants from corporate backgrounds might have been there "to be used," but they also commanded some of the highest salaries in the LGBT nonprofit sector. They were remarkably well integrated within the media institutions they sought to reform and therefore tended to measure the value of movement agents according to the same criteria those institutions employ: one's value to the movement, they believed, closely corresponded to one's value in the corporate world. Accordingly, the more GLAAD positioned itself as a "resource" and a cheerleader to the media industries, the more the organization enjoyed corporate fund-raising success; and as GLAAD's annual budgets increased from year to year, so did the salaries of GLAAD's top staffers. Garry's total compensation in 1998 was $108,302 and stood at $228,250 in 2003, making her the highest-paid executive director of any LGBT movement organization.

That movement leaders should ideally be highly skilled and well paid for their efforts is not at issue, but what is troubling about the rising salaries of GLAAD's upper-level staff over the years is the link between corporate fund-raising success and the organization's increased integration with the media industries. The more GLAAD benefited organizationally from closer ties to media corporations, the more GLAAD employees benefited personally. Far from acknowledging these potential conflicts of interest (or even perceiving them as such), GLAAD's new entrants justified their salaries and professional orientations in terms of the important roles they played in what they saw as overarching historical objectives. They felt that marketing gays and lesbians to America was precisely what the movement needed at this point in time and that people with corporate backgrounds like themselves were therefore in an ideal position to lead the way. As media professionals, they had internalized the limits and rewards of the advocacy structure set up by the media companies to manage and contain the dissent of marginalized or underrepresented groups. Instead of seeing visibility as a precarious, ambivalent, conditional, revocable and market-driven achievement, then, they labored under the impression that they were responsible for great changes in the way the media represents LGBT people. As a result, they often allowed access to media decision makers and homonormative representations of gay and lesbian lives to stand in for meaningful influence and potentially transformative images that might have better reflected the lived circumstances of a wider diversity of LGBT people.

Although these findings support existing accounts of the institutionalized LGBT movement, critiques of movement mainstreaming only tell a part of the story. For example, among the strategic imperatives adopted by the GLAAD board in 1999 in addition to "we want in" was the injunction to "harness the power of diversity," which translated into various attempts to broaden GLAAD's representational reach. These attempts at diversification, however, were hindered by the overarching importance of development objectives and concerns about GLAAD's standing among mainstream media professionals. This situation points to a fundamental tension built into GLAAD's 1999 strategic plan. On the one hand, GLAAD's board recognized that the organization needed to promote movement autonomy and represent a wider array of LGBT people. On the other hand, the board felt obliged—indeed, historically mandated—to advance the externally oriented, narrowly defined objectives of mainstream integration and visibility. Unsurprisingly, as "harness the power of diversity" came into conflict with "we want in," the latter almost always trumped the former.

According to the GLAAD board, harnessing the power of diversity meant to "define ourselves broadly and openly. Affirmatively seek out and incorporate diverse life experiences, talents, expertise, ideas and opinions. Infuse this power into who we are and what we do. Work to knit these together into a whole which is greater than the sum of its parts."[14] As GLAAD's leaders struggled to implement this policy, concerns with professional standing, a competition for resources, and mainstream visibility were like so many strands of yarn that competed with diversity objectives. When diversity objectives did get woven in, they tended to quickly unravel or get lost in the fabric amid many more powerful strands. This was not so much the result of any conscious intention on the part of GLAAD's leaders, but one of the consequences of the narrative they had constructed (and which was constructed for them) that made integration into the mainstream media seem like an evolutionary historical inevitability. This narrative, including its embedded absences, helped to justify what was, in effect, the takeover of GLAAD by stigmaphobic agents oriented to the assimilation of (some) gays and lesbians within the neoliberal world order. While this integration has been beneficial to GLAAD's fund-raising, media prestige, and institution building, it has not necessarily led to more influence in the media advocacy system, especially in periods of conflict, and has also made it more difficult for the LGBT movement to advocate effectively on behalf of diverse constituencies.

How Do You Solve a Problem Like *Queer as Folk*?

The alliance's responses to the Showtime Network's adaptation of the UK's Channel 4 series *Queer as Folk* provides a good example of how the primary importance accorded to mainstream integration objectives tended to structure organizational outcomes, even as GLAAD's leaders made earnest attempts to represent the interests of a broader range of gays and lesbians. *Queer as Folk* presented GLAAD with a unique and challenging set of parameters. It was the first dramatic series on U.S. television to deploy a declaratively LGBT universe. It featured abundant drug use and explicit sex—some of it intergenerational, some of it public, and some of it promiscuous. What was a gay and lesbian media activist organization to do?

In the weeks leading up to the launch of *Queer as Folk*, I conducted interviews with the three GLAAD staff members most responsible for shaping the organization's response to the program. The alliance had been unusually slow to formulate a position on the program because staff members struggled personally and professionally with the fact that much of the sex depicted on *Queer as Folk* did not conform to normative standards of sexual propriety. The show might prove popular with LGBT audiences, they surmised, but how would its sexual frankness play with straights?

Spurgeon told me that he ultimately felt professionally "obliged to give the program support" because he recognized that GLAAD's mission was to promote "fair, accurate, and inclusive" (as opposed to simply "positive") images of gays and lesbians. "I don't see how we . . . as an organization can be so wholeheartedly supportive of what I consider to be highly assimilationist programming such as *Will and Grace*," he told me, "and then not also embrace something that shows another segment of our community." *Queer as Folk*, he said, is "fair, accurate, and inclusive for some people . . . a lot of people are out there making love. You know? I'm sorry, that is a part of what gay life is about. Okay, now here we have the other extreme where people are loving every bush that doesn't move. . . . Okay, fine. But you know what? That happens. We know they're there." On a personal level, however, Spurgeon told me that he would not have supported the program had the decision been solely up to him. He explained that as a "middle-aged man from the conservative Midwest," he believed that in the fight for gay and lesbian equality, "everything is about the undecideds." This demographic, he told me, would have difficulty "embracing the sensibility of the characters on this show." I asked him what in particular might offend, and Spurgeon listed the following: the way the characters call each other "faggots," "use each other for sex," and take drugs, as well as the fact that the program dramatizes what he called "every parent's worst fear: the gay predator as abductor of boys."[15]

Similarly, for Garry, the challenge presented by *Queer as Folk* was deciding whether there is a "sufficient quantity of images out there so that this becomes one of a variety of pictures that people see of gay and lesbian life." *Queer as Folk*, she told me, "in many ways represents . . . the kinds of stereotypes that GLAAD in its early days [was created] to fight against. . . . All the main character seems to think about is really his next trick." And another character, she said, "who happens to be seventeen . . . is equally as predatorial with anyone . . . to whom he is attracted for that moment in time." One of GLAAD's roles, she said "is to really get the word out that this is . . . what some of us are, but . . . there are many of us who are not like this." Like Spurgeon, Garry said that she recognized the program as a fair "depiction of a segment of our community." It is fair for a media company to depict gay men in this way, she suggested, "just as it is fair to show lesbians who live in New Jersey behind white picket fences."[16] (In her public appearances, Garry often refers to the literal white picket fence in front of the house in suburban New Jersey that she shares with her partner of more than twenty years and their three children.) Images of men who frequent sex clubs were therefore acceptable to GLAAD, but only insofar as they were balanced out by homonormative representations. This perspective underscored the extent to which GLAAD's leaders understood mainstream integration, "we want in," to be predicated on assimilationist imagery. Since *Queer as Folk* did not meet this standard with regard to the sexual lives of its gay male characters, GLAAD successfully lobbied Showtime to include this disclaimer at the start of the first episode: "*Queer as Folk* is a celebration of the lives and passions of a group of gay friends. It is not meant to reflect all of gay society."[17]

The organization also opted to distance itself from *Queer as Folk* by turning down Showtime's offer to benefit from the show's Los Angeles red carpet premiere. Seomin, the entertainment media director, told me he thought this decision was "ridiculous" and that he had learned of it from a reporter while on vacation. I asked him what he thought had motivated the decision. He said:

This is a . . . raw, nearly X-rated, certainly R-rated, view of gay men who do drugs and have a lot of promiscuous, meaningless sex. . . . You know, the gay men I know, frankly, they have sex. . . . There's so much in our world, gay and straight, when it comes to sex, it's shame-based, but certainly that's magnified for gay people because we're told that we're sick and wrong and all that. And I feel really bad because I see that here. I see a lot of shame-based decisions. We don't represent absolutely every gay and lesbian person on this planet, but I'd like to think that we could represent the ones that . . . are sexually active.[18]

In contrast to Spurgeon and Garry, Seomin felt strongly that GLAAD had an obligation to defend the sexual cultures of gay men.

When GLAAD finally released its statement about *Queer as Folk* in December 2000, about a week after the first broadcast of the program, it was obvious that the perspectives of Spurgeon and Garry had hardened and prevailed. The statement characterized *Queer as Folk* as a depiction of a "subset of our community" that is "frank and honest" but "falls short of fair and inclusive." It noted the program's inclusion of "both positive and negative images." On the positive side, it mentioned the "camaraderie between the lead characters, a boy's intense coming out, a lesbian couple raising a child fathered by a gay man, and the men's supportive families." On the negative side, the statement bemoaned the "focus on the men's promiscuity, their narcissism and smugness, and the recreational use of drugs."[19]

The statement went on to criticize the main characters as "exclusive unto themselves" and to offer an ambivalent mix of faint praise and not-so-faint condemnation: "This stark and unapologetic depiction of their licentious egocentrism is a bold contrast to traditional media stereotypes of gay men as victims, amusing commentators, or assorted felons. For this core group to all share a shallow dedication to homogeneity is realistic. What is not realistic is how they can all apparently live in Pittsburgh without encountering any people of color—gay or straight. . . . There are numerous missed opportunities to responsibly represent diversity." According to the statement, then, *Queer as Folk* could be deemed "accurate," but fell short of "fair and inclusive" because it depicted a gay world cut off from straight society and from people of color. The alliance's concern with *Queer as Folk*'s depiction of a separate gay sexual world at odds with the values of the majority heterosexual culture was consistent with the views expressed by Spurgeon and Garry prior to the show. The inclusion of criticism about the absence of people of color on the program, by contrast, caught me, and Showtime, by surprise. It seemed as though GLAAD was in the process of attempting to meld "harness the power of diversity" with "we want in."

I interviewed Gene Falk, a former cochair of GLAAD's board of directors who is also one of Showtime's top executives. Falk told me that many people at Showtime felt "ambushed" by GLAAD's criticism of *Queer as Folk*. At the very least, he said, GLAAD should have honored the terms of the implicit agreement it has with the media companies with which it maintains friendly relations:

> This is the access part and it works two ways . . . it gives you responsibility as well as giving you certain privileges. The good news is that Showtime wanted to know what GLAAD thought and let what GLAAD thought help shape the thinking about what should be happening with the show. But then GLAAD has an obligation that if you're gonna say, "Well, we got a problem with this," to alert people to the fact that this is gonna come. Don't ambush people who are inherently your friends. It's not the same thing as "don't criticize people" who are your friends. Don't *ambush* people who are your friends.[20]

Falk was careful to point out that his criticism of GLAAD's handling of the situation was not meant to invalidate the argument about the lack of racial diversity in *Queer as Folk*: "I completely understand why people of color were upset, and . . . the head of Showtime programming was equally upset. . . . That criticism was not something that bothered anyone. It was the way it was delivered." He suggested that a better way to deliver the criticism would have been to acknowledge and celebrate the more innovative aspects of the program ("applaud the good") and tone down the harsh tone of the criticism:

It was a question of balance. If it had been written the other way, if it had said: "this is great Showtime is doing this and we don't even agree with all the things that are in it" . . . and, by the way, we're also really concerned that there are no people of color . . . and you should write to Showtime and tell them that you think that. I think people at Showtime would have applauded.

Falk did not say whether such an approach would have been likely to produce more representations of people of color, but he did suggest that the tone of the statement was reminiscent of a time when GLAAD did not enjoy the kind of access to media executives that it does today:

I spent the last ten years [at GLAAD] getting us beyond this and I [was] completely furious that we [were] going to blow it all up now. You know, it was stupid. And it was stupid not just from Showtime's point of view but from [the point of view of] any media professional. . . . I got calls from friends sort of saying, "What are they thinking?" You know, is this back to the good ol' days of political correctness?

What is "stupid" about the statement is that its wording and the manner of its release (without forewarning) appeared to reinstate the practice of issuing reactive statements critical of media companies with little regard for how these statements might impact GLAAD's relationships with these companies.

Showtime expressed its displeasure directly to GLAAD. Falk said he spent forty-five minutes "just about yelling" at Spurgeon. Some at Showtime wanted GLAAD to publish a public retraction, but, Falk told me, "that had more to do with emotions." The minutes of an emergency GLAAD executive committee meeting to discuss Showtime's reaction to the statement indicated that "Showtime is making some threats, both clear and unclear at this point." (Showtime, like all other major media companies, contributes substantial sums of money to GLAAD, which receives the most corporate funding among U.S. LGBT movement organizations, about $1.5 million in 2000.) The minutes also stated that a meeting between Garry and the chairman and CEO of Showtime, Matt Blank, had been scheduled and that "Garry hopes this meeting . . . will illustrate to Showtime just how important this relationship is to GLAAD."[21]

Shortly after Garry's meeting with Blank, an advertising banner for *Queer as Folk* appeared on the GLAAD Web site. Clicking on the ad sent visitors directly to the Showtime Web site. Later that year, cast members of *Queer as Folk* were present at all four GLAAD Media Awards ceremonies in New York, Los Angeles,

Washington, D.C., and San Francisco. They helped GLAAD raise over $100,000 by presiding over the auctions of walk-on parts on the program. At the Los Angeles ceremony, which was attended by no fewer than seven cast members (in addition to producers and Showtime executives), *Queer as Folk* received a GLAAD Media Award for outstanding drama series, beating out *Buffy the Vampire Slayer*, *Dawson's Creek*, *Felicity*, and MTV's *Undressed*.

The fact that GLAAD's leaders moved so quickly to repair relations with Showtime illustrates the limits of the prevailing discourse that prescribes "we want in" as the path to equality. At the same time, however, the presence of competing perspectives in the data suggests avenues of future queer possibility. A necessary first step for such possibilities to blossom would be for dominant movement agents to come to terms with the history and structural positioning of the organizations they lead. On this point, the Pierre Bourdieu scholar Rodney Benson suggests the importance of making visible the power relations that structure what social agents are able to accomplish in the world: "The first step toward change is to bring to consciousness the invisible structures of belief and practice that lead actors to unwittingly reproduce the system, even as they struggle within it."[22]

The historical narrative by which "we want in" appears to be the natural way forward must be contested on the basis of everyone and everything it leaves out—the subjects and ideologies within the movement whose parts cannot easily be knit together with the existing wholes (and holes) of dominant institutions. The key is to recover some of the autonomy GLAAD has lost in its pursuit of mainstream integration. This is not entirely unfeasible given the media advocacy system as it exists. This system, structurally limited as it is, still provides important mechanisms for marginalized groups to voice concerns about how they are represented. It is crucial for queers to have a strong, well-funded voice within that system, a voice that GLAAD has on many occasions provided and still can provide. For this to happen, GLAAD's leaders will need to acknowledge the value of democratizing their decision-making processes, rendering themselves more accountable to diverse LGBT constituencies and reducing their dependence on the legitimating sanction of dominant (heterosexual) institutions. This will not be easy given the set of ethical commitments and cultural assumptions with which today's movement leaders are endowed. That these commitments and assumptions are themselves the product of a deeply ingrained professional habitus predisposing the movement's new entrants to react defensively to the criticisms leveled against them only adds to the difficulty. As Bourdieu scholar David Schwartz reminds us, however, habitus is not fixed for all time; it is a "kind of deeply structured cultural grammar for action" that, just as grammar organizes speech, "can generate an infinity of possible practices."[23]

Such a conception of social action does not make all cultural practices equally possible or likely, but it does point to the extent to which the habitus of social agents, their "cultural grammar for action," is conditioned by the resources, struggles, narratives, and power relations that structure the fields they cultivate and which cultivate them. It is up to critics of the mainstreaming of gay and lesbian politics and cultures to help foster, through struggle and dialogue, new dispositions and historical narratives in our leaders that might result in more inclusive and transformative representational practices. The stakes of such struggles and dialogue are nothing less than the future of our capacity to imagine new political and cultural possibilities beyond the limits of mainstreaming.

Notes

1. Joan Garry, Speech to Gay and Lesbian Bell Atlantic Employees (GLOBE), location unknown, October 15, 1999. A discussion of Garry's speech also appears in Vincent Doyle, "Insiders—Outsiders: Dr. Laura and the Contest for Cultural Authority in LGBT Media Activism," in *Media Queered: Visibility and Its Discontents*, ed. Kevin Barnhurst (New York: Peter Lang, 2007), 107–24.
2. Lisa Duggan, *The Twilight of Equality? Neoliberalism, Cultural Politics, and the Attack on Democracy* (Boston: Beacon, 2003).
3. Michael Warner, *The Trouble with Normal: Sex, Politics, and the Ethics of Queer Life* (New York: Free Press, 1999); Alexandra Chasin, *Selling Out: The Gay and Lesbian Movement Goes to Market* (New York: St. Martin's, 2000); Eric O. Clarke, *Virtuous Vice: Homoeroticism and the Public Sphere* (Durham, NC: Duke University Press, 2000); Urvashi Vaid, *Virtual Equality: The Mainstreaming of Gay and Lesbian Liberation* (New York: Anchor, 1995).
4. John D'Emilio, "Cycles of Change, Questions of Strategy: The Gay and Lesbian Movement after Fifty Years," in *The Politics of Gay Rights*, ed. Craig Rimmerman et al. (Chicago: University of Chicago Press, 2000), 50.
5. GLAAD, strategic planning document, September, 1999.
6. Garry, Speech to GLOBE.
7. Arnie Kantrowitz, interview by the author, Staten Island, July 18, 2000.
8. Steve Spurgeon, interview by the author, Los Angeles, November 6, 2000. A discussion of this portion of the interview with Spurgeon also appears in Doyle, "Insiders—Outsiders," 110.
9. Quoted in Chasin, *Selling Out*, 209.
10. Chasin, *Selling Out*; Katherine Sender, *Business, Not Politics: The Making of the Gay Market* (New York: Columbia University Press, 2004).
11. Pierre Bourdieu, *Distinction: A Social Critique of the Judgment of Taste*, trans. Richard Nice (Cambridge, MA: Harvard University Press, 1984), 110.
12. Quoted in Chasin, *Selling Out*, 209.
13. Spurgeon, interview, November 6, 2000.
14. GLAAD, strategic planning document, September 1999.
15. Steve Spurgeon, interview by the author, Los Angeles, October 13, 2000.
16. Joan Garry, interview by the author, New York, November 7, 2000.
17. *Queer as Folk*, Showtime, episode of December 3, 2000.
18. Scott Seomin, interview by the author, Los Angeles, October 31, 2000.

19. Gay and Lesbian Alliance against Defamation, "It's Here, It's Queer as Folk," December 7, 2000, www.glaad.org/action/al_archive_detail.php?id=1382&.

20. Gene Falk, interview by the author, New York, May 9, 2001.

21. GLAAD, minutes of executive committee meeting, December 15, 2000.

22. Rodney Benson, "Field Theory in Comparative Context: A New Paradigm for Media Studies," *Theory and Society* 28 (1999): 477.

23. David Swartz, *Culture and Power: The Sociology of Pierre Bourdieu* (Chicago: University of Chicago Press, 1997), 102.

Photo by Katy Raddatz, *San Francisco Chronicle*, 2004. Reprinted with permission

Sex and Tourism:

The Economic Implications of the

Gay Marriage Movement

Nan Alamilla Boyd

What new queer politics are emerging through tourism, and what tourist
practices are emerging from global gay and lesbian activism?
— Jasbir Kuar Puar, "Circuits of Queer Mobility:
Tourism, Travel, and Globalization"

In spite of claims to the contrary, heterosexual capital's gesture of rolling out
the "welcome mat" has less to do with hospitality than with the creation of a
new consumer and a new market both of which must be colonized.
— M. Jacqui Alexander, "Imperial Desire/Sexual Utopias:
White Gay Capital and Transnational Tourism"

On February 12, 2004, San Francisco's mayor, Gavin Newsom, instructed his staff
to grant marriage licenses to same-sex couples at San Francisco's City Hall. Between
February 12 and March 10, 2004, city officials registered over four thousand gay and
lesbian marriages, drawing a frenzy of media attention to the city and its new mayor.
While the legality of these contracts remains in limbo, one outcome of Newsom's
action has been to reinforce San Francisco's spot at the top of a list of favorite U.S.
gay travel destinations, as a recent survey revealed.[1] San Francisco's popularity as a

Radical History Review
Issue 100 (Winter 2008)   DOI 10.1215/01636545-2007-032
© 2008 by MARHO: The Radical Historians' Organization, Inc.

gay travel destination is nothing new, but the dollars attached are increasingly significant as U.S. cities compete for a share of an estimated $55 billion U.S. gay travel market.[2] And as public safety and the availability of civil rights displace the availability of gay bars or a vibrant nightlife as significant travel motivators, gay marriage has become an increasingly important factor in the gay travel market.[3] "We're obviously very encouraged," stated Joe D'Alessandro, the CEO of San Francisco's Convention and Visitors Bureau when he read about San Francisco's high ranking. While once in a position to take gay tourism for granted, San Francisco's Convention and Visitors Bureau is now marketing to gay travelers, both domestic and transnational. "The whole world is waking up to this market," D'Alessandro noted.[4]

Gay travel and marketplace activity raise a set of interesting questions about the relationship between consumption and citizenship, spending and civil rights. A number of scholars, most notably David Evans, Alexandra Chasin, and Katherine Sender, have argued (to varying degrees) that queer consumption functions as an insidious vehicle for civil rights. Indeed, as Chasin argues, "the market eventually undermines the radical potential of identity-based movements for social change."[5] But the role that same-sex marriage plays in this dynamic has not been thoroughly explored. How significant is the link between the gay marriage movement and gay travel markets? How does a city's investment in itself as a gay travel destination impact the viability of marriagelike rights and protections? And how do domestic gay travel markets interact with global markets that work to secure destination points for queer travelers while they introduce and reiterate what Denis Altman has dubiously called a "global gay identity?"[6] This essay explores these questions by looking at the interplay between the U.S.-based gay marriage movement and the growth of an increasingly global gay tourist economy. It examines the economic stakes of the gay marriage movement, the impact of gay marriage on the gay travel market, and the relationship between gay tourism and globalization. Ultimately, this essay argues that the expansion of the gay market via the gay marriage movement interpellates and disciplines consumers by producing a knowable and normalized set of heretofore queer behaviors, values, and identities.[7] In a word, it produces homonormativity—a set of ideologies and behaviors that asserts citizenship rights for gays and lesbians via neoliberal politics and conspicuous consumption.[8]

Weddings are big business. A $70 billion industry in 2005, U.S. weddings now cost, on average, approximately $30,000.[9] Even without its association with travel and tourism, same-sex weddings constitute an important and fast-growing sector of the U.S. wedding industry.[10] In 2004 *Forbes* magazine estimated that the legalization of same-sex marriage in the United States could result in a $16.8 billion market in receptions and catering, flowers and decor, music and entertainment, photography, rings, apparel, invitations, cake, gifts, and honeymoon expenses. The projected "gay-marriage windfall," according to the *Forbes* journalist Aude Lagorce, is based on U.S. Census Bureau data on the numbers of same-sex couples living together—594,000 in 2000—who would, no doubt, marry at the same rate as heterosexual couples. According to Lagorce's calculations, since 92 percent of heterosexual couples living together are married, the same proportion of gay and lesbian couples would probably tie the knot, and they would tie it to the tune of $36,200 per wedding.[11] Leaving aside the question of whether same-sex couples are adequately represented by the U.S. census, or whether same-sex couples exchanging vows would act and spend like heterosexuals, these numbers suggest that the legalization of same-sex marriage has high economic stakes.

Starting in November 2003, when the Massachusetts Supreme Court decided that same-sex marriages would become legal in Massachusetts, but peaking in March 2004 after a flurry of same-sex marriages in San Francisco and elsewhere, journalists speculated about the lucrative gay tourist market and how cities offering same-sex marriage might tap it. In December 2003, the *New York Times* ran a piece entitled "Mining the Gold in Gay Nuptials," which reported a Canadian boom in gay tourism six months after Ontario and British Columbia had legalized gay marriage.[12] "There may be plenty of people excited about the prospect of legalized gay marriage in Massachusetts," the article notes, "but Canadian tourism officials are probably not among them."[13] In 2004, Community Marketing Incorporated (CMI), a San Francisco–based firm that produces data on the gay and lesbian travel and tourism market, published a survey that explicitly linked gay marriage to tourist revenue. The survey, sponsored by the Canadian Tourism Commission, reveals that 50 percent of gay travelers from the United States and Australia see Canada's gay marriage laws as an attractive pull, and "the ability to legally marry in Canada outstrips other travel motivators, such as attending gay pride events, gay ski weeks, or gay circuit parties."[14] Indeed, in 2005 and again in 2006, Canada edged out western Europe, Mexico, and the United Kingdom as a favorite destination for gay Americans traveling abroad according to CMI's eleventh Annual LGBT Travel Survey, and "the legalization of same-sex marriage likely had an impact on Canada taking the top spot," states CMI's marketing manager Jerry McHugh.[15]

The marketing company CMI conducts research on gay spending patterns, produces trade shows, and advises over seven hundred clients a year on how to market to gay and lesbian consumers. Its Web pages recommend that companies seeking gay dollars "get involved in the community" and project a "gay-friendly" attitude. American Airlines and Kimpton Hotels appear on its list of larger clients, but the vast majority of its clients, large and small, are national and municipal tourist agencies seeking to attract gay and lesbian travelers: the French Government Tourism Office, the Greater Miami Convention and Visitor's Bureau, the Canadian Tourism Commission, Switzerland Tourism, the Greater Philadelphia Tourism Marketing Corporation, the Dallas Convention and Visitors Bureau, as well as the tourist offices of Spain, Tahiti, and Curaçao.[16] The company's influence is significant. Most major news articles on gay travel or gay tourism written since 2004 cite CMI's data, as well as the opinions of Tom Roth, the agency's president. On December 5, 2006, for instance, CMI conducted a workshop at the Holiday Inn in Victoria, British Columbia, that drew over fifty local tourism operators eager to learn how to attract GLBT (gay, lesbian, bisexual, transgender) spenders. Tom Roth was there, encouraging tourist industry speculators to think of GLBT travelers as part of a community rather than as a market. "They do not want to be seen as a marketing opportunity only," he stated, suggesting that businesses network with GLBT community members to "identify opportunities and get feedback" on how to build solid relationships with GLBT consumers and gain a gay-friendly reputation. Meanwhile, CMI representatives presented data on the size of the gay travel market and the profits to be gained by reaching out—sincerely and slowly—to GLBT travelers.[17]

Chasin's critique of advertisers who target gay and lesbian consumers, *Selling Out: The Gay and Lesbian Movement Goes to Market* (2000), is useful in this context.[18] Advertisers, she notes, are almost uniformly optimistic about the political rewards of consumption, and CMI's advice to companies seeking gay and lesbian consumers follows this pattern. Indeed, the tactic of seduction plays a key role in CMI's marketing strategies, and the payoff, they claim, is like falling in love (or, more appropriately, getting fucked). Consumers from GLBT communities are known, by marketing strategists, for their intense brand loyalty. Robert Witeck and Wesley Combs underscore this message in their 2006 book, *Business Inside Out: Capturing Millions of Brand Loyal Gay Consumers.*[19] Witeck and Combs are the architects of Witeck-Combs Communications, a marketing and public relations consultancy that specializes in gay and lesbian consumer behavior. In 2000, Witeck-Combs paired with Harris Interactive (the company that produces the Harris Poll) to begin testing gay and lesbian brand loyalty. They found, through telephone and online surveys with thousands of gay and straight consumers in the United States, that gay and lesbian consumers seemed to care more about the internal politics and practices of a particular business than heterosexual consumers. Does the company promote diversity at the worksite? Does the company provide benefits to GLBT employees and their partners? Does the company support nonprofits and/or GLBT community events? An amorphous quality they named "gay-friendliness" emerged from the research, and they demonstrated that a gay-friendly reputation was fundamental to GLBT brand loyalty.[20]

The narrative produced by gay and lesbian marketing professionals attaches marketplace activity to political enfranchisement by equating spending with civil rights. Translating brand loyalty to cities or countries rather than companies or consumer goods demands different strategies, but the basic idea is the same. A March 2004 article in the *Boston Globe* described how some U.S. cities—including Miami, West Hollywood, San Diego, San Francisco, Boston, Washington, DC, and Philadelphia, but also Newport, Milwaukee, and Fort Lauderdale—have begun to market themselves directly to gay travelers. The economic stakes are high. In 2003, for instance, the Greater Fort Lauderdale Convention and Visitor's Bureau spent 7 percent, or $200,000, of its $3 million advertising budget on potential gay tourists, and gay tourists in 2003 accounted for 13 percent, or $700 million, of the $5.3 billion tourist economy there. More recently, Philadelphia completed a three-year, $900,000 campaign to draw gay travelers to that city, and a report reveals that the city has seen a return of $153 in spending for every dollar invested in gay marketing. Philadelphia's branding campaign, which positions the slogan, "Get your history straight and your nightlife gay," alongside images of Benjamin Franklin flying a rainbow kite and Betsy Ross sewing a rainbow flag, has received much press attention. Other cities, seeking similar returns, worked with marketing experts—like those at CMI—to develop gay-friendly slogans to promote their city to gay and lesbian travelers. Boston toyed with the slogan, "Boston Marriages: Invented Here," while Washington, DC, chose, "Celebrate the Freedom to Be" and San Francisco encouraged visitors to "Make a Commitment."[21]

The link between gay marriage and gay tourism is unstable but alluring; it makes for the newest factor in a well-established pattern of gay travel and spending.[22] For instance, even when states ban same-sex marriage, cities within these states continue to vie for gay travel dollars through the production of gay-friendly activities and amenities. In other words, the marketplace activity does not always have to be a destination wedding. A February 2006 *USA Today* article entitled "Cities in Red States Play Ball with Gay Travelers," notes that despite Arizona's proposed ban on gay marriage (which, surprisingly, failed in the November 2006 elections), Phoenix continues to aggressively court gay travelers. Phoenix city and tourism officials met in January 2006 to coordinate their efforts, which resulted in a homoerotic ad featuring a rear-view close-up of a baseball player with the caption, "To the rest of the country, they're the 'Boys of Summer,' to Phoenix, they're the 'Boys of Summer, Spring, Winter, and Fall.'" This ad capitalizes on Arizona's largest tourist draw, major-league baseball's spring training camps, while it advertises the year-round availability of young men to gay travelers. Similarly, Dallas has initiated a marketing campaign to attract gay travelers to a host of activities including the gay volleyball championships and the International Gay Rodeo Association. On the topic of gay tourism, Gregory Pierce, the senior vice president at the Atlanta Convention and Visitors Bureau, states that "around here, we like to say, the color of diversity is green."[23]

The consequence of this economic courtship of the "lavender dollar" is that as the gay tourism industry trumps politics and infuses culturally conservative spaces with new economic interests, the economic implications of same-sex marriage, via its impact on gay tourism, have become increasingly important to thinking about the viability of same-sex marriage as a civil rights issue. Cities like San Francisco with a long history of queer activism can lean on their reputation, but increased competition means smarter business practices. San Francisco now works to expand its share of an increasingly global market, and the February 2004 gay marriages in San Francisco provided a spectacle that no marketing company could dream up: smartly dressed gay and lesbian couples primping inside San Francisco's magnificent City Hall; potential newlyweds waiting patiently with their proud families and, often, small children, in lines that wrapped thickly around an entire city block; and local business owners distributing pizza, cookies, flowers, and balloons to the crowds waiting in the drizzling rain. Journalists documented the stories of gay and lesbian couples waiting to get hitched: one couple had been together for decades; another showed up because their children insisted; a third came all the way from North Dakota.[24] These are compelling images—sincere and heartfelt—and while they demonstrate the complex and often personal meanings swirling around the legal struggle for same-sex marriage, they also secure through reiteration San Francisco's centrality as a gay travel destination. These images cement the link between the idea of San Francisco and the idea of gay and lesbian civil rights, and they insure San Francisco's stake in the increasingly lucrative and globally expanding gay travel market.

Gay marriage can thus be seen as a tourist attraction, an export commodity, and a marketplace activity through which gays and lesbians are schooled in how to participate in consumer culture and be good citizens by a host of teachers, the most familiar of which are celebrities. Rosie O'Donnell's February 26, 2004, marriage to Kelli Carpenter provides a case in point. After a private ceremony in Mayor Newsom's office, the New Yorkers exchanged a kiss on the steps of San Francisco's City Hall while crowds cheered and the San Francisco Gay Men's Chorus serenaded them with show tunes. O'Donnell stated, "I want to thank the city of San Francisco for this amazing stance the mayor has taken for all the people here, not just us but all the thousands and thousands of loving, law-abiding couples."[25]

The U.S. tourist economy is changing to accommodate current U.S. national debates about the legalization of same-sex marriage. As same-sex marriage registers as a tourist attraction and a gay travel indicator—a measure of gay-friendliness— gay marriage becomes part of a larger campaign whereby municipalities market themselves to gay travelers. In 2006, for instance, Tourism Vancouver, which has been working to lure U.S. gay travelers since 2000, offered a "gay-marriage sweep-stakes" to Americans. Over four hundred potential gay and lesbian travelers registered to win a $50,000 wedding package that included an Alaskan honeymoon cruise.[26] Municipalities that offer travelers same-sex marriage as part of a travel or tourism package transform that service or civil right into a commodity, but they are also transformed by it.

The commodification of gay marriage via marketplace activity produces a new kind of queer citizen, one that participates in civic life via the social rituals of marriage and the commercial rituals of conspicuous consumption. As M. Jacqui Alexander has argued, gay tourism functions as a neocolonial enterprise that transforms white gay travelers into global citizens whose consuming practices maintain colonial patterns of production, consumption, and service. "[The white gay tourist] brings with him the potential to develop new and perennially changing needs and desires that capitalism alone can satisfy. Although citizenship based in political rights gets forfeited, they do not disappear. Instead, they get reconfigured and restored under the rubric of consumer at this moment in late twentieth-century capitalism."[27] Alexander's insights help us understand the uneven and complex relationship between consumption and civil rights. For instance, municipalities that do not offer gay marriage as a commodity are increasingly aware of the power of marriage or other civil rights protections to pull gay travelers into new kinds of marketplace activity, but also to brand the municipality's gay-friendliness. Gay marriage thus serves as a marketplace activity (through the sale of hotel rooms, flowers, and so forth), a marketing strategy (through the production of gay-friendliness), and a behavior, as O'Donnell articulated so clearly, that signifies law-abiding, homonormative citizenship.

The historical dimensions of these commercial transformations raise important questions: when, for example, and for what reasons does a city begin to market itself as a gay travel destination? How do municipal or national investments in gay tourism impact the viability of civil rights protections? In San Francisco's history, marketplace activity set the stage for the emergence of nascent political organizations and the eventual assertion of civil rights. The marketability of San Francisco's queer subcultures led to civil rights through the development of a commercial district, a gay spending zone that shifted from San Francisco's North Beach district in the 1940s and 1950s to Polk Street in the 1960s and 1970s to the Castro district—and, to a lesser degree, the Valencia Street corridor where lesbian feminism set up shop—in the late 1970s and 1980s. It was in the Castro district that Harvey Milk received economic and political support and, through district elections, was able to win a seat on the San Francisco Board of Supervisors in 1977. San Francisco's queer subcultures have historically functioned as a vital aspect of San Francisco's larger tourist culture, and it is this development—in combination with the emergence of early homophile organizations—that enabled gay and lesbian civil rights movements to coalesce and make viable appeals to city government.[28]

At the same time, it is important to note that the marketplace viability of San Francisco's queer subcultures emerged in the period between the expansion of global markets after World War I and the reorganization of global capital after World War II. San Francisco's queer nightlife, its male and female impersonator shows, emerged as part of a larger process of colonization—making the exotic familiar—that stimulated new tourist and travel markets, and, ultimately, involved the reorganization of ideas about political subjectivity and citizenship. For instance, in the adjacent districts of Chinatown and North Beach, racialized and sexualized subcultures were colonized and commodified, that is, transformed into a cultural commodity, for the benefit of a developing tourist economy.[29] Through these marketplace activities, a kind of queer citizenship emerged in the 1960s that transformed queer performers and the communities that coalesced around them into a lesbian and gay constituency—that is, a recognizable and intelligible political body. Through their marketplace activity (their role in the production of new capital via the global expansion of San Francisco's nascent tourist economy), gays and lesbians became citizens recognizable to the state through docile and often desexualized notions of sexual subjectivity. The neoliberal trajectory of the gay marriage movement follows a similar pattern, but the economic stakes are higher.

Saskia Sassen has suggested that the development of global cities, linked by superprofits associated with finance industries and specialty services, may occasion new kinds of citizenship claims that deemphasize nationalism against larger economic forces. "The global city [is] a nexus for new politico-economic alignments," Sassen writes, and the valorization of highly lucrative transnational gay tourist industries, especially when set alongside devalued and often informal "native" or "immigrant" services fits neatly into Sassen's analysis. The catch is: What kind of citizenship claims will be made as a result of the production of new capital, and who will be counted as viable citizens? Sassen's critique of the global city as, on the one hand, "a frontier zone for a new type of engagement," asserts, on the other hand, that the undervalued and informal economies that sustain global cities continue to be discounted in the reconfiguration of globalized political constituencies. That is, women and people of color—often configured as immigrants and thus as outside citizenship claims, despite their economic viability with the feminization of the global labor force—continue to be disregarded as peripheral rather than central to the superprofits of corporate capitalism.[30] As was the case in mid-twentieth-century San Francisco, the kind of citizenship enabled by the new capital developments of gay tourism via same-sex marriage will, no doubt, serve the interests of white capitalists rather than people-of-color workers. Or, as Alexander puts it, "the marriage between white gay citizenship and white gay consumption [will have] been efficiently sealed."[31]

The transmission of gay marriage as a kind of export commodity via the gay travel market has important implications for thinking about the production of global gay and lesbian identities that carry neocolonial messages about sexual liberation and freedom. That is, the globalization of gay tourism has the potential to produce the image and reality of a kind of global queer citizen defined by either erotic consumption that depends on neocolonial and racist sexual services or monogamous, marriagelike pairings with predictable and disciplined spending patterns. As Jasbir Puar explains in her analysis of the globalization of gay tourism, "queer tourism underpins and fuels a gay and lesbian rights agenda that assumes the attainment of 'modern queer sexuality' as its ultimate goal."[32] As gay marriage circulates as a commodity on the global marketplace, it attaches new meanings to same-sex sexuality, and these meanings underscore and insist on the intelligibility of modern gay and lesbian subjectivities. But to read this dynamic in reverse, the assertion of gay and lesbian subjectivity and citizenship may work to produce new marketing possibilities.

For instance, since the early 2000s, Cape Town in South Africa has been marketing itself aggressively to gay Australians. Postapartheid South Africa is, of course, the first nation to write gay and lesbian civil rights directly into its constitution; but this marketing strategy may have less to do with a broader civil rights agenda than an effort to tap into the multi-billion-dollar market Sydney has built around its annual gay Mardi Gras celebrations.[33] Gustav Visser, a geographer at the University of the Free State, South Africa, claims that the development of Western-style gay tourism in Cape Town has had a significant impact on the production of gay leisure space in the city. Visser notes that tourist developments have produced transnational or globalized gay leisure spaces that exclude Cape Town's broader gay community; in fact, it excludes virtually everyone who is not a wealthy, white gay man, a situation not entirely different from apartheid South Africa's gay landscape. Ironically, the South African constitutional inclusion of gay and lesbian civil rights seems to have made possible the development of tourist bureau strategies and investments that reproduce apartheid-like conditions, that is, racially segregated leisure spaces.[34]

Another example of the complex relationship between gay tourism, the globalization of gay identities, and the assertion of new citizenship claims can be seen in the shifting tone of conflict around gay cruises in the Caribbean Islands. The Cayman Islands, for instance, became notorious in 1998 for turning away a gay cruise ship, but in 2004 its new tourism minister, MacKeeva Bush, disavowed this practice, asserting that "as a country, the Cayman Islands does not discriminate against any social group and receives all visitors to our shores."[35] In March 2005, a gay cruise ship was barred from disembarking in St. Kitts-Nevis, but the country's tourism minister, Malcolm Guishard, tried to defuse the situation, calling it "unfortunate but isolated" and welcoming "any sexual orientation" to the islands. In response to these events, the International Gay and Lesbian Travel Association initiated a boycott of gay-unfriendly destinations in the Caribbean. A June 2005 *Time* magazine article notes that as a result of the boycott, a "more welcoming attitude is starting to become apparent," notably in Saint Thomas, which now openly advertises gay bed-and-breakfast hotels that cater to gay destination weddings, and Puerto Rico, where both major candidates in the 2005 gubernatorial race pledged to support a gay civil rights agenda. In these examples, the economic power or potential of gay tourism seems to shape both the reorganization of civil society—ideas about tolerance, friendliness, and hospitality—and the renegotiation of certain civil rights investments.

In her analysis of the U.S. "Hispanic market," Arlene Dávila notes that mass-produced representations of Latino consumers reflect U.S. social anxieties about its others, and advertisements featuring Latino shoppers produce "an idealized, good, all-American citizenship in the image of the 'ethnic consumer.'"[36] The production of new markets creates new social identities that reflect the desires of the mainstream or dominant culture to put so-called others in their place, that is, in a position that does not fundamentally challenge the inequities and injustices of global capitalism. Similarly, the U.S. gay travel market is a recognized and lucrative market that is changing to accommodate current U.S. national debates about same-sex marriage, but these domestic markets interact with highly competitive global markets that have important implications for thinking about, first, the relationship between travel, tourism, and the production of new transnational and/or diasporic sexual cultures; and second, the production of global gay and lesbian identities that carry neocolonial messages about liberation and sexual freedom. Gay marriage can be seen as an export commodity in that it has the potential to open new markets via gay travel, but it also attaches neoliberal ideologies to the state regulation of same-sex sexuality. What is produced in the end, through commodification, is a set of modern and global sexual identities that suture sexual citizenship to spending.

As Lisa Duggan and others have noted in "Beyond Same-Sex Marriage," a reconsideration of the politics of same-sex marriage involves tackling questions of poverty head-on, rather than buying into the rhetoric of privatization and individual rights that rewards docile (gay and lesbian) bodies with citizenship.[37] The emergence of gay marriage as yet another fabulous niche market for advertisers to exploit, and the concomitant neocolonial transportation of ideas about gay marriage into globalizing economies via the already fabulously lucrative gay travel and tourism market, add yet more difficult questions to those posed by "Beyond Same-Sex Marriage": Who benefits from the production of ad copy featuring same-sex couples traveling or planning their own wedding ceremony? And what stories are told as marketing professionals increasingly frame the contemporary struggle for justice and civil rights? The stories that are not told are those that frame justice in economic terms and value the integrity of caring relationships—whether they are conjugal, familial, sexual, or not.

Notes

1.   A 2006 poll conducted by Harris Interactive, Travel Industry Association, and Witeck-Combs Communications revealed that the highest percentage (76 percent) of the 2,020 self-identified gay, lesbian, bisexual, or transgender travelers surveyed named San Francisco a gay-friendly city and, thus, a desirable travel destination. "Comprehensive Travel and Tourism Study of Gays and Lesbians Highlights Leisure Travel Insights: New National Survey by Harris Interactive, Travel Industry Association, and Witeck-Combs Communications also Includes Consumer Ranking on Gay-Friendly Destinations," *PR Newswire US*, December 6, 2006.

2. Kathy Bergen, "Chicago Gets Good Grades from Gay, Lesbian Visitor," *Chicago Tribune,* December 6, 2006.

3. Harris Interactive, Travel Industry Associates (TIA), and Witeck-Combs Communications, "Travel and Tourism Study of Gays and Lesbians," 2006. This data challenges earlier findings that a significant travel motivation for gay men, particularly, is "gay social life and sex," rather than "culture and sights" or "comfort and relaxation." Stephen Clift and Simon Forrest, "Gay Men and Tourism: Destinations and Holiday Motivations," *Tourism Management,* no. 20 (1999): 615–25. Consistent with TIA findings, however, are the conclusions reached in Annette Pritchard et al., "Sexuality and Holiday Choices: Conversations with Gay and Lesbian Tourists," *Leisure Studies,* no. 19 (2000): 267–82, which finds safety and an escape from heterosexism to be important travel motivators for gay and lesbian tourists. On the spatial distribution of gay travel and tourism, see Russell L. Ivy, "Geographical Variation in Alternative Tourism and Recreation Establishments," *Tourism Geographies* 3 (2001): 338–55; and Annette Pritchard et al., "Reaching Out to the Gay Tourist: Opportunities and Threats in an Emerging Market Segment," *Tourism Management* 19 (1998): 273–82. For a more recent survey of the global gay and lesbian travel market, see Jasbir Kaur Puar, "Circuits of Queer Mobility: Tourism, Travel and Globalization," in *GLQ: A Journal of Lesbian and Gay Studies* 8 (2002): 101–37.

4. David Armstrong, "No City Like S.F. for Gay Tourists: Key West, New York Are Second Thoughts; L.A. Is Sixth on the List," *San Francisco Chronicle,* December 7, 2006.

5. Alexandra Chasin, *Selling Out: The Gay and Lesbian Movement Goes to Market* (New York: Palgrave, 2000), xvii. See also David Evans, *Sexual Citizenship: The Material Construction of Sexualities* (London: Routledge, 1993); and Katherine Sender, *Business, Not Politics: The Making of the Gay Market* (New York: Columbia University Press, 2005).

6. Dennis Altman, "Global Gaze/Global Gays," *GLQ: A Journal of Lesbian and Gay Studies* 3 (1997): 417–36. See also Dennis Altman, "Rupture or Continuity? The Internationalization of Gay Identities" in *Post-colonial, Queer: Theoretical Intersections,* ed. John C. Hawley (Albany: State University of New York Press, 2001), 19–42. Lisa Rofel provides a satisfying response to Altman's neocolonial thesis in "Qualities of Desire: Imagining Gay Identities in China," *GLQ: A Journal of Lesbian and Gay Studies* 5 (1999): 451–74.

7. As noted in the epigraphs to this essay, both M. Jacqui Alexander and Jasbir Kuar Puar have pointed to these conclusions in their incisive analysis of the evolving global gay tourist market. See Puar, "Circuits of Queer Mobility"; and M. Jacqui Alexander, "Imperial Desire/Sexual Utopias: White Gay Capital and Transnational Tourism," in *Talking Visions: Multicultural Feminism in a Transnational Age,* ed. Ella Shobat (New York: New Museum of Contemporary Art/Cambridge, MA: MIT Press, 1998), 281–305.

8. See Lisa Duggan, *The Twilight of Equality? Neoliberalism, Cultural Politics, and the Attack on Democracy* (Boston: Beacon, 2003).

9. These figures are culled from 2005 wedding industry Web sites. See Vicki Howard, *Brides, Inc.: American Weddings and the Business of Tradition* (Philadelphia: University of Pennsylvania Press, 2006), 237.

10. Ibid., 220–36.

11. Aude Lagorce, "Same-Sex Weddings: The Gay-Marriage Windfall; $16.8 Billion," *Forbes,* April 5, 2004, www.forbes.com/2004/04/05. Lagorce notes that only 85 percent of heterosexual couples hold a reception with guests, so she drops the number of possible same-sex weddings from 546,000 to 464,000: 464,000 x $27,700 + approximately $8,500 per

wedding in gifts ($85/gift x 100 guests) = $16.8 billion. Lagorce gathers her data on wedding costs from two Internet sources: The Knot (www.theknot.com) and WeddingChannel.com.

12. Sarah Robertson, "Mining the Gold in Gay Nuptials," *New York Times*, December 19, 2003.

13. Ibid.

14. "Gay Marriage Brings Tourism Windfall," Community Marketing Press Release, May 10, 2004, www.gaywired.com/article.cfm?section=9&id=2909.

15. Jane Armstrong, "Vancouver Rated Top City for Gay Tourists," *Globe and Mail*, December 5, 2006.

16. "Clients and Endorsements," Community Marketing, Inc., Web pages, www.communitymarketinginc.com (accessed May 12, 2007).

17. Carla Wilson, "Gay, Lesbian Tourist Market Hot: Tourism Operators Are Advised to Look beyond Chasing Bucks and Get Involved in Community," *Times Colonist* (Victoria, BC), December 6, 2006.

18. Chasin, *Selling Out*, 101–43. Katherine Sender's analysis notes more ambivalence on the part of marketing professionals; see her *Business, Not Politics*, 64–94.

19. Robert Witeck and Wesley Combs, *Business Inside Out: Capturing Millions of Brand Loyal Gay Consumers* (Chicago: Kaplan, 2006).

20. Witeck and Combs, "Company Reputation and Brand Loyalty," in *Business Inside Out*, 63–82.

21. Jan Gardner, "Boston Watches as Other Cities Market Themselves to Gay Tourists," *Boston Globe*, March 15, 2004.

22. See Howard, *Brides, Inc.*, 220–36.

23. "Cities in Red States Play Ball with Gay Travelers," *USA Today*, February 10, 2006.

24. See, for instance, *Flowers from the Heartland* (dir. Peter Daulton, US, 2004).

25. Rosie O'Donnell, quoted in David K Li and Aly Sujo, "Here Come the Brides: Rosie and Gay Pal Tie the Knot in San Francisco," *New York Post*, February 27, 2004.

26. Armstrong, "Vancouver Rated Top City."

27. Alexander, "Imperial Desire," 287.

28. Nan Alamilla Boyd, *Wide Open Town: A History of Queer San Francisco to 1965* (Berkeley: University of California Press, 2003).

29. Ibid., 237–42.

30. Saskia Sassen, "The Global City: Strategic Site/New Frontier," www.india-seminar.com/2001/503/503%20saskia%20sassen.htm (accessed March 14, 2007). See also Saskia Sassen, *The Global City: New York, London, Tokyo* (Princeton, NJ: Princeton University Press, 2000).

31. Alexander, "Imperial Desire," 292.

32. Puar, "Circuits of Queer Mobility," 125.

33. On the history of the "gay rights clause" in South Africa's postapartheid constitution, see Jacklyn Cock, "Engendering Gay and Lesbian Rights: The Equality Clause in the South African Constitution," *Women's Studies International Forum* 26 (2003): 35–45. On the history of Sydney's development into a global gay tourist destination, see Kevin Markwell, "Mardi Gras Tourism and the Construction of Sydney as an International Gay and Lesbian City," *GLQ: A Journal of Lesbian and Gay Studies* 8 (2002): 81–99.

34. Gustav Visser, "Gay Men, Tourism, and Urban Space: Reflections on Africa's 'Gay Capital,'" *Tourism Geographies* 5 (2003): 168–89.

35. David Swanson, "Gay, Lesbian Travelers Outward-Bound: More Countries, Companies Put Out Welcome Mat for Same-Sex Tourists," *San Francisco Chronicle*, February 9, 2003.

36. Arlene Dávila, *Latinos Inc.: The Marketing and Making of a People* (Berkeley: University of California Press, 2001), 22.

37. Lisa Duggan et al., "Beyond Same-Sex Marriage: A New Strategic Vision for All Our Families and Relationships: Executive Summary," July 26, 2006, www.beyondmarriage.org.

Mattilda aka Matt Bernstein Sycamore. Photo by Jeffery Walls, courtesy of Mattilda

The Violence of Assimilation:
An Interview with Mattilda aka
Matt Bernstein Sycamore

Jason Ruiz

The writer and activist Mattilda (aka Matt Bernstein Sycamore) never backs down from a fight. As one of the "instigators" of the San Francisco–based activist group Gay Shame and a prolific writer and editor of works such as *Nobody Passes: Rejecting the Rules of Gender and Conformity* (2006) and *That's Revolting! Queer Strategies for Resisting Assimilation* (2004), Mattilda has been fighting what she calls "gay assimilation" since her days as a schoolboy in the early 1990s. Jason Ruiz spoke with Mattilda in snowy St. Paul in March 2007 — in the midst of her grueling cross-country book tour — about her history of activism, the fraught politics of the academy, and the promises and perils of a queer future.

Jason Ruiz: *As we've been putting together this special issue of the* Radical History Review, *I'm curious about what you think about homonormativity as a category of analysis. Is it a word that you use? Is it a term around which we should mobilize?*

Mattilda aka Matt Bernstein Sycamore: Well, it's not a word that I've used. I would say "the violence of assimilation" to describe the ways in which gay people have become obsessed with accessing straight privilege at any cost; it's almost like cultural erasure is the goal. Marriage and military service and adoption and ordi-

Radical History Review
Issue 100 (Winter 2008)   DOI 10.1215/01636545-2007-033
© 2008 by MARHO: The Radical Historians' Organization, Inc.

nation into the priesthood are suddenly "gay issues," whereas things like housing, health care, police brutality, gentrification . . . those? As if to say, "Oh no, we can't be concerned with any of that! We're just so excited about gay cops, because if we have gay cops gunning down unarmed people of color, then we have arrived!" It's the nightmare of identity politics where gay becomes an end point, a rationalization for celebrating the worst aspects of dominant-culture straight identity: nationalism, racism, classism, patriotism, consumerism, militarism, patriarchy, imperialism, misogyny; every other form of systemic violence becomes a hot accessory.

I think the first time I saw the word *homonormativity* was actually in Eric Stanley's essay in *That's Revolting*. But the ideas behind it are absolutely central to the work that I've been doing for all my activist life, and it's definitely something my last several books have engaged. In much the same way that *heterosexist* is really useful for thinking about homophobia, *homonormative* offers us the potential to see the violence that occurs when gays show unquestioning loyalty to many of the things that at this point are routinely challenged even within mainstream straight dominant cultures . . . it's beyond heteronormative because it's on a different level, it's imitating straight people better than they would ever do it, perfecting the tools of oppression and rationalizing it to this extreme violence. I think homonormativity is a great way to look at that because there has to be some way of undoing it.

My politics as a queer person have always been centered on challenging racism, classism, colonialism and imperialism, misogyny, and homophobia — all of that. It's a feminist politics of challenging power that's behind everything I do. This is the approach that I bring to challenging gay assimilation, which tells us that we all should be building this "Gaylandia" where everyone can shop in comfort and buy the right cocktails and the right accessories and the right Hummer and the right kind of dog. Maybe even buy the right kind of partner. Some people are even going abroad to adopt, buying the right kind of kid and saying, "Oh I love these really cute little Asian kids!" It's a consumerist mentality. I think adoption — kid buying — is a fascinating example of the violence that many gay people have absorbed. It legitimates a scenario where people seem to be saying, "I don't have to actually ask any questions about transnational adoption, because I'm a lesbian and I *need* these kids."

Could you summarize some of the goals that you were trying to accomplish with your recent books?

My last anthology, *That's Revolting*, centered on challenging the ways in which the dominant signs of straight conformity have become the ultimate signs of gay success. Marriage and military service and adoption and ordination into the priesthood are suddenly "gay issues." I wanted to expose this fundamental absurdity and offer a radical queer intervention that resisted the violence of a monolithic gay identity. In doing all this work around assimilation, I started to think about passing as a means through which the violence of assimilation takes place and also a way in which difference becomes and remains invisible. And I don't just mean passing in terms of the gay mainstream or commodified gay identity types of passing, but passing across all different lines. That's how *Nobody Passes* came about.

You wrote in the introduction of that book about a struggle with your editor, who saw your focus on different forms of passing as too messy and who encouraged you to focus instead on gender and sexuality. Why the messiness of including all of these varied modes of passing? What do you gain by adding those perspectives?

The messiness is where the possibility for a rigorous analysis emerges. What does it mean to pass as the "right" kind of gender queer or disabled person or immigrant or anticapitalist? For me it just felt too limiting to think only about gender and sexuality. Does that mean that gender and sexuality can possibly exist without race and class and ability? And my editor at Seal Press said, "These themes can emerge as long as the book is centered around gender and sexuality." But for me, it was essential to not limit myself to that framework in a book that is specifically trying to challenge the notion that we should fit ourselves into these narrow identity categories. And as a publishing house that still uses the tagline "Books by Women, for Women," they then asked, "How will this book be relevant to women?" Seal had approached me specifically for my feminist politics, but then they were suddenly questioning me because, as someone assigned the label "male" at birth, I didn't qualify for feminist authenticity of the surface variety. And this is a gender studies publisher that has lately taken an interest in publishing work by transpeople!

When I first saw the work that you've done with Gay Shame and in books like Nobody Passes, *I thought to myself, "Here is an example of coalitional politics across identity categories." Now I am not so sure that the label "coalitional politics" fits. Do you think that coalitional politics is a rubric for the work that you're doing, or do we need to look somewhere else?*

What I'm interested in exploring is how intersections emerge in unexpected ways. Coalitional politics for me often means people sort of tacking on identities to one another, like "My *real* issue is that I'm queer, but I'm also interested in fighting racism and classism." I'm not interested in that. That, to me, is like putting Post-it notes on yourself. Post-it notes fall off, and when they're off they're gone, and you can't do anything with them. I'm much more interested in an intersectional analysis that comes from a core; one that says, "I'm queer *and that means* fighting racism, fighting classism, fighting homophobia; you can't take them apart." I think a lot of people don't understand that. They say, "What do you mean you're fighting police brutality because you're queer? Is it because queers are being abused by the police?" Sure, sometimes queers are abused by the police. But actually white queers are not being gunned down by the cops in New York City or Los Angeles or Minneapolis or wherever; it's happening to people of color. And as a queer person, I have to fight that police brutality because that is the violence that's going on around me.

I know you have worked with Fed Up Queers, a perfect example of queer folks who did activist work against police brutality, especially in the Amadou Diallo case. Gay Shame San Francisco has also done work around gentrification and police brutality that is not focused around the category of sexuality. Can you talk about your personal history as an activist within those organizations in which you practiced what you seem to be describing as an intersectional politics?

For me, the possibility of commonality emerges by expressing the absolute core of difference. That is where the possibility for actually understanding someone comes from. It's not from saying, "I'm just like you because I was abused too." It's from saying, "Here is my experience; how do you relate?" One of the many disasters that ends in identity politics is when activists act like we're all in the same boat together, almost like a melting pot sort of thing, in which our differences will all disappear and then we can become one. No. We actually have to explore the differences in order to find the commonalities, whatever the fuck they are.

In terms of my history as an activist, I think there were a few things that were central to the beginning of my politicization. The first Gulf War started just as I was graduating from high school, and I remember seeing that happening, and just the horror and the hopelessness of it all helped me to realize that we are living under a monstrous government. The Rodney King verdict was also another one of the moments where everything was exposed, not as an aberration but as the violence that the country is built upon.

I joined ACT UP San Francisco in the early 1990s, after fleeing one year at an elitist college. ACT UP San Francisco at that point was very much committed to the idea that you can't fight AIDS without fighting racism, classism, homophobia, and misogyny. That was central for me in developing that kind of politics. The ACT UP that I was part of in San Francisco was also focused on needle exchange programs, prisoners with HIV/AIDS, women with HIV/AIDS, and promoting universal health care. Those were the core issues. It wasn't only about this narrow notion of access to drugs.

Fed Up Queers started in New York after a group of about twenty of us had come together initially to do a political funeral for Matthew Shepard. We only had a week to organize it, and about ten thousand people showed up! People were brutalized by the police, absolutely beaten bloody, and many of these people were not necessarily politicized against the police. We thought, "Oh my God! This is an opportunity to actually politicize people against police violence in a broad way." In the end, we tried to form a large radical queer group, but that didn't happen; it broke down over process issues. But one sort of affinity group that emerged from the political funeral was Fed Up Queers. These were the Giuliani years, and we felt desperate as gentrification and property development and real estate speculation and police tyranny were removing anything about downtown New York that was of any use, especially cultures of resistance that had been there for generations: immigrant communities, public sexual cultures, and outsider queer culture. All this was being erased, and we felt really desperate and driven to challenge all of that violence. This was the time in which I transitioned from an activist who gets involved in struggles that are already going on to becoming an organizer who initiates struggles that I think should be addressed.

Gay Shame emerged in New York as a challenge to the assimilationist agendas of mainstream pride celebrations. We believed that the procession of corporate floats didn't really represent the queer spirit of invention and outsider community building and challenges to the status quo. So we wanted to make something where radical and outsider queers could come together and create culture on our own terms, outside of the mainstream consumerist model. Then, in San Francisco, Gay Shame ended up becoming a direct-action group that centered on challenging the hypocrisy of a mainstream gay elite that sees their desires as everyone's needs. It was our goal to challenge the violence of the happy gay consumer that lies beneath all of those glamorous, sweatshop-produced rainbow flags, Tiffany wedding bands, Grey Goose Cosmo-tinis, and all of the rabid consumption. Beneath all of that is the policing of the borders, as if to say "Oh no, we don't want any trannies; we don't want any of those people of color; we don't want any homeless people; we don't want any of those youth, unless of course it's late at night and you need somebody to warm your bed." The gay elite is perfectly willing to exploit youth and people of color and homeless people when they are useful, but as soon as they are no longer useful, their attitude is, "Oh, we need to beautify this neighborhood," or it's like, "Girl! Get off the yellow brick road! These bricks were not made for you!"

So that's why we started. From there it has become a direct-action group wanting to challenge all hypocrisies. One of the things that should be stressed about Gay Shame is that we're willing to hold mainstream gay people accountable for violence. Mainstream straight people are not going to do that, and neither are mainstream gay people. Part of the point of Gay Shame is to take political stances that other people would like to take but are afraid to. San Francisco is in many ways a nightmare of gay assimilation, but it is also historically a center of radical, queer outsider cultures and, in that sense, even mainstream gay people in San Francisco until recently would never have dreamt of supporting marriage. They would have just said, "That's bourgeois. That's tacky. We might be involved in partnerships that are equally as bourgeois, but nonetheless we would laugh at the idea of marriage." To see how quickly and dramatically that position changed was horrifying and disheartening. People just rallied around Gavin Newsom, who was elected on a virulently antihomeless platform, and exclaimed, "This is the savior of gay civil rights!"

So my politics is a politics of accountability for both the mainstream consumerist monoculture and for gay subcultures.

One of the things that attracts people to and repels them from Gay Shame is the name. Can you tell me about how the organization got its name and the politics of being called Gay Shame?

Gay Shame emerged from a group called the Fuck the Mayor Collective, a little queer group that made stickers and did wheat pastings challenging the Giuliani agenda. I became involved with the Fuck the Mayor Collective just after it had decided to do an event called Gay Shame. The name was the obvious oppositional choice: they have Gay Pride, so let's take Gay Shame. Over and over again, I encounter people who say, "Why are you ashamed of being gay?" or "I love everything you do, but I hate your name. Can't you call yourselves something else?" Of course, that means people are feeling threatened. And that's the point: to be a threat. What's also fascinating is that people will change the name. This happens a lot. In asking me questions or even in writing, they'll change it to "Queer Shame." That's fascinating to me because they don't get that the "gay" part is the part that we're critiquing.

Even after two years, people in Gay Shame in San Francisco were still having arguments about the name and asking whether it's alienating people. I've actually had older people who were politicized in the sixties say to me, "But we did all this work so that you wouldn't be ashamed!" They don't understand that we're talking about being ashamed of the horrible place where gay identity has gone, being ashamed of the violence in the world that gay people are so eager to participate in, and being ashamed of ourselves for being in this space. We are also inspired to take some sort of action because we think we actually can get somewhere else. We don't have to be in this trap that is "LGBT," for example, or even "queer," in the way that the word is used in the mainstream context. We can actually envision something else, or at least try, fail miserably, and create something in that failure.

What really strikes me about Gay Shame—and about you personally—is that you're tremendously pissed off, but at the same time you and the group are tremendously provocative and playful.

At one point I was around (and sometimes still am around) a lot of very earnest activists who are very political and have this certain kind of deadening seriousness. I think it's important to talk about things that are really important in fun ways and to be able to laugh about horrible, horrible things. I mean, if I couldn't laugh at the horrible things that are going on, I'd have to be slitting my wrists, you know? And for me it's about needing some kind of celebration in that challenge. I have to be critical in order to stay alive. And being critical is what gives me hope, and it's not separate from a celebratory thing. It's not like getting smashed and passing out is really fun and celebratory and having a scathing political analysis is a really dry terrible thing. I want the scathing political analysis, and I want to be able to do it in a performative way. I think with Gay Shame what we tried to do was bring that sort of celebration and spectacle into the analysis so that it can be more engaging, certainly, but also so that we can keep ourselves entertained.

While keeping yourselves entertained, you've also inspired your share of critics. What are some of the criticisms of Gay Shame?

Gay Shame is always being accused of dividing our own. And I know that anytime anyone talks against critiquing your own or makes an accusation of divisiveness it means that something is going right! I fully believe in *not* bridging the divide, but in making it wider. Take, for example, gay realtors who advise their clients on how best to evict people with AIDS and old people in order to get more for their property. Those people are not part of anything that I would ever remotely call a community, and I have no interest in finding commonalities with gay realtors who advise their clients to do that. People never say you are being divisive when you say that transgender women don't belong in the streets, or that they should not be in "our" neighborhood. But by saying trans women actually have a right to make a living and by having a public space where they can exist or to say that those trans women were already in the neighborhood before you got there—that would be the divisive thing to say. That's always the notion of unity that's serving the realtors and their ilk. And I'm not interested in preserving that.

In the introduction to Nobody Passes, *you describe the somewhat fraught relationship between activism and academia. Is academia compatible with the type of activism that you practice and promote, or does the academy fall into the category of institutions and people that you just described, those with which you are not interested in bridging the divide?*

I think absolutely they're compatible. But I also think that what I've often seen in queer studies and cultural studies, which allegedly emerged to undo the wrongs of fields like anthropology and sociology, is that they've become edgy, trendy, and elitist ways for academics to do the same thing that's always been done, and get away with it: to appropriate or co-opt people's lived identities and struggles and activisms and then claim to have invented them. Anthropology and sociology now have to answer a lot of these questions. You can't just say that you're an anthropologist; you have to say, "This is how I've done my work without being a monstrous colonialist." Queer theory often gets away with not answering those questions.

One example was this conference that called itself "Gay Shame," at the University of Michigan in Ann Arbor, which explored the concept of shame and how it relates to queer theory. They organized all of these panels, and they contacted people who'd been involved in Gay Shame in New York and San Francisco and asked if we wanted to do a panel. And our response was, "What on earth is this monstrosity? Well, at least they called us, and they know what we do. Our job is to hold people accountable for their hypocrisy, so that must be why they called us here, to engage in this conversation about appropriation." So we went to the panel, and we were ready to stimulate discussion.

I honestly believed that everyone in the audience would just nod their heads and take notes and write a few clever papers and quote us and say, "Oh you're so right." I talked about what I call "trickle-down academia," the process by which academics appropriate anything they can get their hands on and then claim to have invented it. What was fascinating was that people did *not* nod their heads in agreement, and they did *not* want to engage in a conversation. What they wanted to do was to shut us up. I had one academic start screaming at me, "You are just like Cheney!" Of all the silencing lines, implying that by critiquing the academy we were furthering the goals of the Christian Right because the Christian Right is antiacademic! Therefore, all people who are critiquing academia are equivalent to the Christian Right. There were a couple of famous academics that got up and were screaming. The whole room was quiet, and there were several hundred people in the audience. Afterwards, people came up and were quietly agreeing with us, looking over their shoulders because people are very cautious about their careers, and saying things like: "We agree with you. I've had these same problems in academia, of being silenced when I try to articulate something that is outside of whatever the popular thing is." The people who were yelling were so concerned with their credibility and being perceived as outsider or radical academics that they didn't know what to do with us. It was the only panel that was wholly centered on activism at a conference that was allegedly inspired by the activism that Gay Shame has done. Our panel was followed by a session called "Fuck Activism?" It was as if it was too threatening to have an activist panel at a queer theory conference, so they had to immediately follow our panel by questioning the idea of activism, setting up that same sort of polarization—as if we activists aren't always questioning ourselves about the work that we do.

I am worried that we are making distinctions between academics and "authentic" activists. Shouldn't we be careful not to assume that certain people speak from an authentic subject position that academics lack? Because the authentic doesn't only exist on the street.

I'm not interested in saying what is authentic. I don't think anything is authentic necessarily. I absolutely think that there is academic work that is incredibly inspiring for me, such as David Roediger's *Working toward Whiteness*, which I think is brilliant, and Roxanne Dunbar Ortiz's work, which I think is amazing. Samuel Delany's work is brilliant. For me, work that is politicized and historicized and grounded has always been inspiring to me. I think the potential of academia is to take something measured and be absolutely rigorous with it. Marlon Bailey, Priya Kandaswamy, Matt Richardson, and Sara Clark Kaplan organized a panel at the University of California at Berkley that I saw which was about the racism intrinsic to the gay marriage movement, and they were absolutely brilliant in terms of their analysis. They took the concept of gay marriage and went through it methodically, logically, and unsparingly. That kind of academic work for me is totally inspiring. Their work from that panel became a crucial piece in *That's Revolting*.

For me, scholarship becomes appropriation, a fictitious act of creation, when academics say, "We just figured this out." It's creating a word — like *homonormative*, for example — as if this conversation hasn't been going on for a long time. It's a fascinating word, and I think it makes a lot of things clearer in certain ways, but I think there is always a danger that such words are presented to the world as if to say, "We invented this discourse," or, "We invented this way of challenging the violence of assimilation or challenging the ways in which some subcultures imitate dominant cultures," or, "We have discovered the horror of mainstream gay people who are taking on all the worst aspects of the violence, racism, classism and the militarism, the imperialism, and the nationalism of mainstream straight culture in some ways more monstrous than the mainstream."

Let me rephrase the question to more explicitly ask about theory: Do you think activism and theory are incompatible? Do you see these acts of appropriation happening more with queer theory?

I was fascinated by queer theory when I first discovered it right after high school. I found the book *Inside/Out*, an anthology edited by Diana Fuss, that included an essay by Judith Butler, and I was like, "Oh my god! This is brilliant! Performance of gender!" Each page would take me an hour to read. I said to myself, "That's because she's so brilliant." And then I got to a point where I was asking myself why. The actual process of reading was not adding to my understanding at all; it wasn't like a process-oriented experimental film where you are in the process and then you have another understanding of vision and time and space. It just felt elitist.

I think that theory is so often disembodied. It feels just totally disempowering, and that makes me sad. On the other hand, take Delany's *Time Square Red, Time Square Blue*, which talks about cruising sex clubs and porn theaters, but also theorizes about public sex and about sexuality. That kind of theory is amazing to me because it is actually grounded in something. In Delany's case, it is personal experience. I'm not interested in imposing some sort of binary where theory is bad and activism is good. I think we need theory that is activist-based and activism that is theoretical. I think there is absolutely the possibility for all these things to coexist. But I think that doesn't mean that we can't critique the real problems and limitations of theory, or of activism, for that matter.

You describe yourself as a "queer anti-assimilationist." Throughout this interview, you've alluded to several categories of queers that you see as pushing for LGBT assimilation into dominant culture. Who else should we add to this list?

As someone who lives in San Francisco, one of things I have seen is the rapid disappearance of ways of living and being that queers have developed over generations, like loving and lusting and caring for one another, that are outside of the status quo. I see that rapidly disappearing in favor of this foaming-at-the-mouth, marriage-only movement that assumes that marriage will solve all of our problems.

One of the things that has been most horrifying to me is to see the gentrification of Polk Street, the place where really marginalized queer people could formerly find space: drug addicts, runaway teenagers, trans women, those escaping or migrating from other countries and supporting whole families, old queers, disabled queers, queers on welfare. It has been for several generations a space—a fucked-up space like any other, but still a space nonetheless—where people could actually be on the street and figure out a way to survive. And that is what San Francisco has been about for queer people for a long time: a place to create something else.

Being in San Francisco enables me, or anyone else who has lived here long enough, to see what happens when gay people succeed at becoming part of the power structure: to see gay political consultants who have masterminded elections for antipoor, pro-development candidates over and over again. What is perhaps most horrifying is that gay people don't give a shit! Mainstream gay people with power could absolutely not care less. They are so glad to see Polk Street disappear, to see transgender women and old queers disappear. Old queers that don't fit into the model that says, "Oh, we bought this old house in the 1970s, and we renovated it, and now it's worth two million, and the neighborhood has really come up." This doesn't mean anything for old queers who are still on SSI [Supplemental Security Income] and who are living in a hotel room because they can only pay one night at a time. Queer youth who come to San Francisco to escape violence or families where they can't express their gender or sexual or social identities seek out space here, and gay people who made that exact same journey ten or twenty or thirty or forty years ago are anxious to police the borders and say, "Get out!"

These are things that sometimes make me feel incredibly hopeless. But they are also where my anger and drive come from. To see queer people who are marginalized and oppressed in so many ways, not only by their parents and the cops and politicians but by mainstream gay people, still finding a way to be out there on the street and having some sense of a celebratory potential somewhere: that inspires me and makes me feel like that's why I have to do this work, so that other people can go on and find space and create culture and create hope.

So it's time for me to confess something, Mattilda. We've decided to call this issue of the RHR "Queer Futures." I'm reluctant to ask you to prognosticate, but I will anyway. Are you hopeful for a queer future?

I'm in two places at once. One of them is that I feel incredibly inspired by emerging trans, gender queer, gender-defiant, and gender nonconforming cultures, identities, and communities. I'm especially inspired by the possibilities for a really messy fluidity. For me, this is the possibility in being queer, knowing that you can start out one place and end up someplace else. It's not about finding just this one place, but being able to say, "Today this is who I am, and maybe in ten years I'm going to be an entirely different person, and I will also be the person that I am today, and I will have integrated all of it." That is what the potential for queer means to me. Even emerging words like *gender queer* or *homonormativity*, the ideas that they represent are really exciting. So I'm absolutely inspired by evoking a queer future in that sense.

On the other hand, the word *queer* is also a very fraught and fascinating word because it has been totally assimilated into mainstream consumer culture through programs like *Queer as Folk* and *Queer Eye for the Straight Guy*. Despite that, it remains, almost paradoxically, a threat and a challenge and is still a really important word and identity for me. In that sense, that is the potential of a queer future. I guess where I feel less hopeful is when I see identities and ideas that mean something to me — the challenges and the call for accountability and the anger and the defiance and all of that queerness — becoming more and more marginalized. Of course, there is something to be said for the margins. I'm all for being on the margins. But being marginalized is also a scary place to be.

Note

Special thanks to Kevin P. Murphy and David Serlin for guidance and extensive editorial assistance. I would also like to thank Andrea Nordick for her speedy and accurate transcription service, and Mik Kinkead and the Queer Union at Macalester College for bringing Mattilda to Minnesota.

In Memoriam

Roy Rosenzweig

(1950–2007)

—R. J. Lambrose

Radical History Review
Issue 100 (Winter 2008)

Anna M. Agathangelou (PhD, Political Science, Syracuse University) is an associate professor of political science at York University, Toronto, and director of Global Change Institute in Nicosia, Greece. Author of the *Global Political Economy of Sex: Desire, Violence and Insecurity in Mediterranean Nation-States* (Palgrave Macmillan, 2004), Agathangelou is currently working on a book project on "Terror-Necrotic Ontologies of Empire and Capital: Greek Theory and Possibilities for Feminist Substantive Democracy." Agathangelou's geopolitical area of focus is Europe and Eurasia and her research interests are empire, globalization, "permanent" war(s), feminist postcolonial epistemologies of sex and race, and ontologies of revolution, liberation and transformation.

M. Daniel Bassichis graduated from Brown University in 2006 with a BA in Africana studies and English, after completing an honors thesis examining the sexual economies of the U.S. prison regime.

Aaron Belkin is an associate professor of political science at the University of California at Santa Barbara. He has published studies on nudity in military showers, counterfactual thought experiments in world politics, and on coups d'état. He is writing a book on purity and pollution in the U.S. military, focusing on soldiers' embodiment of contradictory ideals such as filth/cleanliness, stoicism/recklessness, and others as sites from which both discipline and empire emerge.

Nan Alamilla Boyd has a PhD from Brown University, and she is currently chair and associate professor of women studies at San Francisco State University. She has published widely in queer studies, and her book, *Wide Open Town: A History of Queer San Francisco to 1965*, was published by the University of California Press in 2003.

Maxime Cervulle is a PhD candidate at Paris 1 Panthéon–Sorbonne University and teaches media and cultural studies at Lille 3 Charles de Gaulle University. He is the editor of *Identités et cultures: Politiques des cultural studies* (2007), the first Stuart Hall reader to be published in France, and has translated into French both Judith Butler's *Undoing Gender* and Eve Kosofsky Sedgwick's *Epistemology of the Closet*. He is currently cowriting, with Nick Rees-Roberts, a book tentatively titled "Homo exoticus: Politiques sexuelles postcoloniales."

Vincent Doyle is visiting assistant professor in humanities and media and cultural studies at Macalester College in St. Paul, Minnesota. He is the author of a book in progress entitled "Making Out in the Mainstream: Media Activism, Queer Autonomy, and the Gay and Lesbian Alliance against Defamation." He is a fellow of the Sexuality Research Program of the Social Science Research Council.

Roderick A. Ferguson is an associate professor of American studies, race, and critical theory at the University of Minnesota. He is the author of *Aberrations in Black: Toward a Queer of Color Critique* (2004). Currently he is working on a book project that analyzes the semantic shifts in capital, state, and the academy caused by the emergence of the antiracist and feminist student movements of the sixties and seventies and by the rise of ethnic and women's studies.

Christina Hanhardt is an assistant professor of American studies and LGBT studies at the University of Maryland at College Park. Her research and teaching focus on the areas of LGBT studies, urban studies, social movements, and cultural geography.

Dan Irving is an assistant professor teaching within the sexualities and human rights streams in the Institute of Interdisciplinary Studies at Carleton University. He is active within trans communities as a community-based researcher and event organizer. His dissertation critiqued the possibilities and limitations of establishing alliances among trans activists and labor, LGBT, and feminist organizations. His current research analyzes the impact of neoliberalism on the formation of trans subjectivities.

Regina Kunzel is a professor in the Department of Gender, Women, and Sexuality Studies and in the Department of History at the University of Minnesota. She is the author of *Criminal Intimacy: Sex in Prison and the Uneven History of Modern American Sexuality* (forthcoming, 2008), and *Fallen Women, Problem Girls: Unmarried Mothers and the Professionalization of Social Work, 1890–1945* (1993), as well as of articles in the history of gender and sexuality.

Patrick McCreery is a PhD candidate in American studies at New York University, and he advises and teaches in the fields of sexual politics and family life at NYU's Gallatin School of Individualized Study. He is completing a dissertation on Anita Bryant's 1977 anti–gay rights campaign. He is the coeditor, with Kitty Krupat, of the anthology *Out at Work: Building a Gay-Labor Alliance* (2001). His writing has appeared in *Social Text*, *GLQ*, and *New Labor Forum*.

Kevin P. Murphy is an assistant professor of history at the University of Minnesota, and he is a member of the editorial collective for the *Radical History Review*. He is the author of *Red Bloods and Mollycoddles: Political Manhood in the Progressive Era* (2008) and is coeditor, with members of the Twin Cities GLBT Oral History Project, of a book tentatively titled "Queer Twin Cities: Politics, Histories, Spaces."

Tavia Nyong'o is an assistant professor of performance studies at New York University. His publications include "Punk'd Theory," *Social Text* 23: 3–4 (Fall 2005). He is currently working on a book about the intersections of punk and queer.

Jason Ruiz is a PhD candidate in American studies at the University of Minnesota. His dissertation interprets representations of travel to Mexico in the late nineteenth and early twentieth centuries and the production of Mexico in the U.S. popular imagination. He is the cofounder of the Twin Cities GLBT Oral History Project and is currently a Consortium for Faculty Diversity Dissertation Fellow at Macalester College.

David Serlin is an associate professor of communication and science studies at the University of California at San Diego and is a member of the editorial collective for the *Radical History Review*. He is the author of *Replaceable You: Engineering the Body in Postwar America* (2004), which was awarded the Alan Bray Book Prize from the Modern Language Association.

Tamara L. Spira is a PhD candidate in the history of consciousness and feminist studies at the University of California at Santa Cruz. She is currently working on her dissertation, which addresses the affective economies of memory and amnesia under neoliberalism through a transnational study of literatures in post-Pinochet Chile and the United States on questions of historical trauma and slavery. She has also worked as a union and community organizer and is involved in anti-prison and immigrant rights struggles.

Susan Stryker is the 2007–2008 Woodward Professor of Women's Studies at Simon Fraser University. She is the codirector, with Victor Silverman, of the Emmy Award–winning documentary *Screaming Queens: The Riot at Compton's Cafeteria* (2005).

Margot D. Weiss is a visiting assistant professor in women's studies at the College of William and Mary, where she teaches courses in queer and feminist studies. Her ethnographic research focuses on contemporary U.S. sexual cultures and activisms. Her forthcoming book, *Techniques of Pleasure, Scenes of Play*, explores the relationships between late capitalism, neoliberalism, and gendered and raced performance in San Francisco's BDSM communities.

Colonial Latin American Historical Review (CLAHR)

Featuring the *COLONIAL ERA*
IN LUSO-HISPANO AMERICA

MANUSCRIPT SUBMISSIONS INVITED
Original essays based on archival sources, max. 25-30 pp. + footnotes
3 copies + disk, Microsoft Word preferred
or PC compatible, English or Spanish

- -

Subscription Form:

Name: _____

Address: _____

Telephone: _____

E-mail: _____

❐ Individual $35   ❐ Institution $40   ❐ Student $30   ❐ Single Issue $9
(Add $5.00 for areas outside of the United States, Mexico, and Canada)

❐ Check or money order payable to: *Colonial Latin American Historical Review*
❐ VISA ❐ MasterCard Acct.# _____ Exp. Date _____

Cardholder's Signature _____

Please send this form with the appropriate payment to Dr. Joseph P. Sánchez, Editor:

Mailing Address:
Spanish Colonial Research Center, NPS
MSC05 3020
1 University of New Mexico
Albuquerque NM 87131-0001 USA

Location/Ship To:
Spanish Colonial Research Center, NPS
Zimmerman Library
1 University of New Mexico
Albuquerque NM 87131-0001 USA

Telephone (505)277-1370 / Fax (505)277-4603
E-mail clahr@unm.edu / Home Page http://www.unm.edu/~clahr

Arab Studies Journal

Send all submissions to:

Arab Studies Journal
CCAS · ICC 241
Georgetown University
Washington, DC 20057
Tel: (202) 687-0904 ·
Fax: (202) 687-7001

ASJ ANNOUNCES ITS RECENT ISSUE

Rethinking Ottoman Frontier Policies:
Marriage and Citzenship
in the Province of Iraq
Karen M. Kern

Pious Stardom:
Cinema and the Islamic Revival in
Egypt
Karim Tartoussieh

Re-Remembering the Dead:
A Genealogy of a Martyrs Memorial
in South Lebanon
Lucia Volk

Palestine on Display:
The Palestinian Pavillion at the British
Empire Exhibition of 1924
Nicholas E. Roberts

BOOK REVIEWS INCLUDE:

One Country: A Bold Proposal to End
the
Israeli-Palestinian Impasse
By Ali Abunimeh
Reviewed by Issa Mikel

CALL FOR PAPERS/REVIEWS

The *Arab Studies Journal* is accepting papers for its Spring 2008 issue. Original work in any social science discipline or literature will be considered for publication. The *Journal* encourages the submission of papers representing fresh and alternative approaches not sufficiently represented in mainstream scholarship.

For more information and online submissions, visit us at:

www.ARABSTUDIESJOURNAL.org

CHARACTER EDUCATION

Transforming Values into Virtue

Holly Shepard Salls

University Press of America,® Inc.
Lanham · Boulder · New York · Toronto · Plymouth, UK

Copyright © 2007 by
University Press of America,® Inc.
4501 Forbes Boulevard
Suite 200
Lanham, Maryland 20706
UPA Acquisitions Department (301) 459-3366

Estover Road
Plymouth PL6 7PY
United Kingdom

Library of Congress Control Number: 2006907503
ISBN-13: 978-0-7618-3612-4 (paperback : alk. paper)
ISBN-10: 0-7618-3612-8 (paperback : alk. paper)